REA: THE TEST PREP AP TEACHERS RECOMMEND

AP* MICROECONOMICS & MACROECONOMICS ALL ACCESS™

Tyson Smith, M.A.
AP Economics Teacher
Iowa City West High School
Iowa City, Iowa

Research & Education Association
Visit our website: www.rea.com

Research & Education Association
61 Ethel Road West
Piscataway, New Jersey 08854
E-mail: info@rea.com

AP MICROECONOMICS AND MACROECONOMICS ALL ACCESS ™

Printed in the United States of America

Library of Congress Control Number 2013941783

ISBN-13: 978-0-7386-1085-6
ISBN-10: 0-7386-1085-2

I13

Contents

About Research & Education Association viii

Acknowledgments viii

About Our Author ix

Chapter 1: Welcome to REA's All Access for AP Microeconomics and Macroeconomics 1

Chapter 2: Strategies for the Exams 7

What Will I See on the AP Economics Exams? 7

Strategies for the Multiple-Choice Section of the Exam 10

Strategies for the Free-Response Section of the Exam 20

Chapter 3: Basic Economic Concepts 29

Economics and Economic Questions 29

Economic Systems and Fields of Economics 30

Scarcity, Factors of Production, and Opportunity Cost 34

The Production Possibilities Curve and Productive Efficiency 37

Comparative Advantage and Trade 43

Marginal Thinking and Allocative Efficiency 47

The Circular Flow Model 48

Demand, Supply, and Market Equilibrium 51

Practice, Practice, Practice! 60

Economic Cycles and Thinking Across Time 63

Quiz 1 .... ***available online at www.rea.com/studycenter***

AP Microeconomics

Chapter 4: The Nature and Function of Product Markets 69

A Closer Look at Demand, Supply, and Equilibrium 69
Households: Consumer Choice and Utility Maximization 81
Firms: Costs of Production and Profit Maximization 83
Four Product Market Structures: An Overview 92
Quiz 2 .... ***available online at www.rea.com/studycenter***

Chapter 5: Factor Markets 125

New Roles in the Circular Flow 125
Demand and Supply of Resources 126
How Firms Maximize Profit 134
Factor Market Graphical Analysis 136
Quiz 3 .... ***available online at www.rea.com/studycenter***

Chapter 6: Market Failure and the Role of Government 147

What Is Market Failure? 147
Externalities 149
Government Provision of Goods 157
Taxes 159
Income Distribution 169
Quiz 4 .... ***available online at www.rea.com/studycenter***
Mini-Test 1 .... ***available online at www.rea.com/studycenter***

AP Macroeconomics

Chapter 7: Measuring Economic Performance 177

Gross Domestic Product and National Income 177

Inflation 189

Unemployment 195

Chapter 8: The Aggregate Demand and Aggregate Supply Model 199

Goal of the Aggregate Demand and Aggregate Supply Model:
Income and Price Determination 199

Aggregate Demand as a Concept 200

Net Export Effect 202

Aggregate Demand's Components and Their Behavior 203

Aggregate Supply 215

Aggregate Supply in the Short Run and the Long Run 220

Short- and Long-Run Equilibrium in the AD-AS Model 223

Quiz 5 .... ***available online at www.rea.com/studycenter***

Chapter 9: Banking and the Financial Sector 229

Money and the Money Supply 229

The Banking Process 232

Interest Rates, Money Demand, and the Money Market 236

The Federal Reserve 240

Chapter 10: Fiscal and Monetary Policies in Action 249

Fiscal Policy Explained 249
Fiscal Policy and Interest Rates 255
Combinations of Fiscal and Monetary Policy 264
Unemployment and Inflation: The Phillips Curve 265
Quiz 6 .... ***available online at www.rea.com/studycenter***

Chapter 11: Economic Growth 275

The Concept of Growth 275
Determinants of Growth 281
Growth Policy 285

Chapter 12: The International Sector, Trade Accounting, and Exchange Markets 287

Trade Accounting and Balance of Payments Accounts 287
Foreign Exchange Markets and Exchange Rates 294
Quiz 7 .... ***available online at www.rea.com/studycenter***
Mini-Test 2 .... ***available online at www.rea.com/studycenter***

AP Microeconomics Practice Exam
(also available online at *www.rea.com/studycenter*) 311

Answer Key 339
Detailed Explanations of Answers 340

AP Macroeconomics Practice Exam (also available online at *www.rea.com/studycenter*) 357

Answer Key 381

Detailed Explanations of Answers 382

Answer Sheets 401

Appendices 403

25 Key Graphs 405

25 Key Formulae 409

Glossary of Key Economic Terms 413

Index 429

About Research & Education Association

Founded in 1959, Research & Education Association (REA) is dedicated to publishing the finest and most effective educational materials—including study guides and test preps—for students in middle school, high school, college, graduate school, and beyond.

Today, REA's wide-ranging catalog is a leading resource for teachers, students, and professionals. Visit *www.rea.com* to see a complete listing of all our titles.

Acknowledgments

We would like to thank Pam Weston, Publisher, for setting the quality standards for production integrity and managing the publication to completion; John Cording, Vice President, Technology, for coordinating the design and development of the REA Study Center; Larry B. Kling, Vice President, Editorial, for his overall direction; Diane Goldschmidt, Managing Editor, for coordinating development of this edition; Transcend Creative Services for typesetting this edition; and Weymouth Design and Christine Saul, Senior Graphic Designer, for designing our cover.

In addition, we thank Rich Wiess for technically reviewing the manuscript; Marianne L'Abbate for copyediting; and Doris Maxfield of Max's Word Services, for proofreading.

About Our Author

Tyson Smith has taught a variety of high school social studies courses for 15 years, the last 10 of which have been spent preparing students for successful performances on AP exams in microeconomics, macroeconomics, and European history. Mr. Smith earned his B.A. in Philosophy and his M.A. in Social Studies Education from the University of Iowa, Iowa City, Iowa. He has also completed post-graduate work in economics and social studies education at several universities.

Recently, Mr. Smith coached the first- and second-place Iowa state champions in the Council for Economic Education's 2013 National Economics Challenge competition (Adam Smith division) and the 2008, 2009, and 2010 Iowa state champions of the Fed Challenge sponsored by the Federal Reserve System.

Mr. Smith has been honored as a Claes Nobel Educator of Distinction by the National Society of High School Scholars and a Joseph B. Whitehead Educator of Distinction by the Coca-Cola Foundation. He has also been named an Educational Leader and Mentor by the National Youth Leadership Forum on National Security. In addition, Mr. Smith has been lauded by the State of Iowa Governor's Scholar Recognition Program on more than one occasion and was the recipient of the Iowa City Area Chamber of Commerce's Excellence in Education Award.

Mr. Smith lives outside Iowa City with his wife, Alison, and two young daughters, Gwendolyn and Eleanor, and spends as much time as possible playing ultimate Frisbee.

Chapter 1

Welcome to REA's All Access for AP Microeconomics and Macroeconomics

A new, more effective way to prepare for your AP exam

There are many different ways to prepare for an AP exam. What's best for you depends on how much time you have to study and how comfortable you are with the subject matter. To score your highest, you need a system that can be customized to fit you: your schedule, your learning style, and your current level of knowledge.

This book, and the free online tools that come with it, will help you personalize your AP prep by testing your understanding, pinpointing your weaknesses, and delivering flashcard study materials unique to you.

Let's get started and see how this system works.

How to Use REA's AP All Access

The REA AP All Access system allows you to create a personalized study plan through three simple steps: targeted review of exam content, assessment of your knowledge, and focused study in the topics where you need the most help.

Here's how it works:

Review the Book	Study the topics tested on the AP exam and learn proven strategies that will help you tackle any question you may see on test day.
Test Yourself & Get Feedback	As you review the book, test yourself. Score reports from your free online tests and quizzes give you a fast way to pinpoint what you really know and what you should spend more time studying.
Improve Your Score	Armed with your score reports, you can personalize your study plan. Review the parts of the book where you are weakest, and use the REA Study Center to create your own unique e-flashcards, adding to the 100 free cards included with this book.

Finding Your Weaknesses: The REA Study Center

The best way to personalize your study plan and truly focus on your weaknesses is to get frequent feedback on what you know and what you don't. At the online REA Study Center, you can access three types of assessment: topic-level quizzes, mini-tests, and a full-length practice test. Each of these tools provides true-to-format questions and delivers a detailed score report that follows the topics set by the College Board.

Topic-Level Quizzes

Short, online quizzes are available throughout the review and are designed to test your immediate grasp of the topics just covered.

Mini-Tests

Two online mini-tests (one for microeconomics and one for macroeconomics) cover what you've studied in the book. These tests are like the actual AP exam, only shorter, and will help you evaluate your overall understanding of the subject.

Full-Length Practice Test

After you've finished reviewing the book, take our full-length exam for microeconomics or macroeconomics (or both) to practice under test-day conditions. Available both in this book and online, these tests give you the most complete picture of your strengths and weaknesses. We strongly recommend that you take the online version of the exam for the added benefits of timed testing, automatic scoring, and a detailed score report.

Improving Your Score: e-Flashcards

Once you get your score reports from the online quizzes and tests, you'll be able to see exactly which topics you need to review. Use this information to create your own flashcards for the areas where you are weak. And, because you will create these flashcards through the REA Study Center, you'll be able to access them from any computer or smartphone.

Not quite sure what to put on your flashcards? Start with the 100 free cards (50 for AP Microeconomics and 50 for AP Macroeconomics) included when you buy this book.

After the Full-Length Practice Test: *Crash Course*

After finishing this book and taking our full-length practice exam, pick up REA's *Crash Course for AP Microeconomics* and REA's *Crash Course for Macroeconomics*. Use your most recent score reports to identify any areas where you are still weak, and turn to the *Crash Course* for a rapid review presented in a concise outline style.

REA's Suggested 8-Week AP Study Plans

Depending on how much time you have until test day, you can expand or condense our eight-week study plans as you see fit.

To score your highest, use our suggested study plan and customize it to fit your schedule, targeting the areas where you need the most review.

Study Plan for AP Microeconomics

	Review 1-2 hours	Quiz 18 minutes	e-Flashcards Anytime, Anywhere	Mini-Test 35 minutes	Full-Length Practice Test 2 hours, 10 minutes
Week 1	Chapters 1, 2, 3	Quiz 1	Access your e-flashcards from your computer or smartphone whenever you have a few extra minutes to study. Start with the 100 free cards (50 for AP Microeconomics and 50 for AP Macroeconomics) included when you buy this book. Personalize your prep by creating your own cards for topics where you need extra study.		
Week 2	First half of Chapter 4				
Week 3	Second half of Chapter 4	Quiz 2			
Week 4	Chapter 5	Quiz 3			
Week 5	Chapter 6	Quiz 4			
Week 6				Mini-Test 1	
Week 7	Review Chapter 2 and Chapter 4				
Week 8					Full-Length Practice Exam (Just like test day)

Need even more review? Pick up a copy of REA's *Crash Course for AP Microeconomics,* a rapid review presented in a concise outline style. Get more information about the *Crash Course* series by visiting *www.rea.com.*

Study Plan for AP Macroeconomics

<table>
<tr><th></th><th>Review
1-2 hours</th><th>Quiz
18 minutes</th><th>e-Flashcards
Anytime, Anywhere</th><th>Mini-Test
35 minutes</th><th>Full-Length Practice Test
2 hours, 10 minutes</th></tr>
<tr><td>Week 1</td><td>Chapters 1, 2, 3</td><td>Quiz 1</td><td rowspan="8">Access your e-flashcards from your computer or smartphone whenever you have a few extra minutes to study.

Start with the 100 free cards (50 for AP Microeconomics and 50 for AP Macroeconomics) included when you buy this book. Personalize your prep by creating your own cards for topics where you need extra study.</td><td></td><td></td></tr>
<tr><td>Week 2</td><td>Chapter 7</td><td></td><td></td><td></td></tr>
<tr><td>Week 3</td><td>Chapter 8</td><td>Quiz 5</td><td></td><td></td></tr>
<tr><td>Week 4</td><td>Chapter 9</td><td></td><td></td><td></td></tr>
<tr><td>Week 5</td><td>Chapter 10</td><td>Quiz 6</td><td></td><td></td></tr>
<tr><td>Week 6</td><td>Chapter 11, 12</td><td>Quiz 7</td><td></td><td></td></tr>
<tr><td>Week 7</td><td>Review Chapter 2</td><td></td><td>Mini-Test 2</td><td></td></tr>
<tr><td>Week 8</td><td></td><td></td><td></td><td>Full-Length Practice Exam (Just like test day)</td></tr>
<tr><td colspan="6">Need even more review? Pick up a copy of REA's Crash Course for AP Macroeconomics, a rapid review presented in a concise outline style. Get more information about the Crash Course series by visiting www.rea.com.</td></tr>
</table>

Test-Day Checklist

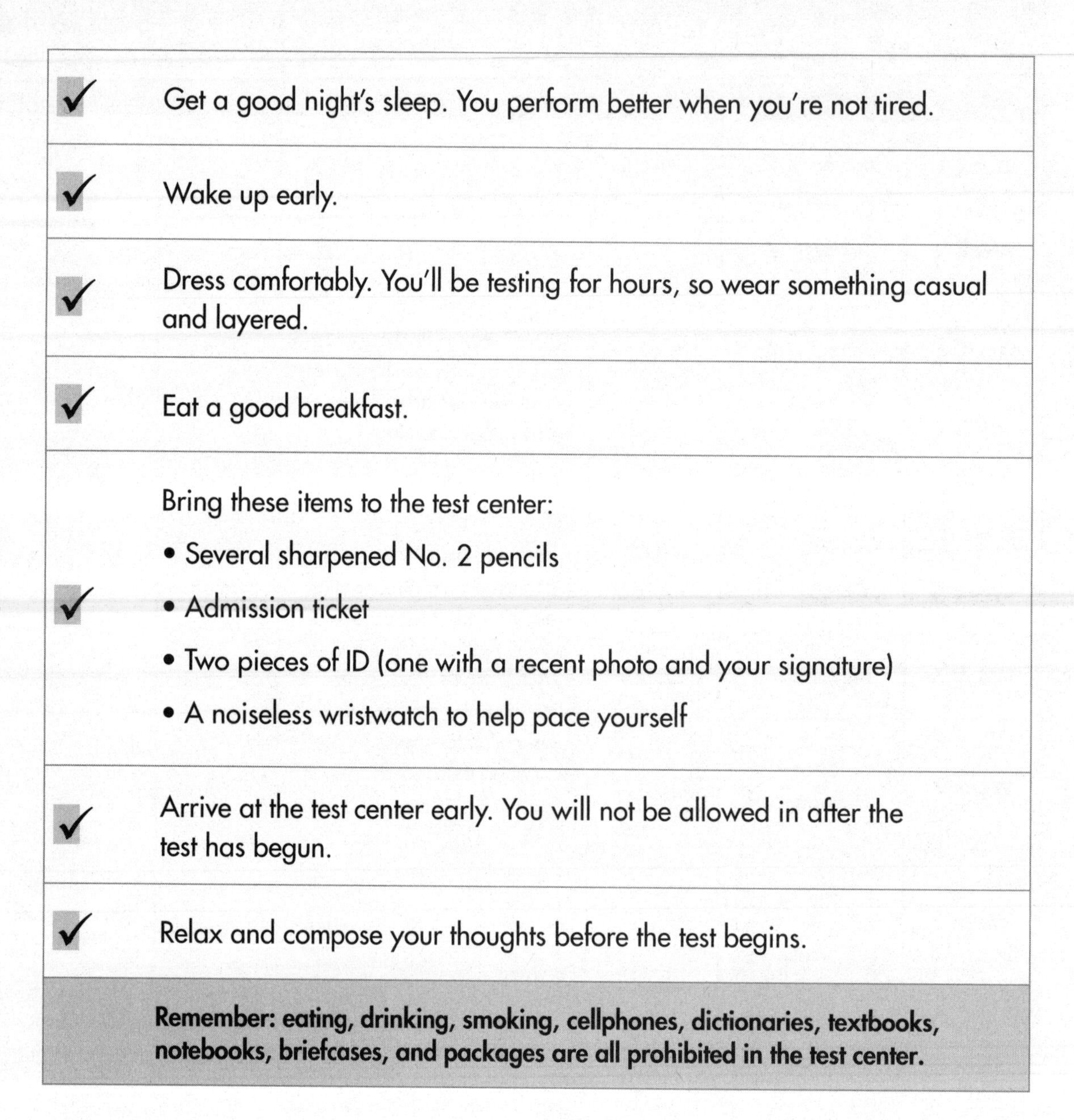

- ✓ Get a good night's sleep. You perform better when you're not tired.
- ✓ Wake up early.
- ✓ Dress comfortably. You'll be testing for hours, so wear something casual and layered.
- ✓ Eat a good breakfast.
- ✓ Bring these items to the test center:
  - Several sharpened No. 2 pencils
  - Admission ticket
  - Two pieces of ID (one with a recent photo and your signature)
  - A noiseless wristwatch to help pace yourself
- ✓ Arrive at the test center early. You will not be allowed in after the test has begun.
- ✓ Relax and compose your thoughts before the test begins.

Remember: eating, drinking, smoking, cellphones, dictionaries, textbooks, notebooks, briefcases, and packages are all prohibited in the test center.

Chapter 2

Strategies for the Exams

What Will I See on the AP Economics Exams?

One fine day in May, you will walk confidently into the testing site for your AP Economics exam(s). You will know the material well: you paid attention in class, read and reviewed graphs in your textbook, and took good, concise notes. Even if you didn't really do all of this, at least we know you are now ready to learn from a special test prep guide. Assuming you've learned the vocabulary, reasoning processes, and key graphs you need to know, what will the test you are prepared for and ready to take look like?

Start with the knowledge that the structure and timing are the same for the AP Macroeconomics and AP Microeconomics exams—each features the same number of multiple-choice items and the same number and style of free-response problems as the other. Furthermore, some of the content overlaps from one exam to the other—over 10% of the concepts and topics are fair game for either exam. If you are preparing for both tests, as many students do, this will save you some study time. If you are only preparing for one exam, be confident that the strategies and techniques explained in this chapter can be used on the test you take.

What Do I Need to Know for My Exam?

Chapter 3 covers material you will need to know no matter which exam you want to prepare for. Questions on this basic economic content can and do appear on both micro and macro tests each year. Chapters 4–6 contain information that will only be covered on the microeconomics exam and Chapters 7–12 contain information that will only be covered on the macroeconomics exam.

Your class at school may have been a full year in length and prepared you for both exams or your class may have been only one semester long and focused on one of the disciplines. If you have been preparing for only one exam in school but find the material interesting, you can use this book to get you ready for the other exam—everything you need to know to earn a 5 on either or both exams is right here! If you know where you are going to college and still have the opportunity to sign up for the other exam, you might find out what score would qualify you for credit and consider whether the benefits of studying independently for the other test would outweigh the costs: as a well-trained economist, you surely will make the rational choice for your own situation.

The Multiple-Choice Section

Your exam will start with a multiple-choice section that will test your understanding of vocabulary, graphs, and cause-effect relationships related to the main topics of that type of economics. This section will require you to answer 60 multiple-choice questions in 70 minutes, meaning you have an average of 70 seconds (a little over a minute) for each question. These questions will be taken from the major categories below in roughly the percentages indicated:

AP Microeconomics Topic Area	%	AP Macroeconomics Topic Area	%
Basic Economic Concepts	8–14	**Basic Economic Concepts**	8–12
Nature and Function of Product Markets	55–70	**Measurement of Economic Performance**	12–16
Supply, Demand, Consumer Choice	20–30	**National Income and Price Determination**	10–15
Production and Costs	10–15	**Banking and the Financial Sector**	15–20
Firm behavior and Market Structures	25–35	**Inflation and Unemployment Stabilization**	20–30
Factor Markets	10–18	**Economic Growth**	5–10
Market Failure and Government's Role	12–18	**International Trade and Finance**	10–15

Your success on the multiple-choice section of the exam will have a lot to do with how well you perform on the test as a whole—it is more heavily weighted than the free-response part. You'll want to budget your time effectively so that you have a chance to answer all of the questions, giving yourself the maximum chance possible to earn your best score.

The Free-Response Section

After time is called on the multiple-choice section, you'll get a short break before heading back into the test room to do the free-response section. In 60 minutes, you will need to analyze, sketch and plan, and write finished responses to three mandatory questions. The first question is longer and worth half of the free-response points, so plan to spend half your time on this question. The other two questions are equally weighted; therefore, plan to spend about 15 minutes crafting your final response to each of these questions.

You won't be expected to write essays—in fact, when asked to explain, you should respond in a single well-reasoned sentence, rather than a long-winded paragraph. Rather than thinking of these as essays, as you are taught in other subject areas, consider them short-response problems that expect you to show a brief line of reasoning. Every year on each test, one or more of the free-response questions will explicitly direct you to create and correctly label a graph—sometimes all of the questions expect graphs in the responses. Questions that don't ask you to create graphs may present you with a stimulus and ask you questions about it. Because the graphing skill is so commonly tested on this part of the test, it is more accurate to think of the free-response section as "explaining and understanding graphs" rather than as an essay section.

What's the Score?

Although the scoring process for the AP exam may seem quite complex, it boils down to two simple components: your multiple-choice score plus your free-response scores. The multiple-choice section counts for two-thirds of your overall score, and is generated by awarding one point toward your score for each question you've answered correctly—60 possible points.

The free-response section counts for one-third of your total score. The first, longer question counts for half of the credit (you can earn up to 15 points) and the two shorter questions allow you to earn up to 7.5 points each. Trained graders will read students' written responses and assign points according to very specific grading rubrics. The number of points you accumulate out of the total possible points for each question will be properly weighted and totaled to form your score on the free-response section.

In the summer, the College Board will report to you a score on a scale of 1 to 5 for each AP exam you took. Individual colleges and universities determine what credit or advanced placement, if any, is awarded to students at each score level.

The table below shows the College Board's qualifications associated with each numeric score and the approximate raw score totals needed (out of the total 90 points possible) to earn each:

College Board Score	College Board Qualification	Earned with a Raw Score Range of:
5	Extremely well qualified	74 or more
4	Well qualified	58 – 73
3	Qualified	48 – 57
2	Possibly qualified	36 – 47
1	No recommendation	35 or below

The exact raw score range needed to earn a final 5, 4, 3, or 2 varies slightly from one year to the next, but these values should give you comfort knowing that you can miss quite a few questions and still earn the overall score you're targeting. If you want to earn a 5, for instance, you might look to earn 50 of the 60 total points on the multiple-choice section and 25 of the 30 points available on the free-response section: you need 5 of every 6 points available to earn a 5. To build your point total toward a score of 4, you'd want to get 40 multiple-choice items correct and earn 20 or more points on the free-response section, meaning you need about two-thirds of the possible score on each part of the test in order to earn a 4. Consider these rough ratios as benchmarks to compare to your own performance when checking your work on the practice quizzes and tests that are part of the REA *All Access* system!

Strategies for the Multiple-Choice Section of the Exam

Because the AP exam is a standardized test, from year to year each version of the test must share many similarities in order to be fair. That means you can always expect certain things to be true about your AP economics exam. Not only will it cover the topics outlined, it will contain questions with a wide range of difficulty levels. Furthermore, there are a number of predictable characteristics all questions will have and there are common question types included every year. You study all the topics covered in order to avoid being caught off guard by material you aren't familiar with—why wouldn't you improve your chances by familiarizing yourself with the characteristics of question types?

Let's get started with a sample question about the test.

Which of the following statements accurately describe the multiple-choice section of the AP economics exams?

I. Every item will have five answer choices.

II. Some items will expect you to apply formulas and perform simple calculations without a calculator.

III. Many items will present you with a graph or table of data to analyze.

IV. Items will range in difficulty from knowledge of definitions to prediction and evaluation of how changing circumstances will affect economic situations.

(A) II only

(B) III only

(C) I and IV only

(D) I, III, and IV only

(E) I, II, III, and IV

Did you pick option "E"? Good job!

What does this mean for your study plan? First, there is the basic goal of understanding the needed vocabulary terms, formulas, and critical graphical models the test will expect you to know. Second, the fact that you cannot use a calculator means that there won't be challenging mathematical calculations: you aren't being tested on your math ability, but rather on your knowledge of how relatively small data sets need to be examined to reveal economic principles. Finally, the toughest questions expect you to apply your knowledge to graphs in new ways. This means that you should consider the connections among ideas and concepts as you study (this book will push you to engage in this kind of thinking).

The format of the question above—the Roman numeral statement—might be unfamiliar to you, but the format will definitely be on the exam. Thinking of it as a series of true-false questions is a simple strategy to conquer these questions that can frustrate many well-prepared students. Let's take a look at another question with this same format, this time over a basic economic concept you will find covered on both AP economics exams.

Which of the following statements are accurate regarding comparative advantage and trade?

> First read the question and be sure you understand it.

I. Countries should avoid specialization because of the high opportunity costs associated with a neighbor obtaining comparative advantage.

II. Goods should be produced in the location where they can be made at the lowest opportunity costs.

> Examine each statement, deciding if it is true or false. If you are not sure if a statement is true or false—put a question mark by it for now.

III. A country able to produce a unit of a good with fewer inputs than a neighbor has the comparative advantage in the production of that good.

IV. A country able to produce a unit of a good with a lower opportunity cost than a potential trade partner has the comparative advantage in the production of that good.

(A) I and III only

(B) II and IV only

(C) III and IV only

(D) II, III, and IV only

(E) I, II, III, and IV

> Next, examine the answer options. Eliminate any choices that include the false statements you identified. For example, if you feel statement I is true, you can only select (A) or (E). Even better, because statement III is false, the only possible correct answer is (B). Remember that the correct answer will include all of the true statements and none that are false.

Types of Questions

You've already seen a list of the general content areas that you'll encounter on each of the AP economics exams. What kinds of multiple-choice items cover those broad topics?

Category	Comment, Strategy, or Explanation
Definition	Know your terms: be able to go from vocabulary term to definition and vice versa—flashcards can help
Marginal analysis	The ideal amount of anything is always where two marginal values are equal or where they intersect on a graph
Formula based	May require basic calculations, algebraic manipulation, recall of formula, or knowledge of when and how it is applied
Multiple true-false	Contains statements with Roman numerals and often doesn't require certainty about all of the statements

(Continued)

(Continued)

Category	Comment, Strategy, or Explanation
Using a provided graph	Tests your ability to recognize a situation, predict effects of a change, or locate and interpret important distances and areas
Using a table of data	Tests your ability to calculate, infer, or maximize and minimize
Problem identification	You may be asked to identify the economic problem in a situation presented in words or a graph and sometimes to know the correct solution to that problem
Cause-effect analysis	Asks you how a given change would influence other concepts or values; many of these are "column questions" and work well for elimination, graphing, and prediction

The following section will give you some tips and tricks for how to make the most of your economic knowledge!

Achieving Multiple-Choice Success

It's true that you don't have a lot of time to finish the multiple-choice section of the AP exam. But it's also true that you don't need to get every question right to get a great score. As previously discussed, answering just two-thirds of the questions correctly—along with a good showing on the free-response section—can earn you a score of a 4 or 5. But remember, you should respond to all of the questions. There is no deduction for answering incorrectly, so there is clearly a benefit to guessing even if you're totally confused by a particular item or if you run short on time. By preparing effectively and working quickly and methodically, however, you'll know the material and have enough time. You have about 70 seconds to answer each item and many of the easier or shorter questions won't take nearly that long. You really do have plenty of time to read slowly and circle key words and sketch graphs in the margins. It is proven that these strategies improve student performance. You may find it helpful to practice some test questions using a timer or a stopwatch to help you get a handle on how long 70 seconds actually is. If timing is hard for you, set a timer for 18 minutes each time you take one of the online quizzes that accompany this book. Let's look at some other strategies for answering multiple-choice items.

Process of Elimination

You've probably used the process-of-elimination strategy, intentionally or unintentionally, throughout your entire test-taking career. The process of elimination involves ruling out choices that aren't accurate and selecting the option that is left over. We used process of elimination to respond to the trade question above—in fact, on that type of question one can often eliminate several options at once! On most questions, there will be a "fatal flaw" with each of the wrong responses—something that is incorrect, inconsistent, or doesn't fit with a key word that was in the stem of the item. Being able to spot those cues is a great timesaver.

Let's examine two multiple-choice questions and use the process-of-elimination approach to work through them—first a macro example and then a micro example. For now, focus more on the process than the content while looking at this problem-identification-solution question.

To control an inflation rate that is higher than desirable, appropriate monetary policy actions include

(A) increasing government spending and decreasing the federal funds rate

(B) decreasing government spending and increasing the discount rate

(C) increasing taxes and increasing the federal funds rate

(D) decreasing the required reserve ratio and increasing the discount rate

(E) increasing the required reserve ratio and increasing the federal funds rate

To use the process of elimination, consider each option and how it fits with the question stem. The goal presented is to decrease inflation, meaning any policy choice that would increase the price level can be eliminated. Thus we won't select choices (A) and (D). A second round of elimination might result from a keen student circling the word "monetary" in the stem. Eliminating any choice that is part of a fiscal, rather than a monetary, policy removes (B) and (C) from consideration. The remaining choice (E) has two examples of contractionary monetary policy and is thus the correct response.

Some questions will ask for the exception to a trend or for you to find the false statement or characteristic that does not belong. These "NOT" and "EXCEPT" questions are nothing to be fearful of: the biggest risk is failing to recognize that you're supposed to be looking for the one *wrong answer* instead of the one *right answer*! To answer these questions correctly, you should carefully read and consider each answer choice, keeping in mind that four of them will be correct and just one will be wrong. Sometimes, you can find the right answer by simply picking out the one that does not fit with the other choices. Other times the correct response is more subtly hidden and you'll need to use the elimination method to figure it out: that's great because the elimination method works quite well for this sort of question. Let's take a look at a multiple-choice question of this type.

All of the following would likely cause a change in the demand for pancake mix EXCEPT

(A) a decrease in the price of frozen waffles, a substitute to pancakes

(B) increased cost of wheat flour, an ingredient in pancake mix

(C) increased popularity of a diet free of wheat gluten

(D) a decrease in the income of pancake consumers

(E) an increase in the price of maple syrup, a complement to pancakes

> To answer a NOT or EXCEPT question correctly, test each option by asking yourself: Is this choice true? You should see four clear examples of factors that DO shift the demand for pancake mix—choices (A), (C), (D), and (E). Even if you didn't spot that (B) would cause supply to shift, you could certainly have reasoned your way there by eliminating the wrong options.

Predicting

Using the process of elimination certainly helps you consider each answer choice thoroughly, but testing each and every answer can be a slow process. Although you want to examine all the options before making a final selection, at times you may find it helpful to try predicting the right answer before you read the answer choices. For example, you know that the answer to the math problem two-plus-two will always be four. If you saw this multiple-choice item on a math test, you wouldn't need to systematically test each response, but could go straight to the right answer. You can apply a similar technique to even complex items on the AP economics exams. To use the prediction method, once you've read the question stem, pause and think about what would be the ideal response. Then, look for an answer choice that matches the one you thought about. Let's look at how this technique could work on questions that could appear on each AP economics exam. Here is an example of a question that could be on the macroeconomics test—an example of a "column question" that falls into the cause-effect category.

> If the fiscal policy authorities pursue an expansionary policy, which of the following are the most likely effects on the budget deficit, demand for loanable funds, the real interest rate, and investment?

	Budget deficit	Demand for loanable funds	Real interest rate	Investment
(A)	increase	decrease	increase	increase
(B)	increase	increase	decrease	decrease
(C)	increase	increase	increase	decrease
(D)	no change	decrease	decrease	decrease
(E)	decrease	no change	decrease	increase

First, notice what is meant by a "column question"—the answer choices are arranged in columns. This is a common way to present cause-effect questions. It lends itself nicely to the process-of-elimination strategy and it works especially well for predictions. As you read the question stem, you might have zeroed in on the key words "fiscal" and "expansionary" to guide your prediction. Hopefully you recognized the four effects the question calls for as the steps in an important process—in this case, the crowding out effect. If so, try to recall the causal chain of events involved. Some students write arrows (up or down) by the column titles and then simply look for the option that matches their prediction.

What should you do if you don't see your exact prediction among the answer choices? Your prediction should have helped you narrow down the choices—at least you should be able to eliminate those that seem to go in the opposite direction as your expectation. Sometimes the best next step is to look for alternative phrasings of your predicted choice. In other situations, you may wish to apply the process of elimination to the remaining options to further home in on the right answer. In this case you could get rid of choices that have the middle two columns going in opposite directions because increases in demand drive up prices and interest is the price of borrowing. These must move in the same direction.

Anytime you're stumped on a column question, consider the causal connections between the columns and the order in which they are presented to you. Usually they are not arranged randomly, but rather in the order that you are supposed to consider them. In this case, borrowing is what drives up the demand for loanable funds, which raises the interest rate, which in turn crowds out investment. If one of the columns seems unexpected to you, see if it is an effect of the prior column!

Learning to predict takes some practice. You're probably used to reading all of the answer choices immediately after reading a question, but in order for the prediction strategy to help save time, you need to avoid doing this. Remember, the test maker doesn't want to make the right answers too obvious, so the wrong answers are all intended to sound plausible. If possible, it may be helpful to cover the answer choices to a question as you practice predicting. This will ensure that you don't sneak a peek at the answer choices too soon. You probably need to know the material better to formulate the right response than to recognize it, so this strategy may help you learn the key topics in a deeper way.

Sketching graphs to predict

Sometimes the best way to predict (or confirm) the right response is to graph the problem. You could have done this with the prior question, but often it is even more essential: the tougher the question, the more strategies you may need to use. Making a planning graph in the margin on the multiple-choice section of the test makes easy questions obvious, turns difficult questions into easy ones, and impossible-sounding questions more approachable. Consider the following question that could appear on a microeconomics exam—another example of a column question that tests your understanding of a cause-effect process.

> A monopolistically competitive firm is in long-run equilibrium producing its profit-maximizing level of output. If the good it sells increases in popularity, what are the most likely short-run results in terms of quantity the firm produces, the price the firm charges, and its level of economic profit?
>
> Quantity — Price — Level of Economic Profit

Notice there are no answer choices? There's a reason for that. To practice the prediction strategy, you have to *think about* the options before seeing them. You could very well know the exact answer that's coming and, if so, that's great. But you might not (you *certainly* won't if you are only preparing for macroeconomics), but you still can figure it out. It is when you're not certain of the correct answer that strategies can help the most. So, when in doubt, graph it out! This graph, which is only for your own help, doesn't need precise labels and can be quick to create. Let's assume that the graph for a monopolistically competitive firm in long-run equilibrium isn't something you remember at all. Can you still get the question right? Yes, you can!

With a limited understanding of basic economic concepts, you could conclude that the question is asking about a rightward shift of demand. A quick sketch of an economic graph in which you move demand to the right will likely involve an increase in both quantity and price. Now, before looking ahead, make a prediction about the firm's profit: will it be positive, zero, or negative?

You might have used the graph to see whether you could spot an area of profit or loss. Failing that, you might simply reason that with the same cost structure and a higher price the firm would likely have a better situation than they did before in terms of profit.

Let's look at the question again, this time with the answer choices.

A monopolistically competitive firm is in long-run equilibrium producing its profit-maximizing level of output. If the good it sells increases in popularity, what are the most likely short-run results in terms of quantity the firm produces, the price the firm charges, and its level of economic profit?

	Quantity	Price	Level of Economic Profit
(A)	higher than initial level	lower than initial level	negative (loss)
(B)	higher than initial level	higher than initial level	positive (profit)
(C)	lower than initial level	higher than initial level	zero (break-even)
(D)	lower than initial level	same as initial level	zero (break-even)
(E)	higher than initial level	lower than initial level	positive (profit)

Perhaps you aren't sure about whether the firm will have a positive or negative profit (or if they'll break even) after this happens. After looking at the complete item with the answer choices, in this example, you find that you don't need to know anything about the last column.

Find the Key Words or Concepts

To use either process of elimination or prediction strategies effectively, you do need one common strategy: being able to identify key words in the question stem that can be used to help you home in on the right response or get rid of the wrong ones. A good approach is to circle or underline those key words—which can reduce the odds that you skip over or accidentally reverse the term. Look for terms that narrow down what you are supposed to consider. Nearly every released AP multiple-choice item contains clues (sometimes several of them) that can channel or guide your thinking if you identify and use them. The line of reasoning laid out in the question stem leads to the right answer a majority of the time. Sometimes there is even a specific word or phrase present in the stem that rules out each of the incorrect options.

Closely related to this strategy is the skill of excluding extraneous information. These facts or statistics (or columns on a table of data or unneeded points labeled on a graph) are distractors that won't help you get to the right answer. On graphs or large tables of information, you're well advised to pay close attention to the marginal values and look for a place where the two of them are equal to one another. Calculation problems in particular tend to include more information than you need. Remember that the most complex calculation type you will need is figuring a percentage change (which only involves subtraction, division, and multiplication, after all) and that you don't have a calculator (so they won't give you nasty fractions or complex numbers). Because the formulas tend to involve easy operations and the numbers have to be neat, the way they can make the questions challenging is by including information that isn't necessary. Calmly consider what you are asked to calculate and what the elements in its equation are—usually there are two values you are given and your job is to find the missing third piece of the puzzle. Which two of the numbers that have been presented are the ones you need to use? Use only those.

Avoiding Common Errors

Remember, answering questions correctly is always more important than answering every question. Take care to work at a pace that allows you to avoid these common mistakes:

- **Don't miss key words that change the meaning of a question, such as *not, except,* or *least.*** Consider underlining these words in your test booklet so you're tuned into them when answering the question. Sometimes they will be capitalized or bolded for you, but you can't take that for granted.

- **Don't spend too much time agonizing over the correct response on any one item.** Remember, on average you have about 70 seconds per question. Some will surely take longer, but on your first trip through the exam, avoid spending more than 2 to 2½ minutes on any given problem. Time beyond that is likely not going to pay off and just might prevent you from analyzing two or more problems that you would have answered correctly and quickly later in the exam. If you get finished with the 60 items before time expires, you can go back to work on the difficult questions.

- **Don't be too eager to change your responses.** Changing an answer is something to be cautious of anyhow—more often students change from a correct answer to an incorrect answer! Looking over your work makes sense. Check for whether you misread or skipped over an important term in the question or even mis-recorded your choice on the answer sheet. However, arguing yourself out of your own best opinion is dangerous. No matter how often you revise your responses, be very careful to erase unwanted marks on the answer sheet completely!

- **Don't over-reason the problem.** The simplest path to victory is the path you want! You are looking for the most direct line of reasoning to get you from cause to effect. In real life, many economic processes balance one another out in the long run or when considering different paths of causation—think in the short run unless long-run analysis is expressly called for in the question. The AP exam is designed to test your understanding of basic causal connections. Test makers are careful to specify somewhere in the question what thought process they want you to use. If you find yourself muttering, "But on the other hand…," then just stop, choose the response you wanted in the first place, and move on.

A Few More Tips

Let's quickly review what you've learned about answering multiple-choice questions effectively on the AP exam. Using these techniques on practice tests will help you become comfortable with them before diving into the real exam, so be sure to apply these ideas as you work through this book.

- Know your vocabulary definitions. Some questions are only about these; other times, you'll need to know them to understand what is asked of you.
- You have about 70 seconds to complete each multiple-choice question. Pacing yourself during practice tests and exercises can help you get used to these time constraints—often it is more time than you think. Bank time on easier or shorter questions to use when asked to calculate or infer, study a graph that is presented to you, or consider long-run effects, all of which require more time.
- Because there is no guessing penalty, remember that making an educated guess is to your benefit. Use the process of elimination to narrow your choices. You might just guess the correct answer and get another point! Even if you can't reason through anything in the prompt, pick a response at random and move forward.
- Know your key graphs. The important ones will be tested heavily on both sections of the exam. Sometimes the important graphs will be presented to you. If so, take a mental snapshot of them at the end of the multiple-choice section—it is possible that the free-response section will include a prompt asking you to draw that very graph!
- Read the question and think of what your answer would be before reading the answer choices. When you get a match, it will almost certainly be right!
- Simplify complicated phrases if you're confused. Sometimes this will involve a sacrifice of meaning, but often it won't. Remember that many economic terms have names that are descriptive and therefore you can often figure out what they mean if you relax and break the terminology down into a simpler form.
- Expect the unexpected. You will see questions that ask you to apply information in various ways or combine ideas from two different units that you've studied. You can do it if you think logically!

Strategies for the Free-Response Section of the Exam

Both AP economics exams always contain three free-response questions. This section allows you 60 minutes to read, plan, and respond to all three questions. The first question will be longer and worth as much as the other two combined, meaning it is worth half your time and energy. Each question is actually a series of prompts and tasks organized in outline form. The individual tasks will relate to a common theme or topic, and frequently you will need to use the results from an earlier part of the problem in a later part. You should structure your response to match the structure of the question: you don't need to respond holistically with a main argument or thesis and there is no bonus for coming up with a creative approach.

Although it's tempting to think of the free-response section as the essay section, that's not correct. Unlike many other AP exams, you don't need to write a formal essay with an introduction, thesis statement, and conclusion to answer the free-response questions on the AP economics tests. Many parts of your response need not even be in complete sentences. You must, however, be on high alert for any time the problem's directives use the word "explain" because it means you need to give a reason for your response. Even then, you'll want that reason to be a short crisp sentence with a "because" in the middle, not a rambling paragraph that loses focus or explains different possibilities.

Achieving Free-Response Success

The single most important thing you can do to score well on the free-response section is to answer the questions that you are asked. It seems silly to point that out, doesn't it? By using the specific process explained below, you'll carefully read all of the elements of each question, identify the key words that direct your thinking, isolate the verbs that tell you how to answer, plan all your responses, and then check them over after you copy the correct parts neatly for your final answer. By thinking and planning more, you'll leave less on the final answer page, but more of it will be well-targeted to the specific questions asked. By answering each of the three free-response questions completely, you'll be well on your way to a great score on the AP exam. Let's look at some strategies to help you do just that.

Follow the process below to maximize the number of points you can earn with your knowledge of economics and minimize your chances of making silly mistakes. Four simple steps will fill your hour.

1. Skim through all the questions

Look for the theme or overall idea of the question, the big topics it tests, and which parts may be tricky or unfamiliar to you. Make a visible note for every time you're directed to produce a graph or give an explanation. This step should take you less than 10 minutes. Don't get too detailed or worry about the answers just yet.

2. Reread all of the questions more closely

As you reread the questions this time, circle the key words that trigger cause-effect processes and terms that help guide your thinking. Take the time to write out what your responses will be in the planning space provided—write out all of your analysis and thought processes. Do not worry about how messy it is, as long as you can read it. Do this for all three of the problems. This may take 20 to 25 minutes. It may seem frustrating that you have spent most of your time and have yet to write any of your final answers, but you have planned well and have given yourself two chances to read each item carefully and accurately. Time well spent.

3. Copy your responses neatly

Now go back to the questions in order and copy your final response down in the space provided. This time, you can relax because you've already planned out everything you will say. Your focus now is on the following three tasks: confirming that you've responded to each subpart of every question thoroughly and in the manner directed; writing your answer neatly and clearly for the grader to evaluate; and looking for places to make your responses shorter, if possible. You should have large, well-labeled graphs and use specific vocabulary instead of vague sentences. Don't be shy about underlining key words in your response. Avoid putting down more information than you were asked for. You want to make it as easy as possible to spot what's right in your answer. This step may well take you less time than the second step because you will write less and because you have already done the reasoning. You might spend about 15 to 25 minutes on this task.

4. Recheck your work

Take the rest of the time to recheck your work. Compare the outline subparts of each question to the structure of your response. Confirm that you labeled every line on each graph and showed changes with arrows and noted changes along axes with appropriate notation. Make sure you included a reason every time you were asked to explain. You should spend about 5 to 10 minutes on this step.

Typical Question Topics

The grid on the next page is a handy reference for some of the major topics that tend to be covered on a regular basis on the free-response section of the AP economics exams. Some topics are predictable and covered in the longer question every year. Other topics make up part of the longer question or appear in short questions from time to time. These are all topics that recur every few years; knowing all of these topics practically guarantees that the free-response section won't contain many surprises for you!

	Microeconomics	Macroeconomics
Long question will...	— Test perfect competition and/or monopoly in the product market — Require that you create graphs and find prices, quantities, and areas on them	— Require aggregate demand–aggregate supply graphing — Test your knowledge of fiscal and/or monetary policy
Long question may...	— Involve an assessment of efficiency — Include a situation with an externality — Involve a tax or subsidy — Include a price ceiling or floor — Involve a change of demand or of costs — Test your understanding of elasticity — Include adjustment into the long run	— Expect use of the money market to show the effects of monetary policy — Expect use of the loanable funds market to show crowding out — Expect use of the Phillips curve graph — Include foreign exchange or trade elements — Require a calculation — Involve one of the multiplier effects — Include adjustment into the long run
Short question may...	— Include price floor or ceiling and surplus areas — Involve deadweight loss — Check your knowledge of factor markets — Involve market failure or correction of it — Cover monopolistic competition — Involve a game theory duopoly problem — Test understanding of costs and production — Expect you to maximize utility — Involve taxes or subsidies — Cover your understanding of elasticity — Be a comparative advantage problem	— Explore a fundamental economic concept in detail, such as... - Gross Domestic Product - Unemployment - Inflation - Interest rates - Growth or long-run aggregate supply — Require a foreign exchange graph — Test the Phillips curve relationship — Involve loanable funds analysis — Include a T-account or money multiplier — Be a comparative advantage problem

Reading, Planning, and Outlining: Plan More to Write Less

Let's take a look at a sample long question from microeconomics and one from macroeconomics for reference, modeling parts of the process described above. We're analyzing long questions, but there are no structural differences in terms of how short questions are written and no special approaches you should use to solve them. Short questions will have fewer parts, incorporate fewer different topics, and contain less complexity and substructure. Otherwise, they are exactly the same. Here's the micro example:

> First, read over the problem quickly. Note that the question requires a graph of perfect competition, a graphical shift, two explanations about factor markets, and three long-run predictions. Parts (c) and (d) look harder and are probably worth more points.

A perfectly competitive, constant-cost industry produces widgets and is in long-run equilibrium.

a. Using side-by-side graphs, show the widget market and a typical widget firm, labeling the relevant cost curves. For the firm and for the industry, label the profit-maximizing price and quantity.

b. Assume that there is a significant increase in the popularity of widgets:

    i. Show the short-run effects of this on your graphs from part (a).

    ii. Show how this will affect the firm's profit-loss situation in the short run.

> Second, read the problem more thoroughly and construct your rough responses for about 10 minutes. In this stage you would start by sketching long-run equilibrium graphs and then complete part (b) on that same graph, showing an increase in demand taking the firm into a profit situation. You will need to construct your graphs for part (a) so that you can show an upward shift in the firm's P = MR = D line; clearly label an area of profit, making sure that prices on the graphs match.

c. Explain how the changes you showed in part (b) influence each:

    i. Marginal revenue product of labor

    ii. The number of widgetmakers the typical firm chooses to hire.

> Factor markets are challenging for many students—if that's true for you, spend a couple of extra minutes sketching graphs for part (c) which can help you reason toward the right response even though the graphs are not required in your final answer. Fortunately, you recall that MRP is demand for labor, so you think you see some connection between the two subparts of (c) and can use the planning graph to help form your reasoning. You're also relieved that part (c) is isolated; any mistakes you make here won't impact your ability to earn full credit on the other three main parts that only require product market analysis.

d. In the long run, how will each of the following have changed from its original level in part (a) as a result of the increase in popularity?

i. The number of widgetmaking firms.

ii. The price of a widget.

iii. The profit-loss situation of a typical widgetmaking firm.

When considering part (d) you see the logical link: the entry of new firms into the widget industry shifts supply to the right, lowering the price and erasing the profit box you drew in part (b). These last changes won't be on your final graph, but you can show or imagine them on your planning graph to eliminate confusion and the need to guess. You can also tell that the big idea of the question is to take the process full circle, ending up in long-run equilibrium once again—everything's the same for each firm, but there are more firms making up a larger industry quantity.

After each of these steps, you'd be wise to spend a couple of minutes considering the other questions on the test before continuing on this problem. Coming back to this item after working even a little on other ones increases the odds that you'll catch a silly mistake in your work or a clue in the question that you missed. Once you've done the second step and then refreshed your vision for this problem by working on something else for a minute, you'll be ready to copy down a neat, trimmed-down version of the answer for the graders.

The example that follows is for macroeconomics, but the process is the same: read and note major tasks, examine and build responses, then trim down and neatly copy. This time, we'll look at what you might have noted during the quick initial reading and then skip to the third step and examine a sample final response, noting the important features along the way.

First, your quick-read: you note that you draw a graph of a recession in the AD-AS model. You'll think of a fiscal solution, and examine its effects on a second graph you are required to draw: the loanable funds model. You spot that parts (c) through (e) test your knowledge of the crowding-out effect and culminate in one of three places you need to explain. Part (f) contains a foreign exchange application and the other two required explanations.

Assume the U.S. economy is operating below full-employment output with a budget deficit and a negative current account.

a. On a correctly labeled aggregate demand–aggregate supply graph, show

   i. current price level

   ii. current output in relation to full-employment output

b. Identify a fiscal policy action that could be taken to restore full-employment output.

c. State the effect this fiscal policy would have on the budget deficit.

d. Using a correctly labeled graph of the loanable funds market, show how the policy you identified in part (b) would affect real interest rates.

e. Indicate how this change in the loanable funds market would influence

   i. Private investment by American firms.

ii. Long-run economic growth. Explain.

f. Explain what effect the change in interest rates you identified in part (d) would have on each of the following

i. the international value of the U.S. dollar

ii. the current account deficit

A Sample Response

a.

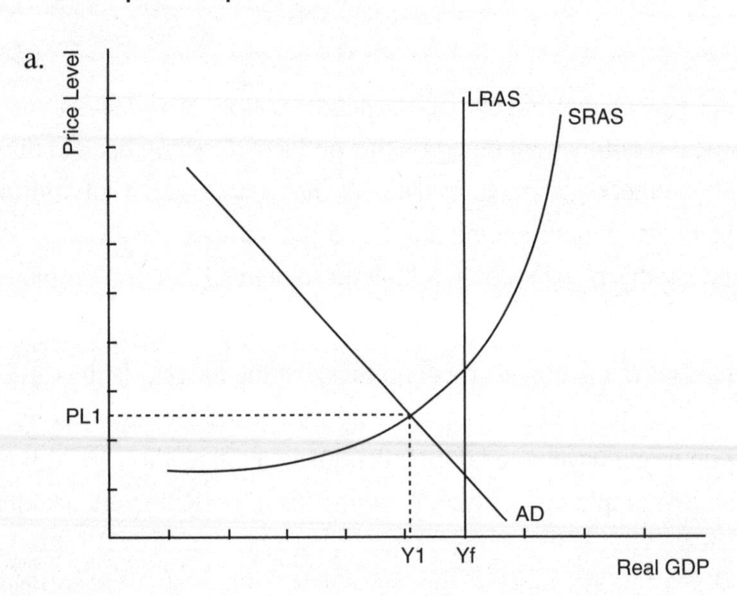

For this macro question, your final answer would ideally look like what is shown here. Note as you examine it, how little is written. The structure of the response matches the structure of the question.

The graphs both have labeled axes and curves; values on both axes are noted and labeled; changes are shown with arrows; numbered labels make clear the before-after relationship.

Parts (b) and (c) are done concisely and directly. The grader won't need to sift through extra words.

b. A tax cut would increase output toward full employment (Yf).

c. The budget deficit would increase.

d.

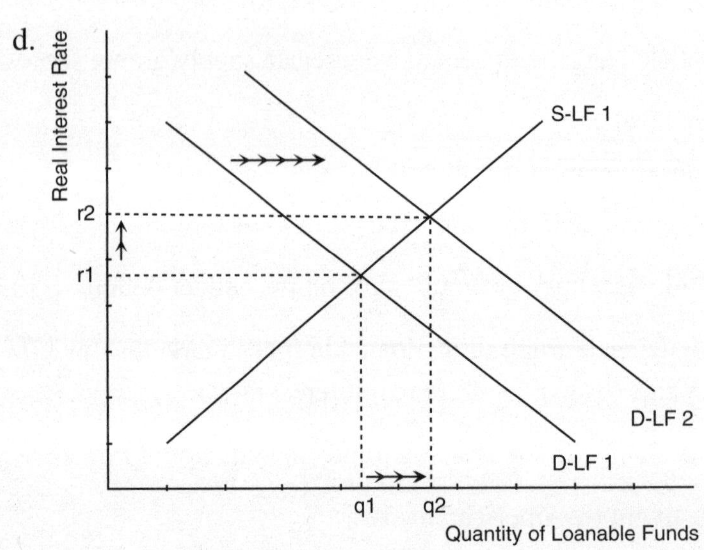

Part (d) shows the effects of the higher budget deficit. You spent time in step two reasoning why to shift demand for loanable funds right—the government demands more funds—but that explanation wasn't requested and you didn't provide it.

e. i. Investment would decrease due to the higher real interest rate.

ii. Decreased investment means less is added to the capital stock, therefore growth rate slows.

Parts (e) and (f) contain your explanations. These are definitely not essays, but short sentences that clearly state the direction of change and the reason for it. Knowing that you have 30 minutes to read and plan with the goal of constructing a response this short should give you the confidence you need to slow down and go through the process described above.

f. i. Higher interest rates increase demand for American assets; demand for dollars shifts right, causing the dollar to appreciate.

ii. The trade deficit grows because the stronger dollar makes imports feel cheaper to Americans and exports more expensive in foreign markets.

Some More Advice

Keep the ideas we've discussed in mind as you prepare for the AP economics exams. Becoming comfortable with these techniques will make you feel confident and prepared when you sit down to take the exam.

- When you are confused, look at the parts before and after the sub-part that have you puzzled. Often the question before is the cause and the one after is the effect of the piece you can't see. You might just be able to infer what the missing piece is!
- Use key economic vocabulary in your answer to improve precision and to make it shorter. One well-placed term or phrase is worth more than two rambling sentences.
- Label, label, and overlabel! Make it easy for the AP reader to award you points by making your response easy to navigate. If you make the reader's life easier, you'll earn the reward! Graphs should be completely labeled. You should mirror the question's outline structure in your response so the grader doesn't need to look for where you answered any particular part.
- Stay on topic and answer the question! Being direct when addressing the question fully is the single most important way to earn points on this section.
- Handwriting and the neatness of graphs are important—everything must be legible! If the AP reader can't read your writing, your knowledge won't translate into the maximum possible points.
- Allow a few minutes to quickly review your answers. You don't need to check the spelling of every single word, but you do need to make sure that all of your ideas

make it onto the page. Double-check that you respond to every part of the question and make your position clear in each case.

Three Final Words: Yes, You Can!

The free-response questions will emphasize the knowledge of the graphs and topics listed in the table on page 23; they are quite predictable and will not present major surprises if you know the models and how they operate. Do your best on all three questions, trying to form partial graphs or answers if you are completely confused. Because the problems are split into parts, even a tricky part can't completely prevent you from earning credit on the other sub-questions. You don't need to know it all to get a high score on the overall test. Relax and let your economics knowledge shine through!

Chapter 3

Basic Economic Concepts

Economics and Economic Questions

Economics is a social science concerned with the study of how scarce resources are allocated. Societies have concerned themselves with fundamental economic questions for a lot longer than there have been people called economists and economic departments in colleges (and certainly a lot longer than students have been studying for economics tests!). The problems economics addresses are fundamental to the nature of humans and our world. What are those problems? And why are they so inescapable?

TEST TIP

This chapter includes a lot of introductory ideas that many students think will be quite easy. Remember that the questions on this material count just as much as those questions that test the more difficult economic concepts. In fact, those of you taking both economics exams will get double payoff for learning these basic concepts because all the concepts in this chapter are fair game for both the microeconomics and the macroeconomics tests.

Because human wants are infinite and the resources people can use to satisfy them are finite, we face **scarcity**. There is no way everyone can have all of what they want given the fact that human labor, land, capital, and entrepreneurial ability are limited. Later, you will need to know more particulars about these four types of resources, but for now think of these as four categories useful for dividing the materials we use in various ways to generate all the products and services that anyone wants to buy.

Three Fundamental Economic Questions

Several results stem from the scarcity principle. One is that all societies must face some challenging questions. Economists generally agree that we must address at least the following three questions:

- What goods and services will we produce with the resources we have? **(What should we make?)** Should societies make the goods that people with money want to buy, or should they attempt to make items that people need, no matter their ability to pay? Should societies continue to make large quantities of goods people want even if those goods do not serve individual or societal interests? How many MP3 players, cars, windmills, and pairs of pink slippers should we make?

- How will we use the resources to make those goods and services? **(How should we make it?)** Should we make goods directly, or do we use roundabout production methods? Do we first spend resources developing high-tech tools and advanced methods that later allow large numbers of finished goods to be produced more quickly and cheaply? Do individuals decide how they perform their work or are private or public institutions in control of choosing production methods? How do the methods used to make goods change over time?

- How should the goods and services we make be rationed or apportioned among people? **(Who gets it? How do we distribute it?)** Are goods allocated according to ability to pay, or are they allocated more equally? What kinds of property rights exist and how are they protected? Does everyone that wants a particular item get one, or do some people get to have all they want while others get none?

As you can probably tell, these are weighty and controversial questions. During the course of human history, these questions have been at the center of ugly family spats, nasty political campaigns, riotous protests, bloody revolutions, and brutal wars. People have fought about how to answer the questions and just as frequently about who gets to answer them.

Economic Systems and Fields of Economics

Probably no two human societies have handled these three questions and related issues exactly the same way. Nonetheless, economists think it is fun to classify societies into groups based on which of two (or three) systems they employ—market systems, command systems, and sometimes also traditional systems.

Economic Systems

One way to respond to these and related questions is to decide that individuals own the productive resources in an economy and can sell them or rent them out to the highest bidder. The idea that when individuals and households pursue this self-interested goal they often serve the collective interest is attributed to Adam Smith, and it is considered fundamental to market-oriented (or capitalist) economies. **Market systems** tend to rest on this notion of private property and generally hold that the big economic questions should be answered, not in one central place, but through interactions among people on a decentralized level. Thus, a market economy typically does not have one person or group of people who decides how many slippers or bowling balls to make, what color they should be, what tools are used to make them, and how they should be distributed among customers. In general, those decisions are made between producers and consumers, with buyers sending signals through their purchasing decisions. As more of a specific type of good is demanded, producers get the message that they should find more resources for making that type of good and generate more units for sale.

DIDYOUKNOW?

Scottish economist Adam Smith's seminal work *An Inquiry into the Nature and Causes of the Wealth of Nations* was published in 1776. Many consider it to be the first articulation of several principles of market economics, and Smith is known to many as the father of modern capitalism.

This market-based approach has some distinct advantages. It tends to encourage production of the goods we are willing to pay the most for by giving owners of resources incentives to put those resources to the uses for which the owners will get paid the most. Because there is no centralized place where these highly important economic questions are answered, it is difficult for one small group of people to engineer a specific self-interested outcome. This suggests that the system as a whole is less susceptible to corruption than more centralized alternatives. In the roughly three centuries since this market-based system has developed and been formally articulated, these advantages have led most of the economically advanced nations in the world to adopt at least significant parts of a market-based system.

However, the market approach has also shown a few drawbacks. In particular, it associates self-interest with the common interest too tightly—many times people take actions that promote their own gain and leave others worse off. It may tend toward overconsumption of resources in the short term without regard for long-run consequences (species extinction, deforestation, and the debate over climate change are notable examples). In its purest form, the market approach has a difficult time distinguishing between wants and needs. People who lack the ability to pay may not get the goods they need, while others who have spending power may be able to have low-level or even frivolous wants met. As a result, market systems have been criticized for inequality and oppression. Remember, however, that many of these problems have existed far longer than market systems and have been features of societies that weren't market-based.

TEST TIP

Whatever its strengths and weaknesses, the exam(s) you are studying for cover your knowledge of market economics, not personal views and debates about capitalism. Disregard those issues when answering practice questions or taking the test.

Alternatively, one could suggest that a more coordinated and centralized decision process leads to a more logical, planned use of resources. **Command systems** attempt to work through economic issues in this way. A central planning group sets goals for what will be produced, rather than let the decisions be made by buyers and sellers acting independently. Typically this planning group is at the top of a hierarchy and wields a mix of governmental and economic power.

In theory, a command system allows more rational use of resources. It can also be a tool for transforming a society toward a specific goal much faster (the former Soviet Union quickly developed heavy industry in the 1930s as a result of Stalin's five-year plans). However, the planners are often far removed from individual consumers, and they are not particularly responsive to consumers' desires. Thus, the command economy suffers from what has been called the economic calculation problem, a tendency to misallocate goods, leading to persistent surpluses and/or shortages (the Soviet Union suffered grain shortages at various times and longstanding shortages of other consumer goods). Another criticism leveled against command systems is that they tend to be more authoritarian and less respectful of humans' desires to self-manage.

Systems that attempt to tell people what they *should* want rather than listening to what they *do* want have been on the decline in recent human history in both the political and economic realms. Thus, market systems have become more common around the world, and several societies, most notably the former Soviet bloc, have begun a transition away from central planning. Command economics currently is practiced in some form in North Korea, Cuba, Saudi Arabia, and Belarus. Many modern industrialized countries today are classified as using a market system, including South Korea, the United States, Japan, Singapore, and the United Kingdom. However, nearly all of the industrial modern economies are better described as using **mixed market systems** because they use elements of governmental regulation and involvement in their markets.

It might be helpful to imagine arranging societies along a spectrum: from those that are more market-based on one end to those that are more command-based on the other. Hong Kong is more market-based than Britain, which is more market-based than Sweden, which is more market-based than Saudi Arabia, which is more market-based than North Korea.

TEST TIP

Don't overthink questions about economic systems—they won't focus on which modern countries fit into which categories or the gray area of mixed market systems. Understand the central features of each system:

—Market: Private ownership of resources

—Command: Central planning of production

—Traditional: Preindustrial, continuity-based

Regardless of which AP economics test you take, the majority of the questions will require you to think *within* the market paradigm and not about the contrasting kinds of societies.

Some scholars and texts cite a third type of economic system—**traditional**—to describe societies of the past and those today that do not have formal economic structures or operate in a manner that does not fit neatly into the two modern categories. Societies using this aptly named approach base most production and distribution decisions on how they've done things in the past. They don't figure too prominently in modern globalized economic trade or in the AP economics curriculum.

Fields of Economics

Economic inquiry can be divided based on the level of analysis on which it focuses. In general, **microeconomists** view matters from the small scale—from the perspective of individual firms and households. They examine how each seeks to maximize its own well-being through selling and buying decisions. They may also study markets for specific goods or services or types of labor.

Macroeconomists view the economy from a larger perspective. They address issues such as economic growth, inflation, and international trade patterns, and they examine how governmental policies can work to improve the function of the economy as a whole.

Both macroeconomists and microeconomists use a similar approach in that they pose questions, study how the world works, and try to use a version of the scientific method to reach conclusions. Both use the *ceteris paribus* or "other things equal" assumption, holding all but one factor fixed at a time. The conclusions they reach are further categorized into positive and normative categories. **Positive economic conclusions** and statements express factual matters and should be capable of being empirically proven true or false. **Normative economic conclusions** and statements express what should or ought to be and are typically based more on judgment and interpretation.

TEST TIP

The difference between positive economic conclusions and normative economic conclusions should be easy to spot once you are aware of these two categories. The distinction between factual claims and opinion claims shows up in lots of areas of inquiry. Practice categorizing news headlines if this concept is a bit fuzzy for you.

Scarcity, Factors of Production, and Opportunity Cost

The scarcity principle is the most important and most fundamental issue of economics and is the reason why societies must ask the three thorny questions. Scarcity is the result of limited resources and unlimited human wants. To be **scarce**, something must be both limited and desirable. **Consumer goods and services** are desirable exactly because they have utility, the economic term for want-satisfying power. But are they limited? They are because the factors of production used to make them are limited, so goods in turn are scarce.

TEST TIP

Even if you aren't a Rolling Stones fan, listen to Mick Jagger sing "You Can't Always Get What You Want" and the concept of scarcity will be easier to remember!

Economic resources absolutely qualify as scarce on both counts: They are finite and we find them desirable because they are used to make the goods we want. (*Goods* is often shorthand for "goods and services.") What are these resources?

- **Land** is the land itself and the natural resources that come with it. Thus, everything from animals, plants, and water on the land to ores and fossil fuels buried deep beneath the surface are all included in the concept of land for economic purposes. Payments made for the use of land are called rent. The amount of land is clearly limited; conflicts over control of land throughout human history are a painful testament to this fact.

DID YOU KNOW?

Land reclamation projects have allowed cities and countries to increase in size for centuries. Much of the Netherlands lies on reclaimed land, as do significant portions of many international cities, including Helsinki, Chicago, Dublin, Beirut, and Rio de Janeiro. However, these projects have had a high cost in terms of economic resources.

- **Labor** is the human effort used to make the goods and services we want. It is a significant component of the production, distribution, and sales process of all that we buy. There are a limited number of people, and thus a limited amount of labor is available for a society to tap into at any given time. The cost of labor varies dramatically throughout the world. Because of this difference and the ease of modern transportation, many firms have focused their production efforts in places where labor is inexpensive. Firms in places with higher wages have thus tended toward focusing on providing services or producing goods with a less labor-intensive method in recent years in order to keep the prices of their goods competitive in global markets. Although some labor is probably of a higher quality or more productive than others, it is best at this level of economic study to think of all labor as undifferentiated.
- **Capital** is the economic term for tools of all types. Capital goods are designed and made by societies for use in the production process. As anyone who has ever used a shovel to dig a hole or an ax to chop wood knows, the effective use of capital goods can drastically increase output quantity and quality in many situations—it makes some jobs possible that otherwise could not be done. **Physical capital** refers to goods used to make other goods and services—tools such as computers, software, scissors, sewing machines, pizza ovens, earthmovers, massage tables, and industrial robots.

  Some of the tools we use and need to make things are not physical capital, but rather are specialized skills, knowledge, and talents that we develop while in school, while being formally trained for a job, or through experience. These specialized skills, knowledge, and talents are considered **human capital** and can have just as big an effect on productivity.

TEST TIP

Capital, especially human capital, and its connection to economic growth are difficult concepts for many economics students. *Education, job training, skill development, vocational enhancement,* and *human resources development* are various ways of referring to the basic concept of know-how (human capital) that you already understand.

A nation's **capital stock** is the quantity of capital at its disposal at any given time. Think of it as the combined contents of a national tool shed. We add to the stock of capital in a process known as **investment**: the production and purchasing of new capital, either human or physical. Investment is important for two reasons. First, over time capital goods deteriorate, wear out, and ultimately break in a process known as **depreciation**. Second, by adding to the capital stock, we increase our capacity to make even more of the goods and services we want tomorrow than we can make today. In fact, all making of capital (whether physical or human) represents a decision to spend resources not for the production of goods to enjoy now, but for the increased ability to produce more later.

- **Entrepreneurial ability** is the name for the talent and vision required to mesh the other three types of resources (land, capital, and labor) in a manner that produces goods and services that have utility. Which materials to use, which mix of capital and labor to employ, and how to guide worker specialization are all decisions entrepreneurs make. The early twentieth-century decision to arrange automobile manufacturing into an assembly line was a breakthrough in entrepreneurship. At face value, this concept may seem like a specific version of labor with some particular organizational skills involved. The crucial difference between entrepreneurial ability and the other factors of production is ownership. Typically the other factors are provided by others, and thus explicit money payments need to be made for them (rent for land, wages for labor, interest for capital), whereas the firm's owner provides his or her own effort and ingenuity *at his or her own risk*. If the revenue generated from the venture is greater than the explicit costs paid for use of resources that belong to others, then the entrepreneur is left with profit; if the revenue generated is less, the entrepreneur takes a loss.

Choices and Opportunity Cost

Resources are scarce and therefore goods are scarce. We must make choices about the goods we want, and when we do that, we are choosing alternative uses of our resources. When we make those choices, we sacrifice other options. The more farmland we spend growing soybeans, the less there is for corn. The more time you spend studying for your AP economics test, the less time you have for studying other academic subjects. Scarcity forces us to make choices, and those choices entail sacrifice or cost. The economic term for this sacrifice is **opportunity cost**. To be more precise, opportunity cost refers to the benefits forgone when we sacrifice the best option not chosen.

Let's explain that definition a little bit using a simple example. You've been invited to go to a movie and to get pizza with some friends. What does this experience cost you? Part of the opportunity cost is easy to see: You have to buy your ticket to the movie and purchase your fair share of the pizza if you don't want your friends to call you a deadbeat. That's the **explicit cost** you face—payments you will need to make to others. But there are lots of things you could have chosen to do with that three hours of time: Read a well-written AP economics review book, play charades with your grandparents, organize your sock drawer, use Hulu to go on a rerun binge. The possibilities are endless, but you can't do them all. Many people work toward some decisions by narrowing their alternatives to just two and then picking between them. Had you not gone for pizza and the movie, what would you have done? If you decided to give up reading this book and spent time with friends instead, then the evening also entailed an **implicit cost**—something you sacrificed but didn't make an explicit money payment for—in this case, two chapters' worth of AP economics knowledge.

In some cases, the implicit cost is easily measured and calculated. If your next best alternative was working a three-hour shift at your job that pays $10.00 per hour, then the missed time from work has a clear $30.00 value, and you would add that to the $20.00 you spend on the movie and pizza to get the full value of the opportunity cost, in this case $50.00. In real life, it is often difficult to estimate the value of time in a manner that allows combining explicit and implicit costs neatly. Economists have several techniques for getting at these types of values, such as having people imagine what kind of payment they'd accept to be without the benefit, or carefully watching their choices and trying to infer an internal value structure, but most are fraught with difficulty. Fortunately for you, any AP problem that expects you to attach a number to implicit cost will make clear the value of that forgone benefit. Remember that opportunity cost is what you sacrifice in order to experience a gain, including not just what you pay out (explicit), but also whatever would have been the best benefit you could have gained doing something else (implicit).

The Production Possibilities Curve and Productive Efficiency

Economists have developed a simple model that depicts both scarcity and opportunity cost. This graphical model, called the production possibilities curve (PPC) or production possibilities frontier (PPF) (these acronyms and the terms they stand for are interchangeable) will be useful to you in visualizing the options available to a society, showing what's gained and lost by making alternative choices, showing change over time, and solving problems related to trade with another society. (Pretty cool that we can show all that on a graph with only one down-sloping curve!)

Look at the two sample PPC (or PPF) graphs in Figure 3-1. Let's walk through the process of figuring out what they tell us.

Figure 3-1. Production Possibilities Frontier

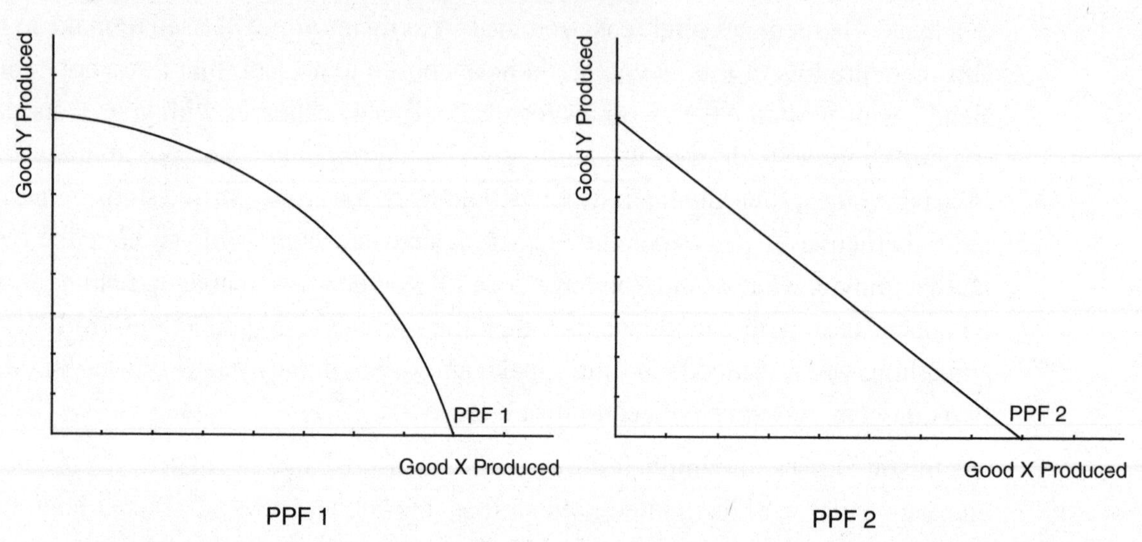

Each graph shows a curve (in economics, a straight line is often called a curve) formed from connecting points, each of which represents production alternatives available to the society; that is, each point is a combination of some units of good X and some units of good Y that the society has enough resources to produce in a given time period (e.g., a year). We might choose the term *frontier* to remind ourselves that points on the frontier represent various decisions to produce all that the society can of goods X and Y in differing amounts. Clearly the society could choose to operate inside this frontier by producing fewer goods than they are able to, and in the extreme case they might operate at the origin, representing the (silly) decision to produce none of either good.

Does any society make only two goods? (Wouldn't that be a weird place to live?) Societies probably produce lots of different commodities, just as all human groups have for a long time. Fortunately, the problems you will be tested on use the assumption of a two-good economy. It's a bit oversimplified, but it makes your work a lot easier. And it can still reveal quite a bit about real economic problems, especially if we keep in mind that each axis could also represent a type of good rather than a single specific product. For example, the categories of capital and consumer goods are sometimes placed on the two axes.

What important similarities can we see in the two graphs of Figure 3-1? Both reveal scarcity and opportunity cost. Each PPF slopes downward (graphical language for an inverse relationship). In other words, if we choose to make more of good X, we can't make as many units of good Y, and vice versa. In a world without scarcity, we could choose more of both goods with no sacrifice at all. Any PPC that has an up-sloping portion violates principle 1 of economics! From each graph, we can see that moving rightward along the curve entails moving downward at the same time. Given points and values, we could calculate the slope so that we could tell just how many Ys we have to forgo in order to have more Xs or even how many Ys the next X will cost us. These are attributes of all production possibilities frontiers, not just the two shown in Figure 3-1. Remember that **all PPCs slope downward** because of scarcity, and that the **slope is the opportunity cost** of X in terms of Y.

TEST TIP

Remember that slope is rise/run. Because of the inverse relationship, the slope of a PPF is negative. When comparing two points on the same curve, either the rise (change in Y value) or the run (change in X value) is negative. We don't have negative numbers of goods in economics, but we can interpret a negative sign in this case as meaning we have less of something, just as a positive sign can symbolize having more of the other good.

What is the important difference between the two sample PPCs in Figure 3-1? Note that PPF 2 is a straight line—a curve with a constant slope—and PPF 1 is bowed outward—its slope gets steeper and steeper the further right one moves along the curve. Economists describe PPF 1 as **concave with respect to the origin**. The difference between the two is quite significant. Because PPF 1 is concave, it tells us that the opportunity cost of each good rises when more units of that good are produced. This contrasts with PPF 2. Because PPF 2 has a constant slope, it depicts a situation in which opportunity cost is the same no matter which combination of Xs and Ys are produced. Most of the time in the real world when we produce more of a good, we experience the **law of increasing opportunity cost**.

TEST TIP

The AP exam will definitely test your understanding of the law of increasing opportunity cost. It will also have questions that operate in the easier (but slightly less realistic) world of constant opportunity cost.

Take a closer look at the curves in Figure 3-2, which shows sample points and specific goods. What happens if we increase food production under two different sets of conditions? In both cases, imagine starting at point A, producing one unit of food. If two more units of food are produced, we would slide right along our PPF and need to move down—and however much we move down is the cost (in terms of clothing sacrificed) of those next two units of food. In the left panel, a movement from point A to point C involves sacrificing about three-quarters of a unit of clothing, whereas in the right panel, clothing production must be decreased by two full units. Now, from point C, with a production of three units of food, imagine increasing food production again by two units, sliding down and to the right to point E. In the left panel, we now need to sacrifice about 1.5 units of clothing (twice as much as before) to get those two more units of food; in the right panel, the cost of those two more units of food remains constant at two units of clothing.

Figure 3-2. Calculating Opportunity Cost

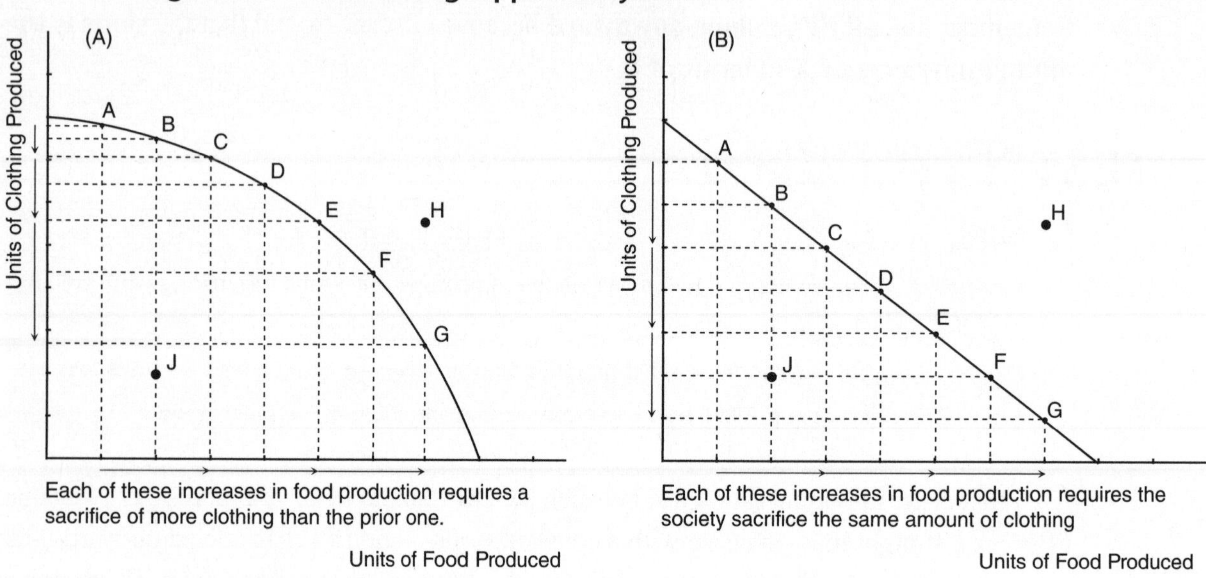

Panel A. Increasing Opportunity Cost

Panel B. Constant Opportunity Cost

Repeating the process once more, we see that moving from point E to point G in the left panel entails forgoing almost three units of clothing (the cost doubled again) to gain two units of food, and again the cost of two more units of food in the right panel remained at two clothing units.

Note points H and J in Figure 3-2. For both societies, point H represents a desirable combination of goods that cannot be produced with technology and resources currently available. Because it lies outside the frontier that represents the societies' production limits, this point is currently unattainable. Conversely, point J lies inside the curve and therefore represents a combination of goods that would not be **productively efficient** for that society—it is attainable, but not desirable, because there would be a way to produce more of both goods with no sacrifice, which represents an underutilization of resources available to the society. Points A to G on both graphs are all productively efficient choices because they all represent situations in which the society cannot choose to have more of any good without sacrificing something else.

TEST TIP

Productive efficiency will be discussed in a later chapter. It is particularly important for AP Microeconomics students. For now, think of it as "making all you can," "not leaving resources idle," or "making each unit at the lowest possible cost."

Examine Figure 3-3 for a moment. Don't worry if it seems complex; you'll rarely, if ever, see a graph with this many curves on it on an AP exam. However, you should feel comfortable using the graph to answer questions like the following:

Figure 3-3. Varying PPF Shapes

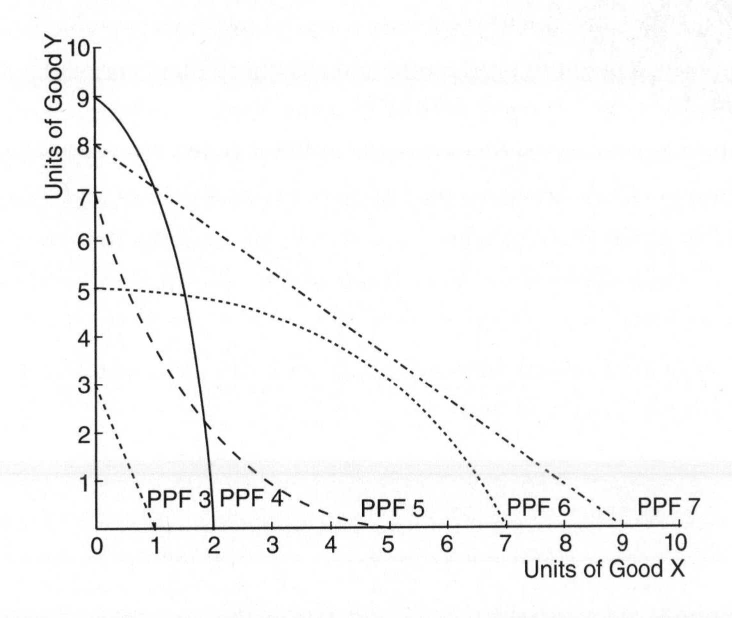

- Which PPFs show increasing opportunity cost? Constant opportunity cost? Decreasing opportunity cost?
- For the society operating with PPF 4, what is the cost of the first unit of good X? The second unit?
- If PPF 5 shows the society's production, how much clothing must be sacrificed in order to produce the first two units of good X? The next three units of good X?
- For each pair of PPFs, make a statement comparing or contrasting production of goods X and Y.

What accounts for the shape of the different PPF curves? Why does opportunity cost generally increase as more units are produced, why does it sometimes remain constant, and why might it actually decrease under unusual circumstances? The answers have to do with the types of resources used to make the goods in question. If all resources are perfectly adaptable to alternative uses, then a society may easily produce extra units of a good at a constant opportunity cost. In other words, as we allocate more and more resources to making that particular good, we don't get less efficient at making it. If you see a linear PPF, you know that opportunity cost is constant and resources in that example are equally suitable for making the two goods.

In most real-life situations, this isn't true. In the real economy, many resources are not so adaptable to alternative uses. Mountainous land with extractable metals would be helpful in making cars, for example, but not corn. Farmland rich in nutrients, however, would not help make cars, but it can be used to grow corn. Capital goods that have already been produced help illustrate the point as well: combines, fertilizers, and hybrid seeds are ideally suited resources for growing corn (they've been engineered that way!). Similarly, large auto production and assembly plants are designed and filled with equipment that could not possibly help grow corn. The training, education, and experience of the laborers in each area result in labor being specialized toward the production of certain goods or services. As a society produces more and more of a good, they start by employing the resources best suited to its production, then move to less useful resources. As a result, opportunity cost (how much of something else is sacrificed for the next unit gained) increases and, as it does, the slope of the PPF gets steeper and steeper. The concave (bowed outward) shape of a PPF tells you that the principle of increasing opportunity cost is at work.

TEST TIP

If opportunity cost decreased as resources were allocated from the production of one good to another, the PPF would bow inward, or be convex to the origin. This situation is not commonly tested on the AP exams and doesn't occur too often in real life because it would mean the society chose to use less efficient resources first as it increased production of a good.

The PPF represents the combinations of goods available to the society at a given time, and it shifts over time as the quantity or quality of its resources change. Bombings that destroy factories, bridges, ports, and offices shift a society's PPF inward. Epidemics that depopulate a society rob it of its labor resources and produce the same effect.

More common is an outward shift of the PPF as a society experiences **economic growth**, the increase in an economy's productive capacity over time. Economic growth can occur with an increase in the land, labor, capital, or technological/entrepreneurial resources available to the society. Better education and training, a healthier or larger labor force, productivity improvements, technological breakthroughs, and discovery of new processes or resources are some of the primary reasons for the growth of the world's economies over the centuries (and they're also the reasons commonly tested on the AP exams).

Figure 3-4. Outward Shift of the PPC Depicting Economic Growth

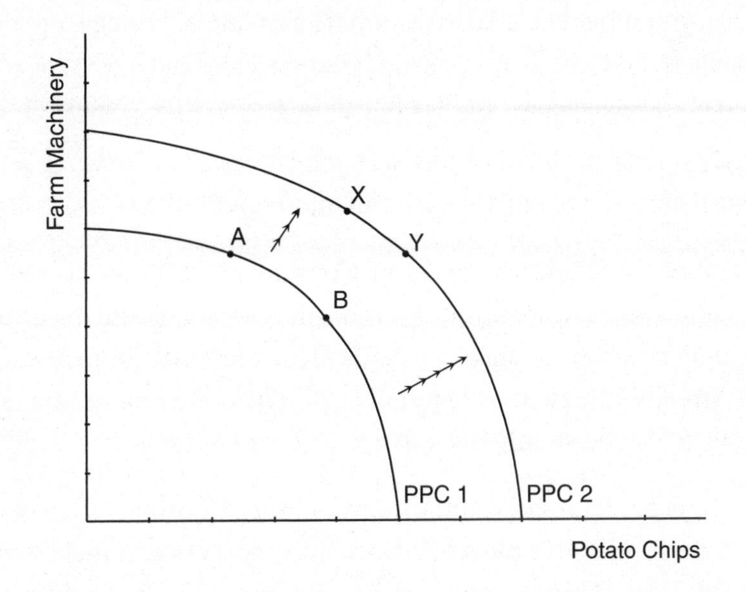

Figure 3-4 shows an outward shift of a PPC that might have resulted from one of these causes. Before the shift, points A and B on PPC 1 were productively efficient, and X and Y were desirable but unattainable. After the shift, points X and Y become available alternatives to the society, and now A and B look like yesterday's fad.

Note that, if the society on PPC 1 were choosing between operating at point A or point B, it might increase its chances of having future growth by choosing point A. Making more potato chips, a consumer good, now doesn't do much to increase future productive capabilities. On the other hand, choosing point A, with fewer chips and more planting and harvesting equipment, would more likely increase the ability to make both goods more effectively in the future—the society would have more practice making combines and more machinery to use on the farms of the future.

Comparative Advantage and Trade

An important principle of economics is that trade can be mutually beneficial, leaving both parties better off. Sometimes, of course, an exchange leaves one party better off and one worse off (think of swindles, Ponzi schemes, and bad sports trades), but often the result is a win-win. Why? The needs of the people or societies diverge enough that they value goods differently. This subjective value of something can be called the **reservation price** one places on a good. This reservation price can be shown mathematically or with reference to the production possibilities curve. The ways societies gain from trade can be depicted as giving them the ability to operate *outside* their PPC, thus appearing to cheat that scarcity monster ever so slightly.

Given the production alternatives for two people or countries making a particular pair of goods, you should be able to determine absolute advantage, opportunity cost, comparative advantage, how production should be specialized, and a possible trading ratio that would be mutually advantageous. We'll define those terms in the context of solving a sample problem.

Data for a problem of this sort can be presented several ways. The following three stimuli are equivalent. Take a moment to confirm that you recognize the similarity.

- Suppose it takes workers in Constanzia six hours to build a hovercraft and two hours to make a bicycle. Workers in Norland require five hours to build a hovercraft and one hour to make a bicycle. This presentation focuses on the number of inputs (in this case, hours) required to produce one unit of output. Call this input data (it can also be summarized in a 2 × 2 grid or table).
- In a production period of sixty hours, Constanzia's workers can make ten hovercraft or thirty bicycles. Norland's workers can make twelve hovercraft or sixty bicycles. This presentation focuses on the various amounts of output each society can produce with the same number of inputs. Call this output data (it can also be summarized in a 2 × 2 grid or table).
- The graph in Figure 3-5 shows the production alternatives for Norland and Constanzia when making bicycles and hovercraft, two forms of transportation used in both societies. We call this the graphical presentation, for obvious reasons.

Figure 3-5. Production Before Trade

Note that the slopes of the PPCs are the costs of a hovercraft in the respective nations.

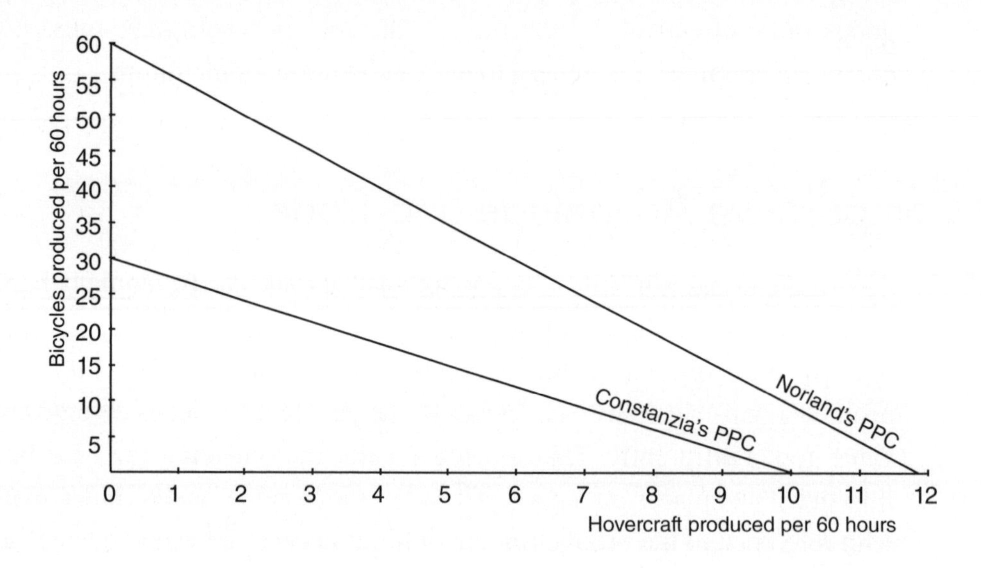

First, you might be asked about **absolute advantage**. This concept is simple and can be phrased two ways: It is the ability of a society to make a unit of output with fewer units of input than a potential trading partner, *or* it is the ability of a society to make more units of output with the same number of inputs than a potential trading partner. The two are logically equivalent. In this example, Norland has the absolute advantage in production of bicycles because its workers can make a bicycle in one hour as opposed to two hours (or because in sixty hours they can make sixty bicycles rather than thirty). Note on the PPC representation that the *y*-intercept for Norland is greater than for Constanzia—this always indicates an absolute advantage in the good on the *y*-axis. Norland also has an absolute advantage in hovercraft production because it can make more craft with the same number of inputs (twelve is more than ten) or make one craft with fewer inputs (five hours is less than six hours). Norland also has a greater *x*-intercept than Constanzia—the greater *x*-intercept always correlates with an absolute advantage in the production of good *x*. It is possible for one country to have an absolute advantage in the production of both goods.

TEST TIP

Sometimes trade problems refer to individual people rather than societies or countries. It makes no difference—solve the problem exactly the same way. Note also that this problem type has always featured constant opportunity cost. It is frequently used as a short free-response question on either the macro- or microeconomics exam and typically appears in some multiple-choice questions as well.

The next step involves converting the data to opportunity cost. Sometimes you'll be asked directly about the opportunity cost of making something in one of the societies. Even if you aren't, you'll need to go through this step to address the remaining aspects of this type of problem—in particular to determine comparative advantage. In this case, the opportunity cost for each country is shown in Table 3-1.

Table 3-1. Opportunity Costs for Constanzia and Norland

	Opportunity Cost of Producing a Bicycle	Opportunity Cost of Producing a Hovercraft
Constanzia	$\frac{1}{3}$ hovercraft	3 bicycles
Norland	$\frac{1}{5}$ hovercraft	5 bicycles

This data can be deduced from any of the presentations above. Recall that the slope of a PPC is the opportunity cost of the good on the *x*-axis. This means the reciprocal of the slope is the opportunity cost of the good on the *y*-axis. For the other methods, the question to resolve is, How many of the other good did I sacrifice in order to get one of these? The opportunity cost is what you give up per unit of what you get. Norland's cost of a bicycle is determined by taking the twelve hovercraft it sacrificed and dividing that number by the sixty bicycles they might now want to produce. We find that each bike is produced at a cost of 0.2 hovercraft, or one-fifth of a hovercraft. An easy way to double-check your work is to remember that, for the same country, the two values must be reciprocals.

Now it is easy to determine **comparative advantage**, the ability to produce a good at a lower opportunity cost than a neighbor. In this example, Norland has a comparative advantage in producing bicycles because it sacrifices 0.2 hovercraft to make one bicycle, while Constanzia must give up 0.33 hovercraft for each bicycle. Constanzia has the comparative advantage in hovercraft production because it must forgo three bicycles to make one (less than Norland's cost of five bicycles). Note that, because costs are reciprocal, a nation could never have comparative advantage in the production of both goods.

It follows that the countries can mutually trade to lower the cost of the good they produce at a higher cost and find themselves better off than they could have been relying exclusively on domestically produced goods—the key is to have each **specialize** or make only the good that they produce at a lower cost, the one they have a comparative advantage in producing. In this case, Constanzia can specialize in hovercraft and Norland in bicycles. To double-check, note that the society with the flatter PPC should always specialize in the *x*-axis good and the one with the steeper PPC should specialize in the *y*-axis good.

Last, you may need to find a **trading ratio** (or **terms of trade**) that benefits both societies between the domestic opportunity costs. There will always be a range of correct answers to this; the best practice is to find one that is relatively easy to work with (the test writers are aware that you can't use a calculator so they won't give you nasty numbers to work with). Because Constanzia will make hovercraft and trade them to Norland, they will want to sell them for more than it cost them to make each one—the residents of Constanzia need more than three bicycles for each hovercraft because that is what they sacrificed to make one hovercraft. Conversely, Norland's residents would never pay more than five bicycles for a hovercraft because they can produce one at home for that cost. So the value of a hovercraft that can benefit both societies would be between three and five bicycles. Trading four bicycles for each hovercraft fits the bill nicely. For Norland, the cost of a hovercraft has dropped from five bicycles to four, and for Constanzia, the cost of a bicycle is lower—now only one-quarter, or 0.25, of a hovercraft rather than one-third, or 0.33. Both countries are now able to choose to consume at points that lie outside their PPCs.

Figure 3-6. Consumption Possibilities Expand as a Result of Trade

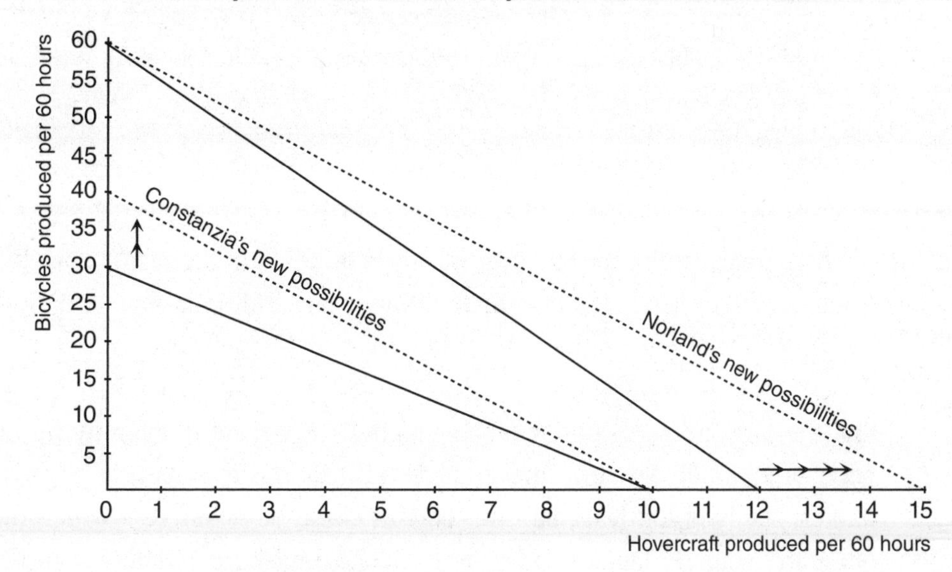

Figure 3-6 shows the original PPFs for both societies as solid lines and the new possibilities curves that result from trading as dotted lines. Note that if Constanzia specializes in hovercraft production, it can have forty rather than thirty bicycles—a ten-bicycle gain due to the trade system used. The dotted trading possibilities curves for both countries have a slope of –4. Why is this? Think about what slope represents in a PPF graph if the answer isn't obvious to you.

Marginal Thinking and Allocative Efficiency

One detail that the PPC can never tell us by itself is which combination of goods we ought to produce. Knowing this detail requires knowledge of our wants, our needs, and how we value additional units of the good. The PPC only tells about making goods, not about the value we place on them. The allocatively efficient point, or the one that suits us best, depends on determining the proper amount of each good. We want to take advantage of all situations in which marginal benefit is greater than marginal cost, and we want to avoid actions that have a higher marginal cost than marginal benefit. The **allocatively efficient** amount of anything is found where marginal benefit equals marginal cost. If we were to follow this rule with everything, we'd end up with the mix of goods that satisfies us more than any of the other available alternatives.

TEST TIP

Marginal thinking is important to all areas of economics, but it is especially vital for those preparing for the AP Microeconomics exam—well over half of the questions on a typical AP Microeconomics exam require some sort of marginal thinking. When you read or hear the terms *next, extra, additional,* or *change in,* it is the economist's code to get you to think marginally.

Marginal values are changes in other values. Let's consider briefly the added personal benefit experienced in consumption of one additional marshmallow—the marginal benefit (MB) of a marshmallow. When marginal benefit is rising, it means you enjoyed the last marshmallow even more than the one before it. When MB is declining, it means that the last one wasn't as satisfying as the one before it, even though it may have still been enjoyable. Anytime marginal benefit is positive, eating another marshmallow makes you happier. But marginal benefit could be negative—which means that eating one more actually made you less happy. The phrase *too much of a good thing* illustrates this situation well.

The idea of balancing marginal cost and marginal benefit should seem intuitive and logical to you—you probably use it all the time. Perhaps by deciding to indulge in richer foods only on special occasions or balancing homework or study time between classes, you have become quite practiced at using marginal thinking even without knowing what it was called or that it was a key economic concept.

The Circular Flow Model

Figure 3-7 provides a simplified picture of the interactions between major institutions in a private, closed economy where firms and individual consumers (households) play roles as both buyers and sellers.

Figure 3-7. Simplified Circular Flow Model

In this simple model, the economy is private (meaning there is no government or public sector) and closed (meaning there is no international trade).

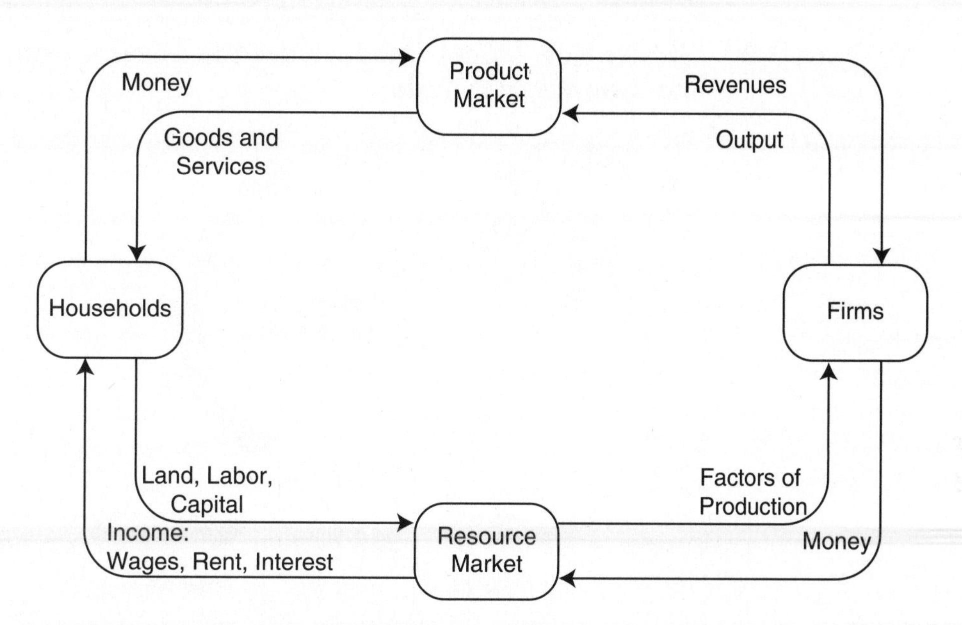

TEST TIP

When preparing for the AP exam, be sure you can draw a simplified circular flow model and respond to questions about what it shows.

Note that the clockwise arrows represent flows of inputs (resources or factors of production) and finished goods. Counterclockwise arrows show flows of money payments for those resources or goods. In product markets at the top, finished goods flow from business firms to households and individuals, who purchase them in a process called **consumption**. In the bottom of the figure, firms act as the buyers, paying households for use of resources they own. In this simple model, the economy is private (meaning there is no government or public sector) and closed (meaning there is no international trade).

Including international trade and governmental and financial sectors in the circular flow model yields Figure 3-8. The government in the center purchases resources and goods, provides public goods and services available to firms and households, taxes firms and individuals in a variety of ways, and regulates many more of the processes that the arrows represent. We purchase imports from other countries, so some spending by individuals and households leaks out of the cycle. Foreigners purchase domestically produced goods called exports, thus injecting spending into the cycle. Purchases and sales of inputs and financial instruments are also ways the foreign sector interacts with our basic circular flow. Some household income is saved in financial institutions such as banks; much of this is lent to businesses for investment, or the purchase of new capital goods.

Figure 3-8. Circular Flow Model That Includes the Government (Public Sector) and International Trade.

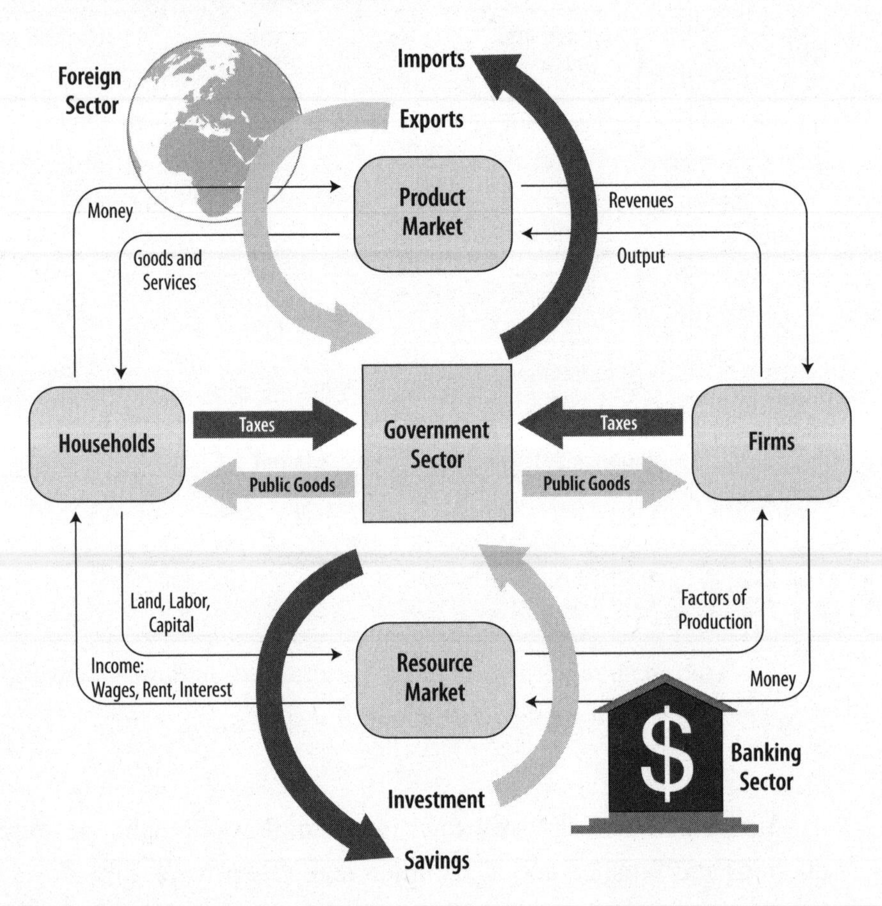

TEST TIP

When preparing for the AP Microeconomics exam, imagine questions, topics, and graphs as happening *inside* the boxes shown in the circular flow model. When preparing for the AP Macroeconomics exam, problems ask about the process as a whole or about the aggregates (totals) of various aspects of the circular flow model.

Demand, Supply, and Market Equilibrium

In analyzing markets, economists typically assume that forces called demand and supply interact and jointly determine the quantity of a good that is traded (bought and sold) and the price per unit of that good.

TEST TIP

You will need to know quite a bit about how supply and demand processes work and what kinds of circumstances can prevent these processes from working efficiently. Transferring demand and supply analysis seamlessly between graphic and written formats is essential for success on both the AP Micro- and Macroeconomics exams.

Demand

Demand is the relationship between the price of a good or service and the amount of it we want to buy in a given time period. It may be presented as data on a **demand schedule**; listed in a table of price-quantity combinations; or graphed as a **demand curve**, with quantity on the horizontal axis and price on the vertical.

The **law of demand** is the idea that consumers want to buy more of a good or service at low prices rather than at high prices. Price per unit and quantity demanded have an inverse relationship, which means that demand curves slope downward. There are three reasons for this relationship:

(1) **The principle of diminishing marginal utility**. After a certain point, the satisfaction we gain from consuming each additional unit of a good declines. As the value of that unit declines, so will the maximum price we are willing to pay for it. We're inclined to want to purchase small quantities of a good if its price is high and find additional units to be a good deal only at lower prices.

(2) **The income effect**. As the price of a good we purchase declines, our unchanged nominal income feels like more—in fact, our purchasing power, or real income, has risen. We feel richer and are therefore inclined to purchase more units of the things we buy.

(3) **The substitution effect**. As the price of a good rises, consumers have an incentive to seek out alternative goods that might fulfill their needs as well as the more expensive good. To whatever degree they can find substitutes that meet their needs, the quantity demanded of the expensive good declines.

DIDYOUKNOW?

The law of demand does not apply in some interesting, theoretical, circumstances. *Veblen goods* supposedly have a snob effect associated with them: a decrease in price leads to a lower quantity demanded because the goods now seem less exclusive. At the other end of the spectrum are *Giffen goods*: under extreme poverty, buyers may purchase less of a good such as a staple grain if it decreases in price because they are now able to choose more desirable alternatives, such as fresh vegetables or meat, with the additional purchasing power.

The demand function is a relationship between quantity demanded and price, assuming other factors are unchanged. However, five other significant factors might change the amount of a good demanded in a market. When any of these circumstances change, the demand function changes and the demand curve shifts; a whole new relationship between price and quantity demanded is now in play.

(1) **Tastes and preferences change**. As fashions and fads come and go, the desires of the buying public change. If a good becomes more desirable because it is perceived as cooler, healthier, tastier, more distinctive, or more popular, then the demand curve for that good shifts to the right.

(2) **Income changes**. If buyers experience an increase in disposable income, then for most goods, known as **normal goods**, demand shifts to the right. For goods that buyers view as less desirable, known as **inferior goods**, a rise in income causes a leftward shift in demand because consumers are now able to purchase more desirable alternatives. For example, a major rise in income might lead to less demand for used cars, bus tickets, and store-brand foods as more buyers purchase new cars or airline tickets and brand-name goods.

(3) **Market size changes**. More buyers means more demand. Conversely, a decrease in population leads to a leftward shift in demand.

(4) **Expectations change**. If buyers believe that a good will become scarce, more expensive, or more difficult to obtain in the future, then typically demand shifts to the right.

(5) **Related goods change in price**. Two types of relationships might alter demand for a good. First, a **substitute good** is one that the buyer might use instead of the good in question. For example, if margarine—a substitute for butter—drops in price, then demand for butter shifts left because some buyers are induced to switch to margarine. A rise in the price of margarine causes demand for butter to shift rightward.

A second relationship is a **complement**—a good that consumers like to enjoy with the good in question. If peanut butter, a complement to jelly, rises in price, then demand for jelly shifts left as consumers find the combination of peanut butter and jelly to be more costly. A drop in the price of peanut butter shifts the demand curve for jelly to the right because the peanut butter and jelly experience becomes more affordable.

TEST TIP

Be able to recognize and explain the reasons behind the shifts in demand curves. Some students like to use the acronym TIMER to recall the five categories of shifters.

Figure 3-9. Demand

Note the difference between a change in demand and a change in quantity demanded. A change in quantity demanded can be caused only by a change in price. A change in demand can be caused by the five TIMER factors explained previously in this chapter.

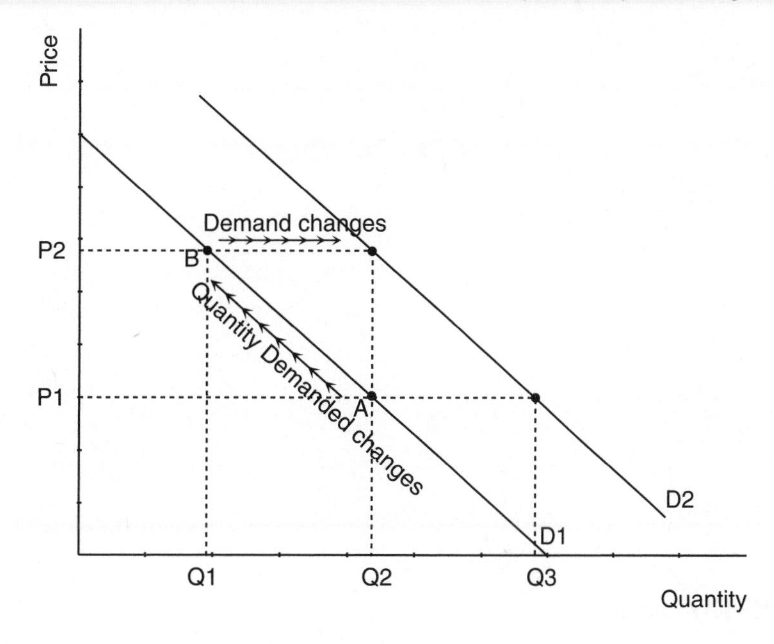

Figure 3-9 shows a demand curve and illustrates an important distinction between a change in demand and a change in quantity demanded. A price increase from P1 to P2 causes a decrease in quantity demanded from Q1 to Q2; in other words, given the same demand curve, buyers now want to buy Q2 units (fewer than Q1) because the price is higher. Note that buyers are operating at a different point along the demand curve, but demand has not shifted.

By contrast, a change in demand—in this case an increase in demand—is shown in the rightward shift from D1 to D2; this type of shift results from one of the five reasons already explained in this chapter. Every given quantity now corresponds with a higher price; if Q2 units are demanded, then the price must be P2 rather than P1. Each price thus corresponds with a higher quantity demanded; at price P1, for example, Q3 (not Q1) units are now demanded.

In sum, remember the inverse relationship between quantity demanded and demand expressed in the law of demand, the three reasons why demand curves slope downward, the five reasons demand can shift, and how to show both a change in quantity demanded (sliding along a fixed demand curve) and a change in demand (a shift from one demand curve to another: rightward for an increase and leftward for a decrease in demand). Figure 3-10 illustrates a decrease in demand.

Figure 3-10. Decrease in Demand

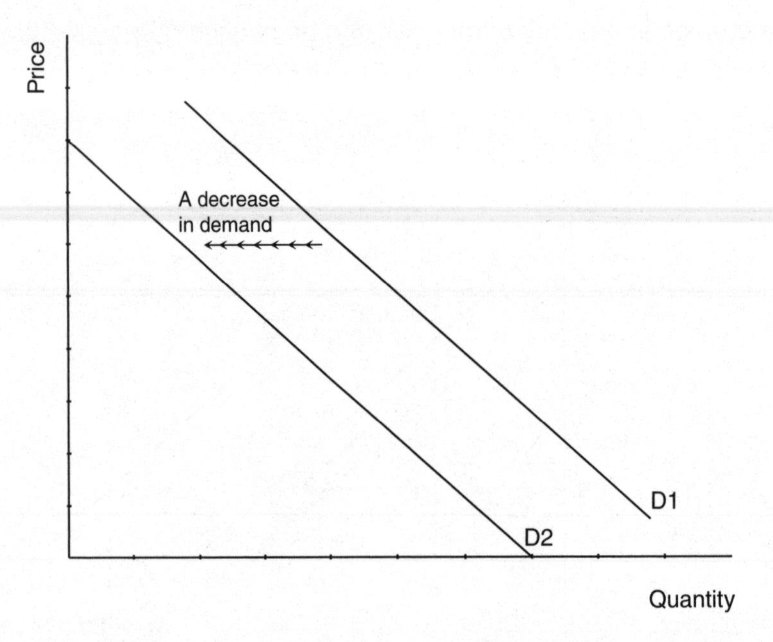

Supply

Supply is the relationship between quantity produced per unit of time and the price of the good. It can be expressed as a function, a schedule, or a graph. According to the **law of supply**, producers make more units of a good or service so they can sell it for a higher price. There is a positive relationship between price and quantity demanded.

Understanding why the law of supply is true involves relating back to the principle of increasing opportunity cost. As we produce more and more of a good, we must bring into use resources that are less and less well suited to its production. This involves less efficient production techniques, less productive labor, raw materials that are more costly to extract, and so forth. The idea that we use the cheapest and easiest resources first and then move on to more costly ones as we produce more is sometimes called the **low-hanging fruit principle** (which fruit would *you* pick first?). As a result, production cost per unit rises as more units are produced. For suppliers to feel that it is worth their time and energy to bring these extra units to market, they must be able to sell them at a higher price. Lower prices induce less production than higher ones do. Just as demand is very closely related to the concept of marginal benefit, supply is very closely related to marginal cost.

Figure 3-11. Supply

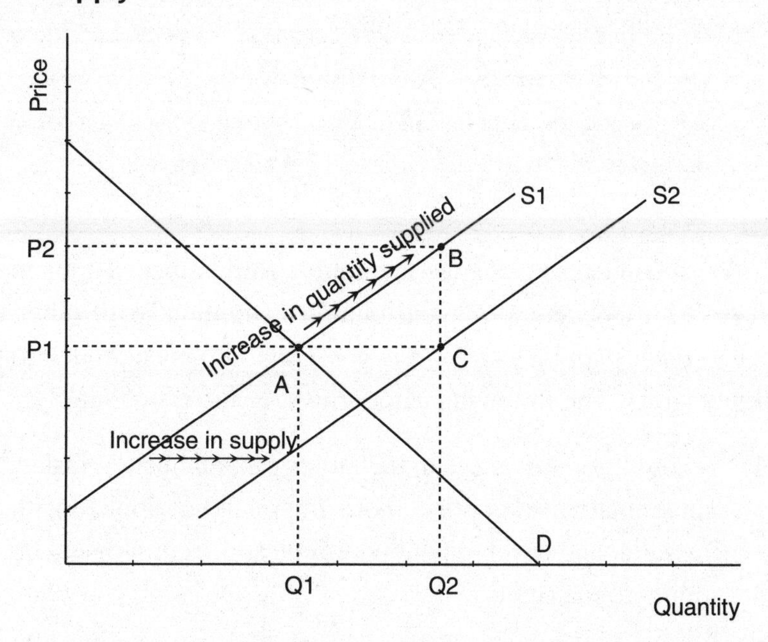

Be careful to distinguish between a change in quantity supplied and a change in supply, as shown in Figure 3-11. A change in quantity supplied is caused by a change in price; it is shown graphically as sliding from one point on a supply curve to another point along the same supply curve. It represents a new price-quantity combination within the same supply function. A change in supply, on the other hand, means that the entire supply function has changed and is shown on a graph by shifting the entire supply curve—either to the right for an increase in supply or to the left for a decrease in supply.

Let's assume that the market is initially operating at point A. An increase in price from P1 to P2 causes an increase in quantity supplied from Q1 to Q2, sliding along the same supply curve S1 to point B. If one of the TIGERS factors (explained below) changes, then supply might increase, shifting from S1 to S2. Note that now a lower price even than P1 would be needed to induce production of Q1 units; note also that, at the original price P1, suppliers are willing and able to bring Q2 units to market (point C).

TEST TIP

Beginning economics students often want to speak of supply and demand moving up or down. This terminology can cause confusion, however, because an upward movement of a demand curve represents an increase in demand, whereas an upward shift of a supply curve is actually a decrease in supply. Train yourself to think of increases as rightward shifts and decreases as leftward shifts to avoid this confusion.

What can cause a change in supply? Remember that a supply curve represents the relationship between price and quantity supplied, with other things held constant. If factors *other than the price of the good* that influence production decisions change, then supply shifts. The following categories are shifters of supply:

(1) **Technology**. Advances in technology enable better, faster, and cheaper production. Thus, at any market price, more units will be supplied with advances in technology. Research and development contributes to technological breakthroughs, which shift supply to the right.

(2) **Input prices**. Changes in the costs of resources needed to produce a good affect the supply for that good inversely—if the land, labor, or capital necessary to make cars gets more expensive, the supply of cars decreases or shifts to the left. Some resources, like labor, electricity, and oil, are commonly used to produce or distribute many goods and services and are considered (near) **universal inputs**.

(3) **Government policies**. If government imposes a **per-unit tax** on a good (think of a per-pack tax on cigarettes, a per-gallon tax on gasoline, or even a simple sales tax), then the convention is to show a leftward shift of supply. Because suppliers collect this tax revenue and are required to transfer it to the government, they need a higher price than before in order to be willing to provide the same quantity of the good for sale. Instead, if the government pays each producer a **per-unit subsidy**

(an amount added to the price paid by the buyer), supply shifts to the right. As each unit is produced, the seller receives the market price and the subsidy payment; thus, a lower market price is required to induce production of the same quantity.

(4) **Expectations**. Sellers' expectations about the future may influence production decisions in the present. The belief that a good's value will decrease in the future may cause some sellers to flood the market now. For goods that do not spoil, the belief that their prices will rise in the future may lead to increases in inventory and fewer goods being sold at the present market price.

(5) **Related goods' prices**. Some goods are related to one another in the production process. Substitutes in production and complements in production are distinct from the related goods that shift demand. Peanut butter and jelly, and butter and margarine are related in consumers' minds, but not in the production process. In this case, consider various disposable plastic products made by one corporation: lighters, pens, and razors are all **substitutes in production** because they can be produced from the same inputs (mostly plastic, electronic machinery, labor, and a little bit of metal) and production of one can be traded with production of another. If cigarette lighters, a substitute in production, decrease in price, then we would expect the corporation's supply curve for razors to shift to the right because they will not find it as profitable to produce lighters. **Complements in production** are goods that are produced together, or one is a by-product of the other. If the price of beef rises, thus increasing the quantity supplied, more leather is supplied to the market at any given price, so the supply of leather has increased or shifted right. As more beef is produced, leather is made as a by-product, and more leather will be supplied at any given market price of leather.

(6) **Suppliers**. If more producers are making a good, supply for that good increases. A decrease in the number of sellers in a marketplace shifts the supply curve to the left.

TEST TIP

Use the acronym TIGERS to remember the six types of causes for a shift in supply. Be sure you can distinguish the factors that shift supply from those that shift demand—they are separate. On the AP exam, each cause tends to have only one effect on a graph, so one change of circumstance won't cause both demand and supply to move.

Figure 3-12. Decrease in Supply

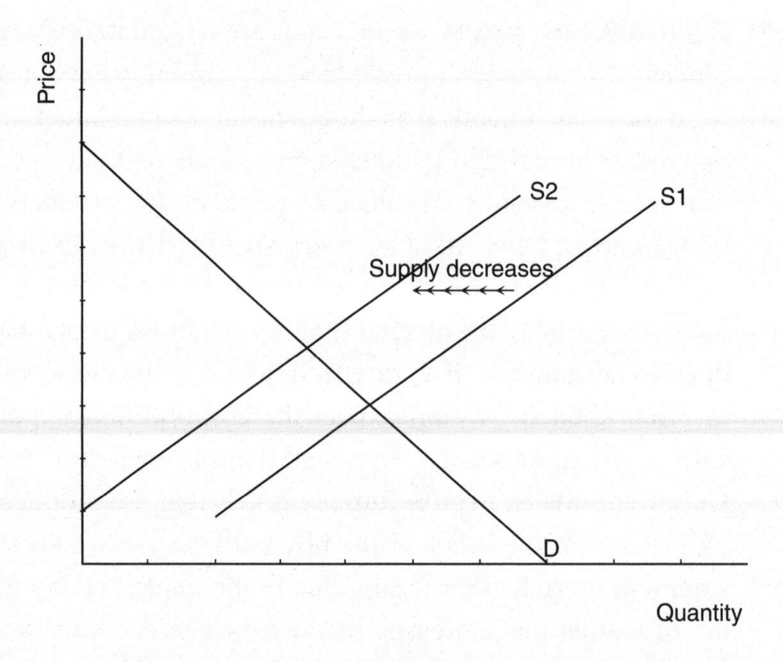

A decrease, or leftward shift, in supply is shown in Figure 3-12. At any given price, fewer units are supplied. To produce the same number of units requires a higher price than before. Such a shift could be the result of an increase in input prices, a rise in the price of a substitute in production, or a decrease in the number of suppliers.

Market Equilibrium

When a market is in **equilibrium**, it is functioning at the intersection of the supply and demand curves: The market price and quantity satisfy the plans of buyers reflected in the demand curve and the plans of sellers reflected in the supply curve. The equilibrium price is the unique price at which quantity demanded equals quantity supplied; therefore, it is also called the **market-clearing price**.

Figure 3-13. Equilibrium Forces in Action

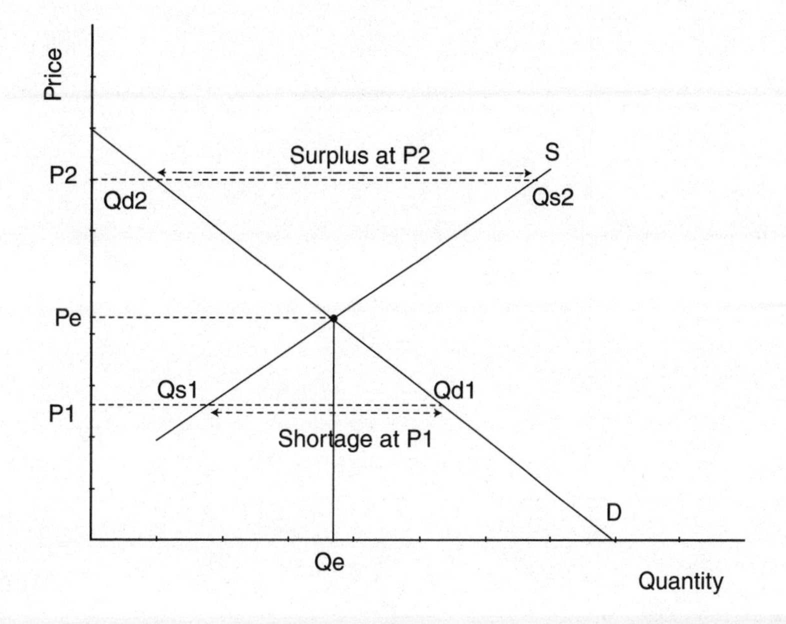

At other prices, misallocations of goods may occur. At Pe in Figure 3-13, the market is in equilibrium with Qe units demanded and supplied. If price is lower than equilibrium (such as at P1), then quantity demanded (Qd1) is higher than quantity supplied (Qs1). Many buyers wish to purchase units, but sellers have little incentive to produce, so **shortages** result. Shortages send signals to both sellers and buyers that the price is too low, and they tend to push prices upward toward the market-clearing price. When the price is higher than equilibrium (as at P2), quantity supplied (Qs2) is higher than quantity demanded (Qd2). Suppliers bring more units to market than buyers wish to purchase at that price and the result is a **surplus**. A surplus tends to push price downward toward the market-clearing level.

Changes in Equilibrium

Market equilibrium changes when either supply or demand (or both curves) shifts. Reexamine Figure 3-12 on the previous page to see that a decrease in supply from S1 to S2 changes market equilibrium from the intersection of D and S1 to the intersection of D and S2, thus reducing equilibrium quantity and increasing equilibrium price.

Figure 3-14. An Increase in Demand Increases Equilibrium Price and Quantity

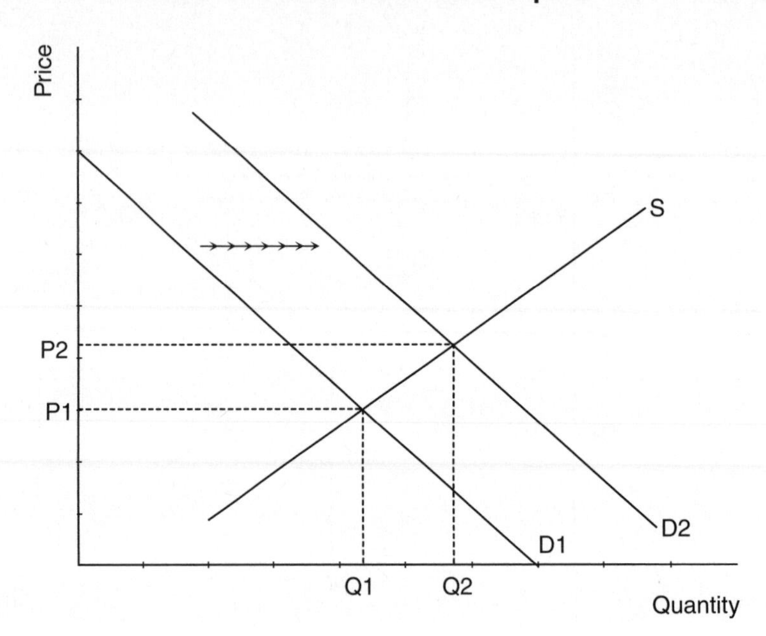

A rightward shift of demand is shown again in Figure 3-14. As demand shifts from D1 to D2, there is a shortage at the old price P1 in the marketplace, with quantity demanded being far greater than the Q1 quantity that suppliers are planning to bring to market. The shortage pushes up the price toward P2, and the rise in price encourages quantity supplied to increase and quantity demanded to decrease. These forces continue to push price upward until a new equilibrium is reached, when P2 is the market price and buyers plan to purchase Q2 units, the number that suppliers plan to produce. An increase in demand causes both quantity sold and price to rise.

Practice, Practice, Practice!

Practice your graphing skills by drawing two basic supply and demand graphs and labeling them—on one, show a decrease in demand; on the other, show an increase in supply. Now indicate along the axes how equilibrium quantity and price are influenced by each shift. Many questions on both AP exams will be based on some version of supply and demand analysis, testing whether you know the causes of curves shifting and the effects on the variables on the axes, in this case, price and quantity. With some work, you will be able to envision these shifts and their effects without actually graphing them on paper, but you'll need to draw graphs neatly on the free-response section of the exam. The ability to sketch a quick graph can help make an impossible multiple-choice question doable, a difficult one easy, and an easy one a guaranteed correct answer. (If you graphed the two examples from earlier in the paragraph, your diagrams should confirm that if demand shifts left, P and Q both decrease; if supply shifts right, P decreases and Q increases.)

Figure 3-15. Simultaneous Increases in Demand and Supply: Three Possibilities

(a) Quantity increases while price remains the same.

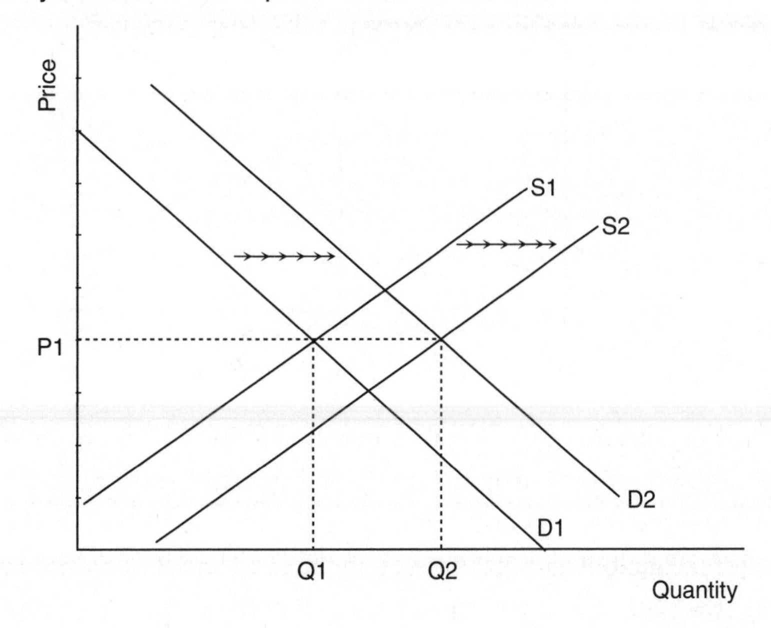

(b) Quantity and price both increase.

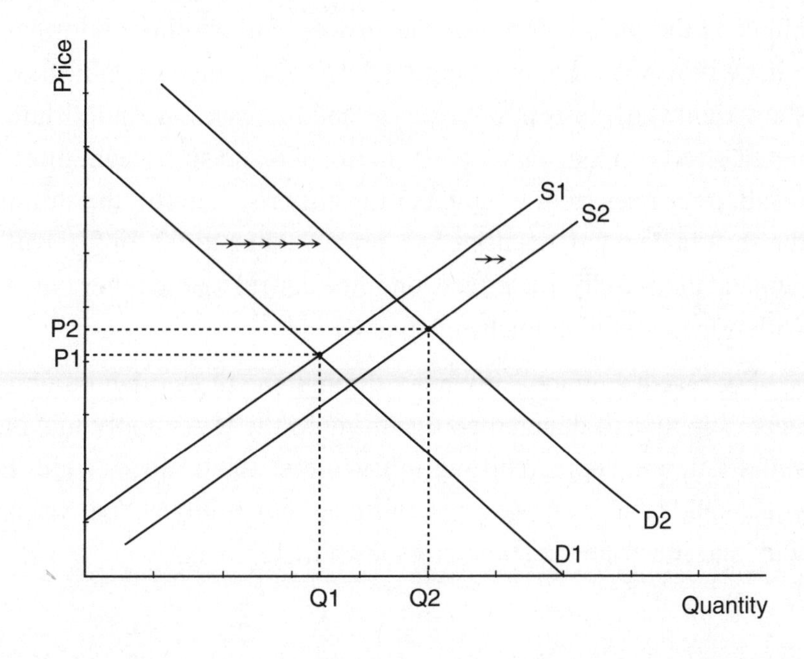

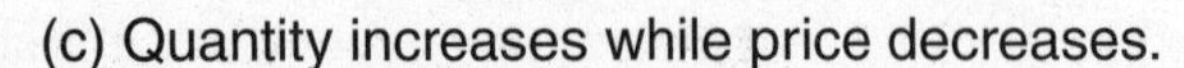

(c) Quantity increases while price decreases.

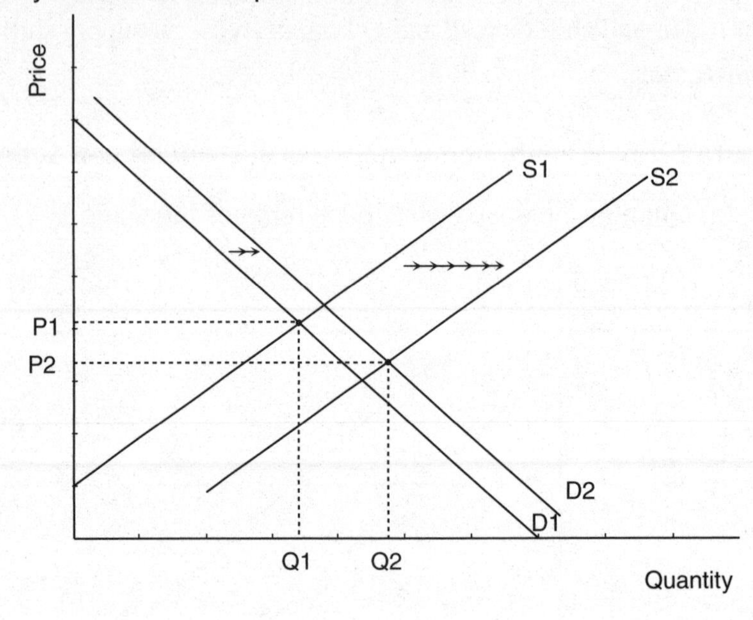

A smaller number of exam questions will be based on whether you can reason through the effects of both supply and demand shifting at the same time. Imagine a question that asks about the effects of an increase in the popularity of hybrid cars and a major technological breakthrough in the production of hybrid cars. The question identifies two causes, and you should know that the first is an example of a factor that shifts demand right and the second is a cause of an increase in supply. Now you are asked to predict the effects of these simultaneous shifts on price and quantity. The relative magnitude of the shifts determines the answer; without more information, it isn't conclusive what will happen. Examine Figure 3-15 to see three possibilities. All parts of the figure show rightward shifts in both curves and increases in equilibrium quantity but with different effects on the market price. In (a), demand shifts right more than supply does; as a result, price rises from P1 to P2 as quantity rises. In (b), the shift in supply is larger than the shift in demand, resulting in a price decline to P2. In (c), with similar shifts in both demand and supply, the effects on price cancel one another out, and quantity increases, with price remaining unchanged, at P1.

For practice, graphically work through the three other combinations of two shifts at once: supply and demand both shifting to the left, supply moving right while demand shifts left, and supply shifting left while demand moves right. For each combination, you should be able to draw three different possibilities. Your graphs should be consistent with and illustrate the summary shown in Table 3-2.

Table 3-2. Effects of Shifts in Both Demand and Supply

	Supply shifts right; tends to increase Q and decrease P.	Supply shifts left; tends to decrease Q and increase P.
Demand shifts right; tends to increase Q and P.	Q certainly increases. P is indeterminate and may increase, decrease, or remain constant.	Q is indeterminate and may increase, decrease, or remain constant. P certainly increases
Demand shifts left; tends to decrease Q and P.	Q is indeterminate and may increase, decrease, or remain constant. P certainly decreases.	Q certainly decreases. P is indeterminate and may increase, decrease, or remain constant.

Economic Cycles and Thinking Across Time

Two additional useful background concepts, no matter which economics exam you plan to take, involve terminology related to economic cycles and the ability to think across time, separating the short run from the long run.

Business Cycles

Economies tend to grow in fits and starts that form cyclical patterns. The general term **business cycle** describes the process of alternating expansion and contraction phases, often with an overall upward trend that reflects long-run economic growth. Economists don't agree about what causes this boom-and-bust pattern, and it certainly isn't easy to predict when the switch will occur, which peaks will be especially high, or which troughs will be especially low.

The contraction periods and troughs may often be referred to as **recessions**, and particularly deep ones may be called **depressions**. During these times, demand for all products is likely to be low, and prices are stable or decrease as economic activity sags and unemployment is high. This could be shown as the economy operating at a point inside of its PPC.

DIDYOUKNOW?

The definition of the term *recession* has actually been the subject of some dispute. Currently, the National Bureau of Economic Research (NBER) is seen as the most credible authority for determining whether the U.S. economy is in recession. Their definition can seem frustratingly vague: "a significant decline in economic activity spread across the economy, lasting more than a few months, normally visible in real GDP [gross domestic product], real income, employment, industrial production, and wholesale-retail sales." This replaced a much clearer, yet unofficial definition of recession as "two consecutive quarters of declining GDP."

Expansion periods feature faster-than-average increases in production and consumption of goods. Because demand is high during these periods, prices often rise as producers struggle to maximize the productive capacity of the resources in the economy. This means firms hire more workers and unemployment tends to be low. This situation could be shown as the economy operating as close as it realistically can to a point on the frontier line.

Thinking Across Time: The Short Run and the Long Run

In each of the AP economics exams, you will undoubtedly encounter questions that use the terms *short run* and *long run*. Unfortunately it isn't as simple as a specific length of time, such as three months, one year, or twenty years. These terms sometimes have specific meanings in context, but the following explanations may help further your understanding of their use.

The **short run** is defined as a time period in which at least one major factor or variable under consideration is fixed. In macroeconomics, we might consider the state of technology or the amount of capital goods the economy has at its disposal (the capital stock) to be fixed in the short run. In microeconomics, where we examine decisions from one firm's perspective, we might consider monthly payments for overhead expenses such as rent or loan payments to be fixed, as would the size of our factory and the amount and type of machinery available for use on a daily basis. In economics, the short run is all about seeing what effects some things (short-run variables) have, while holding other factors (those that are fixed in the short run) constant.

In the **long run**, we typically assume that all these factors are variable. The country can reap the rewards of building more capital stock to have better technology, a farmer can acquire more land, and a firm can choose a factory size (and corresponding monthly rent) that better suits its needs.

TEST TIP

Regardless of which AP economics exam you study for, you'll see a lot of discussion and examples related to the short run and the long run. You will have an easier time with this terminology if you think about what is fixed and what is variable. When it is not specified what time period you are supposed to think about, assume the question is asking you to think in the short run only.

AP Microeconomics

Chapter 4

The Nature and Function of Product Markets

A Closer Look at Demand, Supply, and Equilibrium

The majority of the items on the AP Microeconomics exam require knowledge of demand and supply analysis that goes beyond what was covered in the basic concepts chapter. In particular, a great many questions expect you to show your knowledge of how firms and households that interact in markets make decisions. To do so, we'll need to journey behind those seemingly simple supply and demand curves you read about in Chapter 3. Let's begin.

Total Revenue and Marginal Revenue

Demand curves tell us the quantity demanded at a variety of prices. From this information, we can figure out several other principles. To begin, let's consider the price and the quantity multiplied together. The product of these two values yield the total expenditures made purchasing that good. Total expenditure is also the **total revenue** that the firm or firms selling the goods brought in. This total revenue is shown in Figure 4-1 as the area of the rectangle bounded by the origin in the lower-left corner and any particular point on the demand curve in the upper-right corner.

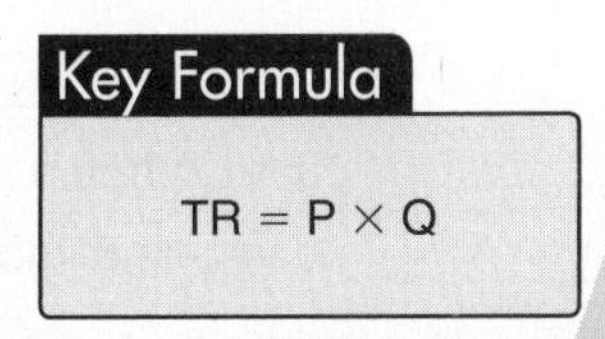
Key Formula

$TR = P \times Q$

Figure 4–1. Demand and Total Revenue

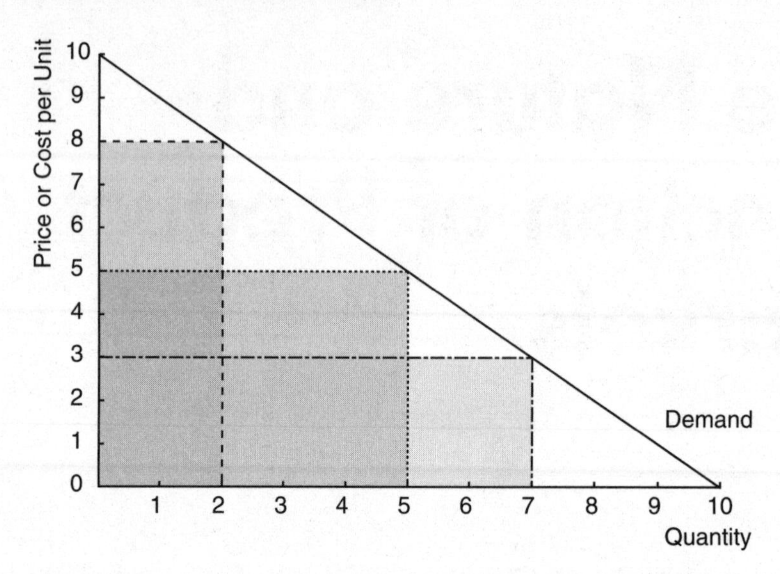

If we assume that the demand curve is linear, then plotting the total revenue against quantity on a separate set of axes generates a downward-opening parabola with its maximum value at the same quantity as the midpoint of the demand curve.

TEST TIP

Demand curves are not linear very often in real life. Fortunately, on the AP exam, you can draw graphs and work out problems under the assumption that they are linear. In the few cases where this isn't true, a clue in the problem will let you know.

Note that total revenue (TR) is zero at the two endpoints or intercepts of the demand curve when a quantity of zero is produced and when price is zero. In between, TR rises, peaks, and then falls. Its slope is clearly changing, and the rate at which this function changes is called **marginal revenue (MR)**, it represents how much revenue increases or decreases (if it is negative) when one additional unit is produced. In Figure 4-2, MR is plotted with demand and TR. Note that at quantity Q_r, MR = 0 and TR is maximized. This quantity also corresponds with the midpoint of the demand curve. This will be true for linear demand curves no matter what slope they have, meaning that MR starts at the same y-intercept as demand and descends twice as fast as quantity increases.

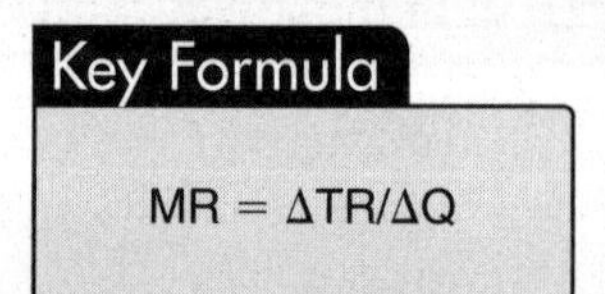

Marginal revenue is one of two key elements in a firm's decision about how many units it should produce because it represents the marginal benefit to the firm of producing one extra unit.

Figure 4–2.

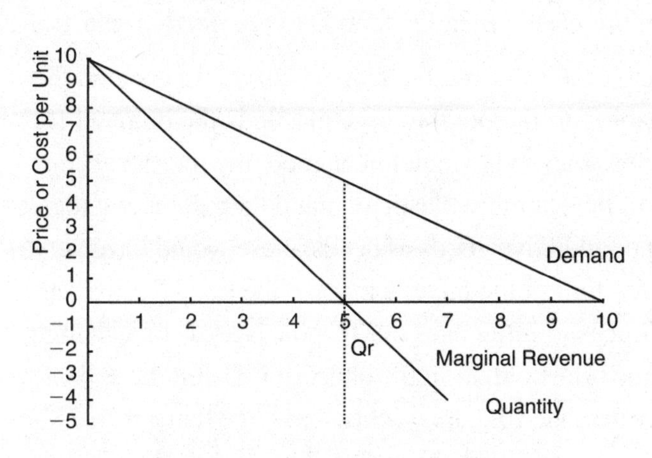

Panel A. Demand and Marginal Revenue

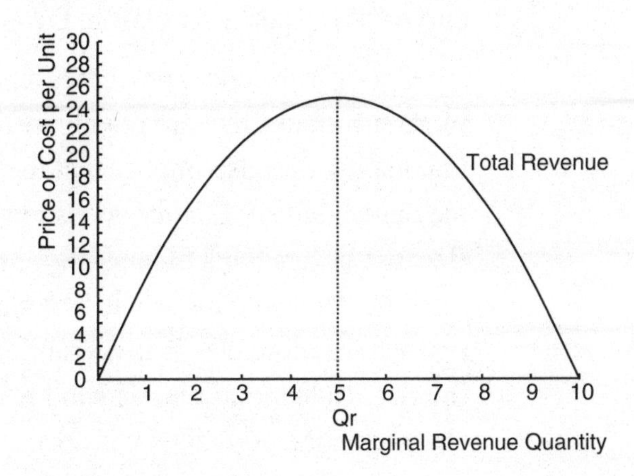

Panel B. Total Revenue

Elasticity: Measuring Responsiveness

Along with price, the TIMER factors that you read about in Chapter 3 govern how much of any given good consumers want to buy. The effect of these factors on quantity demanded can be measured in several ways. *Elasticity* is the general term for measurements that are designed to gauge the level of responsiveness that quantity demanded has to various factors. In each case, we are measuring how much quantity changes given a per-unit change in another variable, such as price or income. Some of the tougher multiple-choice items on the AP Microeconomics exam feature applications of elasticity, and a version of this concept frequently appears in the more challenging parts of one or more free-response items.

Price Elasticity of Demand

The first and most commonly tested type of elasticity is price elasticity of demand. (If the term *elasticity* is used without specification, assume that it refers to elasticity of demand.) **Price elasticity of demand** (ε_d) tells us how responsive quantity demanded is to a change in price. In some situations, as price rises, consumers do not decrease the quantity they buy much; in other words, they are not so responsive to a change in price. In these cases, demand is said to be price inelastic (or simply inelastic). If the price rises and quantity demanded decreases rapidly, demand is price elastic (or simply elastic). In these situations, consumers are highly responsive or sensitive to a change in price.

When comparing two demand curves, the more inelastic (or less elastic) demand curve has the steeper downward slope. Flatter demand curves are more elastic than more steeply sloped ones. In extreme cases, we could describe a horizontal demand curve as perfectly elastic and a vertical one as perfectly inelastic. Figure 4-3 shows four demand curves. D1 is perfectly elastic, D2 is more elastic than D3, and D4 is perfectly inelastic.

Goods with certain properties tend to have more elastic demand curves. In general, the more substitutes that are readily available for a good, the more elastic is the demand for that good—this also implies that the more narrowly we define a good, the more elastic is the demand for it. Luxury goods tend to have a more elastic demand than do necessities. Because buyers think of habit-forming or addictive goods as needs, these would have very inelastic demand curves. The larger a fraction of the buyer's income the good's price represents, the more elastic is demand. Time also influences our responsiveness to a change in price. In the long run, demand is more elastic than in the short run. Using these basic characteristics, you might consider why demand for cars, yachts, and large flat-screen TVs are relatively elastic and why demand for electricity, eggs, paper clips, rice, and cigarettes are relatively inelastic. See if you can explain why your demand for gasoline is likely to be very inelastic during the next month, but much more elastic during the next decade.

Elasticity varies along a demand curve and can be measured at a particular point or along a short range (arc) of a given demand function. Because demand curves have a negative slope, sliding along a given curve always involves Q and P moving in opposite directions. Thus, the elasticity coefficient (ε_d) is always negative, but standard economics convention has us drop the negative sign. This result is then compared to 1.

Figure 4–3. Elastic and Inelastic Demand Curves

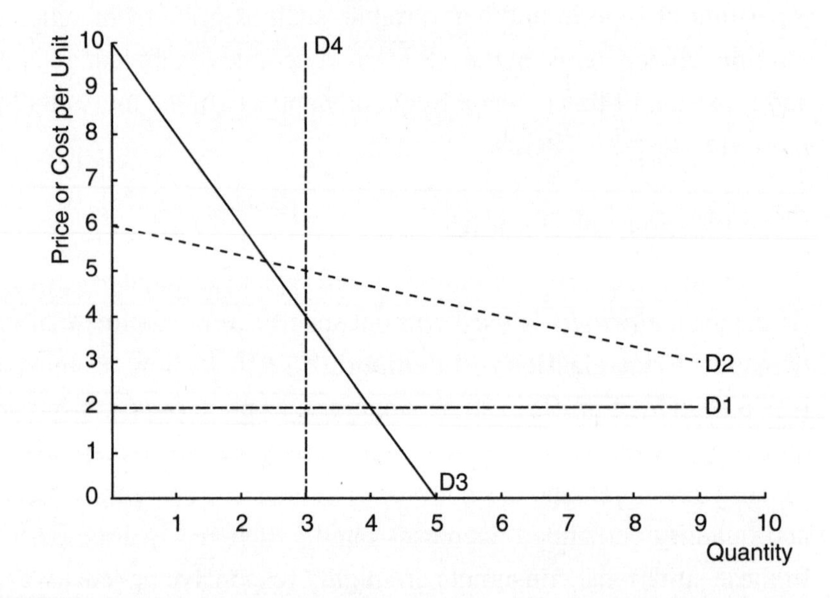

Figure 4-4 shows the behavior of this elasticity coefficient along a linear demand curve. It is important to be able to connect price elasticity of demand with total revenue and marginal revenue.

For all linear demand curves, elasticity at the top of the curve by the y-intercept approaches infinity. Demand is highly elastic. In mathematical terms, quantities are very low so small numerical changes in Q are very large percentage changes, producing a large numerator. Price is high, so numerical changes in P produce a small percentage change and a small denominator. So ε_d is large and demand is elastic. As quantity increases, Q rises by a larger percentage than P falls, so total revenue increases, meaning that marginal revenue is positive. The top or left half of any linear demand curve is elastic with a ε_d value greater than 1, corresponding with a positive MR and an up-sloping TR function.

Key Formula

$$\varepsilon_d = \frac{\%\Delta Q_d}{\%\Delta P}$$

When $\varepsilon_d = 0$, demand is perfectly inelastic.
When $0 < \varepsilon_d < 1$, demand is inelastic.
When $\varepsilon_d = 1$, demand is unit elastic.
When $1 < \varepsilon_d$, demand is elastic.
ε_d approaches infinity when demand is perfectly elastic.

At the midpoint of any linear demand curve, ε_d equals 1. This midpoint is also the unit elastic point directly above the *x*-intercept of MR and at the same quantity as the maximum TR value. It is also the upper-right corner of the largest TR rectangle bounded by any of the points on that demand curve.

Figure 4–4. Elasticity Ranges Along a Demand Curve

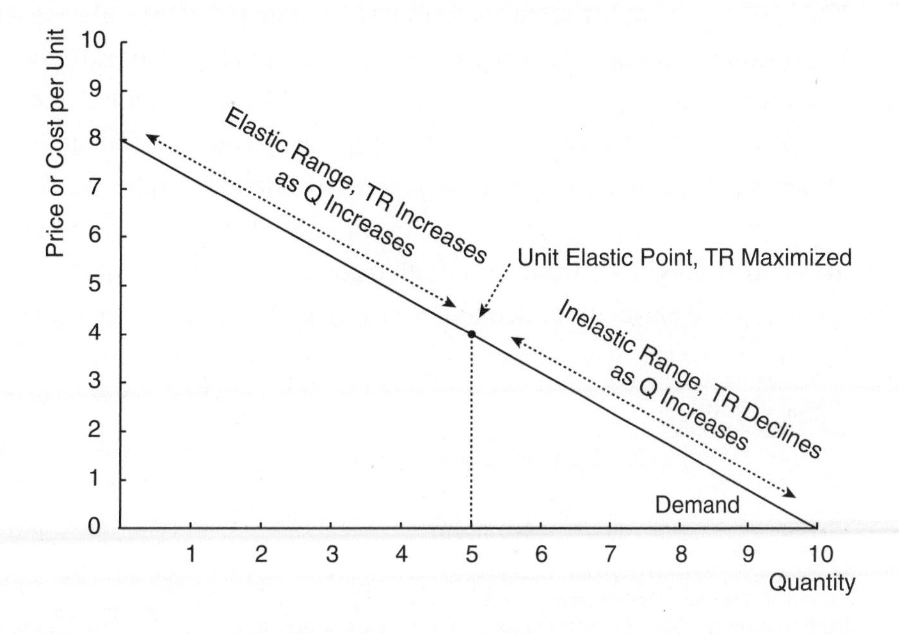

TEST TIP

If a test question gives you values for P and Q rather than percentage change values, use this easier, mathematically equal method to find ε_d.

In the lower or right half of the demand curve, ε_d is less than 1 because, at low prices, percentage changes in P are large, and at high quantities, percentage changes in Q are small. This inelastic section of the demand curve corresponds with quantities at which MR is negative and TR is declining as Q increases. Visualize the size of the TR rectangle bound by the demand curve getting smaller and smaller until it has no area at all because its height is zero.

If you are asked to calculate ε_d over a range or arc of a demand curve, standard practice is to use the mean values for Q and P. This is known as the midpoint method and ensures the ε_d value is the same for a given arc whether sliding up to the left or down to the right along the demand curve. Many test questions will ask if a given change in output might increase or decrease total revenue. Streamline your thinking about these questions by sketching a fast graph and determining whether the movement would be toward or away from the unit elastic point where total revenue is at a maximum. If toward, TR increases; if away, TR decreases.

Key Formula

$$\varepsilon_d = \frac{P}{Q} \times \frac{1}{\text{Slope}}$$

Income Elasticity of Demand

Recall that a change in income is one of the factors that can cause a change in demand. The type of effect a rise in income has on demand is not always the same, however. **Income elasticity of demand** is a measurement of how responsive demand is to a change in income. The typical pattern is for demand to shift right if income increases. This means that, at any given price, a greater quantity is demanded, and the income elasticity of demand is positive. This pattern applies to **normal goods**. We would purchase less of some goods, however, if we got a raise in salary because they are goods we have to buy rather than goods we want to buy. If income rises and demand shifts left for a certain good, income elasticity of demand is negative; the buyer regards this as an **inferior good** because he or she is wealthier and purchases a smaller quantity of it at the same price. For many buyers, bus tickets, used cars, and off-brand clothing might be inferior goods—if income were to rise, these individuals might buy more airline tickets, new cars, and designer brands, substitutes they regard as more desirable.

Key Formula

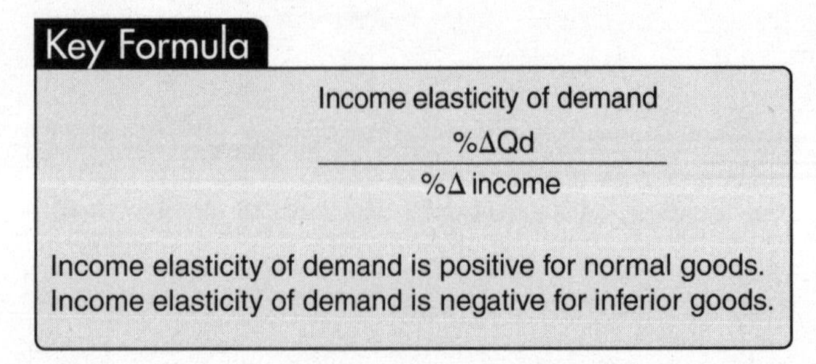

Cross-Price Elasticity of Demand

A change in the price of related goods can also shift demand. Cross-price elasticity allows us to measure the effects of one good's change in price on demand for another good. Again, this type of elasticity is a reflection of how responsive quantity demanded is, this time to a change in the price of a related good.

Key Formula

Cross-Price Elasticity of Demand

$$\frac{\%\Delta\, Qd_{good\ x}}{\%\Delta\, P_{good\ y}}$$

Cross-price elasticity of demand is positive for substitute goods.
Cross-price elasticity of demand is negative for complementary goods.
If cross-price elasticity equals zero, then the goods are unrelated.

Elasticity of Supply

Just as some buyers in some situations are more responsive to changes in price than in other circumstances, a rise in price sometimes encourages suppliers to make many more units and sometimes a rise in price generates only a small increase in quantity supplied. Goods that do not require specialized inputs or particularly scarce raw materials as part of the production process are likely to have more elastic supply curves—the more complex and time consuming the production of the good, the more inelastic the supply curve is likely to be.

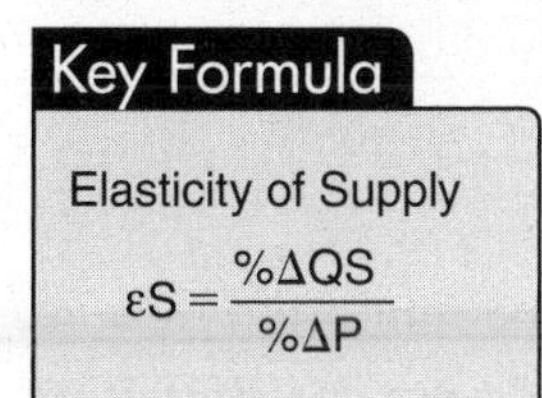

Reservation Price and Economic Surplus

Reservation Prices, Marginal Benefit, and Marginal Cost

Recall from Chapter 3 that reservation price comes from the subjective value a buyer or seller places on a particular unit of a good. From a buyer's point of view, the reservation price is the highest price she or he would pay for that unit—generally a bit lower than for previous units. You wouldn't pay more than your reservation price for a pair of shoes because that would mean paying more than they were worth to you. A buyer might well be saying to himself, "At *that* price, I'd just as soon keep my money." Reservation price, therefore, is a reflection of how much extra gain (marginal benefit) you'll get from buying one more pair of shoes.

From a seller's point of view, reservation price is the lowest price he or she would accept to part with a particular unit of a good. It bears a close relationship with marginal cost—the amount that producing that good increased the seller's costs. Generally it would not make sense to sell a good for less than making that unit cost the producer. A seller in this situation might well be saying to herself, "If *this* is all I'll get for it, then I may as well take this product home and try again next time." (Making this sort of a decision is far easier for the producer if the good does not spoil!)

In economics, we typically assume that if market price is equal to or below a buyer's reservation price, the buyer will make the purchase. Likewise, we assume that sellers always produce units for which market price equals or exceeds the reservation price. The vast majority of the time that sellers sell or buyers buy, they feel they are getting a good deal, or reaping **economic surplus**, a gain in value as a result of the exchange.

Consumer Surplus

When consumers purchase units of a good for less than the maximum they are willing to pay, they experience a gain called **consumer surplus**. This is a nonmonetary gain that comes from exchanging something (the money price) for something else of greater value. Figure 4-5 shows the area of consumer surplus and producer surplus in a market functioning at equilibrium. On a graph, consumer surplus is always the area under the demand curve, above the price paid, and to the left of quantity purchased.

Producer Surplus

When producers sell units of a good for more than the minimum they are willing to accept, they experience a nonmonetary gain called **producer surplus**. Refer to Figure 4-5 for a depiction of producer surplus in a simple market functioning at equilibrium. On a graph, producer surplus is always the area above the supply (or marginal cost) curve, below the price received, and to the left of the quantity sold.

Figure 4–5. Consumer and Producer Surplus

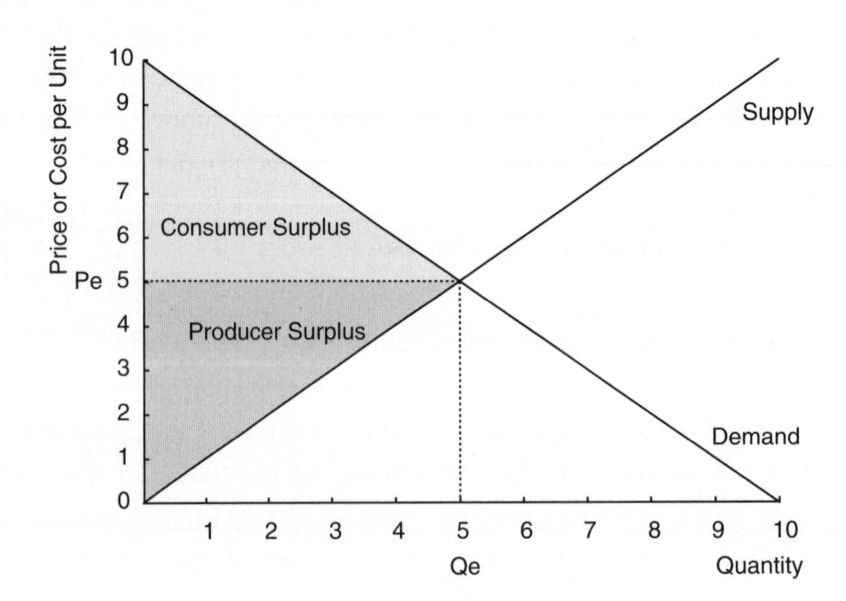

TEST TIP

AP questions frequently test your ability to find producer and consumer surplus or explain how it changes in situations when markets are not functioning at equilibrium. These situations include price floors and ceilings or the imposition of taxes. Keep in mind the three conditions for finding the areas, and you'll be well positioned for these questions.

Total Economic Surplus

If consumer surplus is the total amount of gain experienced by buyers and if producer surplus is the total amount of gain experienced by sellers, then total economic surplus is the net gain to all of society. In a simple market functioning at equilibrium, total economic surplus is the sum of the areas of consumer and producer surplus. However, in situations where the rest of society experienced a net gain (tax revenue is raised from transactions in the market) or a net loss (production of the good causes an externality such as pollution), then those would be factored in as well when calculating total surplus.

Allocative Efficiency and Deadweight Loss

In Chapter 3, the term **allocative efficiency** was introduced to describe production of the quantity of each good where marginal cost incurred producing the last unit equals the marginal benefit gained in its consumption. When this condition is met, all opportunities for voluntary gain have been realized. Thus, under normal circumstances, the market equilibrium quantity is the one that maximizes total economic surplus and is thus allocatively efficient and considered to be socially optimal.

When an allocatively inefficient quantity is traded, some of the opportunities for mutual gain through exchange have not been seized. If too few units are sold, then chances for net gain were bypassed. If too many units are produced, then the marginal cost (representing what society sacrificed to get the last unit) exceeded marginal benefit (the gain experienced from enjoying that last unit). Either way, the result is an unrealized gain that economists refer to as **deadweight loss**—it is an area on a graph that shows how much worse off we are as a result of misallocating resources to the production of a good.

TEST TIP

Deadweight loss that results from underproduction of a good are common in the free-response questions. You will find deadweight loss below the demand/marginal benefit curve, above the supply/marginal cost curve, and to the right of the quantity produced. It looks like an arrow pointing you to the right: right toward the socially optimal quantity and price!

Look for the connection between deadweight loss and allocative efficiency. The AP exam uses *socially optimal* and *allocatively efficient* interchangeably. Deadweight loss is evidence that a market is not allocatively efficient; if the socially optimal quantity is being sold, there will be no deadweight loss. Allocative and productive efficiency are two important criteria used to evaluate different market structures, government policies, and short- and long-run outcomes.

Price and Quantity Controls

A price or quantity control is a government action to restrict a market legally by regulating either the price or the quantity traded, thus preventing function at equilibrium. Other things being equal, these policies lead to inefficient outcomes and misallocation of resources toward production, and create deadweight loss as a result.

Price Ceilings

If a government sets a legal maximum price, or **price ceiling**, below the equilibrium price, then sellers have less incentive to produce units, and quantity supplied decreases as a result of the new lower price. Quantity demanded increases to Qd, but not enough units are available—because a transaction requires a willing seller for every buyer, quantity traded decreases, as does the area of total economic surplus. As Figure 4-6 indicates, fewer units (Qs) are produced and sold at the lower price Pc. Because consumer and producer surplus are the result of transactions they actually engage in, the area of total economic surplus is narrower, and an area of deadweight loss is present between Qs and Qe, indicating that society underallocated resources to the production of this good.

DIDYOUKNOW?

Rent controls in some urban housing markets, notably in New York City, are classic examples of price ceilings.

Figure 4–6. A Price Ceiling

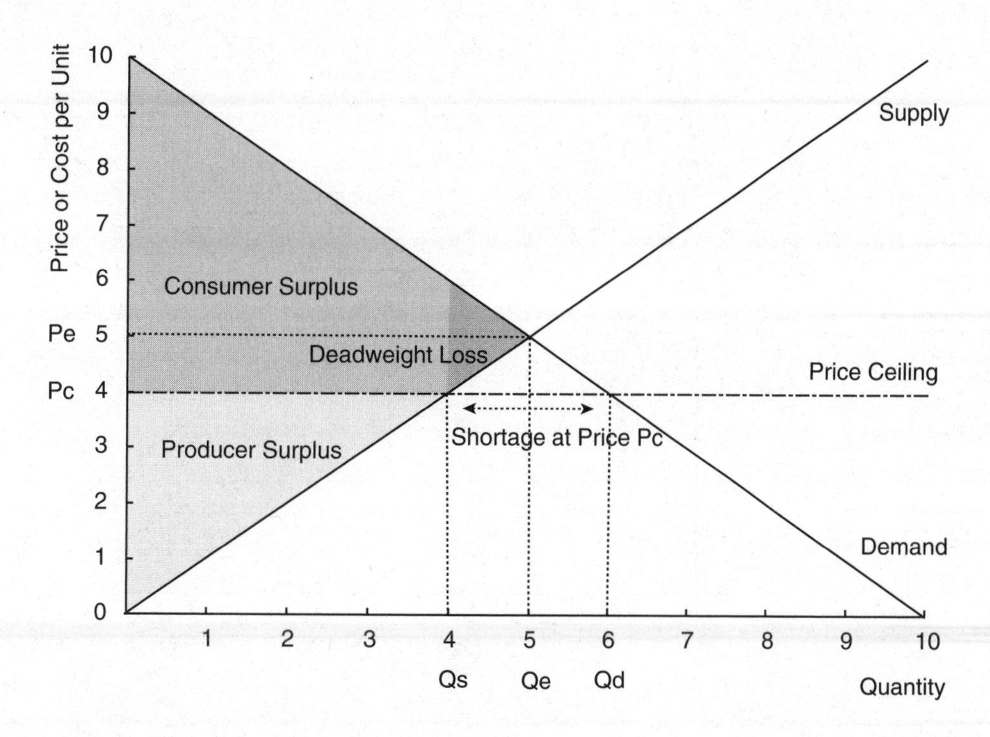

Price ceilings can cause other costs as well. Buyers may need to wait in long lines or waste time searching for goods. Producers, knowing there are more buyers than sellers, may have an incentive to sell units of low quality. Black markets may develop in which goods are traded above the legal maximum. Buyers may fear shortages and hoard goods. The few units that were produced and sold are not likely to go to those who value them most.

Price Floors

Legal minimum prices, called **price floors**, create misallocation of resources and deadweight loss for many of the same reasons that a price ceiling does. If a price floor is set above the equilibrium price, then quantity demanded decreases due to the higher price, and quantity supplied increases. At the legal minimum price, more units are available than are desired. Figure 4-7 illustrates the situation: quantity traded decreases from Qe to Qd—yet again quantity traded is at a lower quantity than socially optimal, and opportunities for mutual gain are forgone. Black markets in which goods are sold below the legal price floor may result, and it is likely that some of the units made will not be produced as cheaply as they could have been. The most commonly cited example of a price floor is one in the labor market: the minimum wage.

Figure 4–7. A Price Floor

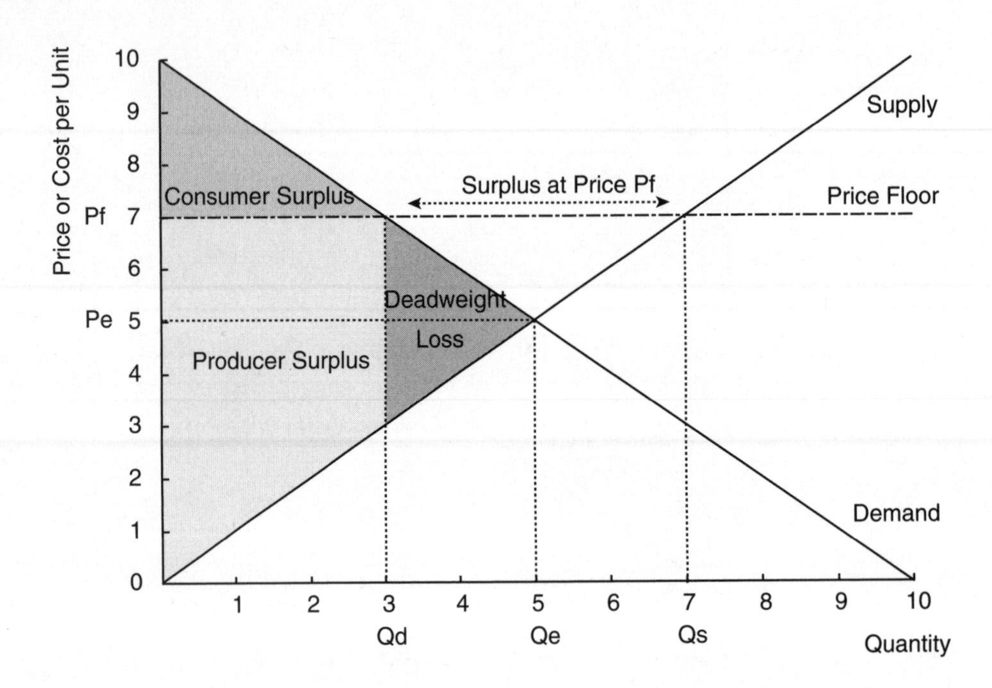

Quantity Regulations

A **quota**, or legal limit on the quantity of a good that may be sold, works very much the same way. Governments might require licenses and limit the number of licenses available, as is done in many large urban taxicab markets. Taxi operating licenses (sometimes known as medallions) limit the number of cabs in the city, and in many markets can be traded as commodities. The quota is also the basic idea behind the cap-and-trade concept designed to reduce carbon emissions.

To show a quota on a graph, use a vertical line rather than the horizontal line used for a price control because the quota represents a restriction on quantity. If the quota is to the left of equilibrium quantity, it limits the number traded: Sellers now are able to charge a high price because buyers are willing to pay a price well in excess of the marginal cost of the last unit produced. Units between the quota's limit and the equilibrium quantity have a higher marginal benefit than marginal cost but are not produced, leading to deadweight loss.

Effective and Ineffective Controls

Both price and quantity controls may be effective or ineffective—and this characterization has nothing to do with how well they might work! Effective controls are ones that take effect, and ineffective ones do not influence how the market operates.

A price ceiling set above the equilibrium price does not take effect because buyers and sellers continue to trade at the normal price, which would be in effect without the legal maximum. Similarly, neither a price floor below the market price nor a quota greater than the typical quantity traded would take effect. After all, how much of a constraint is a law making it illegal to sell a luxury sedan for less than $10?

Households: Consumer Choice and Utility Maximization

Consumers in product markets are individuals who organize into households. Individuals in households make many buying decisions about, for example, housing, food, transportation, and utilities, together, so it may be more appropriate to consider the household as the fundamental consumer unit (sometimes the terms *consumers* and *households* are used interchangeably). Whether speaking of individuals or households, economists typically assume that these consumers are self-interested and logical creatures, always seeking to maximize their happiness, sometimes through meeting their own needs and sometimes gaining satisfaction by helping people. The assumption that buyers maximize utility allows some nifty mathematical analysis of consumer behavior, which you'll need for the AP exam (even if measuring your happiness with a number sounds silly to you and setting up a proportion seems like it would take the joy and spontaneity out of the shopping experience).

Total Utility and Marginal Utility

Utility, or the want-satisfying power that goods have, is usually gained as we consume more units of all the things we enjoy. However, we don't keep gaining utility at the same rate, and we can sometimes have too much of a good, feeling less happy than we did with the first unit. The **total utility** gained from consuming four units of a good is the happiness felt from each of the units, added together. **Marginal utility** is defined as the gain in utility the fourth one gave, over and above the level of satisfaction associated with consuming three. Marginal utility is the change in total utility that results from one additional unit—thus, it is also the slope of the total utility function. As a rule, marginal utility diminishes as more units of a good are consumed, meaning total utility is increasing at a diminishing rate.

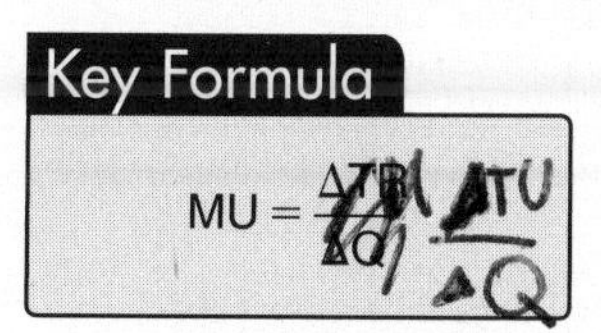

When total utility peaks, marginal utility equals zero, and marginal utility is negative when total utility is decreasing as additional units are consumed. Table 4-1 shows a sample relationship between total and marginal utility derived from consumption of marshmallows.

Because marginal utility is the marginal benefit the next unit yields for the consumer, it is an important consideration in deciding whether to purchase a good. Thus, it is closely related to demand.

Table 4–1.

Marshmallows	Total Utility	Marginal Utility
1	4	4
2	7	3
3	9	2
4	10	1
5	10	0
6	9	−1

Utility Maximization

Consumers want to get the best deal they can from each dollar they spend; in other words, they want to maximize their utility. This fundamental assumption allows you to determine the quantities of two separate goods if given utility information, like that in Table 4-1, for two goods and the prices of both. A utility-maximizing consumer will purchase quantities of any pair of goods so that the marginal utility of the last dollar spent on one good is equal to the marginal utility of the last dollar spent on the other.

Be sure to find marginal utility (change in total utility) if it is not given, then divide each good's marginal utility by its price. A consumer on a budget will first purchase the item that yields the greatest marginal utility per dollar, then the next greatest, and so forth, until no money remains.

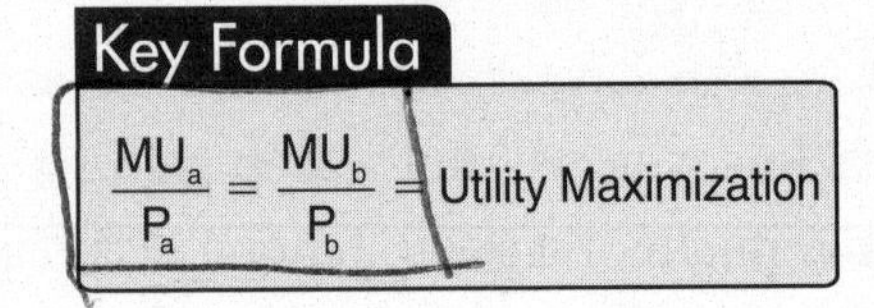

Table 4–2.

Cups of Lemonade	Total Utility	Marginal Utility
1	7	7
2	12	5
3	15	3
4	17	2
5	18	1
6	18	0

Assume a consumer experiences satisfaction from consuming lemonade and marshmallows, as listed in Tables 4-1 and 4-2. You might be provided with a budget of $6.00, and told that marshmallows cost $0.50 each and cups of lemonade are priced at $1.00. If asked to determine the utility-maximizing combination of goods the consumer will purchase, you could reason that the first purchase would be the initial marshmallow, yielding eight utils per dollar (4 utils gained for a cost of $0.50). Next the consumer would buy a cup of lemonade, adding seven utils and costing a dollar. The second marshmallow costs $0.50 but gives an additional three utils, so at six utils per dollar, it is the next-best purchase. Continue making purchases at the highest gain per dollar until the budget runs out. In this example, the consumer ends up with four marshmallows and four cups of lemonade because she will have spent the entire budget taking advantage of every opportunity to gain two utils per dollar, but she will never have spent a dollar that yielded less than that marginal benefit.

Utility and Demand Curves

You may find it silly that economists try to explain our buying behavior by thinking of us purchasing one more unit of a good and then stopping to divide our marginal utility by price to decide whether to buy another unit. However, it can also be seen as the basis of the downward slope of the demand curve. This consumer's demand curve for lemonade has a point at which the price is $1.00 per cup and the quantity demanded is four cups. Now let's imagine holding other factors (a budget and the price of marshmallows) constant and increase the price of lemonade to $2.00 per cup. At this price, the consumer will purchase four marshmallows and only two cups of lemonade, having made all purchases that exceeded or equaled two utils per dollar (the last marshmallow yielded 1 util at a cost of $0.50 and the last lemonade yielded 2 utils at a cost of $1.00). From this information, we can plot the point on her individual lemonade demand curve at a price of $2.00 per cup and a quantity of two cups. While you won't be asked to derive demand curves, you may be asked how a utility-maximizing combination of goods would change if prices changed, or you might be tested on the fact that the principle of diminishing marginal utility is a reason why the demand curve slopes downward (see Chapter 3 for more explanation of this).

Firms: Costs of Production and Profit Maximization

Business firms are presumed to make operating and production decisions in order to maximize profit, just as consumers are presumed to maximize utility. They generate revenue by selling finished goods and incur costs by buying resources from households. **Profit**, or revenue minus costs, might be at a maximum when it is positive, zero, or negative (a loss), and sometimes it might be maximized by producing a quantity of zero units!

TEST TIP

Many of the questions on the AP exam each year are designed to test your knowledge of how various costs behave and your understanding of profit maximization in a broad range of conditions.

Short-Run and Long-Run Production Decisions

Firms can make certain decisions only at a moment's notice; other plans can be realized only with time. The **short run** is defined as the period of time in which most of a firm's costs are fixed and only one is variable. For example, firms might have short-run fixed costs for rent, insurance premiums, or loan payments on the purchase of capital equipment. Those costs don't change in the short run, but their production process has only so much land and capital equipment to use on any given day. Typically most resources are variable in the short run; often labor is the resource used this way. Imagine a clock-making business with a fixed-size factory and machinery that can choose to hire whatever number of workers it wanted in the short run. Choosing to hire zero laborers would be the way to produce a quantity of zero clocks. By adding laborers, the firm can produce a higher quantity of finished clocks.

In the **long run**, the period of time far enough into the future that all resources and variables can change, the firm would be able to purchase or rent more land as its lease comes up for renewal, operate in a bigger factory, or add machinery to the production process. Conversely, the firm could choose to operate on a smaller scale—it could even decide to use no resources and exit from the industry altogether! Because the short run involves fixed costs, firms might sometimes operate while taking a loss for a while. In the long run, however, a firm would choose to exit the industry or adjust its size if it forecast a loss.

Short-Run Production and Marginal Product

Because the amount of fixed factors available to the firm cannot be changed, adding units of a variable resource does not uniformly increase production. Generally, production increases quickly and then more slowly. At some point, adding units of a variable resource may not increase production at all. The **principle of diminishing marginal returns** states that, after some point, fixed inputs will be overtaxed and adding units of a variable resource will increase short-run production more and more slowly. As more and more of a variable input is added to a set amount of fixed inputs, marginal product declines. **Marginal product** (MP = change in total product divided by change in a variable input) thus declines and pulls average product down with it. Note that these principles are revealed in the data of Table 4-3 and are shown graphically in Figure 4-8.

Table 4–3.

Workers Hired (Labor)	Clocks Produced (Total Product)
0	0
1	8
2	18
3	27
4	32
5	35
6	36

Figure 4–8. Average and Marginal Product Curves

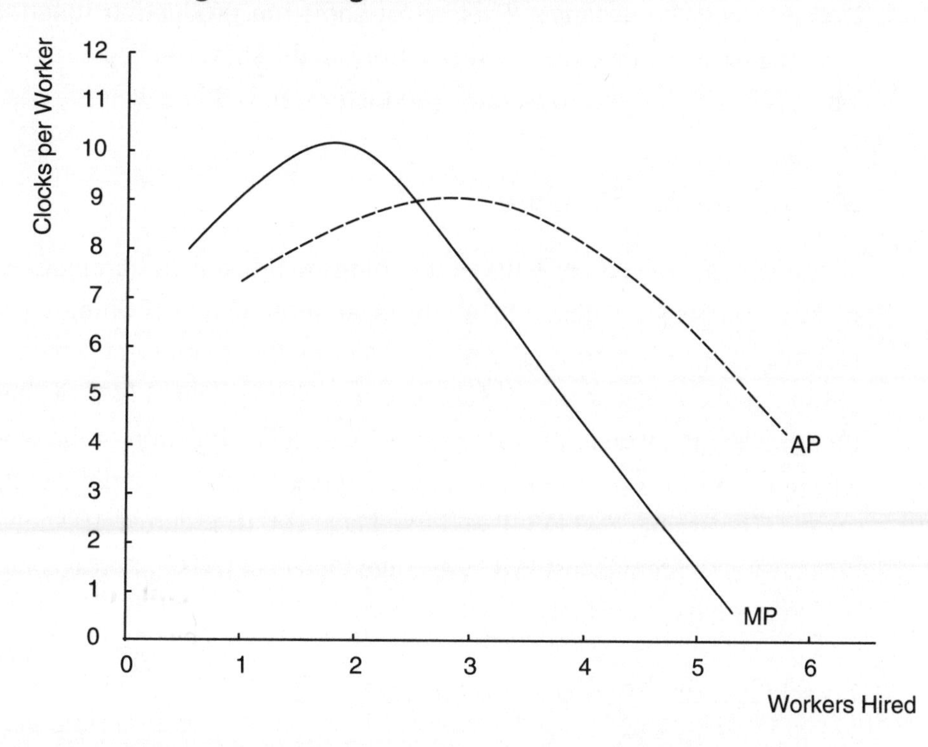

The clockmaker can produce more clocks by hiring additional workers—to get more revenue—but it also increases costs. Remember, what we're really after is profit, so we want to see if increasing production will add more to revenue than it does to cost. Adding the first few units of labor will increase total product dramatically, especially if workers can specialize, but as the machinery becomes fully used and the workspace becomes more crowded, the added production (marginal product) each new worker brings the firm decreases. When the third worker is hired, the firm's total product (TP) increases by nine, one fewer than it did with the second worker's addition. As marginal product declines to five with the fourth worker's hiring, it drags average product (AP) per worker down from nine (twenty-seven units produced by three workers) to eight (thirty-two units produced by four workers). If hired, the fifth worker, with an MP of only three clocks, brings AP down to seven clocks per worker. Hiring the sixth worker adds one clock and decreases AP to six. Average product is always rising when marginal product is above it—workers hired who add more than the average—increasing AP. The average product curve is at its maximum when it crosses marginal product, and thereafter MP is below AP, and AP is declining. This is because workers are being hired who add less than the average to the total product (TP).

One can easily imagine adding a worker to a crowded shop and witnessing a decrease in the total number of clocks produced. In that case, the marginal product of that last worker would be negative. This set of short-run production functions (MP and AP) form the basis for the firm's cost functions in the short run because, for the firm, adding workers is the only way to increase production, and adding workers costs the firm money.

Short-Run Cost Structure

How many clocks (or units of anything) will this firm (or any other firm) choose to make? The answer is that a firm will make more clocks if doing so adds more to total revenue than it does to total cost. It produces the quantity at which marginal revenue (MR) equals marginal cost (MC). The more complicated half of that puzzle involves thinking about a variety of costs, each of which is a function of the quantity (Q, same as TP) of clocks the firm chooses to make. Figure 4-9 shows sample total cost curves (total cost [TC], variable cost [VC], and fixed cost [FC]); Figure 4-10 shows sample per-unit cost curves (marginal cost [MC], average total cost [ATC], average variable cost [AVC], and average fixed cost [AFC]) for a firm.

Fixed Cost and Average Fixed Cost

Fixed cost (FC) is constant no matter the quantity produced. The payment a firm needs to make for rent and capital loan installments is the same whether the firm stays

Figure 4–9. Total Costs of Production

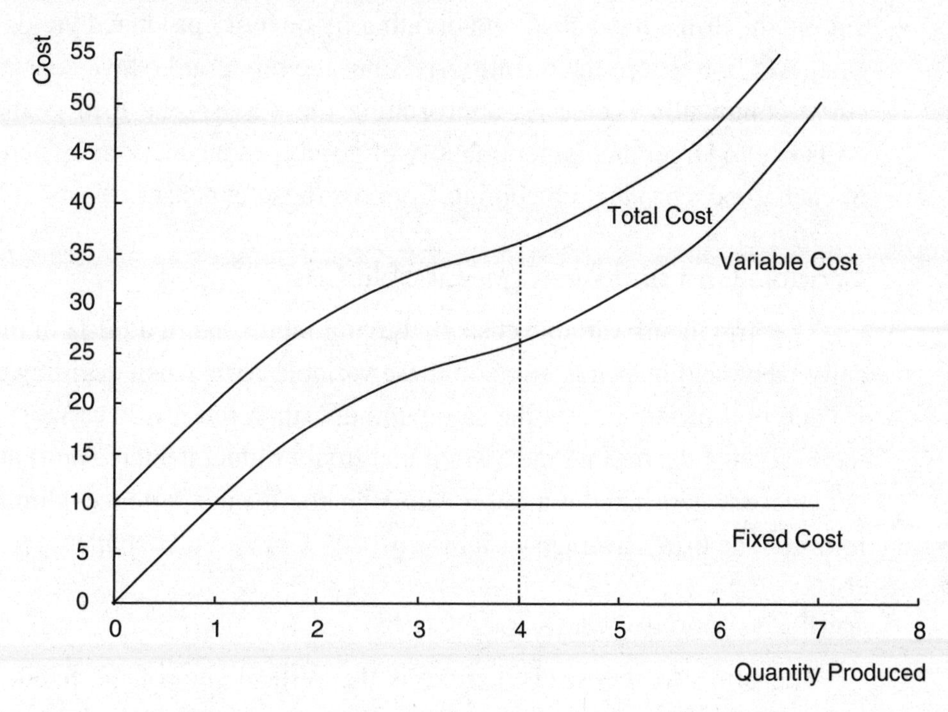

Figure 4–10. Per-Unit Costs of Production

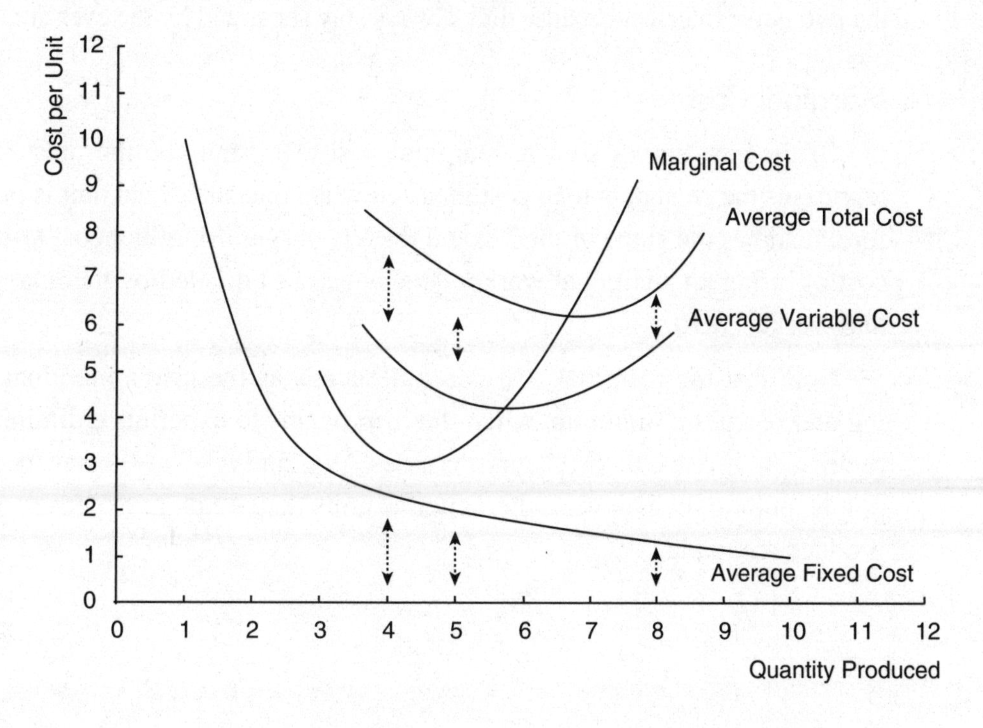

open twenty-four hours a day or shuts down, producing zero units on a given day. Taking the firm's fixed costs and dividing by quantity produced yields its average fixed cost (AFC). Because the quantity rises but the numerator stays constant, a firm's AFC curve continually decreases, approaching the *x*-axis—the firm is spreading its fixed costs over a larger and larger quantity of goods produced, with less and less of the cost of each good's production coming from overhead expenses.

Variable Cost and Average Variable Cost

The firm incurs variable costs by buying inputs that it adjusts in the short run, typically labor, and it spends more on these variable costs when deciding to produce more. If each unit of labor costs the same amount, then the firm's variable cost (VC) curve increases at a decreasing rate (when marginal product is increasing) and then begins to get steeper, increasing at a faster rate after the firm experiences diminishing marginal returns. The firm's average variable cost (AVC) takes a U-shape.

Total Cost and Average Total Costs

The firm's total cost (TC) curve is the vertical sum of the fixed and variable cost curves. It takes the same slope as the VC curve and lies above it by a distance equal to fixed cost. The firm's average total cost (ATC) is also U-shaped. Because it is the vertical summation of the AFC and the AVC curves, it approaches AVC as quantity increases, but the two never intersect because they always stay separated by the ever-smaller AFC value.

Marginal Cost

Of the cost curves shown, marginal cost (MC) may be the most significant. MC represents the change in total cost incurred when one additional unit is produced. Therefore, it shows the slope of the TC and the VC curves. Marginal cost also represents the cost of hiring an additional worker (the wage rate) divided by the marginal product of that worker (MP).

Note that the marginal cost curve descends as the firm's marginal product is rising and reaches a minimum when the firm begins to experience diminishing marginal returns. As it rises, the MC curve crosses AVC and ATC at their respective minimum points, pulling them upward thereafter as units that are more expensive than average to produce are made.

TEST TIP

Take the time to practice drawing the fundamental cost curves on the same set of axes. Draw MC, AVC, and ATC so that MC reaches its minimum first, then crosses AVC and finally ATC. Be sure that AVC and ATC get closer and closer together, but do not cross as quantity rises. (AFC is often not drawn on this graph because it isn't really necessary—it can be inferred from the distance between AVC and ATC.) Keep working on the cost curves: Repetition is truly the best teacher in this case.

Long-Run Cost Structure

The cost curves presented in this chapter represent what happens as a firm tries to increase production quantity while holding some factors of production constant. Once we extend our analysis to the long run, these factors are variable and thus the behavior of cost functions differs. As a firm increases its production by using more of its resources, it expands in size. As it does so, it shifts all of its cost curves, in particular its short-run ATC curve, to the right. Of interest to the economist is whether this short-run ATC curve shifts up or down (or neither) as it moves right.

Economies and Diseconomies of Scale

As a firm grows, initially it may become more productively efficient, reducing per-unit cost as workers specialize or learn by doing, bulk prices of raw materials are negotiated, and lower interest loans are available. When these forces are at work, the firm is experiencing **economies of scale**—a decrease of the short-run ATC function as the firm grows. Another way this can be described is increasing returns to scale. If the firm adds 10 percent more to all the resources it uses, perhaps it produces 15 percent more output. As the firm grows, it also grows more productively efficient.

At some point, the firm will grow but experience constant returns to scale—an increase in output proportional to the amount it increased all the inputs. After this range of sizes, the firm begins to experience negative effects associated with growth—the need for more communication channels, expensive managerial positions, duplication of efforts, and inefficient office politics. These forces cause **diseconomies of scale**, also known as decreasing returns to scale, because the firm experiences an increase in ATC as it increases in size, getting back perhaps only 5 percent in increased output in return for a 10 percent increase in all resources used.

Figure 4–11. Economies of Scale, Constant Returns to Scale, and Diseconomies of Scale

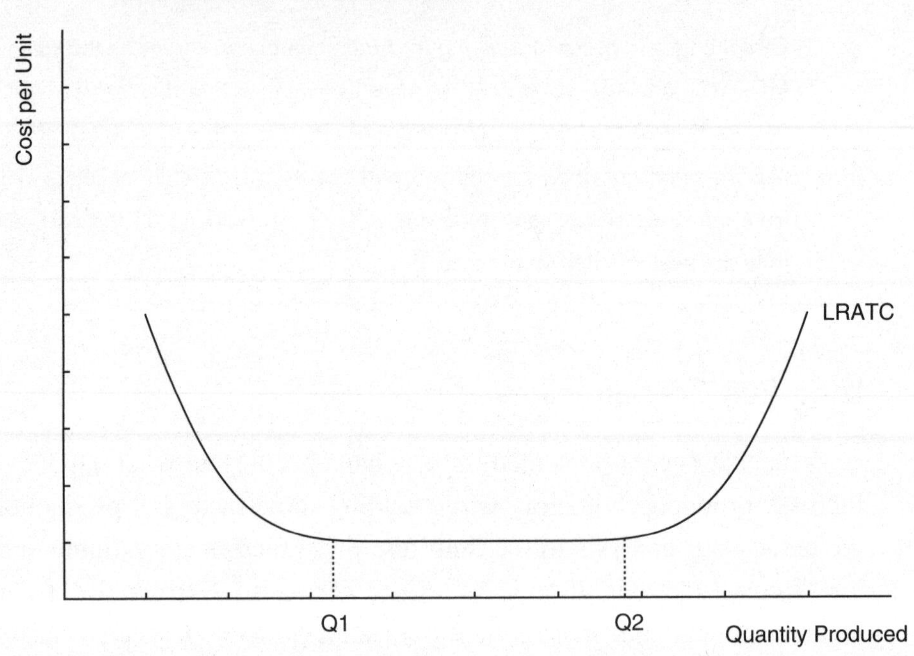

Figure 4-11 shows increasing, constant, and decreasing returns to scale. At quantities below Q1, the firm experiences economies of scale as it grows and sees a decrease in ATC. Between Q1 and Q2, the firm experiences constant returns to scale—as it shifts its short-run ATC to the right, it moves neither up nor down. At quantities beyond Q2, the firm gets less productively efficient as it grows and therefore experiences diseconomies of scale.

Efficient Scale, Firm Size, and Market Structure

A firm operating on an ATC curve that has its minimum point at Q1 on Long Run Average Total Cost (LRATC) would be the smallest firm in that industry that would be able to minimize per-unit production costs; it is said to be of **minimum efficient scale**. A firm operating on an ATC with its minimum at Q2 is the biggest firm that can produce at this minimum cost; it is said to be of **maximum efficient scale**. We would expect, in the long run, that all the firms in this industry would fall between these sizes because outside this range, they incur higher per-unit costs and would be encouraged to resize in order to compete in the market. In some industries, the shape of the LRATC curve dictates that the firms will all be small. Sometimes the shape of the LRATC curve leads to small and large firms operating with very similar per-unit costs. In other industries, it may lead to a few very large firms or, in the extreme, one **natural monopoly**, a firm that is more productively efficient than any smaller combination of firms could ever be. As described later in this chapter, the number and size of firms in an industry is one of the major factors separating competitive markets from monopolies and oligopolies.

Revenue, Costs, and Profit

Profit-maximizing firms want to make their total revenue (TR = price × quantity) exceed total cost by as much as they possibly can. In the event total costs exceed total revenue, the firm hopes the gap between the two is as narrow as possible.

The Idea of Profit

Profit compensates the entrepreneur for his or her efforts and risk. While everyone calculates profit as revenue minus cost, there are distinctions among different kinds of profit that the AP Microeconomics test consistently expects you to know. The divergence in views comes from the fact that accountants and economists differ in how they calculate costs.

Accounting, Normal, and Economic Profit

Accounting profit is total revenue minus only explicit costs. Explicit costs are costs that the firm must make money payments for because they are costs incurred from using resources that belong to someone other than the proprietor of the firm. This number is probably useful in calculating tax liability or for reporting to shareholders, but it is less relevant to an economist because economists believe that explicit costs don't represent the whole cost of running a business.

An entrepreneur surely could earn some salary by selling her labor to another firm. Many business owners use other resources they own for the firm rather than put them to other uses (e.g., an old family car that becomes the company car, or family savings lent to the business interest-free rather than saved in an interest-bearing account). In these cases, the entrepreneur incurs an implicit cost and must earn a **normal profit**, or profit just equal to this implicit cost, in order to feel she is breaking even. Economists consider this normal profit to be a cost (the market cost associated with entrepreneurial ability, measured mostly by what that person would have been worth in the labor market), and thus figure **economic profit** as accounting profit minus normal profit. If there is an opportunity cost, then a firm's economic profit will always be smaller than its accounting profit. A firm that brings in $10,000 in revenue in a given month and has $4,000 of explicit costs is earning $6,000 in accounting profit. However, if the owner's labor could have earned her $5,000 that month if she worked for another firm, then her economic profit would only have been $1,000—that is how much she earned in accounting profit *over and above* what she could have earned working for someone else.

Economists probably favor this less exact manner of thinking about profit because it better explains the desire of entrepreneurs to flock toward or away from an industry—they'll generally move into an industry if they can earn above-normal profit and move out of industries in which they earn less-than-normal profit, so seeing whether economic profit is positive or negative is a better indicator of their choices. For this reason, the graphs in this book that show areas that represent profits or losses are depicting economic profits or losses, not accounting profits or losses. Whenever the term *profit* is used without specification, it should be interpreted to mean economic profit.

Profit Maximization at MC = MR

No matter how big the firm is, and whether it is the only seller or one among thousands, every firm needs to adhere to a simple rule in order to maximize economic profit: Produce units for which marginal revenue exceeds marginal cost and never produce units for which marginal cost exceeds marginal revenue. For some firms, this is the start of the process; for others, this is the whole story. The reason for this should be clear: When revenue rises more than cost, profit increases; when cost rises more than revenue, profit falls.

Profit and Loss in Graphical Representations

An important skill in many AP problems about product markets is being able to identify in graphs the areas that represent costs, revenues, profits, and/or losses. Because the vertical axis is price or cost per unit, vertical distances are per-unit distances. At a given quantity, the distance between price and average total cost represents per-unit profit (or loss if ATC is above price at that quantity). Quantities are horizontal distances. Areas represent total costs, total revenues, and total profits (or losses). These areas are always as wide as the number of units sold, extending horizontally between the y-axis and the firm's production quantity.

Four Product Market Structures: An Overview

Essential Characteristics of Each Structure

How a firm chooses its profit-maximizing price and quantity and how it behaves in other respects depend on the type of market in which it sells its goods. Based on the number of firms selling goods, the degree to which they differentiate their products from one another, and the relative ease or difficulty new firms face when joining the industry, markets for various goods can be grouped into four general categories: perfect competition, monopolistic competition, oligopoly, and monopoly.

In real life, many industries exhibit mixtures of these characteristics, and many of them may actually be blends of these types. Several products are produced under conditions that blur these lines quite a bit. The structures in the middle ranges are probably most common, but those at the extremes are the most commonly tested, so we will examine those first and in the most detail.

Table 4-4 shows the basic characteristics of the four market structures and the resultant behaviors expected of firms selling goods in each market. These basic characteristics are certainly fair game for the test, and the consequences explained influence the way the graphs presented in this chapter look and behave.

Table 4–4. Characteristics of Four Market Structures

	Perfect Competition	Monopolistic Competition	Oligopoly	Monopoly
How many firms?	Very many (infinite)	Many firms	Few firms	One firm
Therefore...	Each firm is a price taker, facing a horizontal demand curve.	Firms can choose price within a narrow range.	Firms make interdependent price-setting decisions.	The firm is the industry—it faces the entire market demand curve.
Are goods differentiated?	Goods are homogenous, undifferentiated.	Goods are differentiated or heterogeneous.	Goods may be homogenous or differentiated.	Firm sells a unique good with no close substitutes.
Therefore...	Firms don't engage in nonprice competition.	Nonprice competition is widespread.	Some oligopolies advertise heavily and others don't.	Firms would only advertise to boost demand for product.
Can new firms enter in the long run?	Yes, entry and exit are easy and relatively cheap.	Yes, entry and exit are easy and relatively cheap.	Generally not, entry is difficult because big firms control market share and have lower per-unit costs.	No, entry is blocked by law, control of resources, or extensive economies of scale.
Therefore...	In the long run firms will earn zero economic profit.	In the long run firms will earn zero economic profit.	Long-run economic profits are possible.	Long-run economic profits are possible.

TEST TIP

These market structures (perfect competition, monopolistic competition, oligopoly, and monopoly) and how firms within each decide what quantity to produce and how to maximize profit are the bases of almost half of the content covered on the AP Microeconomics exam. In particular, challenging questions focus on the way each type of market reacts to a change. Comparisons between market structures, especially contrasts between the extremes of monopoly and perfect competition, are the bases for another group of difficult items on the exam. Questions focus on evaluating the consequences of the different market structures in terms of efficiency. You'll be expected to know whether monopoly is allocatively efficient or if monopolistic competition is productively efficient in the long run. You may have to give your response in graphical form. The information in Table 4-4 and the graphs and explanations in this chapter are all the information you'll need!

Perfect Competition

Perfectly competitive markets feature many suppliers producing identical products. Entry of new firms and exit of failing firms from the industry in the long run are both presumed to be relatively easy, meaning that fixed costs are low. We usually further assume that every firm faces an identical set of cost curves. While real-world examples of pure competition are rare, some agricultural products are traded in ways that come close. Most of the time there is no distinction between soybeans grown on one farmer's field compared to soybeans grown on another's. Each grain seller is providing only a tiny sliver of the market share. It isn't costless to enter or exit agricultural production, but in a given season, farmers might be able to choose to devote less land to production of soybeans in order to plant more corn.

Firm and Market

Because there are many—possibly thousands—of firms, each single firm produces and sells very few of the overall market quantity. For this reason, the demand curve seems different from a single firm's narrow point of view than it does to us, seeing the market from a wide-angle lens. We know that demand for soybeans slopes down because when they are expensive, purchasers' limited dollars don't go as far in buying them. However, to the single producer, the demand curve appears to be a horizontal line. Why? Each producer is a **price taker**. The market price is not influenced by the production quantity of an individual seller—each may produce any quantity at the price determined by the market. The individual farmer cannot sell beans for a penny per bushel more than the market price because buyers would desire a quantity of zero, having many perfect substitutes (the soybeans of every other farmer) available more cheaply. Nor would the farmer have any interest in selling at a lower price than the market determines: If you could sell all you had at the market price, why would you cut your price? The price taker concept is fundamental and unique to perfect competition.

Because the firm's demand curve is a horizontal line and equal to price, this same value serves as the firm's **marginal revenue** curve. Every time the firm produces and sells one more unit, it adds the same amount to its total revenue. In fact, for this firm, price, demand, marginal revenue, and average revenue are all appropriate labels for the single horizontal line.

Figure 4-12 is a graphical depiction of perfect competition. The graphs are placed side by side because the price determined in the market graph (at right) becomes the D = MR = AR = P curve in the graph from the perspective of a typical firm. The ability to draw the market or industry graph next to the graph for a sample firm in horizontal alignment shows that you know changes in one graph have effects on the other. You might use the handy acronym "Mr. Darp" to remind yourself to include marginal revenue, demand, average revenue, and price when you label the graph.

Aside from this alignment, each graph has some important features that you'll want to replicate as you practice drawing these from scratch for yourself. Note the quantity in the industry graph is an uppercase Q, whereas in the firm graph, a lowercase q is used. This shows the grader that you know the market quantities may well be in thousands or millions, but the quantities for representative sellers might be in the tens or hundreds—there are a couple of orders of magnitude difference because there are so many firms in the industry. In the market graph, demand slopes down for the reasons restated in this chapter. Supply is up-sloping because at higher prices, each producer is induced to supply more

Figure 4–12.

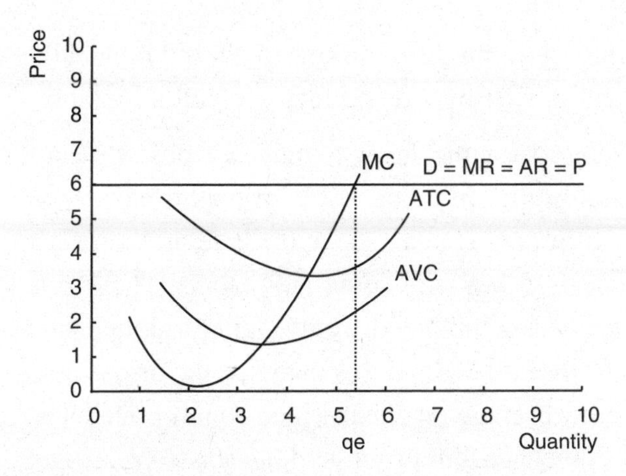

Panel A. Perfectly Competitive Firm

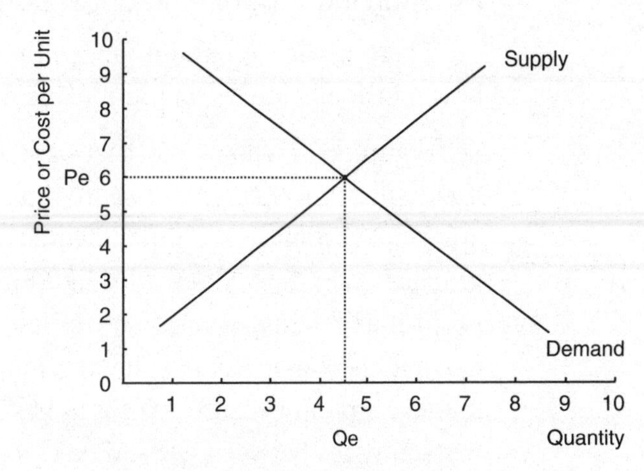

Panel B. Perfectly Competitive Market

units to the market. Consistently higher prices may encourage soybean farmers to acquire more land or capital specific to soybean farming, or even draw farmers who haven't grown soybeans before to begin to do so. Just as a market demand curve is the horizontal sum of all the buyers' individual demand curves, this market supply curve is the horizontal sum of all the firms' supply curves.

On the firm graph, we've covered the D = MR = AR = P line. Other than that, you'll need to have three important cost curves: marginal cost, average total cost, and average variable cost. Marginal cost should be drawn to descend a little and then rise rapidly as quantity increases. The intersection of marginal cost and marginal revenue is the point that determines the firm's output quantity. AVC and ATC are U-shaped and converge as quantity increases, with each function's minimum point located at its intersection with MC. The placement of ATC relative to the D = MR = AR = P line is what determines whether the firm is able to make a profit, has to settle for breaking even (including only a normal profit), or must take a loss. When price is extremely low, the AVC curve tells us when the firm should decide to produce zero units, shutting down in the short run.

TEST TIP

The following definition has appeared almost verbatim on released versions of the AP Microeconomics exam. It's also fundamental to figuring out a lot of other questions that use different terms or present material graphically. It is definitely worth committing to memory: **The short-run supply curve of a perfectly competitive firm is the portion of its marginal cost curve that lies above minimum average variable cost.**

Maximizing Profit in the Short Run

There are three circumstances in which you might be asked to show graphically how a firm maximizes its profit using a pair of side-by-side perfect-competition graphs.

Figure 4-13 shows the best-case scenario for the firm: It makes a positive economic profit in this type of short-run equilibrium. In other words, it makes more than a normal accounting profit and earns a profit area we can see and shade on the firm's graph. Figure 4-13 looks a lot like Figure 4-12 but with some new labels. The firm's profit-maximizing quantity, q_1, is labeled and is indicated by dropping a dotted line down to the x-axis from the intersection of MC and MR. At this quantity, the firm is able to make a profit because ATC at q_1 lies below average revenue (which equals price). The vertical space between AR and ATC represents per-unit profit, and the shaded rectangle is the area of total economic profit—per-unit profit is its height and the number of units

Figure 4–13.

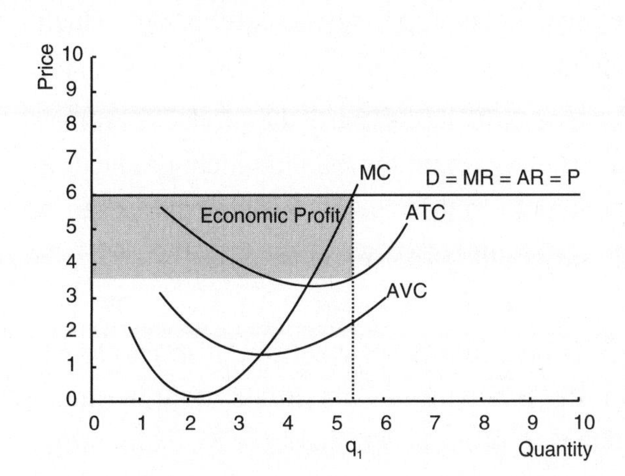

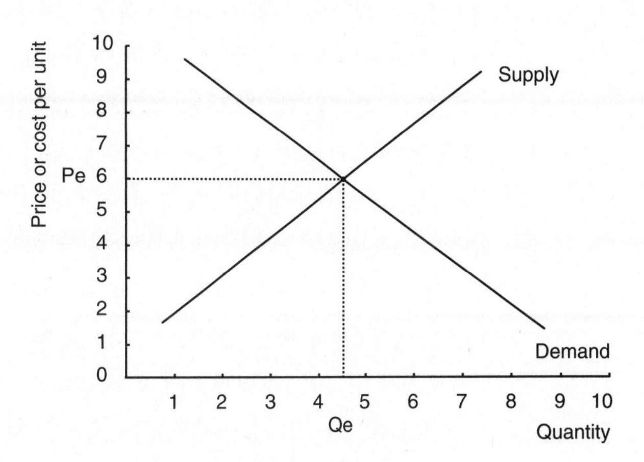

Panel A. Perfectly Competitive Firm Maximizing Short Run Profit **Panel B.** Perfectly Competitive Market

produced is its width. You should be able to spot the situations in which the firm can make a positive profit because the D = MR = AR = P line slices through the ATC curve, crossing it twice. It is in the space between those two intersecting points that the firm can find quantities that allow profit opportunities because that's where AR is above ATC.

Figure 4-14 shows the next-best possibility for the firm: It can find a quantity allowing it to cover all explicit and implicit costs, so it can break even economically. All other quantities the firm could choose to produce would leave it in the red, making less than normal profit and with an area on the graph of economic losses because ATC would lie above AR. Note that the firm is producing fewer units, q_2, than it did before because this lower D = MR = AR = P line crosses MC further to the left, telling the firm to produce

Figure 4–14.

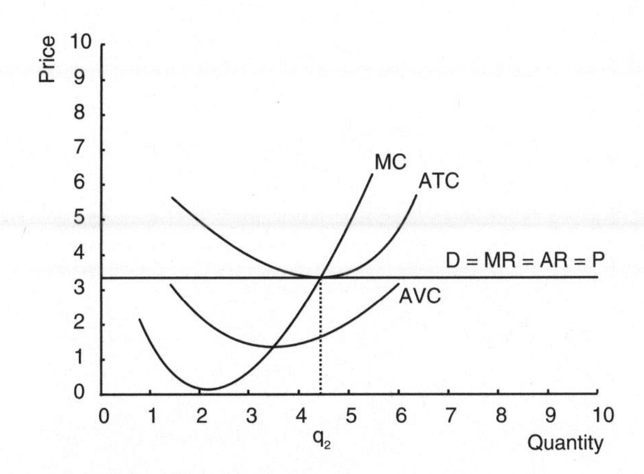

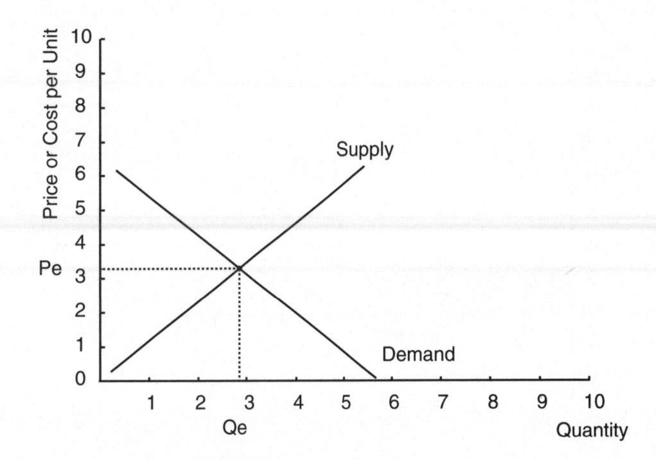

Panel A. Perfectly Competitive Firm Breaking Even **Panel B.** Perfectly Competitive Market

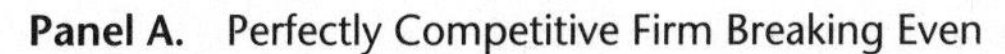

a smaller quantity than when prices were high enough to earn a profit. This situation, in which each firm maximizes profit by breaking even, is also long-run equilibrium, which is explained in more detail later in this chapter.

Now imagine that the market demand curve shifts left because the product becomes less popular. Market quantity declines, but more important for the individual producer is the decline in market price. Because the producer is a price taker, this new market price becomes his D = MR = AR = P curve, and the result isn't a welcome one!

The short-run equilibrium, when reached, is shown in Figure 4-15. Now, ATC lies entirely above the AR line, meaning there is no quantity at which the firm can break even, let alone earn positive economic profits. It must try to maximize profit by minimizing its losses. Once again the firm's decision process is to look for MR's intersection with MC. That establishes the firm's quantity (as long as AR exceeds AVC at this quantity—for the reasons why, see the section called The Shutdown Rule in this chapter). This new quantity is a bit lower than q_2 because price has decreased—the firm is responding to the law of supply, just as we should expect. The vertical space from AR up to ATC at the quantity q_3 now represents a per-unit loss. When this height is multiplied by the quantity q_3, the result is the shaded area of economic losses. From this graph, it is impossible to tell whether the firm is making positive, zero, or negative accounting profit because we don't know the size of the normal profit relative to the size of the economic losses.

Many students find it difficult to understand why a firm would produce units if selling those goods would generate less revenue than making them cost the firm. The explanation depends on referring to the distinction between fixed and variable costs.

Figure 4–15.

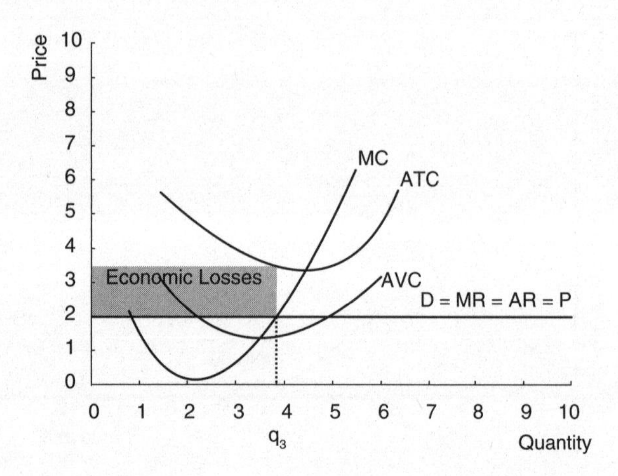

Panel A. Perfectly Competitive Firm Minimizing Losses

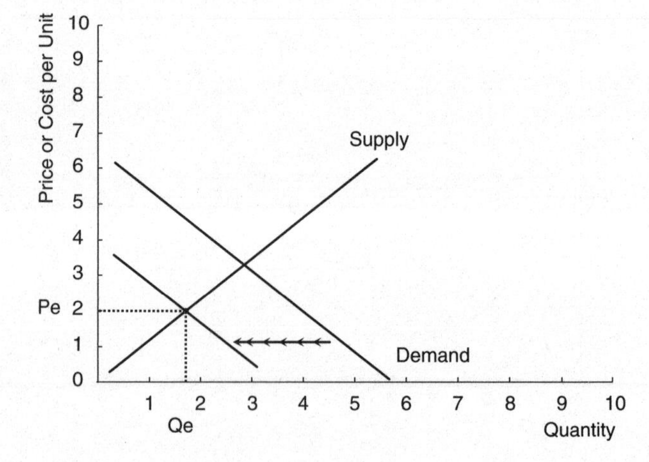

Panel B. Perfectly Competitive Market

Fixed costs are **sunk costs**—they can't be avoided no matter what quantity is produced; even if zero units are produced, these costs apply. In situations in which price exceeds AVC, producing at the MC = MR quantity involves a smaller negative profit (losing less money) than producing zero units, incurring zero variable costs but all fixed costs, and earning zero revenue. Under those circumstances, losses would equal fixed costs. The firm should produce some units if it can offset these lost sunk costs even partially.

The Shutdown Rule

What happens if the price should fall so far that AVC exceeds AR for all quantities? Now the balance has tipped and producing goods doesn't look like such a good option any longer. The firm has already made irreversible decisions that mean fixed cost has been spent. But now every time a unit is produced, more variable costs are incurred than revenue is obtained. The result is that the losses become larger than the fixed cost—the opposite of the situation in Figure 4-15, when production offset at least some of those costs. The choice is clear: The firm should incur no variable costs, earn no revenue, and face losing exactly the fixed costs because any quantity it might choose to produce would worsen this outcome. Deciding to produce a quantity of zero in the short run is called **shutting down** (distinguish this from exiting the industry, which a firm can decide to do only in the long run).

To visualize this situation, examine Figure 4-16. We can spot that this is a shutdown situation right away because the D = MR = AR = P line never crosses AVC or ATC—it always lies underneath both average cost curves. Let's imagine the alternative to the shutdown idea and say, for the sake of argument, that the firm produced at the MC = MR quantity instead. The resulting quantity would be q_0. At this quantity, ATC lies above AR—the distance between the two curves is per-unit loss. But note that this difference is greater than the gap between AVC and ATC, which represents average fixed cost. The firm is losing more than just fixed costs on a per-unit basis. Examining totals rather than per-unit values yields the same unfortunate result. The losses the firm would take if producing no units can be shown as AFC times any quantity because that equals fixed cost. If the firm makes quantity q_0, then losses are larger than this area: Its loss would include the whole fixed-cost rectangle and the shaded one below it. So when average variable cost is greater than price, the firm would prefer to choose not to produce any units because its losses would be smaller. This is the **shutdown rule**. It also shows us why the points on a firm's MC curve that lie below the AVC minimum point are not part of its supply curve: At prices that low, they'd produce a quantity of zero!

Figure 4–16.

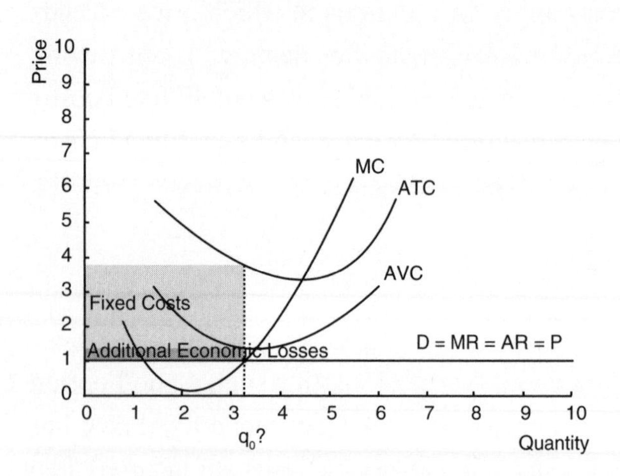

Panel A. Perfectly Competitive Firm Facing Shutdown

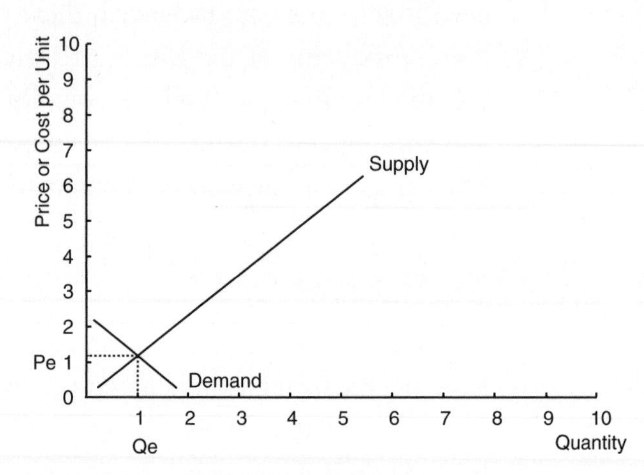

Panel B. Perfectly Competitive Market

Changes in Demand

Changes in market demand for the product result in either a higher or lower market equilibrium price. If the market price determined in the industry graph rises, then the firm experiences a higher D = MR = AR = P curve; it responds by choosing a higher quantity to produce at a point up and to the right along its MC curve at the new intersection with that ever-important horizontal price-taker line. This is one way that an economic loss can turn into a situation in which the firm breaks even or earns profit. Figure 4-17 shows the effects of an increase in demand.

Conversely, if market demand declines, the firm sees a lower demand curve, responds by finding the point at which this lower marginal revenue crosses the marginal cost curve, and produces a smaller quantity. This would create a smaller area of profit or increase losses—it's never good for the firm if the market price of its good decreases. Practice drawing the pair of graphs and showing the effects of a decrease in market demand—it is quite doable with some practice, but it is also easy to forget a step or leave something unlabeled. The more you practice drawing these graphs, the more skilled you will become. If you have trouble, examine Figure 4-17 more closely.

Because changes in price lead the firm to produce new quantities and each price-quantity combination lies on the firm's MC curve, this curve functions as its supply curve as well as its marginal cost. At this point, the definition in the last Test Tip should make complete sense to you, and you should understand why it is written the way it is. If you do, you are well on your way to a strong understanding of perfect competition, the most commonly tested of the four market structures.

Figure 4–17. Perfectly Competitive Firm Can Make a Profit Because of an Increase in Market Demand

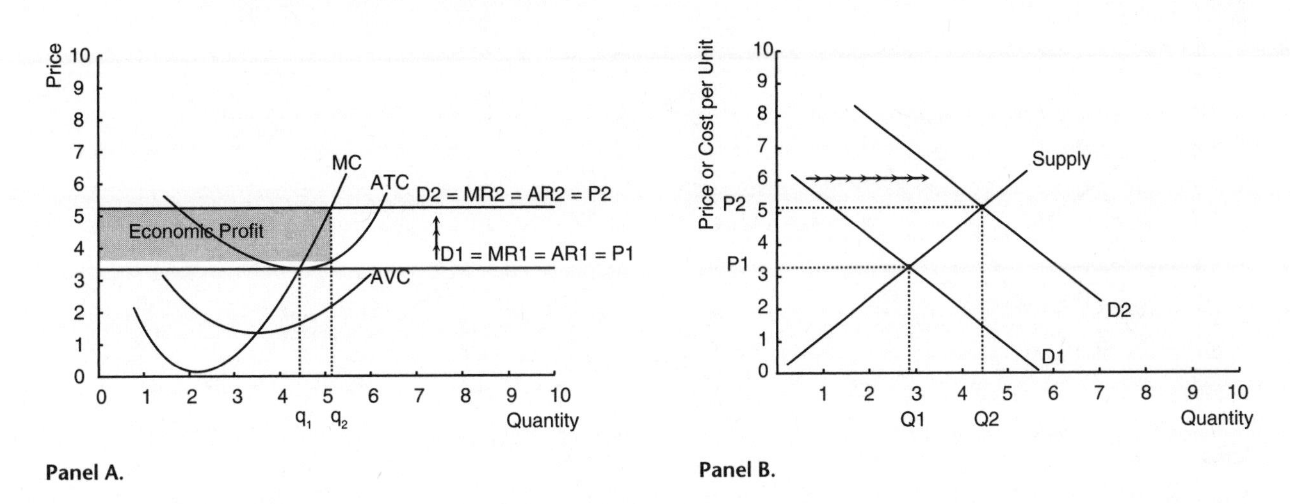

Entry, Exit, and Long-Run Equilibrium

Every bit of our analysis of perfectly competitive industries so far has focused on possible short-run equilibrium situations and how they might change in the short run. The essential feature that changes when we add the element of time is that firms can choose to leave the industry entirely if conditions are not good or, if circumstances are favorable for producers, new firms can join the marketplace as producers. Firms do not have any unavoidable sunk fixed costs in the long run, meaning the decision about joining the action is a bit simpler: Join the industry if you believe that price will be equal to or greater than average cost, in other words, if you can break even or better. (You, the careful economics student who has read Table 4-4 carefully, know that the firm will break even exactly, with no economic profit in the long run. But because you're a curious creature, you also want to know why.)

Under what circumstances might firms decide to exit the industry? If firms are able to earn a better rate of return doing something else, it makes sense that they would exit the industry. This means that the concept of normal profit comes into play again. Normal profit represents the gain that the entrepreneur could have had doing something else, perhaps working for another person's business, selling labor for wages or a salary. In some cases, normal profit may be higher because, perhaps, nonmonetary benefits are associated with knowing you built your own business. In other cases, the stress and risk of having no stable income may feel like an extra cost; then the normal profit would be lower than the forgone salary. Generally we won't need to calculate this; we can simply recall that ATC on all our graphs is drawn to include a normal profit. If we're showing an economic loss, then the business owners in that industry, given time, will consider closing down altogether.

Figure 4–18. Losses Disappear Due to a Price Increase as Firms Exit the Industry

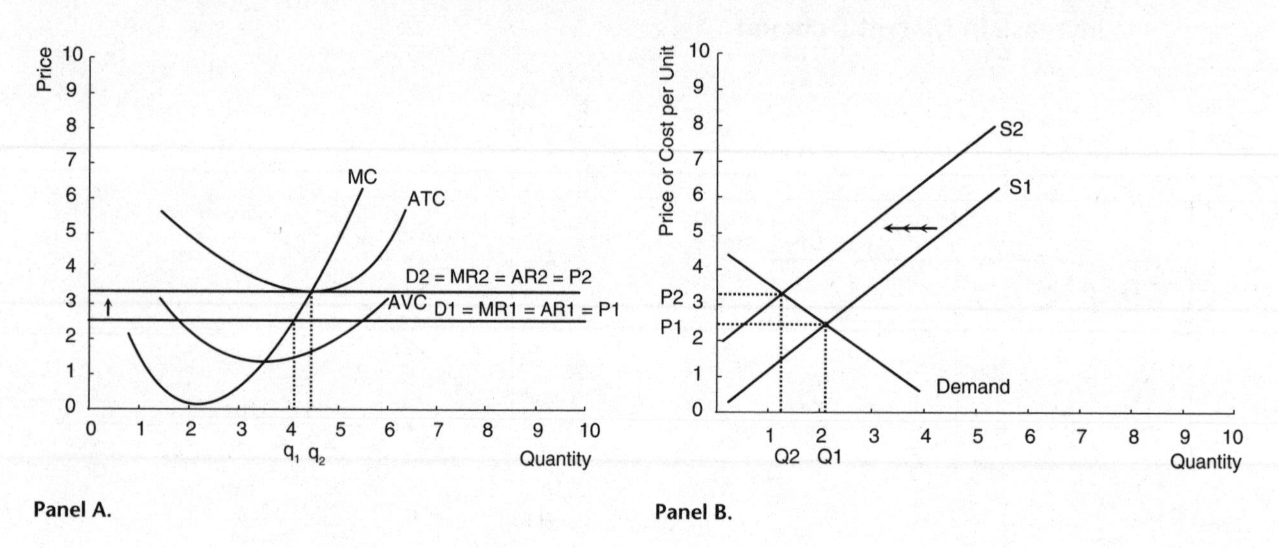

Panel A. Panel B.

As firms leave, the loss situation for each firm remaining in the industry improves. Because the market supply curve is formed from the horizontal summation of each firm's individual supply (marginal cost) curve, fewer firms means fewer units produced at any given market price. Recall also from Chapter 3 that an industry with fewer suppliers causes the supply curve to shift leftward. As market supply shifts left, price increases on both graphs. Now demand is higher than it was before (and marginal revenue and average revenue have also increased). This process will continue until price is just equal to minimum ATC, and the situation looks as it did in Figure 4-14, with each firm breaking even and producing exactly q_2 units. In this way, economic losses encourage firms to seek opportunities elsewhere, thus decreasing the supply in the market, pushing up prices until each firm is a price taker at a price that allows it to just break even and to earn exactly normal profit once long-run equilibrium is reached. Figure 4-18 shows a loss leading to exit from the industry and the resulting increase in the firm's D = MR = AR = P curve, which encourages an increase in quantity produced from q_1 to q_2, the long-run quantity.

Now let's consider the opposite set of circumstances: the entry of new firms into the market. When would this be likely to occur? If positive economic profit is expected in the industry, savvy entrepreneurs are likely to try to start new firms and earn the higher rates of return available for producing the good.

Try it yourself: Draw side-by-side graphs showing an industry and firm in which the market price allows a profit, just as was shown in Figure 4-13. Now show what happens in the long run. If you have difficulty, refer again to Figure 4-18 and try to reverse the process, showing the effects of firms who are entering the market rather than leaving it. Once you've got your graph the way you want, check whether it shows a picture of the process explained in the next paragraph.

As the new firms enter, market supply shifts right (more suppliers mean more supply) and the price declines. Firms will continue to enter as long as there are opportunities to earn more than a normal profit. Once the economic profit chances have all been squeezed out and price declines to long-run equilibrium level, tangent to the bottom point on each firm's ATC curve, there is no incentive for new firms to enter. There are more firms in the industry so market quantity is higher, but each firm is producing exactly q_2 units, just as they would in any long-run equilibrium situation. Note also that the market price is the same at every long-run equilibrium point: equal to the minimum of each firm's ATC. In an odd twist of fate, the market dictates the price to the firm in any given short-run equilibrium, but in the long run, the market equilibrium price is determined by the bottom point on each firm's ATC curve. Distinctions between the short run and long run can be tough, but one helpful hint is to remember that, in the long run, the number of firms can change. So when a question asks for long-run analysis, usually thinking about entry or exit of firms is a core piece of the reasoning you'll need to figure out the problem. The entry or exit of firms is how the market reaches long-run equilibrium, and it is the reason why no firms can earn positive economic profits in the long run.

TEST TIP

When showing entry or exit of firms, start on the firm graph even though it shows the result. Draw in the new breakeven D = MR = AR = P line tangent to the bottom of the firm's ATC curve first. Extend it to a dotted line on the market graph. See where that line crosses demand to determine industry quantity, and make a new supply curve that intersects demand at that quantity. By drawing the effect before the cause, you'll be sure that you shift the market supply curve the right distance every time.

Efficiency of Perfect Competition

For each market structure, it will be important for you to be able to assess both its allocative and productive efficiency. **Allocative efficiency** implies that the last unit produced yielded as much marginal benefit (marginal utility to the consumer is reflected in the demand curve) as it involved marginal cost (the sacrifice involved in producing the last unit is shown in the marginal cost curve). When asked about allocative efficiency, relate back to price (which comes from demand) and marginal cost (P = MC). For perfect competition, a profit-maximizing firm is always allocatively efficient: The price charged to consumers equals the marginal cost of the last unit produced. This is true in the short run and in the long run. Perfectly competitive markets produce the allocatively efficient quantity and do not result in deadweight loss. Perfect competition is the only market structure to have this feature; this contrast with the other structures is a subject that AP test writers are fond of checking several times to see that you understand it.

For **productive efficiency**, the condition is whether the firm is producing at the quantity that minimizes ATC. If it is, units are produced with the fewest resources possible. Anytime a perfectly competitive firm is breaking even, it is operating at the minimum point on ATC. If, in the short run, the firm is taking a loss, its production quantity is smaller than the productively efficient output. If the firm is earning positive profit, it produces more than the productively efficient quantity. But we know that entry or exit of firms results in the breakeven situation as time passes. So perfectly competitive firms are always productively efficient when in long-run equilibrium.

Monopoly Markets

Monopolies are markets in which one single firm sells a good that has no close substitutes and is effectively able to block the entry of new firms. Because this one firm *is* the market, there won't be a need for separate side-by-side graphs as in perfect competition. Because the number of firms doesn't change over time (if new firms entered the market, it wouldn't be a monopoly any more!), the short run *is* the long run. Balancing these factors may cause students to view monopoly as easier than perfect competition, but a couple of features make learning about monopolies more complex: the difference between demand and marginal revenue, deadweight loss, the ability of some monopolists to charge a variety of prices for the same good, and the dilemma associated with regulating natural monopolies.

Examples of monopolies are somewhat easier to find in the real world than are examples of perfect competition, but because public policy in many countries is intended to foster competition, most markets are not truly monopolies even if there is one firm that controls a substantial share of the market. The DeBeers Company held near-monopoly power over the world's diamond trade for a long time. At one point, Standard Oil controlled a gigantic share of the gasoline market in the United States. Today, pharmaceutical corporations enjoy monopoly power over newly approved drugs, but only for the limited life of their patents. Looking on a more local level, you might live in a small town with only one movie theater or a larger city in which one company owns all the theaters. In many cases, even in large markets, one firm provides a given category of services (i.e., cable TV, electricity, natural gas, a single daily newspaper, etc.).

How Monopolies Form

Three different causes can give rise to monopolies. First, they may form because of legal barriers. If only one firm has the legal authority to operate because of an exclusive contract with the government or a sole license, then the market is a monopoly. Patents, trademarks, and copyrights are all examples of monopoly power because they grant exclusive rights to one seller over the intellectual property they are aimed to protect.

DIDYOUKNOW?

The Mexican government owned and operated two large monopolies, Pemex and Telmex, for decades. Pemex, a petroleum and fuel corporation, is still a primary source of revenue for the Mexican government. Telmex, a communications company, was privatized in the early 1990s. While Telmex does face competition from other providers of landline phone service, it still controls over 90 percent of the phone lines in Mexico City.

Second, monopolies can arise when one firm controls the access to an input vital to the production of a good. A major reason why DeBeers could control the world's diamond trade was ownership of the land on which the diamonds were mined. Ownership of oil fields and/or refineries can lead to significant power in the gasoline and diesel markets. This was a major factor in Standard Oil's success in the late nineteenth century and is at the core of the Organization of the Petroleum Exporting Countries' (OPEC's) power over the global oil market to this day, though its power has declined since the 1970s. (OPEC is not quite a monopoly; it is a cartel that acts like a monopoly.)

Third, monopolies can come from the cost structure associated with producing the product itself. If fixed costs are high enough and marginal cost is nearly constant (sometimes close to or actually zero), then one large firm will be able to experience a lower average cost of production (and therefore offer a lower price) than any combination of smaller competitors. Thus, one firm can drive out the others, prevent the effective rise of challengers, and enjoy extensive economies of scale. The result is a **natural monopoly**. Cable television and natural gas service are good examples of industries that gravitate toward natural monopolies because the high fixed cost of creating a network that connects to every house in a market prevents other challengers from entering the market on a competitive basis. See the section called Natural Monopoly and Regulation Options for more on the distinct way to draw this situation graphically and why it poses difficulties for regulators who want to promote markets with more competition.

Demand and Marginal Revenue in Monopoly

Because the monopoly is the entire industry, it faces the whole market demand curve, which is down-sloping. For the firm, picking a price and picking a quantity are now linked. To sell more units during a certain production period than the period before, the firm must reduce its price. We typically assume for all firms that the units they sell are all sold at one common price (the exception to this is explained in the section called Price-Discriminating Monopolies). Because the monopolist must reduce price to encourage more people to buy their product, all units must be sold at this new, lower price. The effect is that marginal revenue lies below demand, starting at the same *y*-intercept and descending faster. Each time the firm increases quantity by one unit, the gain in revenue that the new unit brings is offset by the decrease in revenue resulting from selling a number of units at the lower price.

If the demand curve is linear, marginal revenue descends twice as fast and thus crosses the *x*-axis halfway between the origin and the lower-right endpoint on the demand curve. The point where the MR curve crosses the *x*-axis represents the quantity at which the firm has maximized its total revenue: That last unit neither added to nor subtracted from the firm's inflow of money for selling its goods. This quantity therefore corresponds with the unit elastic point on the demand curve, which always lies directly above the *x*-intercept of the MR curve.

Figure 4-19 shows the demand and marginal revenue curves that a monopolist might face. Note that, as the firm increases production from Q1 to Q2, the area of total revenue (price times quantity) grows, but not by the full amount that the new units are sold for; the horizontal rectangle between the higher price P1 and the new lower price P2 that is

Figure 4–19. A Monopolist's Demand and Marginal Revenue

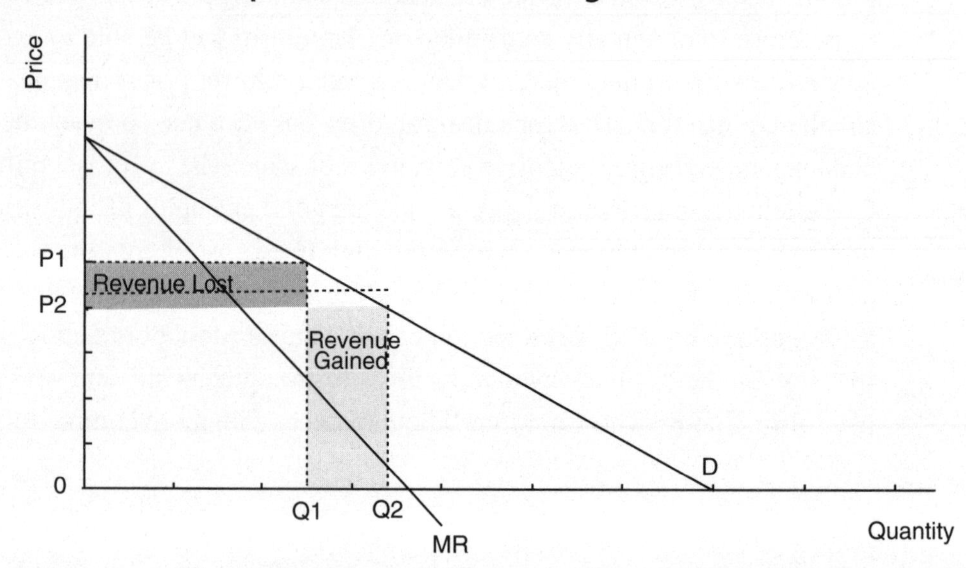

Q1 units wide represents the decrease in revenue that came from selling those first Q1 units for a lower price. This partially offsets the gain in revenue represented by the vertical rectangle between Q1 and Q2 that is P2 units in height. The resulting total revenue rectangle (Q2 wide and P2 high) is only slightly larger than the original one (Q1 wide and P1 high). The marginal revenue curve shows the change in total revenue that results from increasing production to Q2 units directly. Because MR is positive for this range of quantities, total revenue increases when the firm produces more units.

TEST TIP

Free-response questions on the AP exam often require students to explain the relationship between demand and marginal revenue for a monopolist, to identify the quantity that maximizes revenue rather than profit, or to draw conclusions about the elasticity of demand at the firm's level of output. You will do fine on these questions if you remember the relationship between total and marginal revenue, and recall that the demand curve is elastic when marginal revenue is positive, unit elastic when marginal revenue is zero, and inelastic when marginal revenue is negative.

The significance of this relationship between demand and marginal revenue is twofold: It makes the firm into a price setter and it leads to underproduction of the good.

Maximizing Profit and Minimizing Loss

Just as any firm should, the monopolist fixes its quantity where MC and MR intersect. Unlike the perfect competitor, however, the monopolist now has a second decision to make: determining a price. This firm, as all imperfect competitors do, seeks a price along the demand curve it faces *directly above* the point where MC = MR. For the perfect competitor, the way to maximize profit was merely to find a quantity; the monopolist's method is a two-step process (determine quantity and then go up to find price). This firm's quantity-price combination does not lie on its marginal cost curve; in fact, a monopoly does not have a supply curve at all.

The ability to set price above marginal cost does enhance the odds that the monopolist may make positive economic profits. Just as a perfect competitor does, however, a monopolist might face conditions that force it to choose from among quantities, all of which result in negative profit, and thus select the one that minimizes loss. This may come as a surprise, given that the monopolist can change output in order to control the market price, but sometimes there just isn't enough demand for the firm to be able to charge a price that allows it to earn profit.

As in the case of perfect competition, the relationship between price (which is average revenue) and average total cost is the graphical factor that distinguishes these situations. Train your eye to look for it.

If ATC is above demand at the profit-maximizing quantity, the firm is forced to minimize its loss, as shown in Figure 4-20. Note that ATC never crosses demand; if it did, the firm would be able at least to break even. This is because the demand curve represents average revenue and price as well. If ATC is above AR for all quantities, profit will be negative because per-unit profit is AR minus ATC.

If market demand were to shift right due to a rise in consumer income, the firm would face a new marginal revenue curve, encouraging it to make a few more units, and thus sliding down along ATC and increasing price. Figure 4-21 shows a possible result. Note that ATC is above demand at the profit-maximizing quantity and that the shaded box represents positive economic profit.

Figure 4-22 shows a profit achieved through different means. If the firm experiences a decrease in fixed cost (perhaps due to a lump-sum subsidy or a decrease in its rent costs), its ATC curve slides down along the same marginal cost curve. Note that, in this case, the quantity produced does not change: Factors that move the MR or MC curve result in new quantities because their intersection point determines the profit-maximizing quantity. In this case, neither curve shifted.

Figure 4–20. Monopoly Minimizing Losses

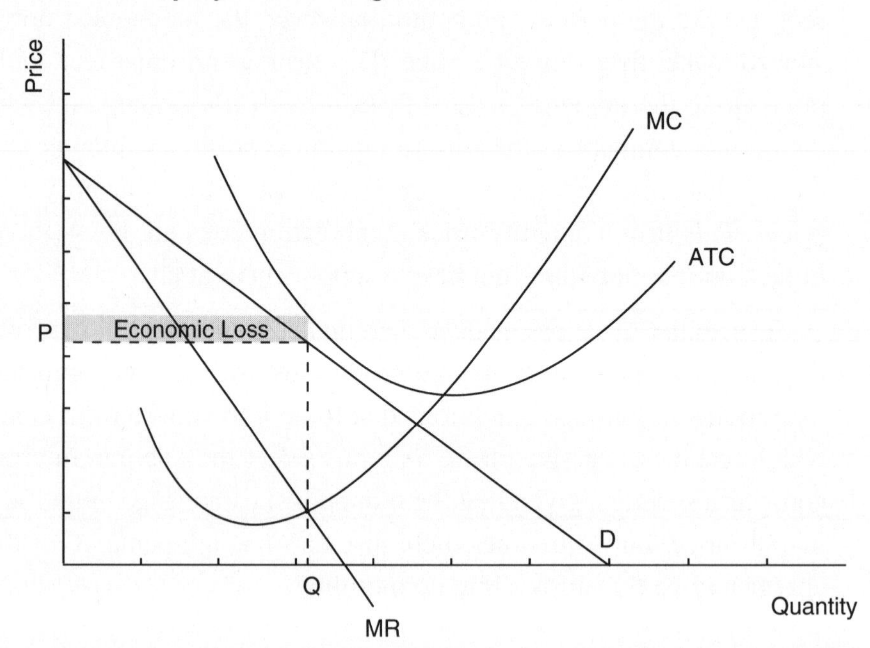

Figure 4–21. Increase in Demand for the Monopolist

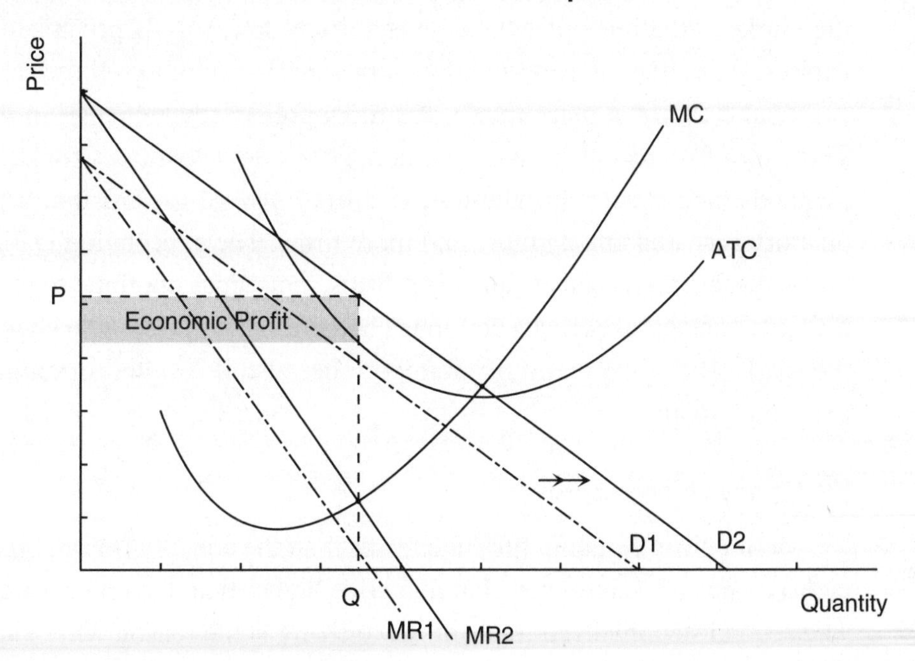

Figure 4–22. Lower Fixed Costs Turn Losses into Profits

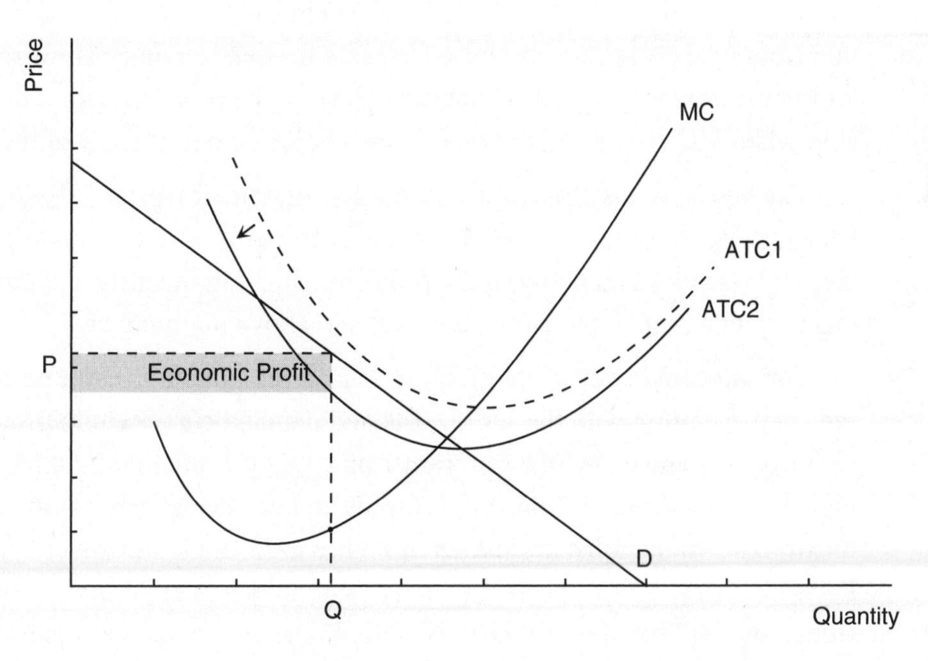

In the long run, nothing really changes for the monopolist. Because entry into the industry is blocked, you won't need to think about profits or losses evaporating. Despite this, some circumstances might threaten monopoly power (and prior AP exams have sometimes featured questions about this possibility). If firms are allowed to flood the market (which happens when a state-run monopoly is privatized or when a patent expires, thus allowing generic drug companies the right to sell the same exact chemical compound as a pharmaceutical), the monopolist sees a change in the demand curve. The curve flattens out because the new goods are substitutes for the product, making demand more elastic. In addition, it shifts leftward toward the origin as the market quantity is shared among more and more firms. The expectation is that profit decreases under these circumstances; however, firms sometimes continue to enjoy a name recognition advantage over rivals and thus charge a higher price. The change, however, took the market from the realm of monopoly because it resulted in multiple firms making the same product.

Efficiency of Monopoly

Monopolists certainly produce fewer than the socially optimal (or allocatively efficient) quantity because they charge a price higher than the marginal cost of production. The second step involved in profit maximizing is the reason why. The allocatively efficient quantity is found where the demand curve crosses marginal cost (where P = MC), meaning that the last unit produced yielded just as much benefit to the purchaser (a buyer's reservation price is reflected in the demand curve) as was sacrificed to create that unit (marginal cost is a record of added cost for that last unit). However, the monopolist will never produce a quantity that high because the profit-maximizing incentive says to stop when MC crosses MR, which it does below and to the left of the demand curve.

The result is that, when a monopolist maximizes profit, deadweight loss exists because opportunities for gain have not been realized due to underproduction. Deadweight loss is located between the profit-maximizing quantity and the allocatively efficient quantity, under the demand curve, and above marginal cost.

The allocatively efficient quantity is also the quantity that a perfectly competitive industry operating with the same costs and demand curve would produce. Because the quantity is produced by one firm rather than many, a smaller quantity is produced and a higher price is charged. Consumer surplus and deadweight loss associated with a profit-maximizing monopolist are shown in Figure 4-23. If Q_{ae} units were produced and price P_{ae} were charged, as in perfect competition, no deadweight loss would exist, and consumer surplus would be a larger triangle. Some consumer surplus has been transferred to producers and some is lost due to underproduction at quantity Q_m, leaving the smaller shaded triangle above price P_m.

This situation may explain a motive for governments to try to break monopoly firms into smaller components, increasing competition in the market in order to push quantity

Figure 4–23. Monopolist Earning Profit

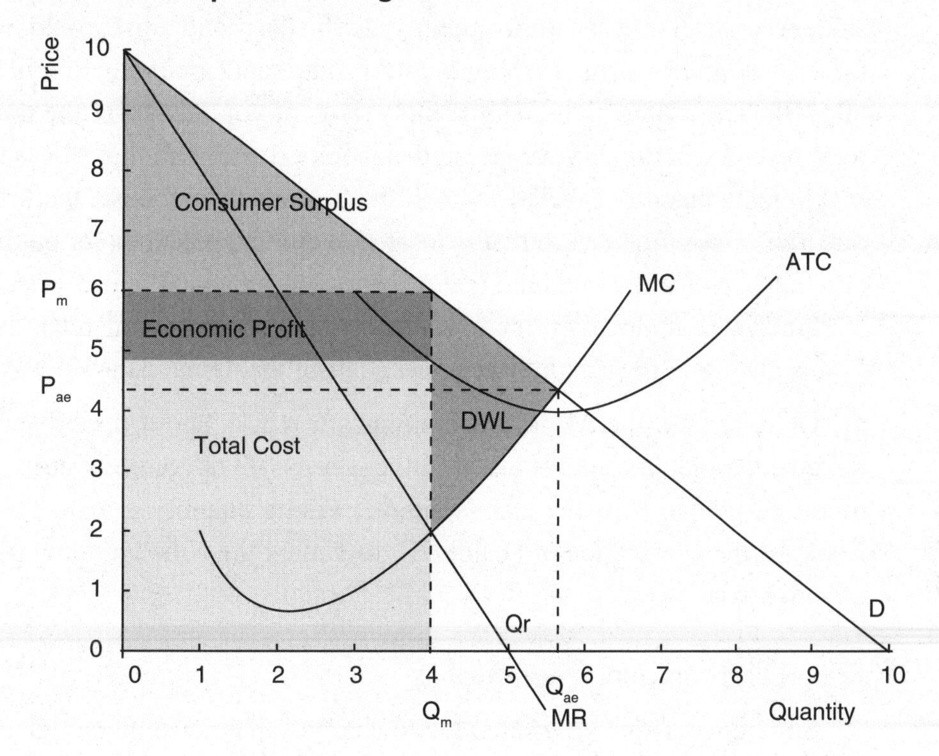

closer to allocatively efficient levels. Standard Oil and Bell Telephone suffered exactly this fate during the twentieth century.

Another solution for the government seeking a socially optimal level of output is to set a price ceiling at the allocatively efficient price. Doing so puts the firm in the position of being a price taker, conveniently at the right price. Now the firm's demand curve is flat, meaning its MR curve is as well. To find how a firm facing this regulation would maximize profit, follow the price ceiling to the demand curve where it intersects MC. The regulated price shifted the firm's MR curve so it now produces the "right" quantity by itself.

Monopolies are rarely productively efficient when maximizing profit. Producing the quantity that minimizes ATC would lead to a large economic profit indeed. Try to draw it: You'll need MC to intersect MR at the minimum point on ATC. The whole distance up to demand is per-unit profit! This would be quite a rare coincidence.

Revenue-Maximizing and Breakeven Quantities

The goal of a firm is presumed to be maximization of profit: When asked, you should respond clearly with this answer. We know the firm does this by making the number of units at which MC = MR. However, the AP exam frequently tests your ability to locate and compare other possible quantities. In particular, the test has asked students to label or discuss the quantity at which a monopolist would maximize revenue rather than profit—actually these questions have appeared rather regularly because they allow the test writers to use subtle hints to see if you recognize the relationship among total revenue, marginal revenue, and elasticity. Just recall that MR = 0 at the revenue-maximizing quantity, labeled as Q_r. If that is what they choose, the firm operates at the quantity-price combination that is located at the unit elastic point on the demand curve. Of course, typical firms would make fewer units, charge a higher price, earn a little less total revenue, and incur far fewer costs: The profit-maximizing quantity-price combination is always in the elastic (left-upper) half of the demand curve.

Occasionally, the AP Microeconomics test asks about the breakeven quantity (or the quantity that just allows the firm to cover its full opportunity cost: explicit costs and a normal profit). Now the task is simple: Find a quantity at which price equals ATC. Look for the intersection of D and ATC and mark the corresponding point below on the quantity axis.

Price-Discriminating Monopolies

Sometimes monopolies are able to charge some consumers higher prices than others for goods that cost the same to produce. Often, theaters or museums charge children and senior citizens a lower price, knowing that the movie, play, or art on the wall doesn't cost any less to show to the young and the old. It is a form of discrimination, and in some cases, it has been found to be an unfair business practice. It's called **price discrimination**: charging different prices for units that cost the firm the same amount to make. To make this work, a firm needs to have some power and some information. It also doesn't hurt if they find a sneaky way to restrict the people who buy their goods as well! If it works, however, a firm experiences increased profit, and the deadweight loss associated with monopoly decreases, even disappears. Could discrimination really have these positive effects? Yes, but it means consumers experience no surplus as a result.

Price discrimination depends on three factors. First, a firm must have the ability to choose price. This means it must be facing a down-sloping demand curve. We know perfect competitors face a horizontal demand curve, and they clearly can't price-discriminate because they can't choose any price at all. This is the power firms need to price-discriminate: the power to set or choose a price.

Second, a firm must be able to separate its potential customers into groups or gain information about their reservation prices. The goal for the firm is to know who is willing to pay a lot (in order that they might be charged a high price) and who is willing to pay only a little (so that their price might be set lower), thus taking from each customer a price close(r) to the maximum he or she is willing to pay. Consumers with an inelastic demand and who are not price-sensitive are charged a high price; those with more price sensitivity, whose demand is more elastic, are able to purchase at the lower price(s). Firms desire information in this area.

DIDYOUKNOW?

The vast proliferation of consumer information-gathering firms, who sell data about you, your earnings, and your buying preferences to all kinds of producers, is evidence of firms' desire to price-discriminate.

Third, the firm needs to be able to keep the low-price buyers from reselling the good to those who would otherwise pay a higher price. Otherwise, nobody would be willing to pay the higher price, instead finding deals in secondary markets. This is where firms get crafty: They find ways to block the resale of their goods. Firms providing services find it easier to block resale; others ask for identification or have various complex methods to ensure that the original purchaser cannot pass the low price to other potential buyers, undercutting the producer.

Firms able to make these three conditions work in their favor tend to produce a higher quantity and make more profit: Otherwise, they wouldn't be so eager to do it. If a firm is able to **price-discriminate perfectly**, it charges each consumer exactly her or his reservation price, and there is no consumer surplus at all. However, this firm would experience a marginal revenue curve equal to its demand curve and therefore produce the quantity at which MC = D, leaving no deadweight loss.

TEST TIP

Few questions on the AP exam will ask about price discrimination, and it is important to keep it in its place. Always assume a firm will sell all its output at the same price unless there is clear language in the problem stating that the firm can sell units at various prices to different consumers.

Natural Monopoly and Regulation Options

The last of the spinoff creatures spawned by monopoly, **natural monopoly** (sometimes called pure monopoly) differs from the typical variety because the cost structure is the source of monopoly power. This type of firm has extremely high fixed costs and very low or even constant marginal cost—so much so that any combination of smaller firms would not be as productively efficient as this one giant can be. Put another way, the natural monopoly's long-run average total cost curve declines indefinitely, meaning the firm experiences economies of scale as it grows, and those become a barrier to any new firms entering the market. The new firms would be smaller, so they would not be able to produce for as low an average cost. Mail delivery, cable television, and utilities are all examples of natural monopolies because they involve setting up and operating large networks; adding additional units (letters delivered, houses on cable, or kilowatt hours) doesn't cost very much and the cost of those units doesn't rise very fast.

Figure 4-24 shows a natural monopoly. Let's walk through the features and aspects of it that you need to know. First, note that the cost curves look different. If MC rises, it does so at quantities far bigger than this market's demand curve requires us to consider. Because MC is low and not rising, it is below ATC for the entirety of the graph, meaning that we see only the down-sloping part of ATC. This firm, if left to profit-maximize on its own at the point (Q_m, P_m), would create a large area of deadweight loss, which is triangle ABC on the graph.

However, the typical solutions to monopoly won't work quite so well here because any combination of smaller firms would have a higher set of cost curves than the one large provider. Breaking the firm up, or trust-busting, won't work—the smaller firms that would result would need to duplicate all of the fixed cost infrastructure.

Figure 4–24. Natural Monopoly: Regulation Options

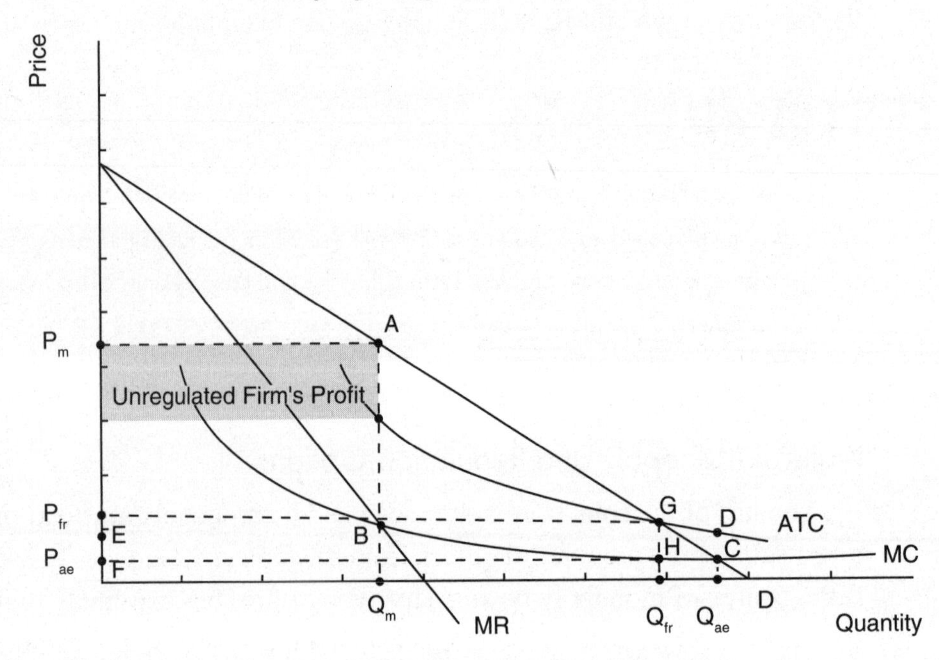

The other usual solution, regulating the monopolist by using a price ceiling, has unfortunate results as well. If the price is set at P_{ae}, the firm could produce Q_{ae} units, but at that quantity and price, the firm takes a large loss (area CDEF). Given the loss, the firm might refuse to produce at all, exiting an industry that would require it to lose money in, not just the short run, but in the long run as well, or challenge the legality of the price ceiling in court. If the firm produces nothing, there is no surplus at all, and all of the area below demand and above marginal cost would be deadweight loss (look for it—it's a huge triangle).

The result is known as **fair-return pricing**; set a price equal to the firm's ATC (at P_{fr}, where it crosses demand) and allow it to be a price taker at a price that yields a normal profit but no more, producing Q_{fr} units. The monopolist is able to earn, as the name suggests, a rate of return equal to that available elsewhere, and stays in business. Society doesn't quite get all that deadweight loss converted back into surplus (area CGH remains as deadweight loss), but the compromise is as good as we can do. The potential gain sacrificed is far smaller than if the natural monopoly were left unregulated.

Monopolistically Competitive Markets

From Table 4-4 and from the name *monopolistically competitive market*, you already know that monopolistic competition has characteristics of both a monopoly and perfect competition. Many firms are selling products that are differentiated from one another, but the products work fairly well as substitutes for their rivals' goods. Firms have low startup and other fixed costs so that entering and exiting the industry is relatively easy for firms in the long run.

Nonprice Competition and Advertising

The distinguishing feature of monopolistic competition is that each firm is trying to convince consumers that its product is better in some way than its competitors to maintain a slightly higher price and not lose market share. This effort at **product differentiation**, because it is designed to justify a higher price, must take the form of **nonprice competition**. Firms make explicit or implicit claims that their service is friendlier, their production process is more environmentally friendly, or that their goods are more durable, and so forth. In the short run, the firms attempt to make the competitors' goods seem less like suitable substitutes in order that their own demand curves will be steeper, thus allowing them to act more like monopolists. Every producer envies the monopolists. Second, in the long run, firms try to prevent the entry of new competitors into the industry, which would cause a leftward shift or a decrease in their own demand curves and reduce their profits. To the extent that they are effective, they extend the short run in which they can operate, forestalling the eventual outcome of monopolistic competition: a long-run equilibrium in which each firm breaks even.

Demand and Marginal Revenue for a Monopolistic Competitor

Because there are several firms, each only serves a small fraction of the market quantity—perhaps 1 to 2 percent per firm. Each firm faces a demand curve that is downward sloping but more elastic than monopolists face. Because substitutes are available, some consumers would find other suppliers if the firm raises its price. And if the firm increases its quantity, it must lower its price in order to sell that quantity. Either way, it means reducing price.

Because demand slopes downward, even slightly, it will create a separate marginal revenue curve lying below it. This has all the same important implications as it did with monopoly. The firm is a price setter, but within a much more narrow range of prices than the monopolist was.

Maximizing Profit in the Short Run

The firm chooses to produce the quantity at which MC = MR and then searches upward to find the point on the demand curve that corresponds with this level of output. In terms of the two-step process for maximizing profit, this firm acts just as a monopolist would. As with any firm, the placement of its ATC curve relative to demand at this level of output determines if a profit can be made or if a loss must be minimized.

Figure 4-25 shows the profit maximization case. Note that at Q, the firm's demand curve lies above ATC; the space between the two is per-unit profit. The shaded area represents short-run profit. However, this economic profit opportunity attracts new firms to open in the long run. As they do, the individual firm we see in this graph experiences a leftward shift of its demand curve until it is just tangent to the ATC curve; at this one point, the firm can choose a quantity that allows it to break even, as shown in Figure 4-26. The new demand curve creates a new MR curve, leading the firm to decrease its production quantity to this level of output.

Figure 4-27 shows the loss minimization case. Note that at Q, the firm's demand curve lies below ATC; the space between the two is per-unit loss. The shaded area represents short-run losses. In the long run, however, these losses encourage firms to leave the industry and seek their fortune elsewhere. Again, the exit of firms shifts this firm's demand curve, this time to the right, until it is just tangent to the ATC curve, and the firm's MR curve moves upward so that it crosses MC at quantity Q_{lr}.

Figure 4–25. Monopolistic Competition Maximizing Profit

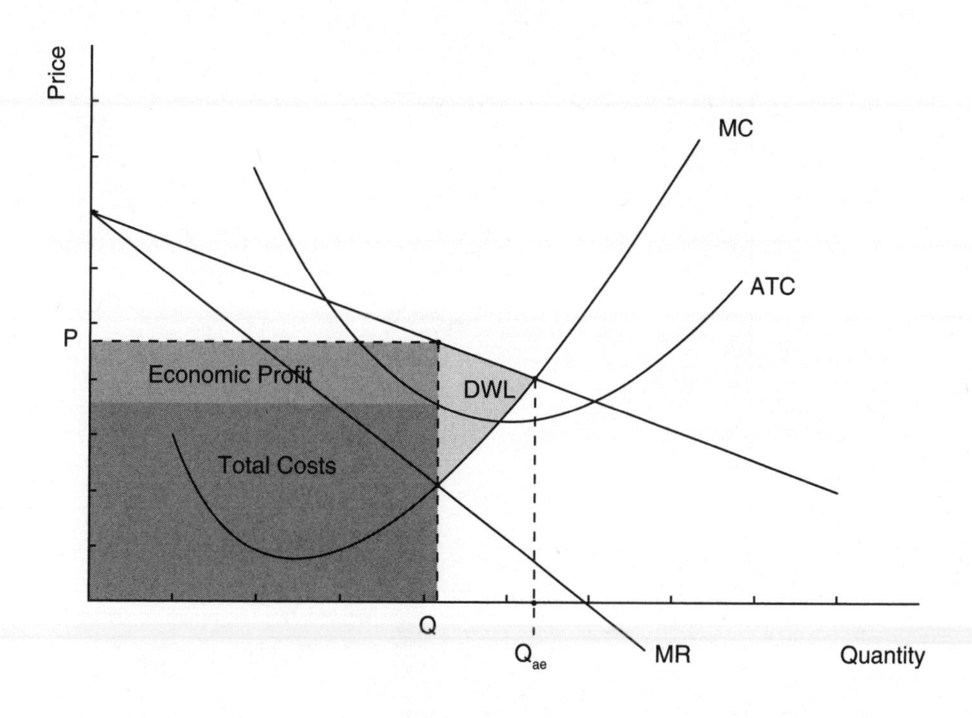

Figure 4–26. Monopolistic Competition in Long-Run Equilibrium

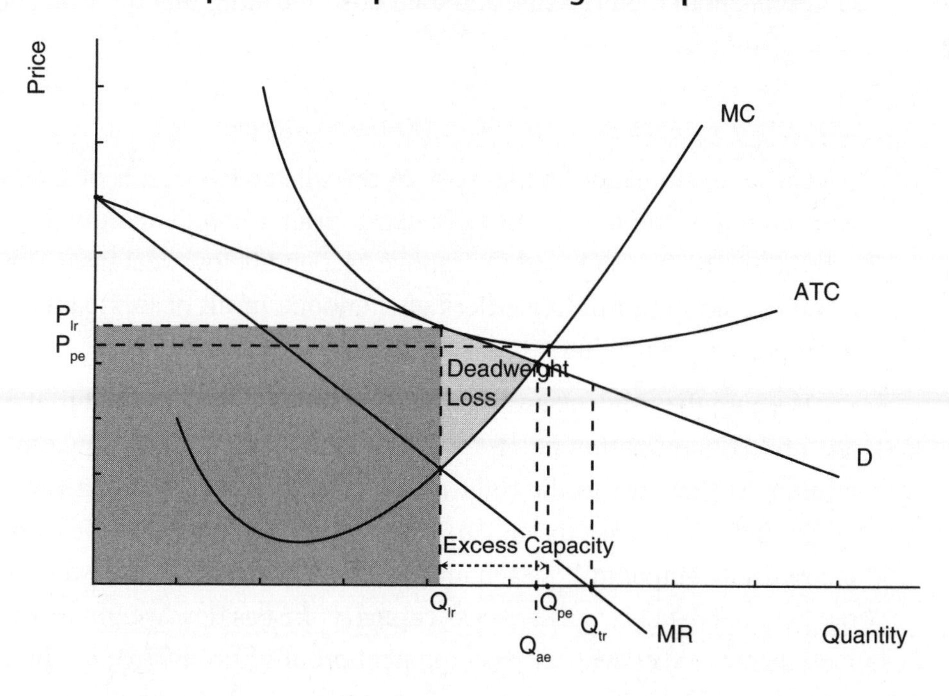

Figure 4–27. Monopolistic Competition Minimizing Losses

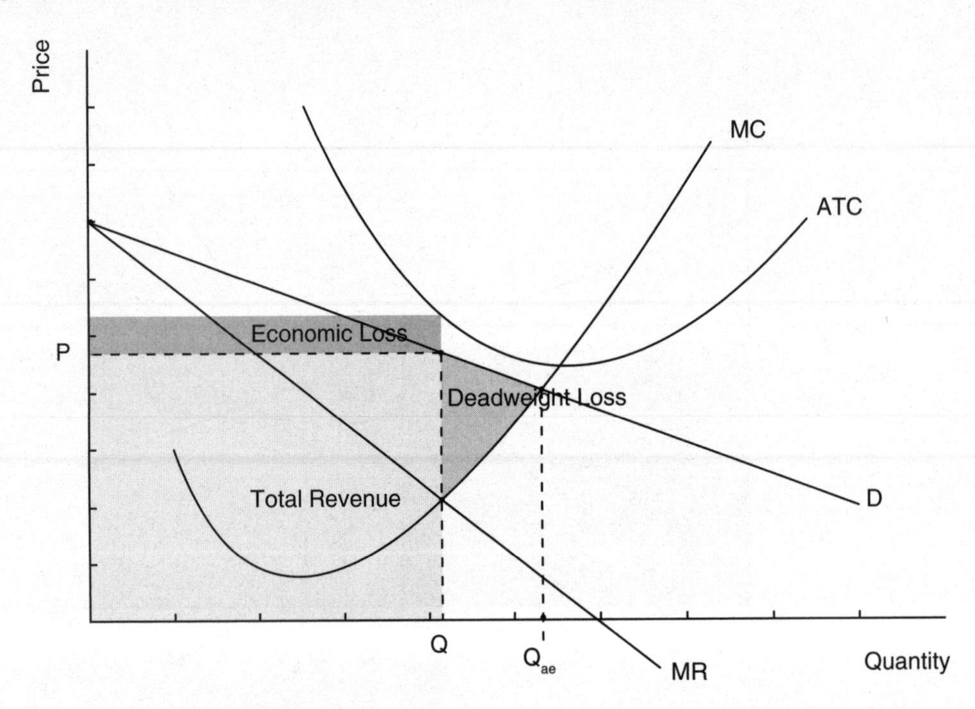

Breaking Even in Long-Run Equilibrium

Whether profits or losses exist for firms in the short run, in long-run equilibrium, each firm shows no economic profit; each charges a price just equal to its ATC curve, and each produces Q_{lr} units, as depicted in Figure 4-26. Note that the shaded rectangle represents both total revenue and total cost, meaning that the firm is earning zero economic profit.

Efficiency Assessment of Monopolistic Competition

Closer examination of Figure 4-26 reveals the two levels of inefficiency associated with monopolistic competition. Because price exceeds marginal cost, there is deadweight loss between Q_{lr} and Q_{ae} (above MC and below demand). This deadweight loss results in the short run (regardless of economic profit or loss) and in the long run for a monopolistic competitor.

Because the firm's demand curve slopes down, it is tangent to the ATC curve to the left of ATC's minimum point. Q_{pe}, the productively efficient quantity at which ATC is minimized, lies just to the right of Q_{ae}; the horizontal gap between the firm's output at Q_{lr} and Q_{pe} represents underuse of this firm's productive capabilities. If the firm increases its output to P_{pe}, each unit would be produced at a lower cost. For this reason the horizontal gap is called **excess capacity**. Just as deadweight loss indicates allocative inefficiency, excess capacity is graphical proof of productive inefficiency.

TEST TIP

Students are often asked to draw areas of profit (or loss) for firms in the short-response section of the AP exam. The following four steps to finding this area will work for perfect competition, monopolies, and monopolistic competition:

1. Find the intersection where MC = MR and draw a vertical line down to the *x*-axis to find profit-maximizing quantity.
2. Follow your line from Step 1 back up to the demand curve, because it represents price.
3. Draw a line up or down to the ATC curve.
4. Draw a line to the left (from the point you found in Step 3) until you reach the *y*-axis. You should now be able to see a rectangle that represents the area of total profit (or total loss) for the firm.

Note—for monopolies and monopolistic competition, you will need to draw an additional line over to the *y*-axis in Step 2 (from price) in order to see this rectangle.

Oligopoly: Strategic Behavior and Game Theory

The term *oligopoly* comes from the Greek words "few" and "sell," so it is no surprise that oligopoly markets have a few large firms. Entry of new firms is difficult because startup costs present a high fixed-cost barrier. To match the low per-unit costs of the existing firms, a new firm would have to enter the industry as a large player, which doesn't happen very effectively or very often. Some oligopolies are industries with differentiated products and, in many cases, firms spend a lot of money accentuating differences that may not be all that significant (the duopoly of the cola market certainly qualifies as an example). However, other industries have a few producers that make goods that are indistinguishable and that do not bother with nonprice competition. Because entering the market involves difficulties, firms are able to sustain short-run profits into the long run in some cases.

Many industries that fall into the category of oligopoly don't work in the same manner. Some factors that influence the way the market functions are the number of firms, the relative size of the firms, the number of options presumed to be available to each firm, and the way in which firms react to one another's changes in behavior. All of these factors mean that the study of oligopoly is both highly relevant to our world and extremely complex and unsettled. For our purposes, it is reassuring to know that the vast majority of that difficulty is not tested on the exam and that the coverage of this market structure, while increasing slightly over the last few years, is not as extensive as the simpler ones covered in this chapter.

Interdependence and Strategic Behavior

The key feature that drives the AP exam's coverage of this market structure is that firms are engaged in interdependent strategic decision-making situations with one another. This **interdependent** behavior means that each firm's best choice about output quantity (and therefore price) depends on the decisions of the other firm(s). Firms need to be able to analyze these situations, predicting the actions of their rivals in order to make their own profit-maximizing price and quantity determination.

The fact that a manageable number of firms (or other actors) choose from among a variety of options and influence the outcomes for themselves and others has also led economists to find ways to connect other areas of strategic decision making to the study of oligopoly. This concept, called **game theory**, has been used to explain the behavior of suspected criminal conspirators, game show contestants, and even the nuclear posture of the cold war superpowers! Fortunately, the increased coverage of oligopoly on the AP Microeconomics exam all falls into the area of game theory and involves problems that make some wonderfully simplifying assumptions.

Three Versions of Oligopoly

Three different conceptual kinds of markets all have a few firms. In this case, the number of firms is not as important as whether they work together, all following a leading firm that sets a general price, or each works independently, occasionally backstabbing one another and potentially jeopardizing its profits.

If a few firms (consider *few* to mean somewhere between two and a dozen or so) work together to determine a price and/or industry quantity target, they are acting **collusively**. This collusion can take the form of a **cartel**, which is a more formalized agreement between rival firms. Cartels (of which the Organization of the Petroleum Exporting Countries, or OPEC, is the most noteworthy example), typically work to limit the quantity produced, thus ensuring a high market price for the good or service they provide. In this regard, they are functioning just as a monopoly would, maximizing profit and creating deadweight loss because they are charging a price well above marginal cost.

Cartels are not stable because each firm (or producing nation, in the case of OPEC) has an individual incentive to produce slightly more than the agreed-upon quantity. The firm who cheats gains revenue, but doesn't reduce the market price of the commodity. Unfortunately, each rival may be engaging in the same thought process. If all increase production, the market price falls and each has played a role in harming the whole industry's profits, including their own! So the incentives of the cartel are inconsistent with the incentives of the individual members. Cartels, price fixing, and other collusive behaviors are illegal in many countries, including the United States.

DID YOU KNOW?

In December 2011, authorities in France discovered a huge laundry detergent price-fixing scheme. Colgate-Palmolive, Procter & Gamble, Unilever, and Henkel were using code names in communication with one another to fix prices in eight European countries between 2002 and 2005. They were fined a total of €361 million, or nearly $500,000,000!

A second type of oligopoly is one in which a single firm sells a significant enough share of the market quantity that it is recognized as a price leader. In the **price leadership** model, the dominant firm determines its price much as a monopolist would and then the other firms in the industry follow, choosing a similar price, or perhaps one slightly lower (for a generic or off-brand good) or slightly higher (for a gourmet or luxury version). However, the remaining fringe firms do not threaten the industry leader because their overall market share is small.

Often it is to the advantage of the price leader to allow the fringe firms to continue to exist and earn normal profit, even in situations in which they could put those competitors out of business. Doing so might draw the attention of regulators enforcing antitrust laws to promote competition (these regulators also take a close look at potential mergers and acquisitions to determine if they would significantly reduce competition in a market). Regulation for this firm, which would become a monopolist if it put competitors out of business, would surely decrease profits. In some cases, the firm could be broken into smaller firms. Leaving the small players on the edge of the market can have its advantages.

The third oligopoly model is the **kinked demand model**. It has fallen slightly from favor, at least in terms of coverage on the AP exams. The basic idea is that firms of a balanced size are likely to match a rival's price cut, but they ignore a rival's price increase. This does seem to explain the behaviors of some firms at times. For example, it is common in the airline industry for firms to match others' fare cuts, even to the point of a fare war. However, the typical result in this analysis is that firm output and price remain rather constant, even when costs increase over time, because raising its price will cost the firm such a large share of its sales.

TEST TIP

Based on recently released AP exams, oligopoly coverage will not require you to draw graphs and is not likely to present you with graphs. However, it will present problems about game theory, and you will need a clear procedure to solve game theory problems.

Solving Game Theory Problems

In economic analysis, a **game** is considered to be a situation with a finite number of identifiable players, each of whom can pursue a strategy from among a certain number of options, and with a value placed on the various outcomes for each player. These values (for example, profit or loss over a given period of time) are usually displayed in the form of a **payoff matrix**. The idea is to use the information in the payoff matrix to come to conclusions that allow you to respond to questions about what each firm will choose to do. The AP exams are also likely to test whether you know some of the basic vocabulary associated with game theory.

Before we work on that, let's get three simplifying assumptions out of the way. These assumptions will make your life easier even if they make the problems you'll be solving a little less applicable to the real world. First, there will be two firms (or perhaps two people, countries, etc.) in the industry or in the problem. Don't create third parties: think only about the two firms involved. Second, each firm will have two choices of strategy to pursue. (Yes, your life got a whole lot easier because that means you will need to consider a maximum of four scenarios for a given problem!) Third, each firm is interested only in doing the best it can for itself—not in hurting the rival, not even beating the rival. In other words, if a firm could make a change that would result in gaining $2.00 of profit but leave their rival with $200.00 more profit, they would jump at the chance.

Here's a sample problem that we can use to define the terms we'll need to know and to develop a procedure for solving problems of this sort. Imagine a town with two service stations at which to purchase an oil change, one run by Jean and one run by Lyn. Each is deciding whether to charge full price or offer a sale on oil changes. The payoff matrix in Table 4-5 displays the daily profit for each station and is information that the two firms can access in making their pricing decisions. The first number in each cell is the profit for Jean; the second is the profit for Lyn.

Table 4–5.

	Lyn has a sale	Lyn charges full price
Jean has a sale	$125, $225	$175, $150
Jean charges full price	$100, $150	$125, $175

At the most basic level, you might be asked to read the grid and interpret the question: "If Lyn charges full price and Jean has a sale, how much will Jean earn per day?" (Answer: $175). At the next level of difficulty, you might be asked about one firm's **best response** to a specific choice from their rival: "What is Lyn's best response to Jean charging full price?" (Answer: Charge full price because she'll earn $175 rather than $150.)

This leads nicely into the idea of a **dominant strategy**, an option that exists if a player always chooses the same strategy for him- or herself regardless of the opponent's choice. Sometimes a firm has a clear choice that results in more profit, regardless of the other's decision; that is the firm's dominant strategy. In this example, Jean has a dominant strategy: She should have the sale. Why? If Lyn charges full price, Jean prefers the sale because she will earn $175 rather than $125. If Lyn has the sale, Jean would still prefer to lower her price because she'll earn $125 rather than only $100. So if Jean is a rational firm trying to maximize profit, she'll always choose to have the sale.

From Lyn's point of view, the situation is a little more complex. Lyn has no dominant strategy because her best choice depends on Jean's decision. If Jean were to charge full price, Lyn would want to keep the high price because she'd earn $175 rather than $150. However, Jean having a sale changes a lot for Lyn. Now she wants to have a sale because she would be able to earn $225, far better than the $150 she'd earn keeping the higher price. We can't really be sure what Lyn will do by thinking only about her outcomes.

What we can do is figure out what both will do because we do know Jean's choice. Assume that Jean will follow her dominant strategy of having the sale. Lyn will know this and have a sale herself. The square in the upper-left corner of Table 4-5 is the **Nash equilibrium**, the position that neither party has any incentive to alter.

Some games you might be presented with will not have a Nash equilibrium at all. Some could have more than one, and many might have only one. Figuring out where the game will end up is mostly a matter of comparing the result for each rival with what he or she could have obtained had he or she made the other choice.

The simplest are games in which both players have a dominant strategy, and they both pursue it: That's the Nash equilibrium. The game featured in Table 4-5 has a Nash equilibrium because one player has a dominant strategy and the other has a clear best response to it.

A special type of game that has a Nash equilibrium and in which both players have dominant strategies is called the prisoners' dilemma. It doesn't have to involve prisoners; it merely describes a situation in which each player selecting her dominant strategy results in a worse outcome for both than if they both had selected their inferior option.

Try checking your knowledge by making a grid and putting some values in it. Test yourself to find out whether either player has a dominant strategy. Can you predict a square in which the players would not want to alter their choices? If so, that is a Nash equilibrium.

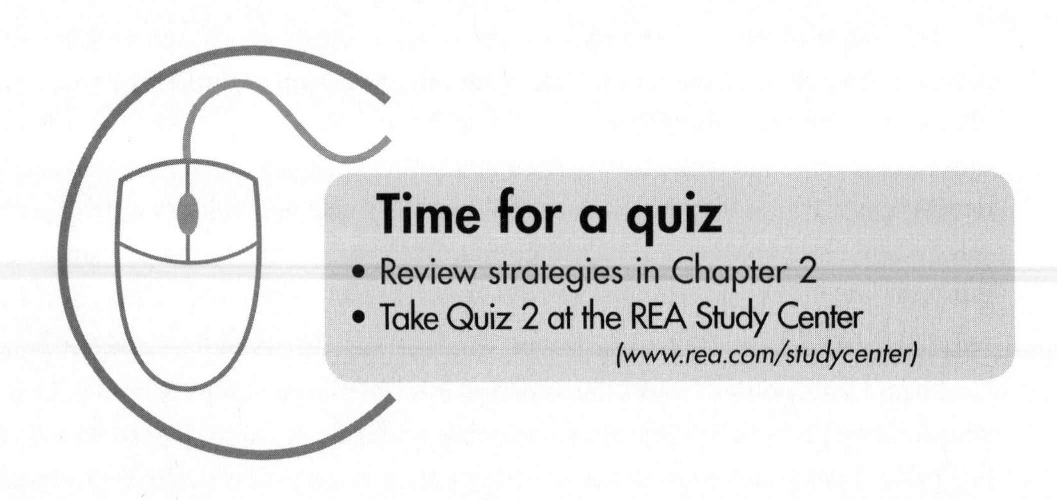

Chapter 5

Factor Markets

New Roles in the Circular Flow

Revisiting the circular flow presented in Chapter 3 allows us to see the connection between the product markets discussed in Chapter 4 and the factor markets we examine in this chapter.

Factor markets, also called resource markets, involve the same supply and demand analysis. Both firms and individuals interact according to marginal analysis. Firms are the buyers, and individuals and households are the sellers, so several concepts should seem familiar to you. They are often concepts you have learned before, but now you will see them from a different angle.

Firms combine the four resources—land, labor, capital, and entrepreneurial ability—in order to make units of output. Each time a unit of one of the factors is purchased, the firm would like to ensure that it improves their profit. The firm, as you know from examining it in the product market, wants to make the profit-maximizing quantity of goods, and it isn't hard to imagine that it also wants to produce that quantity as cheaply as possible.

We will examine how to measure what each unit of a resource is worth in added output and in added revenue, and then focus on how firms determine the profit-maximizing amount of each factor to employ. We'll use the labor market as a case study in graphing a firm's decision about how many workers to hire in various situations.

Demand and Supply of Resources

Derived Demand

Derived demand is the idea that demand for resources comes from demand for the products those resources can produce. This is the most fundamental connection visible when looking at the circular flow shown in Figure 5-1: The costs firms incur when making goods are payments they make while buying the labor and capital used to produce their products. You might look at the relationship as something of a chicken-and-egg situation: Firms want to sell certain goods, so they seek resources needed to produce those goods. On the other hand, our desire for certain kinds of products can be seen as guiding firms into purchasing specific kinds of resources designed to produce those specific products.

Figure 5–1. Simplified Circular Flow Model

In this simple model, the economy is private (meaning there is no government or public sector) and closed (meaning there is no international trade).

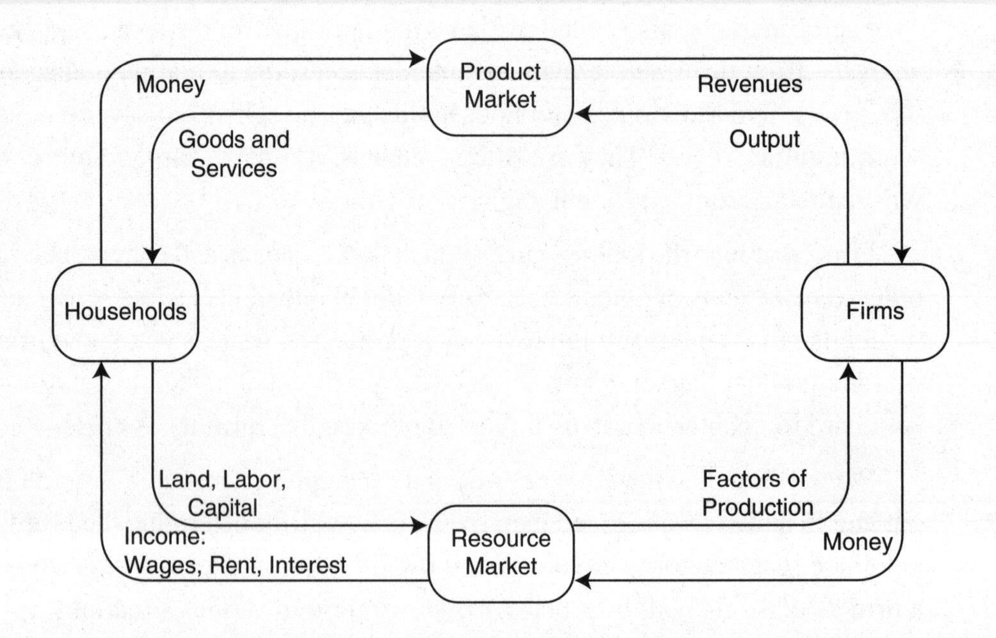

When the demand for a good increases in the product market, the equilibrium quantity and price both tend to rise. Firms respond to the increase in demand by producing a higher quantity, and they are also able to charge higher prices. Both are reasons that the firm's demand for resources increases: More resources are needed, and each unit helps contribute to a product that is more valuable too.

For example, if it becomes popular for teenagers to hang out in coffee shops, the demand for coffee drinks is likely to increase. Coffee shops close to high schools and college campuses will likely sell more cups of coffee and perhaps even be able to charge higher prices. As a result, those businesses will need to purchase more of several variable inputs used in the production process. They'll certainly need more coffee beans, filters, and cups. They will also need more units of labor (whether requiring the current staff to work more hours or hiring additional workers) to make drinks, wash dishes, and clean up. Derived demand is the first concept that links demand for the product to demand for the factors used in its production.

Marginal Revenue Product

It is not always enough to know that a firm's demand for a resource, say, labor, has increased. Sometimes you will be expected to calculate how much hiring a specific worker, say, the fifth laborer, will affect revenue or even profit.

The Value of Hiring Another Laborer

Marginal revenue product (MRP) answers the question of how much another unit of a given resource changes total revenue gained by the firm. It is the value in dollars of added revenue gained when a firm adds one more worker. MRP is a version of marginal benefit and, in many situations, is equivalent to the demand for a resource. Let's take a look at where this comes from and then how it behaves, using labor as our example. Understand that we could examine the same concept for any other resource—often land, capital, and entrepreneurial ability are considered fixed in the short run—which is one reason we typically use labor as the variable input.

The marginal product of labor tells us how much total revenue increases with the employment of one more worker; the marginal revenue product of capital would tell us how much total revenue would increase with the addition of one more machine: perhaps another coffee roaster or grinder or espresso machine in the coffeehouse.

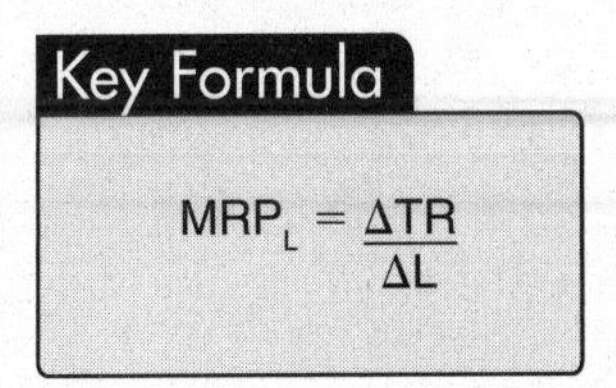
Key Formula

$$MRP_L = \frac{\Delta TR}{\Delta L}$$

Most firms have certain inputs that are fixed: These inputs can't be increased in the short run. To make more units of output in the short run, the firm adds more of its variable input(s). Increasing the amount of a variable input employed increases output, but the firm will experience diminishing marginal returns because the fixed inputs become overused in some way—the fixed kitchen size limits the number of meals that can be cooked even as more chefs are hired, or the number of espresso machines prevents another barista from adding many drinks to the total product. The added output when another worker is hired is the **marginal product** or **marginal physical product** of that worker. Marginal physical product might increase with the hiring of the first few workers as they specialize, thus increasing efficiency and lowering per-unit cost. However, at some point, a firm with fixed inputs will find that adding more of the variable input yields a smaller and smaller marginal product.

Key Formula

$$MP_L = MPP_L = \frac{\Delta TR}{\Delta V} \text{ or } \frac{\Delta Q}{\Delta L}$$

Marginal (physical) product, or the added number of units of output the next worker hired adds, slopes upward initially and then descends (see Figure 5-2). It may even be a negative value if the firm were to hire too many workers that actually decreased output!

Figure 5–2. Marginal (Physical) Product

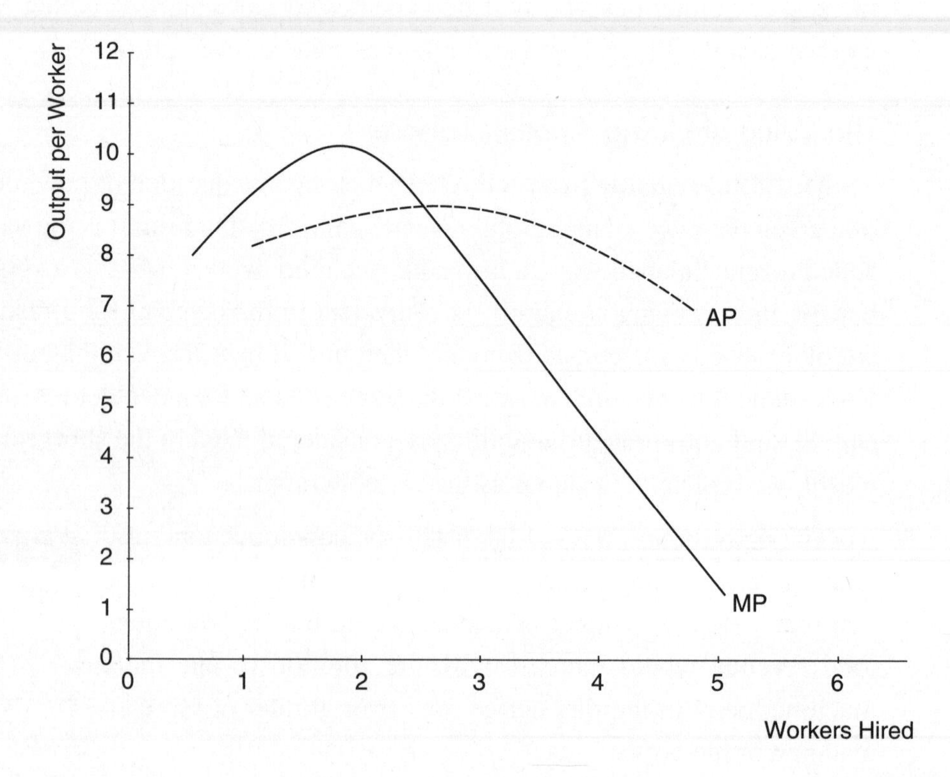

TEST TIP

Keep the following acronyms clear: MR, MP, and MRP. Marginal revenue (MR) is the added revenue when the firm makes one more unit of output. Marginal product (MP, the same as marginal physical product [MPP]) is the added output when the firm adds one unit of an input. Marginal revenue product (MRP) is the gain in revenue when one unit of an input is added. Although the three are related, each is distinct. MR is strictly for use in the product market. MP is a function that helps explain where both marginal cost and MRP come from. MRP is the most essential new concept for you now: The demand for a resource is its marginal revenue product.

MRP for a Price-Taking Firm

A firm that sells its goods in a perfectly competitive market is a price taker. As a price taker, the firm may sell as many units of output as it wants without lowering its price; a price taker faces a perfectly horizontal demand curve that also represents its marginal revenue function.

Calculating the MRP for a price-taking firm is easy: The output the worker adds (MPP) is multiplied by the product price. To practice, imagine that you are presented with data for a coffee shop like the one shown in Table 5-1. The firm can sell as many drinks as it chooses without influencing the market price of $3.00 per drink.

Table 5-1.

Workers Employed (L)	Coffee Drinks Sold (TP or Q)
1	20
2	50
3	70
4	80
5	85
6	87
7	88

To calculate how much each worker is worth to the firm in dollars, we first need to calculate how much that worker is worth in extra cups of coffee served. When the firm adds the second worker, quantity increases from twenty to fifty, so that second worker's marginal product (MP_2) is thirty drinks. The second worker's marginal revenue product is the value of these thirty drinks in dollars of potential revenue they might bring to the firm. At \$3.00 each, those thirty drinks represent \$90.00 of value, so MRP_2 = \$90. After hiring this second worker, the firm experiences diminishing marginal returns to labor, which you can see by the decrease in the rate at which TP rises as more workers are hired, beginning with the third worker. Do your own calculations to verify the values of MRP_3 (\$60.00), MRP_4 (\$30.00), and MRP_5 (\$15.00). Plotting the firm's MRP_L curve yields a function similar to that shown in Figure 5-3.

Figure 5–3. MRP for a Price-Taking Coffee Shop

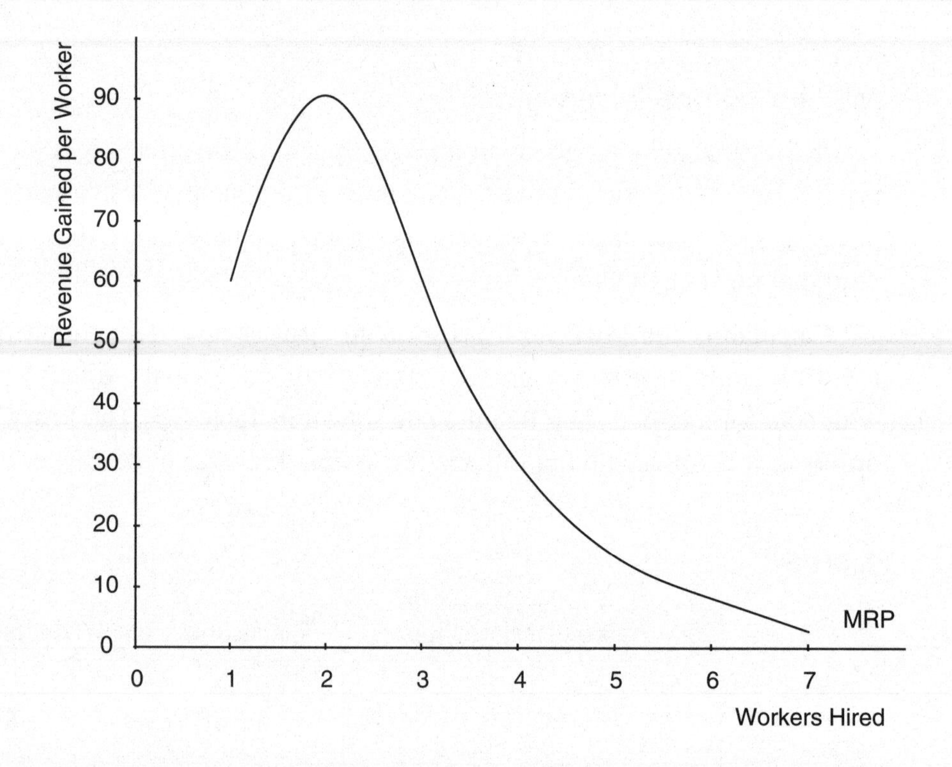

TEST TIP

It is fine to simplify when drawing MRP. In reality, firms probably would have a function that slopes upward initially and then turns downward, changing slope along the way. However, on the AP exam, you can draw MRP as a down-sloping line. It is easier and the results of your graphical analysis will be the same.

MRP for Imperfect Competitors

For a price-taking firm, MRP declines after the firm experiences diminishing marginal returns for one reason: The additions to total product are smaller and smaller. However, the product price did not change as the firm hired more workers and produced more units of output. For many firms, selling additional units required that price be decreased because the firms face down-sloping demand curves.

In a smaller town where there aren't so many coffee shops, firms probably do not face horizontal demand curves. To sell more coffee drinks, these firms must reduce the price charged per drink. Let's contrast their marginal revenue product with the firm above by examining Table 5-2.

Table 5-2.

Workers Employed (L)	Coffee Drinks Sold (TP or Q)	Product Price (P)
1	20	$3.30
2	50	$3.00
3	70	$2.80
4	80	$2.70
5	85	$2.65
6	87	$2.63
7	88	$2.62

Now, this firm has the same production function as the one shown in Table 5-1, meaning that marginal product functions for these two firms are identical. However, because price declines as quantity increases, we'll see that MRP is quite different: It declines faster than for the price-taking firm above.

MRP can no longer be calculated by multiplying the marginal physical product by the price because price is changing. Instead, we'll need to calculate the total revenue earned with various numbers of workers and see how it changes as each one is added.

MRP_2 is therefore the change in TR when the firm adds the second worker. With one worker, the firm earned $66.00 in total revenue (twenty cups times the price of $3.30). After hiring the second worker, the firm earns $150.00 (fifty cups times the price of $3.00) in revenue, for an increase of $84.00, the second worker's MRP. The third worker increases revenue to $196.00, meaning MRP_3 is only $46.00. Confirm that MRP_4 = $20.00, and MRP_5 = $9.25. Comparing these values to those of the price-taking firm illustrates the principle: Any firm that faces a down-sloping demand curve will have an MRP function that slopes down more steeply than it would if it were a price taker.

Changes in MRP

Whether a firm faces a down-sloping demand curve or a horizontal one in its product market, the same basic factors shift its MRP or labor demand curve. First, an increase in demand for its product increases MRP. By the concept of derived demand, this idea should be pretty intuitive. However, thinking about how MRP is calculated should give you another connection: the product price. A worker who adds the same number of units of output is more valuable if each of those outputs can be sold at a higher price. Consider the MRP function of the price-taking coffee shop shown in Table 5-1. Each worker's MRP might now be found by multiplying his or her marginal physical product by a new higher price, say, $4.00. That second worker who used to be worth $90.00 in added revenue still enables the firm to sell thirty more drinks, but now he adds $120.00 in revenue because each of those drinks sells for a dollar more than it did before.

Second, MRP increases if the resource becomes more productive. Increases in MPP mean each worker is worth more in output than he or she was before. A worker who adds more output units also adds more revenue; therefore, the firm finds workers more valuable when worker productivity rises.

MRP is the demand for a factor of production, so when MRP rises, that means the firm's demand curve in the resource market has risen. This leads firms to find it profitable to purchase more of that resource. For example, an increase in worker productivity encourages a business to hire more labor because each worker is more valuable to the firm in terms of extra output and therefore also in added revenue.

Supply in Factor Markets

Individual and Market Labor Supply

For individual laborers, the decision about whether to work (and the decision about how much they want to work) is determined by the value of wages that might be earned compared to the value of the leisure time that one must give up to earn them. Both the value of added wages and the value of the time sacrificed change as the person works more and more.

While every dollar earned has the same nominal value and can probably purchase the same goods as the dollar earned before it, dollars do decline in marginal value as we have more of them. The first earnings might determine whether we have fundamental necessities such as food and shelter. As income rises, we can start to satisfy desires rather than basic needs, and eventually we enter the realm of buying luxury goods, but only when income is quite high. Similarly, the more we work, the less leisure time we have; when we don't have much of it, leisure time can be quite precious to us. You've likely perceived this yourself; when you're busy, you'd really like a small break, but at other times, perhaps you've had so little to do that you were actually bored and wished for less leisure time.

DIDYOUKNOW?

As wages rise, workers want to work more because each hour of leisure time entails a larger opportunity cost, or the wage forgone by not working—the substitution effect at work. However, at some wage, the added income doesn't entice workers to work more, but rather encourages them to "purchase" more leisure time. Above this wage, the income effect predominates: workers are richer and therefore want to "buy" more normal goods, including leisure time, which is "purchased" by working fewer hours.

In a market, higher wages encourage workers to supply more labor. This means **market labor supply** slopes upward, showing a positive or direct relationship between quantity of labor supplied and the wage rate. Why? First, the new higher wage rate encourages a greater percentage of the population to join the labor force. As the wage rate climbs above a worker's **reservation wage**, the lowest wage she or he would be willing to work for, a worker tends to want employment because employers are now willing to pay what a worker feels her or his efforts are worth. Second, those who are already employed may want to work more hours or shifts. More labor is supplied at higher wage rates—an up-sloping supply curve isn't a new concept for you by now!

Total and Marginal Factor Cost

Two ideas that closely relate to supply in resource markets are total factor cost and marginal factor cost. **Total factor cost** is the amount on all the units of that resource or factor that the firm purchased. If four workers were hired at $8.00 per hour each, the total factor cost for those four units of labor is $32.00. **Marginal factor cost (MFC)** or **marginal resource cost (MRC)** is the amount that hiring one more unit of the input increases cost. It's the amount total cost rises when that last or next worker is hired.

Key Formula

$$MRC_L = MFC_L = \frac{\Delta TC}{\Delta L}$$

For the firm, MFC (or MRC) is much more important. Whether we are thinking graphically or numerically, firms evaluate the purchase of any resource by comparing the marginal factor cost to the marginal revenue product. A firm should pay to use units of labor, capital, or land only if doing so increases revenue by more than it increases cost. Any resource purchases that push up total cost by more than they increase total revenue decrease the firm's profit.

How Firms Maximize Profit

Let's examine two formulas that provide sensible mathematical rules for a firm wishing to make wise decisions in resource markets. Keep in mind that, in a given short-run situation, a firm might be able to add units to just a few of its many inputs. However, firms should also have longer-run strategies that enable them to balance the smart purchasing of all the inputs they buy. The really tough part is keeping close records and trying to infer from tons of data how revenue and cost would change given other decisions that might have been made. Fortunately, this aspect of entrepreneurship is not tested on the AP exam; however, you will need to apply two simple rules to data that is provided. These rules should sound familiar to you if you recall how smart consumers maximize their utility and how smart firms decide how many units to sell.

Least-Cost Rule

The first rule helps the firm determine the best way to make a specific given quantity. If, for example, you ran a mowing business, you might be faced with a decision about how to serve new clients. On one hand, you might hire more units of labor, either paying your workers for more hours, or having more workers take shifts with your current stock of lawnmowers. On the other, you might consider upgrading the lawnmowers you have so, with the same amount of labor, you can have your employees mow more lawns. Of course, it would also be possible to add some capital and some labor. What should you do to find the cheapest way to service 100 clients rather than your current fifty?

If you know the marginal factor cost and marginal revenue product for both labor and capital when selling a quantity of 100 mowed lawns, you can determine if you got the balance right. Any specific quantity can be produced at the least cost if, and only if, the ratio of MRP to MFC for each input is the same.

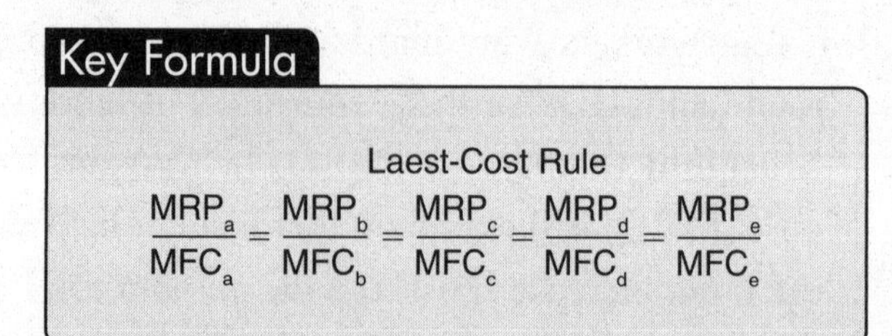
Key Formula

Laest-Cost Rule

$$\frac{MRP_a}{MFC_a} = \frac{MRP_b}{MFC_b} = \frac{MRP_c}{MFC_c} = \frac{MRP_d}{MFC_d} = \frac{MRP_e}{MFC_e}$$

The reasoning behind this is the same as the utility-maximizing rule for purchasers in the product market. Just as the ideal place is where the ratio of marginal utility (a version of marginal benefit) to price (a version of marginal cost) is equal for all the goods that the household purchases, it is the same with the firm purchasing land, labor, and capital (or even a wide variety of each basic resource). The gain that is experienced per dollar spent on each factor should be the same. Keep in mind that marginal benefit here is MRP and marginal cost is MFC.

If the ratios aren't equal, the firm should purchase a few more units of the input with the higher ratio and a few less of the one with the lower ratio. This should bring them closer to equal. If, for example, fewer units of labor are employed, the marginal product of labor should increase. At the same time, if the firm purchases more capital, the marginal product of capital should decline. If the firm rearranges its spending in this fashion, the same quantity can be produced for a lower total cost. This is the same way buyers rearrange their spending in order to maximize utility.

Profit Maximization Rule

It is possible for the firm to make a specific quantity at the lowest possible cost and yet fail to maximize profit. Of course, you knew this because you've mastered the product market material in Chapter 4, meaning you know that a firm wants to make the number of units of output at which marginal cost equals marginal revenue.

Put another way, this rule can imply that any factor used in the production process should be purchased until its marginal benefit of adding units of that input equals the marginal cost of adding units of that input. Thus, MRP for a given resource should equal MFC for that resource. Simple algebraic manipulation, combined with the least-cost rule explained above, allows us to show in one formula how many of all the inputs the firm should buy. If any of these ratios is greater than 1, it implies that the firm could increase profit by adding more of that input because it would add more to revenue than to cost (the firm isn't making enough units). If any fraction is less than 1, the firm has employed too many units of that resource and therefore overproduced. If these fractions are not equal to each other, it suggests that there is a way to make the same number of inputs at a lower cost and therefore increase profit because revenue would remain the same. The formula looks complex, but you can remember that it is saying the firm should make sure MFC = MRP for every resource it purchases.

Key Formula

Profit Maximization Rule

$$\frac{MRP_a}{MFC_a} = \frac{MRP_b}{MFC_b} = \frac{MRP_c}{MFC_c} = \frac{MRP_d}{MFC_d} = \frac{MRP_e}{MFC_e} = 1$$

Many of the problems on AP exams will test your knowledge of this rule as applied to only one factor of production at a time. Based on information such as that found in Table 5-1 and a product price and a wage rate, you should be able to figure out how many workers a firm should hire to maximize profits. Take your time converting total product data given to marginal product and then to marginal revenue product. Compare marginal revenue product with marginal factor cost for each successive worker (hire every worker for whom MRP > MFC and do not hire a worker for whom MRP < MFC). At a wage rate of $45, the firm in Table 5-1 would hire 3 workers, but not 4. The third worker adds $60 in revenue and adds $45 in cost, therefore increasing profit by $15. However, the fourth worker would not help the firm; adding $45 in cost in order to gain $30 of revenue would reduce their profits by $15.

Factor Market Graphical Analysis

Situations dealing with a factor market graph are fairly common on the AP Microeconomics exam. Every two or three years, one of the short free-response questions will be on factor market analysis, and often these questions require graphing or interpreting a graph. Several multiple-choice items will present you with a factor market problem. These will be easier if you sketch a rough graph before answering the question.

TEST TIP

Only one variable input for the firm in any AP exam question will expect you to think in the factor market. Usually this input will be labor, so all the examples in this section will be about the labor market. There have been a few times in which students have been asked to consider capital as the variable input, but a well-prepared student like you won't be fooled by that. Instead of wage, use "price of capital." Instead of MRP_L, think of the marginal revenue product of capital units. Instead of facing the fundamental question, How many workers should the firm hire?, try to determine how many units of capital it should buy or rent.

For these graphs, note the axes: Using price and quantity will probably not be enough. The horizontal axis represents the quantity of labor units purchased, so it should be labeled Q_L (sometimes shortened to L). The vertical axis still gauges price, but price of the input rather than the output. Thus, "wage" (W) is probably best to use in labor market situations, though you may also use P_L for "price of labor." Just as we might categorize businesses by the different structures in which firms sell their products (price taker, monopolist, etc.), we can categorize firms by the structure of the market in which they purchase their labor.

Perfectly Competitive Factor Markets

In a perfectly competitive market for any resource, there are a great many firms purchasing units of the factor from a common pool. For example, many restaurants, hotels, and stores seek to purchase undifferentiated labor from an unskilled pool of possible workers. You learned in perfectly competitive product markets to show the market on one graph and the point of view of one firm (in the role as seller) in side-by-side graphs. The same approach is used for the labor market graph and the graph showing the hiring decisions from the point of view of an individual firm.

Firms as Wage Takers

Because each firm is hiring only a small portion of the total labor units that are hired in the market, individual firms are **wage takers**. This means that each can hire additional units of labor at a given market wage; one firm's hiring decisions do not influence the overall wage rate determined by the interactions of hundreds or thousands of workers and their employers. Any firm that hires its labor in a perfectly competitive factor market is a wage taker.

A wage taker faces a horizontal curve that represents market wage, the supply curve, and marginal factor (or resource) cost. Wage comes from the intersection of supply and demand in the market graph and is a constraint each firm cannot control. The supply curve shows the quantities of labor available to this firm at various wage rates—but this firm can choose any quantity it wants and the wage rate is the same. That's why supply seems horizontal for the individual firm. When supply is horizontal, so is MFC: The added cost incurred when hiring one more unit of labor is just the wage paid to the added worker.

Examine Figure 5-4(a), which shows the situation of an employer in a perfectly competitive labor market. The wage rate, in this case \$8.00 per hour, comes from the market. This graphical situation is analogous to the horizontal line facing a price-taking firm in the product market that represents price, demand, and marginal revenue. In Figure 5-4(b), the labor supply curve, formed from the willingness of workers to provide labor at various wage rates, intersects with the market demand curve to determine the equilibrium wage rate and the quantity of labor hired in the market. Because each firm's demand for labor is the MRP curve, the market labor demand curve is the horizontal summation of the MRP curves for each of the individual firms. In this case, we'll assume that there are 1,000 similarly situated firms hiring undifferentiated labor. At the market wage rate of \$8.00, each firm hires four units of labor, so the equilibrium quantity in the market is 4,000 units of labor. This is the reason why the market graph is labeled L and the firm graph is labeled *l*.

Figure 5–4.

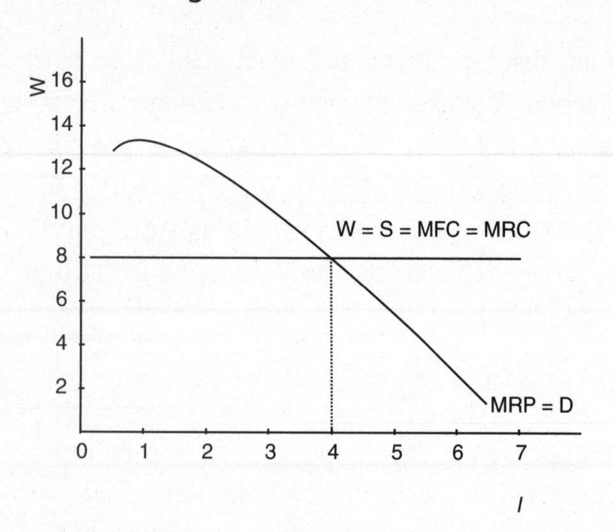

Panel A. A Wage-Taking Firm

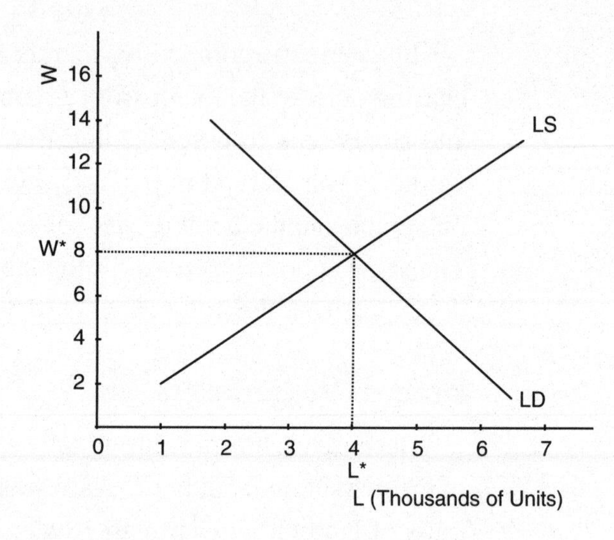

Panel B. A Perfectly Competitive Labor Market

How Much Labor to Hire

The firm chose to hire four units of labor because that is the quantity at which MRP equals MFC. The hiring of each of the first three workers adds more to total revenue than to total cost, whereas any hiring beyond four units yields less added revenue than the increase in cost. Hiring the third unit of labor adds roughly $10.00 to revenue but only $8.00 to cost, so profit will increase by $2.00 if the firm chooses to hire. For the fifth worker, the firm experiences a constant increase in cost of $8.00, but only about $6.00 is added to revenue. Hiring this worker would decrease profit because it would add more to costs than to revenue. In any factor market situation, the intersection of MRP and MFC determines the profit-maximizing quantity of the resource to purchase.

You might be asked to draw and manipulate side-by-side graphs using this model in a free-response question. Often, sketching this set of graphs helps answer multiple-choice questions as well. Therefore, you'll need to know the circumstances that shift the lines on each graph. Let's start by looking at the market graph.

Labor supply shifts when there is a change in the number of suppliers or in workers' willingness to trade away leisure time in order to earn wages. If the population increases or if people feel that they need to work more, then the labor supply shifts to the right. The supply curve shifts left if the labor force decreases in size or if workers feel they need higher wages in order to work the same number of hours. Demand for labor shifts right with an increase in the number of firms that hire labor or an increase in the MRP curves of all the firms.

On the firm's graph, the $W = S_L = MRC_L = MFC_L$ curve shifts upward or downward with movement in the market equilibrium wage rate or if a minimum wage takes effect (see below). The firm takes the market wage, so whenever the market wage changes, that horizontal line shifts. The firm's MRP curve changes based on the factors explained in this chapter: It increases if product price rises or if labor productivity increases.

The Monopsony Model

Just as a product market in which there is only one firm selling a good works differently, so does a resource market in which only one firm is buying an input. Just as in the product market, quantity is lower than in the competitive version of the market, but in this case, the equilibrium wage is lower.

The Firm as a Wage Seeker

A monopsonist is the only firm hiring labor in the market. Therefore, it faces the entire market supply curve, which is up-sloping. To hire more workers, the firm must raise the wage rate it offers. The firm must either encourage more people to join the labor force or encourage some of the workers it currently employs to work even more hours. Either way, the inducement is a higher wage. Interpreting the supply curve facing the firm in two ways, we can conclude that by choosing the wage it pays, the firm is also choosing its quantity of labor, and that by choosing the quantity it hires, the firm is also choosing a wage. This firm is therefore able to select the wage that suits its profit-maximizing goal best—it is a **wage seeker**.

We will presume that the firm cannot offer new employees a higher wage while continuing to pay the previously hired workers their prior lower wage rate; the firm cannot **wage-discriminate**. Because of this, marginal factor cost is higher than supply, sloping up faster. Consider the firm shown in Figure 5-5, which is hiring its fourth unit of labor, as an example to illustrate why MFC is steeper than supply. The firm previously had three units at $6.00 per hour for a total factor cost of $18.00 and now must pay four employees almost $8.00 each. If total factor cost is about $30.00, then the MFC of the fourth worker is $12.00, well above the supply curve.

Figure 5–5. A Monopsony Factor Market

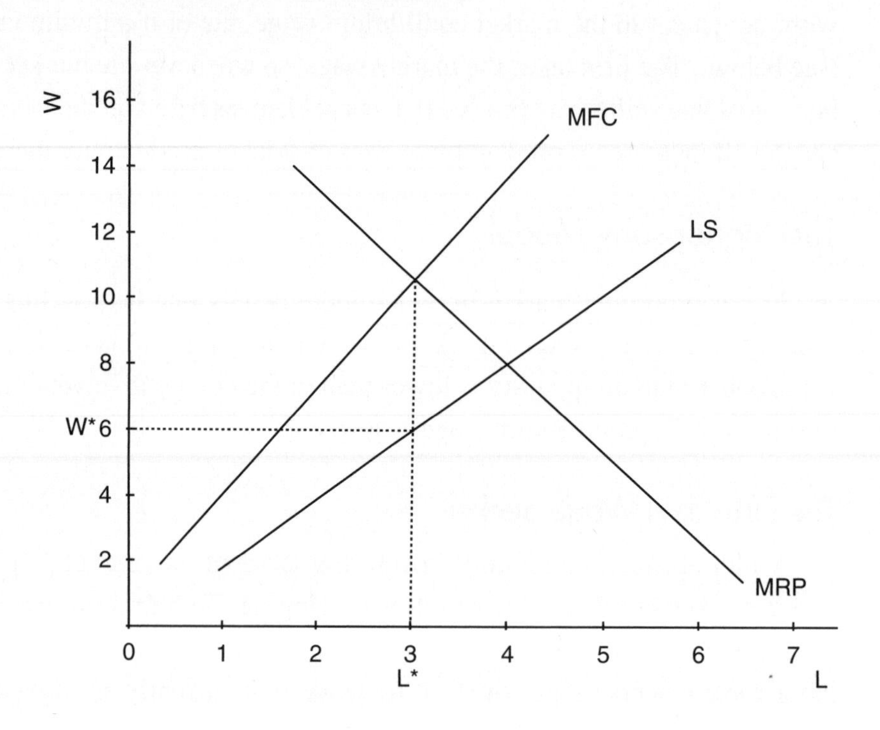

DIDYOUKNOW?

Overtime wages enable the firm to wage-discriminate. The regular hours come at the lower rate, and the increase in hours comes at the higher rate. The firm effectively avoids paying the higher wage for all its units of labor when it is profitable to hire more labor.

Labor and Wage Determination

This firm's process for deciding how many workers to hire is the same as the wage taker: Compare marginal revenue product and marginal factor cost. For the firm shown in Figure 5-5, the two curves intersect at a quantity of three workers.

Note that the firm does not pay the full value that the third worker added to revenue in wages. The third worker yielded a marginal revenue product of over $10.00 but was paid a wage of only $6.00. Why? The firm finds (seeks out) the lowest wage rate that will allow it to hire the desired quantity of labor. In this case, the wage is $6.00 because that is where the quantity of workers (three) the firm wishes to hire intersects with the supply curve. The effect of the firm's inability to wage-discriminate means the firm hired fewer workers and paid them a lower wage rate than it would have in a competitive labor market.

This firm operates below its MRP curve; therefore, MRP doesn't quite represent the demand curve for a monopsonist. While a firm buying in a monopsony market doesn't technically have a demand curve, you should think of MRP as the closest thing when it comes to recognizing reasons for curves to shift. Question prompts that make you think of derived demand are good situations in which to shift MRP and then find the new profit-maximizing quantity of labor to hire and the lowest wage rate that the firm can offer to obtain that number of workers. The quantity of labor hired will increase if the product price or the output in the product market rises.

Unions, Minimum Wages, and Wage Disparities

Goals and Strategies of Unions

Unions, or worker associations, can be formed for a variety of reasons, but two of the goals that they typically strive to achieve are increasing the wage rate and the quantity of labor hired. To achieve both of these goals simultaneously, a union might take or encourage actions that increase the demand for its members' services. This **demand enhancement strategy** might include encouraging customers to purchase union-made goods or securing training that makes member workers more productive and in higher demand. Graphically, this type of strategy would aim to shift marginal revenue product to the right, encouraging firms (whether wage-taking or wage-making firms) to hire more workers and to pay a higher wage.

At times when this type of strategy seems unlikely to work, a union may be forced to choose which goal (increasing the number of jobs or pushing for higher wages) is more important. An **exclusive union model** might seek to make entry into the labor pool more difficult, attempting to shift labor supply leftward to push up wages at the cost of some jobs. If a union were to push for more rigorous tests or qualifications to enter that specific job market, then the particular form of labor in question would be scarcer and therefore more costly for firms to purchase. This strategy was long employed by guilds and may be better suited to particularly skilled kinds of labor.

Another approach is to try to gather all the employees into an **inclusive union** and negotiate for a wage (and perhaps other nonwage benefits or working conditions) through **collective bargaining**. Workers have used this strategy to enhance safety and to force employers to have specific hiring and firing procedures. For your purposes, the important effect of the collective bargaining process is that it can result in a union-negotiated wage below which the firm or firms cannot hire any units of labor. In the next section, you'll see that the way a union-negotiated wage influences the firm's decisions about how many workers to hire and how much to pay in wages is exactly the same as if the government had set a legally binding minimum wage at the same level.

DIDYOUKNOW?

Unions have experienced a major decline in their economic and political power over the last several decades. Overall, the percentage of the labor force that belongs to a union is about 11 percent—its lowest level since before the United States entered World War I!

Union Negotiated Wages and Minimum Wages

The effects of a wage rate set by contract with a collective bargaining unit and a legally binding minimum wage are the same: Both make a hiring firm into a wage taker, influencing the firm's labor supply and marginal factor cost curves. In the context of a union or minimum wage, the term *effective* is used to mean "takes effect" and is not a judgment about the suitability of a policy. To be effective, a minimum wage must be higher than the wage the firm would pay without any restrictions.

For a firm that is already a wage taker, an effective minimum wage shifts the $W = S_L = MRC_L = MFC_L$ curve upward to the level of the set wage. A perfectly competitive firm responds to the higher mandated wage by hiring fewer workers, at the level where the same MRP function intersects the new MFC curve. For the firm shown in Figure 5-4, a wage set at $10.00 would make only the first three workers profitable for the firm to hire. The fourth worker's MFC is now $10.00, which is higher than the added revenue paying that worker would generate.

The perfectly competitive market shows perhaps more interesting results. At the new proposed wage rate of $10.00, about 3,000 workers are demanded, but over 5,000 workers wish to be employed. The difference between quantity supplied and quantity demanded is the unemployment caused by the minimum wage.

For the monopsonist, a binding wage above its profit-maximizing wage is slightly more complex. The minimum wage transforms the firm into a wage taker, effectively moving the supply and MFC curves facing it. While the wage paid always increases to the new set wage, the quantity of labor hired may decrease or stay the same, and in many cases, it actually rises! Let's set up a new graph to help understand why.

Take the various wage rates presented in Figure 5-6 one at a time, imagining what the firm sees as its supply and marginal factor costs under each possibility and then determining how much labor will be hired. First, for the purposes of comparison, confirm that, if there is no legal or union minimum wage, the firm will hire L2 workers and pay a wage of W1. Now, we'll examine the effects that progressively higher and higher wages might have on this firm's hiring decisions.

Figure 5-6. Set Wage Rates in the Monopsony Model

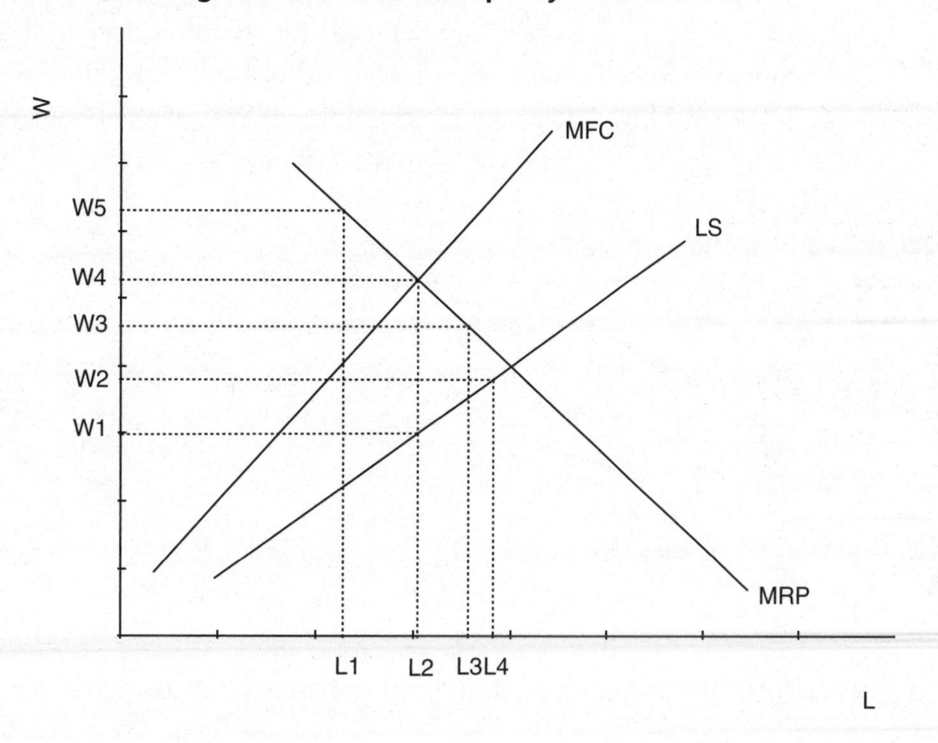

At a set wage of W2, the firm is a wage taker until it hires L4 units of labor. After that point, no more workers are willing to work for a wage of W2. For the first L4 units of labor, the firm faces a perfectly elastic $W = S_L = MRC_L = MFC_L$ curve. If the firm wanted to hire additional labor, it would need to raise the wage further for all its workers, therefore facing the old supply curve and the old MFC curve. L4 is, in fact, the number of workers the firm would hire (any additional units would have MFC > MRP and should not be hired). Note that the wage and the quantity of workers hired both rose.

At a set wage of W3, the firm is a wage taker whose profit maximizes by hiring a quantity of L3 workers. Beyond this point, the set wage and constant MFC exceeds the marginal revenue product. Note, however, that the wage rate and the quantity of labor hired both increased.

At a set wage of W4, the firm uses the same procedure to decide how much hiring to do but ends up with exactly L2 workers, just as it did when it wasn't regulated. However, these workers now receive a much higher wage, W4 as opposed to W1. The union (or the political group seeking to help workers) has achieved its goal of higher wages without sacrificing jobs. In fact, this is the highest wage that can be set without any loss of employment.

At a set wage of W5, MRP crosses the $W = S_L = MRC_L = MFC_L$ curve at a low quantity, and only L1 workers are demanded by the firm. Under these circumstances, a union's push to help its members has at least partially backfired: While the L1 workers who are employed do earn a nice high wage (W5), the horizontal distance between L2 and L1 represents employees that the firm may lay off due to a higher supply and marginal factor cost.

TEST TIP

If you need to figure out how employment and wage changes with a union or legally set wage, follow this simplified procedure. Draw a horizontal line rightward from the vertical axis at the level of the binding wage. Stop when you hit labor supply or marginal revenue product, whichever comes first. That is the quantity you want, and the wage is at the level of your horizontal line.

Marginal Productivity Theory of Income Distribution

Trying to map the conclusions reached in the simple models contained in this chapter onto the complex real world can be difficult. How might these models, which all seem to show one universal wage rate, explain how some jobs pay so much more than others (surgeons earn far more than sandwich artists, for example) or how unskilled laborers in some parts of the world can be paid so much less than in other parts? Analyzing the supply of different types of labor and considering marginal productivity can provide some explanations.

If we think of several markets for different types of labor all existing at once, we can imagine why there are different equilibrium wages for nurses, teachers, and electricians. The pool of potential workers is separate in each of those cases, and the firms who hire those workers are mostly separate as well. Then there might be an overall unskilled labor pool for workers who don't have a particular skill and from which many types of firms might hire workers in order to use them in various ways after a brief training period. Because anyone can be part of the labor pool in the unskilled market, supply is much farther down to the right than in the market for electricians or surgeons; there are simply fewer trained electricians and surgeons, and their labor is more valuable because it is scarcer.

Even the same worker might get a far lower wage in some situations than others. Differences in the wage rate for the same work between the developed and developing world are quite stark. Sometimes the same level of overall productivity may translate into more revenue for firms if they are able to sell goods for a higher price—a factor in the differences in earnings between workers around the world.

Another explanation is that education, training, and more powerful tools within developed economies means that additional units of labor yield a higher marginal product than those same labor units would yield when mixed with less technology and less powerful tools in other settings. This **marginal productivity theory of income distribution** predicts that workers receive more or less income based on the differences in what they add to the production process and how valuable that output is wherever it is eventually sold. While this theory can explain some differences in income, it tends to break down in circumstances where workers aren't paid the full value of what they add to the production process, which is what happens in monopsonies.

DIDYOUKNOW?

If you want to be paid well, get education and training (human capital) that not too many other people possess—the labor supply for your labor submarket will then be up and to the left. If you add lots of marginal physical product to the process and if the good or service you help make sells for a high price, then you will generate a healthy marginal revenue product. So if you want to be well paid, develop rare and valuable skills!

Chapter 6

Market Failure and the Role of Government

What Is Market Failure?

The term *market failure* refers to situations in which markets fail to yield the outcome we want. The general expectation of economists is that markets formed of self-interested buyers and sellers create results that are in the general social interest. While this may sometimes be true, it probably doesn't happen as often as introductory economics would suggest. Frankly, the real world is more likely to have the kinds of complexities that this chapter just begins to explore. Fortunately for you, the topics in this chapter, while the stuff of wonderful public policy debates, do not appear on too many AP Microeconomics exams.

A Fresh Look at Allocative Efficiency

The major theme present in all the issues addressed in this chapter is the failure of markets to generate the "right" quantity of various goods. What constitutes the "right" quantity? Generally, the **socially optimal quantity** is the one that is **allocatively efficient**: the quantity at which marginal benefit equals marginal cost. When this quantity is produced, there is no deadweight loss. All the good deals that buyers and sellers can reap from interacting in the marketplace have been done, so total economic surplus is maximized. The socially optimal level of anything is the level at which marginal social benefit equals marginal social cost.

Major Reasons Markets Fail

You've already studied some of the reasons that resources are misallocated. When examining price floors, price ceilings, and monopolies, you discovered that output was low enough that deadweight loss resulted: Units that would have yielded mutual gain to both sellers and buyers weren't produced. These are just a few of many reasons why markets can produce results that aren't socially optimal.

Imperfect competition, whether because of too few buyers or too few sellers, can lead output to be below the optimal level. Government policies, such as taxes and price or quantity restrictions, can also result in underproduction. When there are high transaction costs to the buyer or seller, as in the case of real estate purchases, sales may be more difficult to complete and therefore may decrease market quantity.

Sometimes markets create deadweight loss because of overallocation of resources. When some of the costs associated with producing a good aren't borne by the seller, overproduction is the result. Industrial pollution and carbon emissions are two serious examples of this sort of external cost. Likewise, a subsidy can encourage production even when it doesn't make sense according to the rules of marginal analysis.

TEST TIP

Some of the same factors that can cause market failure can also be used as policy tools to remedy those failures. If the market makes the efficient quantity, a tax or price ceiling would create market failure because it would lead to underproduction. However, if that same tax or legal maximum price were implemented in a market that was already overproducing a good, it might fix that misallocation. If it is difficult to imagine a specific cause being able to both create and solve a given problem, consider vaccines. They are formed from a small amount of a disease, and when they are doled out in a timely and measured way, they can prevent the illness!

Asymmetric or incomplete information can hamper a market's ability to function properly. If buyers or sellers don't really know what they are trading, then unwise decisions about both the desirability of an exchange and the appropriate price are likely. Similarly, a lack of knowledge of the tendencies of the market can lead to unwise decisions: Many people who have made a purchase in an unfamiliar situation or in a new place, only to discover later that they didn't get the best deal possible, can attest to this!

Showing Deadweight Loss

Because deadweight loss is an indication that resources have been misallocated, it can be found in the space between the quantity that was produced (or the private market quantity) and the quantity that should have been produced (the socially optimal quantity). Now that we have a version of deadweight loss that results from overproduction and one that comes from underallocating resources toward making a good, it's worth a moment to revisit what deadweight loss represents and how to locate this space on a graph.

With underproduction, the market quantity is below the allocatively efficient one because not enough units are made. Deadweight loss in this situation represents the potential gains that some of the units that weren't sold might have yielded to buyers and sellers if they had been produced and exchanged in the marketplace. On a graph, look for a shape that lies to the right of the market quantity and shows that some unproduced units would have yielded more marginal benefits than they would have required in added costs to produce.

If a good has been overproduced, market quantity appears to the right of the optimal quantity: Too many units have been created. In circumstances like this, deadweight loss represents the wastefulness associated with making some units that didn't yield as much added satisfaction as the marginal costs associated with making them.

TEST TIP

Locating deadweight loss in monopoly or market failure is a challenging component of many past free-response problems, based on comments by the lead exam grader that the College Board releases each year. Students seem to have a lot of trouble locating and explaining the meaning of this region on a graph. If you know whether the market is making too many or too few units, you can interpret the deadweight loss in the proper context. If you can find the socially optimal price and quantity point, then you can find the deadweight loss space. The secret is that deadweight loss looks like an arrow pointing from the quantity you got toward the quantity you should have. Practice seeing this space on the graphs provided in this chapter. Once you get the hang of it, you'll relax your eyes and the shape will pop out at you.

Externalities

When we analyze markets, we usually make relatively simple, but often unstated, assumptions: The gains from a good benefit only the buyer, and the costs associated with making the good burden only the seller. It seems to create an intuitively fair situation.

Buyers pay the cost in the marketplace (the price) but gain the benefits when they consume a good. Sellers, on the other hand, are paid the market price but bear the costs of production.

Sometimes the distribution of costs and benefits isn't so simple. Externalities are situations in which there are spillover costs or benefits to third parties to the transaction. Generally, the people directly involved in the transaction (buyers and sellers) consider only their own benefits and costs. When there are significant benefits and costs to others, the private marketplace misallocates resources, either underproducing or overproducing the good.

Marginal Social Benefit and Marginal Social Cost

To help measure and graph these situations, we will distinguish between marginal cost as it is felt by the producer and marginal cost as it is felt by society. **Marginal private cost (MPC)** denotes the added cost the supplier feels when producing one more unit of a good. **Marginal social cost (MSC)** refers to the added costs that all of society feels when another unit is produced. In parallel fashion, **marginal private benefit (MPB)** describes the added utility or satisfaction that the buyer reaps when enjoying another unit of a good, whereas **marginal social benefit (MSB)** is the total of all the benefits that the next unit of a good yields to the buyer as well as to any other affected parties.

Demand and Benefits

Demand curves show the marginal benefit that consumers expect to obtain from consuming goods. Recall that one of the three reasons why the law of demand is true is because marginal benefit diminishes as more units are consumed. Each consumer, as a generally self-interested creature, is primarily motivated by the benefits he or she will gain. Therefore, demand and marginal private benefit is always shown as the same line on the graph. If marginal social benefit is the same as marginal private benefit, you know that there is no externality associated with buying the good. If you see a separate MSB curve, there is some important effect on nonbuyers.

Supply and Costs

Supply curves reflect the marginal or per-unit costs of production. Firms seek to maximize their own profits; they respond to incentives that influence *their* revenue or *their* costs. As a result, supply is based on marginal private cost, and the two are represented by the same curve on problems related to externalities. If you see a separate marginal social cost curve, there are spillover costs to others. If MSC is the same curve as supply and MPC, all the costs associated with production are borne by the seller.

Negative Externalities

A Spillover Cost

Given the new vocabulary you learned in the preceding section, it is easy to understand what a negative externality is: It is a spillover cost imposed on someone not involved in the transaction. The producer has avoided paying the full costs associated with production and has externalized some of those to other individuals or to society at large: When industrial chemicals are produced, groundwater can become contaminated; when electricity is generated, carbon emissions increase; and when more taxis are on the streets, traffic is congested for everyone. All of these production situations suggest a negative externality associated with the production of the good or service. Now the marginal social cost (the marginal cost to all of society of producing the forty-seventh gallon of a pesticide, for example) is greater than the marginal private cost the firm experiences. The difference between the two is called the marginal external cost—the costs imposed on others.

Figure 6–1. Production Generates an External Cost

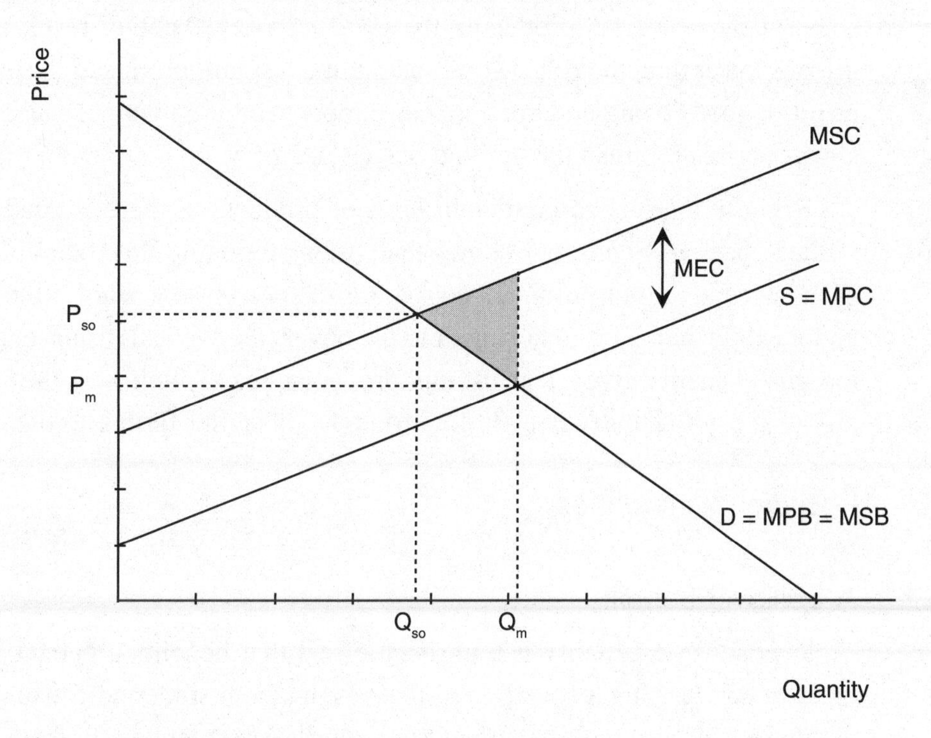

Showing a Negative Externality

This situation and others like it can be graphed, as shown in Figure 6-1. You can see the negative externality right away: MSC has its own separate curve above the S = MPC curve. The distance between the two is the marginal external cost (MEC) and represents effects on others as a result of the production of each successive unit. This is the reason that there is a separation between the quantity the market produces (Q_m) and the allocatively efficient or socially optimal level of output (Q_{so}).

TEST TIP

Remember that the private market produces the quantity where marginal private cost and marginal private benefit intersect (yes, each includes the word *private*). And the socially optimal quantity is where the marginal social benefit and the marginal social cost intersect (and those contain the word *social*). (Imagine that—economics terms that make logical and intuitive sense!)

Inefficient Price and Quantity

From examining the graph in Figure 6-1, we see that the good has been overproduced: The market quantity exceeds the socially desirable one. Negative externalities result in overallocation of resources because they stem from the producer failing to bear some of the costs that producing the good imposes. Another result is that the market price is lower than the full cost of making the last unit produced. Negative externalities result in goods being underpriced; consumers want too many because they get each for a lower price (P_m) than the optimal one (P_{so}).

Because there is an inefficient level of production, there is deadweight loss. This shaded space in Figure 6-1 shows that, after producing the socially optimal quantity, each successive unit produced cost more to society as a whole (the vertical distance under MSC) than it brought benefit to the buyer (the vertical distance under the demand/marginal benefit curve). The last unit produced, the Q_m unit, was the biggest mistake of all—that's why the deadweight loss triangle gets taller farther to the right.

Positive Externalities

A Spillover Benefit

A positive externality is a pleasant effect that benefits a person who didn't buy a good or service. It's a social good that results from someone consuming a product. If you have beautiful landscaping around your house, you benefit from enjoying it every day, but so might others who pass by your house. Your neighbor, who is selling her house, may reap a financial benefit because the neighborhood appears to be well kept. Education and immunizations are other examples of goods that, when consumed, confer benefits on others. Just think how much lower your chances of getting sick would be if everyone you interacted with got the latest vaccines! The marginal external benefit, or benefit not reaped by the buyer, therefore separates marginal social benefit (what we might wish demand were) from marginal private benefit (what demand is).

Figure 6–2. A Positive Externality

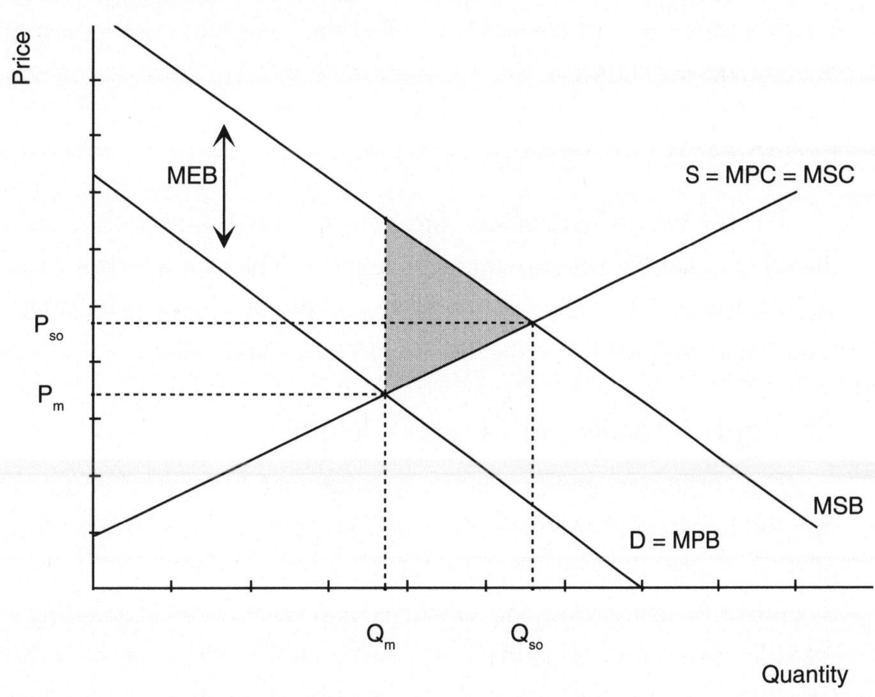

Showing a Positive Externality

Figure 6-2 depicts a positive externality. You likely notice immediately the two down-sloping lines representing different types of marginal benefit. Because marginal private benefit is below marginal social benefit, you know that those not directly involved in the market yield a positive spillover benefit. The **Marginal External Benefit (MEB)** is the vertical displacement between MPB and MSB and the reason that resources get underallocated in markets of this sort.

Inefficient Price and Quantity

You should be able to tell that the good has been underproduced when you see Q_{so} is greater than Q_m. This results because demand is lower than it ought to be if it reflected the full benefits the product yields to everyone. Positive externalities fail to allocate enough resources to the production of a good; too few units are made. The equilibrium market price is lower than it would be if all the benefits took external benefits into consideration instead of only private benefits.

Deadweight loss is again the result of misallocation of resources, but this time it takes a more familiar shape. As in the case of monopoly, the inefficiency is because too few units are produced and therefore represents gains that were not realized because of the failure to make units that should have been produced. The space shaded in the graph in Figure 6-2 shows that for units between Q_m and Q_{so} the marginal benefit to the buyer and the rest of society exceeded the marginal cost—these are units we should have made, but didn't.

Fixing Market Failures

The big idea when considering how to fix externalities is getting the quantity produced to equal the socially optimal quantity. The first question you will need to clarify is, Will too much or too little be produced by the marketplace? The answer determines which way to change the incentives of buyers and sellers.

Changing Incentives to Change Output

The consumers and producers who interact in the market do so by comparing their marginal costs and marginal benefits. In general, a good way to change the quantity of those trades is to manipulate those costs and benefits. Governments can alter these incentives by using taxes and subsidies, and price floors and ceilings. On the more forceful side, governments can directly limit quantity with a quota or break up monopolists (or trusts and cartels that act like monopolists) to address the externality.

Because taxes add to production costs, they discourage firms from producing the taxed goods. You'll read more in the section in this chapter called Taxes, but for now focus on the difference between a per-unit tax (also called an excise tax) and a lump-sum tax. The per-unit tax feels like added marginal cost for a firm, shifting all the firm's cost curves up vertically and leading to a lower profit-maximizing quantity for each firm. In markets, supply shifts left, reducing quantity. When used appropriately, this can shift supply (or marginal private cost) upward by the same amount at the marginal external cost and encourage the market to function at the socially optimal output level. Lump-sum taxes don't change marginal cost because they represent a fixed cost, independent of output. Firms produce the same quantity because marginal costs and marginal revenues have not changed.

A subsidy works like a tax in reverse: Per-unit subsidies shift marginal cost downward, encouraging a greater quantity to be traded. The most appropriate use of these subsidies is as a remedy for a positive externality. If the per-unit subsidy is the same amount as the marginal external benefit, the firm may be encouraged to produce the socially optimal output quantity. As with taxes, lump-sum subsidies might influence the number of firms in an industry in the long run, but they do not change quantity produced in the short run because they change fixed costs and don't influence the point at which marginal cost and marginal revenue intersect.

DIDYOUKNOW?

Per-unit taxes have been used for a very long time: salt was taxed on a per-unit basis 2,000 years ago. Goods and services as varied as alcohol, paper, tobacco, coffee, gambling, and prostitution have been taxed on a per-unit basis over the years by various governments.

Price floors and price ceilings reduce the quantity of a good that is traded in the market; therefore, both can be used to offset the misallocation that results from a negative externality. It may seem unexpected that a minimum legal price set above the market price and a maximum legal price set below the market price could both have the same effect, so it is worth a moment to consider why. Price floors, or minimum legal prices, set the price above the market equilibrium and therefore make the good more costly for buyers. Because quantity demanded decreases, the higher price imposed by the price floor decreases the quantity sold in the market. A price floor that crosses demand at the same point that marginal social cost does could be an effective solution to a negative externality.

Price ceilings are legal maximum prices that take effect when they are set below the market equilibrium level. Setting a low price lessens the incentive to produce: Firms can't charge as high a price so they choose to produce fewer units. Quantity supplied decreases and reduces the quantity traded. The appropriate price ceiling for a negative externality crosses the line representing supply and marginal private cost at the socially optimal quantity.

Other solutions that government can pursue include regulating or breaking up monopolies to make them more efficient. You learned when studying market structures that monopolies tended to underproduce and charge too high a price when they are not regulated. Two strategies might be used to encourage a greater production level. First, the government can break up the firm into smaller companies—the more competitive a market structure is, the less deadweight loss there will be. Second, the government can set a price ceiling at the socially optimal price and transform the monopolist into a price taker. The firm faces a horizontal demand and marginal revenue curve after the regulation, so it will produce where marginal cost meets the regulated price.

The most direct and blunt tools are a bit simpler. If there will be too many units of a particular item, set a firm limit on how much can be produced. If there won't be enough units, provide the efficient quantity publicly. Quotas give certain suppliers the authority to produce a specific quantity or can limit the number of suppliers. Because quotas limit the quantity traded directly, they can be used as a remedy for a negative externality. Some goods with certain kinds of positive externalities are well suited to be distributed as public goods. (This topic is discussed later in the chapter in the section called Public Goods.) Because government becomes either a major or the only supplier of the good or service, it can produce enough units to raise the market's output to the level it deems allocatively efficient.

DIDYOUKNOW?

Quotas have been used for several decades to limit the number of taxicabs that can operate in major cities, notably New York City. Carbon emissions have been the focus of much debate because of their role in contributing to climate change; the cap-and-trade concept is based on a fixed number of tradable quota permits.

Market-Based Solutions

If certain conditions are met, private actors can sometimes solve the effects of an externality without an intrusive governmental role. London School of Economics and University of Chicago professor Ronald Coase argued that government can clarify property rights effectively and then ask private parties to negotiate in order to reduce the misallocation of resources. This was part of the theory that won him the Nobel Prize in Economics in 1991. His idea, called the Coase Theorem, is that the party who bears the social cost will be willing to pay an amount less than that cost so that the producer will not produce the good. The producer needs a payment greater than the potential marginal benefit forgone, so private actors have an incentive to find the allocatively efficient quantity. As long as the harm exceeds the gain the seller can get from the extra (inefficient) units, there should be room to negotiate a private payment to prevent overproduction.

This type of solution requires three conditions. First, there must be clearly defined property rights. Second, there must be few enough parties that each can be identified, each can feel ownership over the problem, and each stands to gain or lose significantly based on the market's production. Third, the parties must be able to negotiate payments privately and expect that contracts are enforceable. The Coase Theorem therefore suggests that, in certain situations, the government need not regulate a market directly but can play a more passive role by clarifying property rights and effectively enforcing them and the contracts on which they are based.

Government Provision of Goods

Many goods that create positive externalities have specific properties that make them poorly suited to private markets. Based on two fundamental questions about the nature of a good's consumption, we can classify goods and thus shed light on which ones might best be provided by a government and funded through taxes rather than traded in a market and paid for by the consumers of the good.

Rival and Shared Consumption

The first question to ask is, Can more than one person enjoy a given unit of the good at the same time? Is the good subject to shared consumption or rival consumption? With gallons of gasoline, cheeseburgers, apples, and T-shirts, one person uses one unit of the good, which means others can't. Those goods are characterized by rival consumption: One more unit that I consume is one less unit that you can enjoy.

Other goods are enjoyed jointly and therefore are subject to shared consumption. Non-rival goods include videos on YouTube, a movie in a movie theater, or a sculpture in a park. Another person admiring the sculpture, watching the same video, or attending the same movie doesn't prevent you from experiencing the same unit of that good at all in most cases.

Excludability and the Free-Rider Problem

A second question to resolve is, Can the benefits of the goods be denied to those who don't pay for them? If so, the good is excludable; only those who choose to purchase it can reap the gains associated with its consumption. If not, people can draw the benefits whether they've bought it or not. Those who enjoy a nonexcludable good but do not pay for it are referred to as free riders. The **free-rider problem** describes a situation in which a number of people refuse to purchase a good, instead enjoying the external benefits derived from those units that are purchased by others. Most public parks, roads, and bridges are nonexcludable goods, as are national defense and common resources like fish in the open ocean. Major architectural works are also nonexcludable because anyone can look at the structure without paying for it. Goods that are not excludable are common sources of positive externalities because the demand or marginal private benefit curve that shows utility captured by all the buyers is likely to underrepresent the real benefit to buyers and nonbuyers alike.

Excludable goods include most physical products: The sporting goods store can deny you a new soccer ball, pair of skis, or new putter if you aren't willing to pay for it. Lots of services are excludable as well: You won't be shown to your seat at the opera unless you present a ticket. Toll roads and bridges are examples of goods that have been made excludable.

Public Goods

A pure public good is neither excludable nor rival. These two characteristics make goods such as national defense, parks, streetlights, and flood prevention systems well-suited for removal from the typical marketplace. Instead, many governments provide them and fund their production with tax revenues. Shared or nonrival consumption means people won't have an incentive to overuse the good—it won't run out or be used up if others use it first or alongside a given consumer. Pure public goods are also not excludable. This means that any system for providing them does not generate enough revenue to produce all the units that society desires because some of the benefits of their use go to free riders who don't pay. The fact that these people cannot be excluded means that it might make sense to charge them anyway by using a tax system. In fact, no distinction between buyers and nonbuyers can be made—everyone is entitled to the benefits because everyone takes part in paying for the good to be produced.

The provision of public goods has a few problems because consumption is sometimes not truly shared or the benefits aren't distributed evenly among members of a community. The categories presented in this chapter are convenient, but the goods and services we trade in the real world don't always fit perfectly into one category or the other. Many goods are somewhere between shared and rival consumption in real life, or their use is rival in certain circumstances.

If you're ready to watch a parade, enjoy a nice day in the park, or relax on the beach, you aren't really affected by the other people doing the same thing. All can enjoy the same parade, park, or beach sunset at the same time without diminishing each other's experience at all. Crowding is one problem that may impair shared consumption: At some point, the parade route is so full of people that your ability to see the performers diminishes. Normally one more person in the theater doesn't affect your enjoyment of a play or movie, but as those facilities reach or exceed their intended capacity, you are negatively affected. Now you and your friend might need to sit in separate rows because there aren't any sets of empty seats next to one another in a crowded theater.

Last, we often see examples of people overusing or misusing goods that are publicly provided. People are sometimes inclined to damage, take away, or dirty an environment that isn't privately owned. Because someone else is likely to be the next user, people don't feel the same level of responsibility for the care of the resource. You've likely noticed more graffiti and less toilet paper in publicly accessible restrooms than those in people's houses and apartments. When a commonly held resource is overused or misused, it means that resources are consumed suboptimally—either too quickly or in the wrong way. This problem has been called the tragedy of the commons by economists and is a tough one to solve.

DIDYOUKNOW?

Some jurisdictions have become quite creative in their management of public goods. Roads have long been considered a public good, but population growth and increased use of automobiles have combined to make consumption less a shared experience and more of a rivalry—also leading to a huge negative externality—traffic jams! Because some roads get a lot of usage at only one time of day, many cities have lanes that run in one direction during morning rush hour and the other way during the evening rush hour.

Societies differ in the choices they make regarding which goods to provide publicly. In some places, free citywide transit, healthcare, education, and high-quality museums and libraries abound. In other situations, police and fire services may underallocate resources so much that private markets emerge for these goods we think of as public in nature. The most important facts to keep in mind about public goods is that they are nonexcludable and nonrival in consumption and that using this strategy of providing a good may sometimes be the right way to correct for the underallocation that results from positive externalities.

Taxes

Taxes have been controversial for a long time. They have been the subject of many famous and oft-cited quotes. Benjamin Franklin said, "[N]othing can be said to be certain, except death and taxes." Oliver Wendell Holmes referred to taxes as "the price of civilization." The AP Microeconomics exam will test you on only a few topics related to taxes, and the basics you need are discussed next.

Theories of Collecting Taxes

There are two basic philosophies behind collecting tax revenue, each appropriate for a slightly different set of objectives. The **ability to pay principle** and the **benefits received principle** represent two different answers to the fundamental question, Who should pay a tax? The ability to pay principle suggests that taxes should be paid by those who have the most resources (the most wealth or the highest incomes) because they have a greater ability to bear the burden of taxes—they won't be in a position to go without basic needs if taxed. The benefits received principle suggests that those who directly benefit from the service or good should bear the cost and therefore be the ones to pay the tax that funds it.

Which theory to use in a given situation depends on a government's objectives and the type of good or service it is providing. It would make no sense to fund a food stamp program for the poor or build a homeless shelter by taxing the same people who are to receive the benefits—the reason such programs are needed is because the groups who will benefit from the programs don't have enough resources in the first place! Any program targeting inequality in society is far more likely to make sense if it is funded by the ability to pay philosophy. On the other hand, some government-funded transportation programs may benefit some members of the community far more than others. If that is the case, it would make sense to use the benefits received principle, charging those who ride a rail line, drive on a toll road, or cross a bridge a per-use fee and use those funds to pay for the publicly accessible good.

TEST TIP

Studying taxes can be intimidating because there are so many different types of taxes. Many countries, states, or cities have a complicated system of revenue collection because societies have long known that raising revenue through taxation is both necessary and unpopular. AP questions about taxes tend to focus on three details:

- who bears the burden of the tax;
- how the taxes affect incentives and, therefore, production and purchasing decisions
- how the tax affects efficiency

Types of Taxes

Income Level and the Tax Burden

Taxes often affect those with high incomes differently than those who earn less. If the percentage of one's income paid in taxes rises as income rises, the tax structure is **progressive**. The U.S. federal income tax is a progressive tax because those with low incomes are in lower tax brackets than those making higher incomes. For the year 2012, a single income-tax filer with a taxable income below $8,900 owed 10 percent. A single taxpayer with a taxable income of $225,000 payed approximately 26 percent of that taxable amount in income taxes.

A **proportional tax** structure is used when income is taxed at a constant percentage rate regardless of income level. Note that if everyone in a community paid 20 percent of her or his earnings in tax, the rich would still contribute more in taxes, but the payments would be proportionally the same for everyone. Sometimes this is referred to as a "flat" tax, perhaps in misleading fashion.

A **regressive tax** implies that those with higher incomes pay a smaller portion of their income in taxes than those with lower incomes. If every citizen were presented with an identical tax bill (a true "flat" tax), the result would be a regressive tax: owing $20,000 would be a far smaller percentage of LeBron James's income than it would be of the average doctor's or lawyer's income. A new schoolteacher might be paying close to a 50 percent tax rate, and someone working at a minimum wage job would owe more in taxes than he or she earned in income, for a tax rate over 100 percent! Some taxes function regressively even if they aren't designed that way. For example, income taxes are regressive because the rich can afford to save a substantial fraction of their incomes, so they pay the tax only on some of what they earn. Poorer households don't have the ability to save much or at all because (nearly) all the income earned is spent on basic necessities; therefore, they end up paying a greater fraction of their overall income in taxes.

Taxes as Fixed or Marginal Costs

Taxes on production are the focus of most of the exam questions you will face on this subject. All of the microeconomics questions asking you to consider or show the effects of taxes on graphs will be about production taxes. A tax on producing a good is considered an added cost for the firm. The key question for you to consider is, Does the tax represent an added fixed or added marginal cost for the firm? Either way, the firm's costs will increase, but because output decisions are based on marginal cost and marginal benefit, the two approaches have different effects on the firm's incentives.

A **lump-sum tax** is a tax of a particular amount placed on each producer in a market. It's called a lump-sum tax because the amount taxed is one total that is independent of that firm's output; just like the lump-sum income tax of $20,000 was independent of income, the amount of this production tax does not depend on the quantity the firm produces. A one-time licensing fee, such as the liquor license a restaurant or bar might purchase, constitutes a lump-sum tax. To the firm, a cost that does not vary with output is a fixed cost. Therefore, lump-sum taxes increase the firm's fixed costs. If you are asked to show this process on a graph, the result would look like Figure 6-3. Note that a firm faced with this new tax won't change its level of output, whether it is a price taker selling in a perfectly competitive market or a monopolist. Because marginal cost is the same as it used to be and marginal revenue is the same as it used to be, the level of output is unchanged. However, the firm now experiences a lower total profit at every output level than it did before. In competitive industries, therefore, a lump-sum tax may reduce the number of firms in the long run.

Figure 6–3. A Lump-Sum Tax

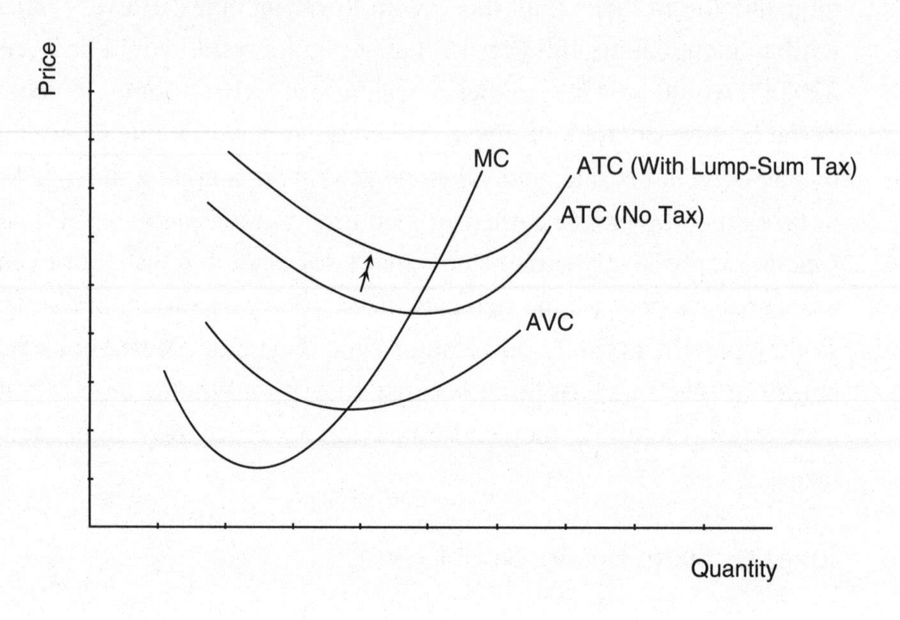

Last and most important is the **per-unit tax**, which acts as an added marginal cost for the firm. A $1.00 per-box tax on crayons is an example of a per-unit tax, which might also be called an excise tax or a specific tax. From the firm's perspective, this pushes up all of the common cost curves by the amount of the tax. The firm's new marginal cost curve is above and to the left of the old one, meaning that its profit-maximizing quantity decreases. Figure 6-4 shows how this per-unit tax of $t influences a monopolist. Initially, the firm produced Q1 units and charged a price of P1. The per-unit tax shifts marginal cost and average total cost up by a distance of $t. Because the new MC with tax curve intersects MR further to the left, the firm makes a smaller quantity. At the new lower quantity Q2, the firm finds its price at P2, above the old price. Another thing to note is that this firm has gone from making positive economic profit to the unfortunate situation of minimizing losses—their new ATC curve lies above the price they now charge at Q2. It isn't likely that you will need to draw this graph on the AP exam, but you might be asked to think about how such a tax influences output, price, or profit for a specific type of firm, and visualizing how the per-unit tax affects the firm's world is sure to help you reason through such questions and come to the right response.

Figure 6–4. A Per-Unit Tax on a Monopolist

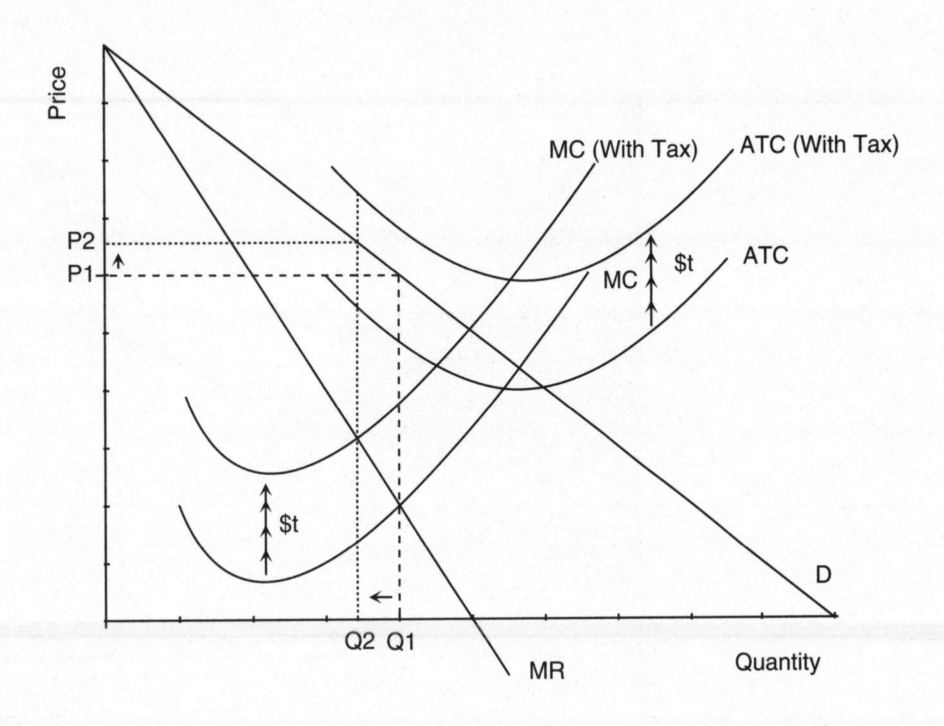

Elasticity, Deadweight Loss, and Tax Incidence

Taxes and Deadweight Loss

Because per-unit taxes and subsidies influence output, they affect whether a market's quantity aligns with the socially optimal quantity. If a market produced the socially optimal quantity initially, then imposing a tax would decrease output and create deadweight loss—the tax discouraged production of the good in such a way that too few units were produced.

Examine Figure 6-5 to see the effects of a tax in a marketplace. It is somewhat common for the AP exam to ask students to replicate this graph either partially or completely, or to locate various areas on a graph presented in the question. First, consider that, before the tax, Q1 units were traded at an equilibrium market price of P1. The tax creates a new marginal cost, shifting the supply curve upward by the amount of the tax. Next, locate the new level of output, Q2, by finding point B, where demand intersects the supply curve after the tax is imposed. Buyers will pay price P2 and purchase Q2 units.

Figure 6–5. A Per-Unit Tax

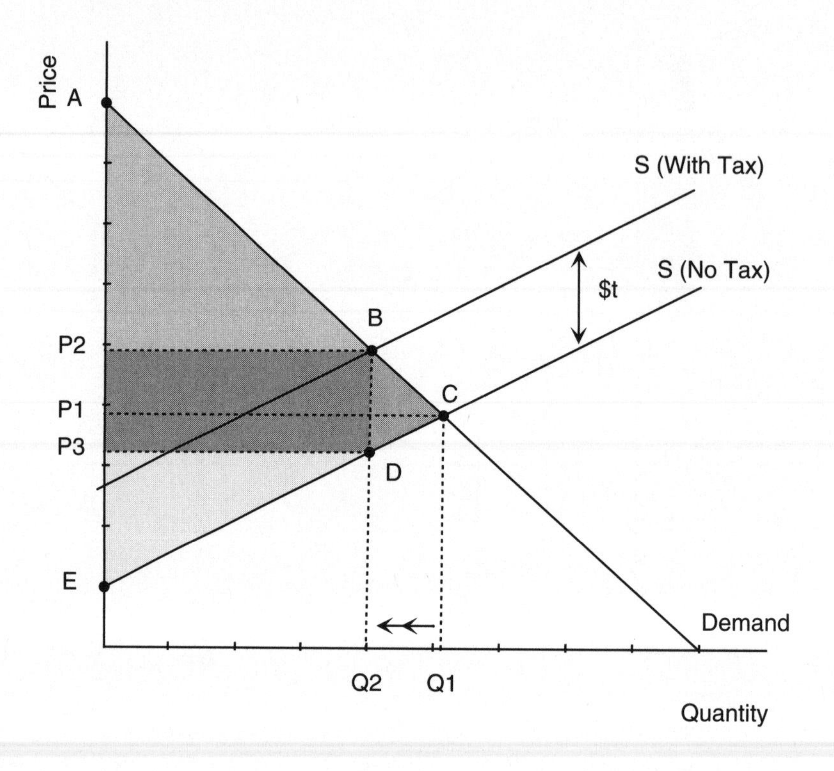

With a tax, however, any question about price immediately becomes more complicated because there are two relevant prices: the one buyers pay and the lower price (less the per-unit tax) that sellers actually receive and can use to pay for the actual costs associated with producing the good. P3 is the price sellers receive after the tax, found from the point at which the old supply curve passes quantity Q2 (at point D). The per-unit tax has created a price wedge between buyers and sellers. Sellers act as they would have if there were no tax and a market price of P3.

You may be asked to identify regions on such a graph that represent deadweight loss, consumer and producer surplus, and total revenue that the tax raises. The area of triangle BCD represents deadweight loss. Q1 was the efficient quantity, and now only Q2 units are produced; because units between Q2 and Q1 have a greater value to society (as seen in the segment of the demand curve between B and C) than it cost to produce them (the part of the original supply curve between D and C), they should have been made and sold. They weren't produced because the tax decreased output, so the potential gain that those trades would have yielded to buyers and sellers is now deadweight loss associated with the tax.

Consumer surplus is the area that shows the sum total of all good deals that all buyers have experienced by interacting in the market. It can always be found below demand, above the price paid, and to the left of the quantity purchased. Prior to the tax, the area of triangle ACP_1 was the total consumer surplus. However, now buyers purchase only Q2 units and pay the higher price P2. Thus, consumer surplus is the shaded area of the smaller triangle ABP_2.

Producer surplus shows the gains to sellers of interacting in the market. It is the area above supply, to the left of quantity sold, and below the price received. An excise tax reduces quantity sold and decreases the price sellers receive. In Figure 6-5, producer surplus was reduced from area P_1CE to area P_3DE by the per-unit tax.

Tax revenue is generated whenever any sort of tax is imposed. We might see tax revenue raised by the government through taxes as a social surplus because it can pay for goods and services we want. Here, the money paid in taxes is visible as area P_2BDP_3. The height of the tax revenue box is the amount each unit is taxed, $t per unit; when a buyer pays the higher price at point B, segment BD of that money goes to the government and the part below point D stays with the producer. The width of the box is the number of units traded after the tax, Q2.

Considering the effects of the tax overall, we can see that consumers and producers each get a bit less surplus, and most of that loss in surplus is transferred to the government, which can use that surplus to provide something of benefit to the community: more law enforcement or a new library, school, or courthouse. Some of the lost surplus disappears entirely in the transfer process because the tax decreased the traded quantity: That's the deadweight loss.

If this type of tax is used to correct for the effects of a negative externality, however, the tax can eliminate rather than create deadweight loss. Refer again to Figure 6-1 and examine the way a negative externality looks. Remember that the firm has neglected a cost of production equal to the marginal external cost (MEC) per unit. If a per-unit tax in that same amount were imposed, the MSC curve would now also be labeled Supply with Tax and the quantity traded would decrease from Q_m to Q_{so}. Buyers would pay a higher price, P_{so}. Of that price, the amount equal to the marginal external cost is paid to the government and the remainder (the portion below MPC at Q_{so} on the graph) is left for suppliers to cover the costs of production they bear.

TEST TIP

Reverse it! Subsidies are like negative taxes. When asked about a subsidy, imagine the opposite effects as those of a tax. Lump-sum subsidies shift ATC downward, but they leave marginal costs unchanged. Per-unit subsidies are shown on a graph as a rightward shift of supply and marginal cost curves: They increase quantity traded. A subsidy introduces two relevant prices as well, but this time the price sellers receive is greater than the price buyers pay by the amount of the subsidy. If a subsidy is introduced when a market is already producing the optimal quantity, however, it will create deadweight loss, as happens with a tax. A subsidy used in a market that is underproducing a good can be used to increase quantity to the efficient level and therefore eliminate deadweight loss.

Elasticity and the Tax Burden

Will the producers pay the tax or pass the increased costs incurred from paying the tax to their consumers? The answer depends on how elastic supply and demand are in the affected market. To understand this better, let's break the tax revenue area into two parts, using the old price as the dividing line, as shown in Figure 6-6. The lighter-shaded portions are the deadweight loss and the tax revenue above price P_1 and the darker shaded parts below P_1. The top part of the deadweight loss and the tax revenue used to be part of the consumer surplus before the tax was imposed. It's reasonable to think of them as having been sacrificed by buyers. Thinking on a per-unit basis, we could say that the distance between P_1 and P_2 represents the part of the per-unit tax that buyers pay because it is the amount of the increase in price for them.

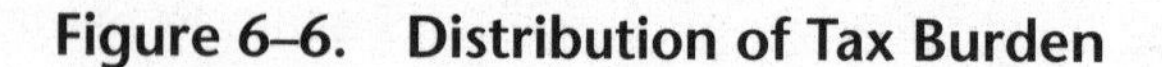

Figure 6–6. Distribution of Tax Burden

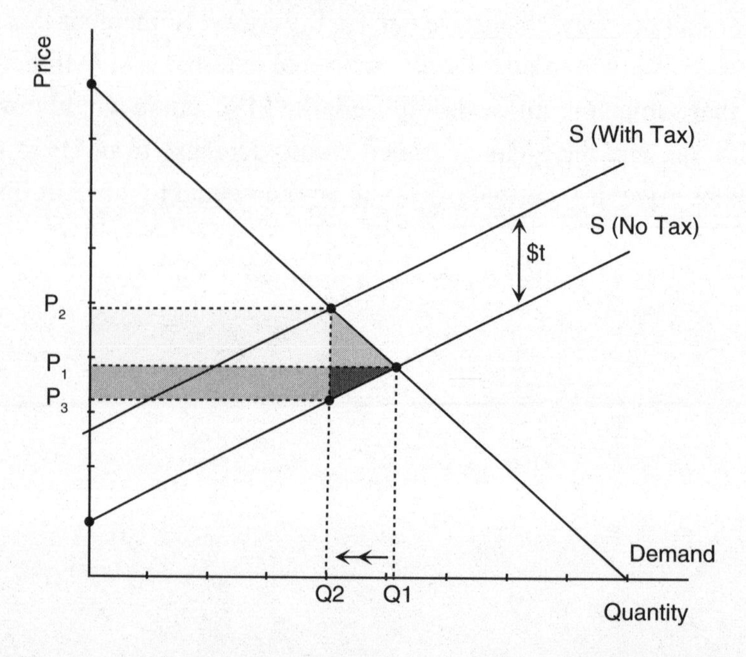

Sellers sacrifice the darker-shaded parts below those given up by buyers. Producer surplus shrinks by the space between P_1 and P_3 so that part of the tax revenue and deadweight loss areas come at sellers' expense. Suppliers end up paying the part of the per-unit tax between P_1 and P_3 because that is the decrease in price they experience as a result of the tax. In this case, buyers contribute a bit more in tax revenue than sellers because price rose for them more than it fell for those producing the good.

Figures 6-7 and 6-8 explore how the relative tax burdens (known as **incidence of tax**) depend on whether demand or supply is more elastic. Remember that elasticity stems from responsiveness: how responsive or sensitive buyers and sellers are to changes in price. In Figure 6-7, with the same supply curve and the same value of the tax, $t, we can see that the result of a more inelastic demand curve is that the tax is borne almost entirely by the consumers of the good. Note that P_2 is now far above P_1, and the price that sellers receive, P_3, is only barely below the original market price. Buyers in this example are insensitive to an increase in price, so the tax falls mostly on them. The upper lightly-shaded portion of the tax revenue rectangle is far bigger than the lower, more darkly shaded part. Consumer surplus took a big hit, whereas producer surplus is only slightly smaller than before. Note that the area of deadweight loss is smaller than it is in Figure 6-6 because quantity didn't decrease as much as when buyers were more responsive to a price change.

Figure 6–7. Buyers Pay with Inelastic Demand

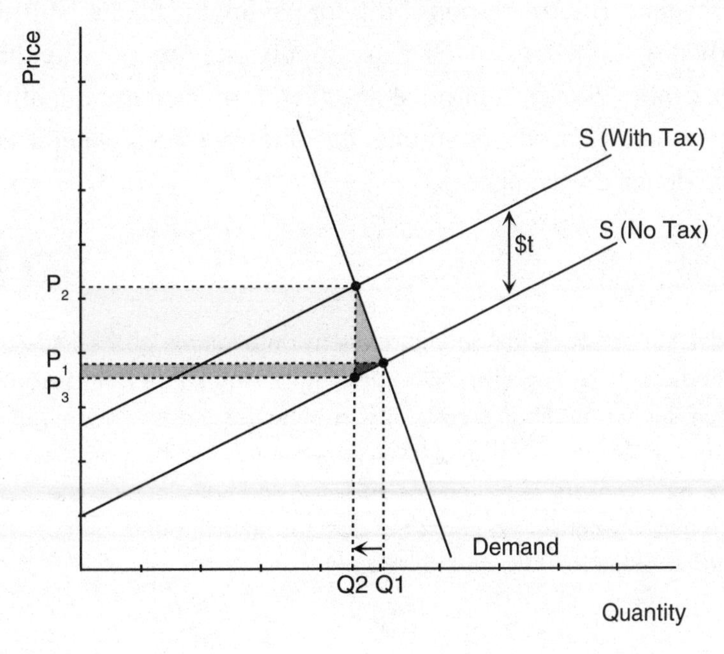

Figure 6–8. Elastic Demand Shifts the Tax to Sellers

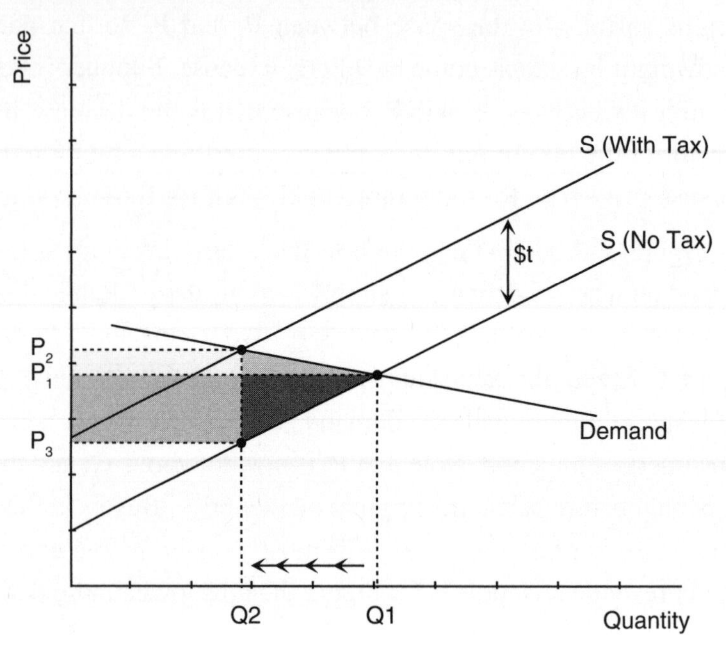

In Figure 6-8, the situation is reversed. Now demand is extremely elastic; buyers care a great deal about price. The tax decreases quantity far more in this example than it did in Figure 6-7. There is a larger area of deadweight loss and a smaller area of total tax revenue. But the responsibility of paying the tax has shifted: Now the suppliers are saddled with the burden. Because supply is more inelastic than demand, sellers experience more of a drop in price and therefore decrease quantity supplied even more. A larger share of producer surplus becomes both deadweight loss and tax revenue than when demand was inelastic.

DIDYOUKNOW?

Consider the per-pack tax on cigarettes as an example of the issues discussed in this section. The good creates a negative externality in the creation of both secondhand smoke and, in the long run, higher healthcare costs. It is a behavior that society might want to discourage to a lower, more allocatively efficient level. A per-unit tax shifts supply leftward, decreasing quantity a lot for new smokers who aren't as addicted and have less income. For addicted lifelong smokers, the quantity consumed might not decrease much, but a lot more tax revenue is raised and the burden of the tax falls on those smokers.

Thinking at the extremes, you could reason through and even draw what happens when either demand or supply is perfectly elastic (horizontal): that group (buyers if demand, sellers if supply) would bear none of the tax. If either curve were vertical (perfectly inelastic), the tax would fall entirely on that group. In this special case, a tax doesn't reduce quantity at all and therefore can be levied without any resulting deadweight loss. For this reason, some economists in eighteenth-century France and the nineteenth-century United States were strong advocates of taxes on land (which was presumed to have a perfectly inelastic supply curve).

Income Distribution

Income inequality can stem from several different sources and varies greatly from one society to another. Some countries work to change the level of inequality over time, for both moral reasons and out of an instinct for regime preservation (inequality has, at times, caused revolts against governments). Policies designed to decrease income or wealth gaps can be quite controversial and may decrease overall efficiency and output in some cases.

Sources of Inequality

Income and wealth end up in equal distribution for many reasons. Identifying the reasons is not difficult if you remember that income comes in exchange for providing resources or factors of production. Because the resources aren't equally divided and are of unequal desirability and value, the income they generate is likely to vary greatly.

Over time, uneven amounts of wealth are inherited by younger generations, and prior wealth is often a major source of income. Interest, dividend, or rental income is far more possible with previous wealth. Only those who can afford to buy stocks, bonds, and real estate in the first place can possibly earn money from buying these assets at low prices and selling at high prices. Past discrimination and uneven ownership of productive resources contribute to the differences in wealth, and those differences allow for continued differences in this sort of income.

Income earned from providing labor varies quite a bit as well. Wages and salaries depend on the characteristics of the markets in which the labor is sold. If there are very few people with a highly specific skill that requires years of difficult and expensive schooling to gain, the supply curve will be high and to the left in that particular labor market. If the good they produce or the service they render is in high demand and they have a high marginal revenue product, the wage rate will be extremely high. The market for brain surgeons might have roughly these characteristics. A broad market for unskilled labor in a densely populated region might yield a far lower wage rate. The quantity of capital stock available to magnify the productivity of labor and the value of the good produced are factors that also influence the distribution of income.

The Lorenz Curve

Measuring the level of inequality in a society can be done with two basic tools: the Lorenz curve and the Gini coefficient. Both can be useful for comparing the level of inequality present in two different countries or for seeing how income inequality has changed over time.

The Lorenz curve has the percentile rank of all households (or individuals earning income) on the horizontal axis and the percentage of the total income earned on the vertical. A 45-degree angle reference line represents a society with all earners having equal income. Inequality is shown by the degree to which a society's Lorenz curve dips below the reference line.

Figure 6-9 shows two Lorenz curves, each of which might represent two different countries. In country 1, the bottom 50 percent of all households earn 20 percent of the national income, and the top 10 percent earn 37 percent. In country 2, the bottom 50 percent of income earners collect only 10 percent of the total earned, and the top 10 percent earn 60 percent of the total income. Country 2 has more unequally distributed income and therefore a Lorenz curve that sags or bows more below the line of perfect equality.

Figure 6–9. Two Lorenz Curves

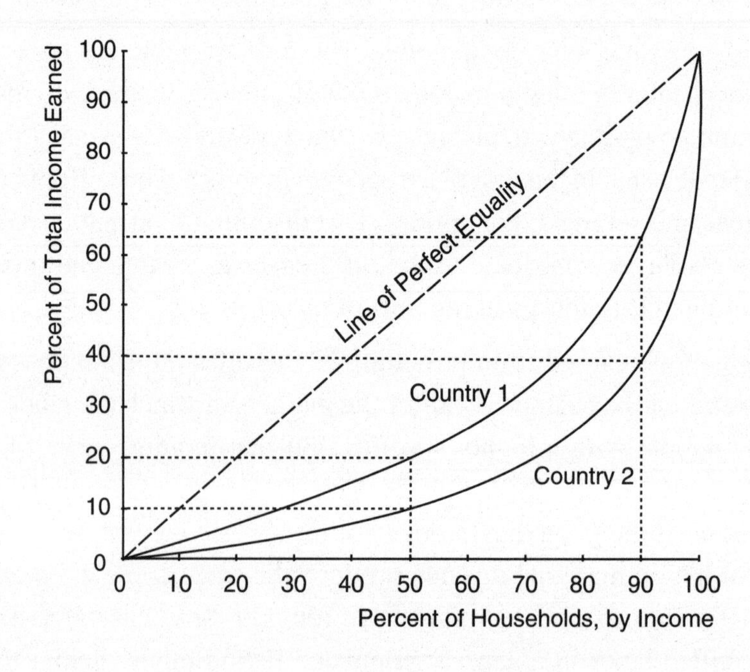

Progressive tax structures and social programs for the needy can push a country's Lorenz curve upward, reducing the problems associated with large rich–poor gaps. Societies with lower gaps between the richest and the poorest usually have lower crime rates, more trust in fellow citizens, and better physical and mental health rates. However, some of these policies remain controversial because they can be perceived as class warfare or weakening the incentive to work and therefore inefficient and a drag on production.

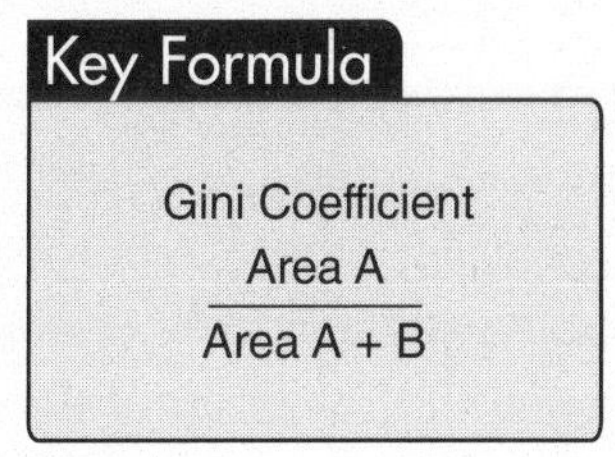

The Gini coefficient is a decimal value between 0 and 1 that correlates to the level of inequality in a society. It is found by taking the area above a country's Lorenz curve and dividing by the total area under the line of perfect equality. Figure 6-10 shows country 1's Gini coefficient areas, and Figure 6-11 shows the same areas but for a more unequal country 2. As the society approaches the line of perfect equality, the size of area A approaches zero, but A + B stays the same. A perfectly equal society has a Gini coefficient of 0. Country 2 has a higher Gini coefficient because area A is relatively large and therefore takes up a bigger percentage of the whole triangle than the comparable area for country 1. A perfectly unequal society would have a Gini coefficient approaching 1.

Figure 6–10. Gini Coefficient: Country 1

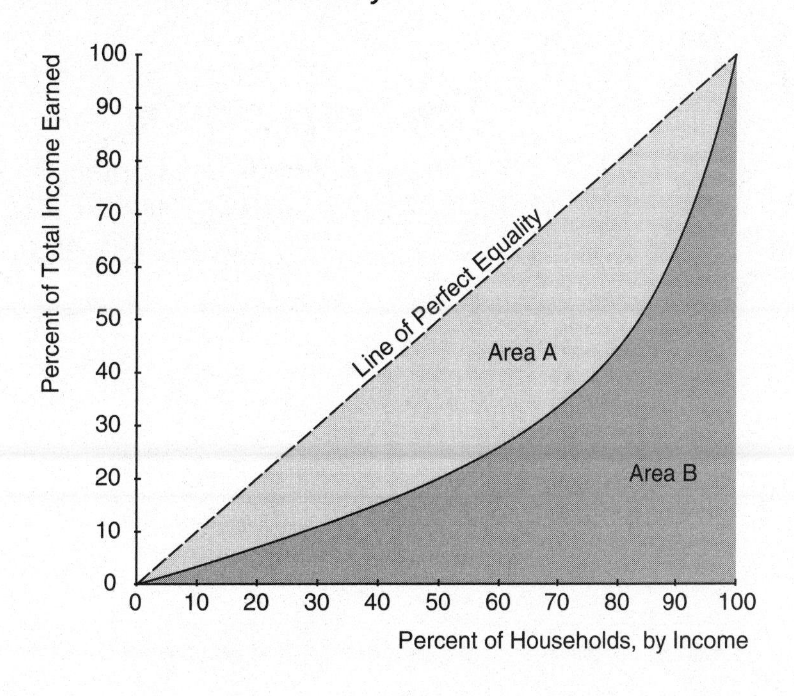

Figure 6–11. Gini Coefficient: Country 2

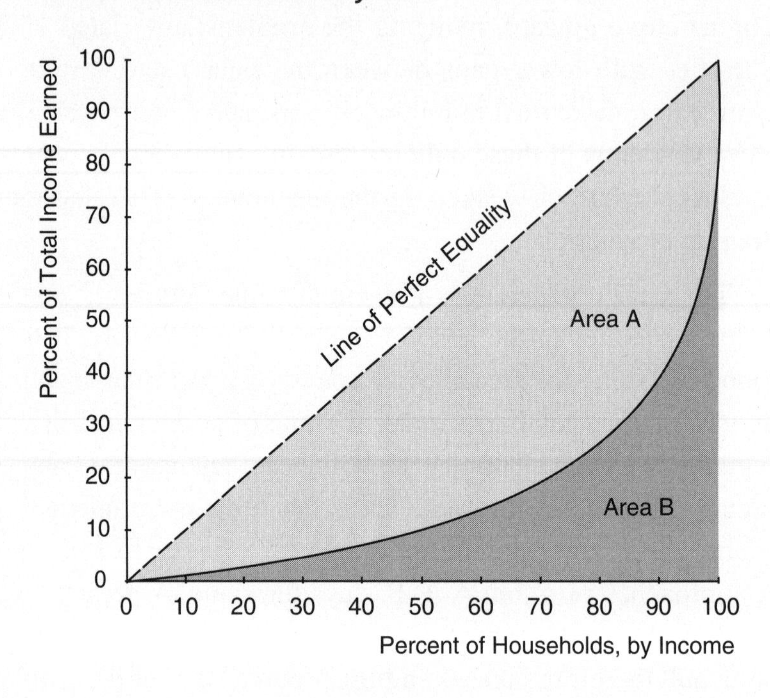

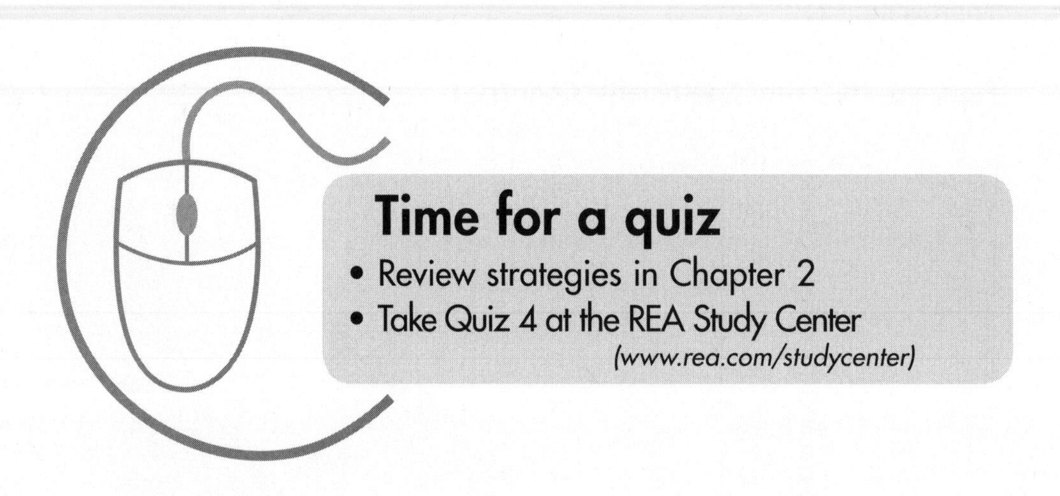

Take Mini-Test 1

on Chapters 3–6

Go to the REA Study Center

(www.rea.com/studycenter)

AP Macroeconomics

Chapter 7

Measuring Economic Performance

In macroeconomics, the fundamental tasks are to understand a nation's economic situation and to analyze how various factors influence that economy. In particular, you'll be faced with questions about how governmental policies might influence the total production of goods and services in an economy or the average price at which those goods are traded. Most economists begin judging the overall health of an economy by taking into account three major factors: the value of goods it produces, how its prices are changing, and how many of its workers cannot find employment. **The three fundamental measurement tools you'll need to know are gross domestic product (GDP), the inflation rate, and the unemployment rate**. In this chapter, these measurement tools will be introduced, defined, and explained. Later chapters will focus on how to show changes in these measurements in various graphical models.

Gross Domestic Product and National Income

Calculating the total value of the production in an economy is a large, complex, and rather controversial job, and there are several ways to measure this value. What items to count and where in the production process we choose to count them change the nature of the calculation process. There are also arguments about how to modify it in order to render it most meaningful for comparisons across time or to other economies' production totals.

Are We Measuring Output or Income?

The short answer to this question of whether we're measuring output or income is that we are measuring both. When we calculate the value of the finished goods and services that are produced in a country in a given year, that total should represent not only what we collectively paid for those goods in the product markets, but also what we *were paid* in the factor markets for helping to produce them. Thus, aggregate expenditures should equal aggregate income and aggregate output. This is known as the **fundamental identity of national income accounting**: total production, total expenditure, and total income are equal. Because market values are used to add unlike products together, the value we pay for goods is the same as the value of what we make and is also equal to the income earned from providing resources that were used in the creation of those goods.

Three Measurements of Production, Income, and Expenditure

Gross Domestic Product

Gross domestic product (GDP) is the main tool economists use to measure the production of an economy. Despite some limitations, this raw total is seen as the best for determining the size of an economy. GDP is the total market value of all final goods and services produced in a country within a specified period of time.

GDP represents the total income earned from producing goods in an economy and also the total expenditure made in the economy during the time period, usually a year. There are two primary ways of calculating GDP: the **expenditure method** and the **income method**. The first is an attempt to figure out how many goods a country made by adding up all the amounts that are paid for them when they are finally sold. The second is a method of getting the same figure by totaling the amounts earned for providing the resources that help produce those goods. These two methods are described in more detail in this chapter in the section entitled Two Methods of Adding It Up: GDP's Components.

TEST TIP

The formal definition of GDP is a case in which verbatim memorization is a wise use of time. Taking a word-by-word approach gives you built-in reminders about what is included and what is excluded from GDP. "Market value" reminds you that, to be counted, the goods and services must actually be sold. "Final goods and services" reminds you that intermediate goods are excluded. "Produced" suggests that we account for changes in inventory. "In a country" reminds you to add exports and subtract imports, and specifying the period of time reminds you to exclude resales and can reinforce the idea that GDP is a flow, not a stock, meaning that it is a measurement per unit of time.

Gross National Product

GDP wasn't always the main measure of output used to track economic progress. Prior to 1991, the Bureau of Economic Analysis (BEA) used **gross national product (GNP)** as the main indicator of output. GNP is the total market value of final goods and services produced *by* a country in a specified period of time. Note the difference: GNP assigns production by the ownership of the resources used to create a good. GDP assigns production by the location of the production. **Foreign factor income** is the term for the earnings accrued by citizens of a nation outside their nation. The difference between GNP and GDP is the net foreign factor income. This means we add the income earned from production outside the country by its citizens and subtract the income earned domestically by foreign nationals. If you work while living abroad, you'll be contributing to your homeland's GNP, but your new home's GDP.

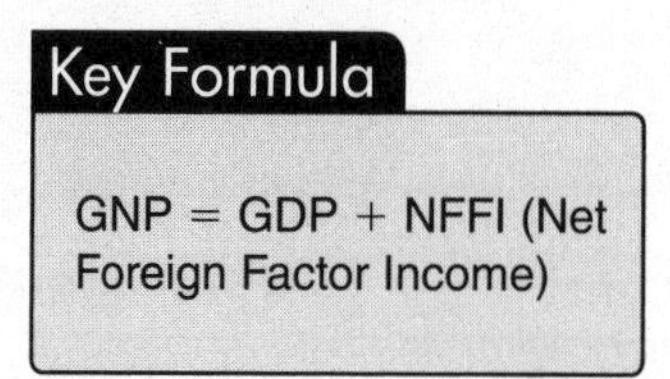

National Income

National income (NI) is the total of payments a country's households have received in a given period of time for providing resources used to make goods and services. Households earn wages and salaries for providing labor, rental payments for providing land, interest for loaning money that will be used to buy capital, and profits for providing entrepreneurial ability. Economists regard national income as a fairly accurate gauge of what a country's citizens spend in a year; in fact, with the earned money left over after taxes (disposable income), consumers really have only two choices: spend or save. NI is also very closely correlated with GDP: Only three adjustments distinguish the income method of calculating GDP from national income and, fortunately for you, they are not emphasized heavily on the AP exam.

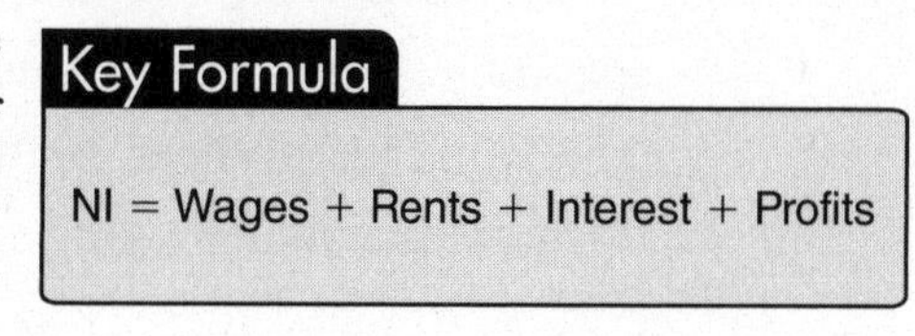

Two Methods of Adding It Up: GDP's Components

Of the various methods used to calculate a country's GDP, two are more directly emphasized on the exam and are comparatively more useful in explaining graphs. These two methods are the expenditure method and the income method.

Expenditure Method

The **expenditure method** of aggregating GDP involves tracking all production by measuring who pays for goods and services at the point of sale. The value of all spending on consumption, gross private investment, government purchases, and net exports is a country's GDP for a given period of time. Many questions will require that you apply formal definitions of each component to either determine which payments are counted in GDP or deduce how a change in one will influence other economic indicators and trends. We'll take each of these components one at a time, addressing its scope and the major factors that cause it to change.

> **Key Formula**
>
> Gross Domestic Product – The Expenditure Method
> $$GDP = C + I + G + (X - M)$$

Consumption (C) is the spending by households on final goods and services that give them satisfaction (or utility). It is the largest of the components, accounting for roughly 70 percent of U.S. GDP annually. Consumer spending can be divided among spending on durable goods, purchases of nondurable goods, and expenditures for services. Durable goods that last many months or even years include cars, furniture, and appliances. Food, newspapers, and gasoline are examples of nondurable goods. Service expenditures range from haircuts and taxi rides on the cheaper side to thousands spent on health care or legal services. Most consumption comes from regularly budgeted household disposable income, but it can come from dipping into savings or from household borrowing. In these latter cases, the amount spent depends in part on the interest rate and is referred to as **interest-sensitive consumption.**

Gross private domestic investment (I) is primarily comprised of business firms spending money to purchase new capital goods. This might involve purchases of physical capital (computers, industrial machinery, delivery trucks, or even new factories) or of human capital (buying training for the firm's workers, for example). Often, firms borrow to make major physical capital purchases, but some of these payments come from saved earnings. Typically new capital machinery has an expected life span and is considered to **depreciate** evenly over that period. Therefore, some investment spending merely replaces the natural wear and tear of tools and machines that form a country's **capital stock**. Net investment is what remains, or the amount by which a nation's capital stock grew (or shrank, if negative) during that year. Two other types of expenditures are included as investment: households purchasing newly constructed homes and changes in business inventories. In this book, use of the term *investment* typically means gross investment: We want to count capital goods that we made and purchased no matter if they were used to replace worn-out old tools or were new additions to the toolkit.

Government purchases (G) includes government spending on salaries for employees; goods bought by the various levels of government; investments made in public infrastructure like roads, bridges, schools, and libraries; and government spending on healthcare, prescription drugs, and the military. Government purchases are distinct from government spending because they do not include **transfer payments** made by the government to individuals. These transfer payments, such as Social Security and unemployment insurance, are not made in exchange for current production and therefore are not counted in GDP.

Net exports (NX or X_n or X − M) include the value of goods purchased by the foreign sector minus the value of foreign goods purchased. **Exports**, or goods produced domestically and sold abroad, are included in GDP because they are goods produced in the nation. **Imports** are goods purchased in a country but made abroad. Why subtract these rather than simply not counting them? The simple answer is that they have already been counted and thus now need to be subtracted. Some of the consumer goods included before, or the capital goods that were counted as part of investment, were produced in other nations. These goods that were picked up along the way are now subtracted, leaving only those produced domestically. The value of net exports for many countries (including the United States) is negative, meaning these countries have a **trade deficit**—they import more than they export. Other countries—China, for example—have trade surpluses because their exports exceed their purchases of imported goods.

Income Method

The **income method** works the other way to determine what we produced in a year: It involves examining all the money payments received for helping to create goods and services rather than thinking about who paid for the goods at the time of purchase. The reasoning goes this way: We know that goods are produced from land, labor, capital, and entrepreneurship. So by adding together wages and salaries, rental payments, interest income, and the different categories of profit, the same total should be reached as when using the expenditure method. With a few minor adjustments, it does. The income method of calculating GDP is quite similar to the measure of national income (explained previously in this chapter). In fact, it is only minor adjustments that separate the two.

Key Formula

Gross Domestic Product - The Income Method
GDP = Wages + Rents + Interest + Profit + Indirect Business Taxes + Depreciation − Net Foreign Factor Income

Wages and salaries (often shortened to simply wages) are the payments made to workers in exchange for labor. Wages include hourly and salaried employees' earnings as well as the market value of nonmonetary compensation such as healthcare benefits. Wages are the largest component of GDP when using the income method.

Rental payments, or **rents**, are payments made in exchange for the use of land. If firms pay private individuals for the use of land to run a store, factory, or office building, the rent is a direct payment. Some firms own the land they use, but rent is still a relevant cost for them: It represents the cost of using their own land because it is a benefit the firm could have realized if it had rented the land to someone else.

Interest payments are made from borrowers to lenders in exchange for the use of money over a period of time. Savings by households are channeled through banks (and other firms in the financial sector) and into investment when businesses borrow to purchase capital equipment or into consumption when, for example, a household takes out a car loan. It will be helpful to think of interest as the price of money from the borrower's point of view. Another useful hint is to simplify by remembering that businesses pay interest for capital: Then the main components in national income and the income formula for GDP all match perfectly with the four economic resources or factors of production.

Profits take different forms depending on the type of corporation. *Proprietors' income* and *corporate profits* are probably the most common terms used to describe types of profit. **Proprietors' income** refers to income earned by those who own sole proprietorships or are members of partnerships. **Corporate profits** are often distributed as dividends to the owners of stock according to their holdings of shares. Corporations, partnerships, and sole proprietorships are taxed slightly differently, distribute risk and liability differently, and have varying levels of flexibility in structuring. These distinctions are typically outside the scope of the AP Macroeconomics exam, however. All you need to know is that profit is what's left over after the firm pays for its costs and that it is the income earned by providing the entrepreneurial ability needed to run a business firm.

These four components form national income, but not quite all of the expenditures we make in a year are included yet. Three adjustments are made to reach GDP. First, indirect business taxes are added. These taxes, like a state's sales tax, are part of expenditure, but they are not received as income in any of the categories above. Adding these to national income yields net national product. Second, a capital consumption allowance for depreciation of capital goods is added. This represents part of the total expenditures made, but because that spending was gobbled up as part of the normal wear and tear on machinery, it wasn't distributed back to households in any of the four categories of national income. Adding in this figure for depreciation generates gross national product. Third, net foreign factor income needs to be subtracted. To be precise, we need to add payments received for domestic production by foreigners and subtract income earned by the country's citizens for providing resources used to produce goods internationally.

Even with these three adjustments, the income method and the expenditure method for any large economy are unlikely to be exactly equal. This can be due to rounding or simply to the volume and variety of transactions completed. The remaining statistical discrepancy is not considered significant; however, the expenditure method is widely regarded as being more accurate.

DIDYOUKNOW?

GDP is quite large. According to the World Bank's 2011 statistics, U.S. GDP was the world's largest, at slightly over $15,000,000,000,000 (that's $15 trillion!), or about twice the size of the next largest economy: the People's Republic of China.

The Circular Flow Revisited

The circular flow of economic activity enables us to visualize both formulas for calculating GDP and to see why they should lead us to equivalent totals. Figure 7-1 (which is repeated from Chapter 3) shows the circular flow again. Now that you know about GDP and the two methods used to calculate it, look for the arrows that represent the components of each formula.

Figure 7-1. Circular Flow Model That Includes the Government (Public Sector) and International Trade

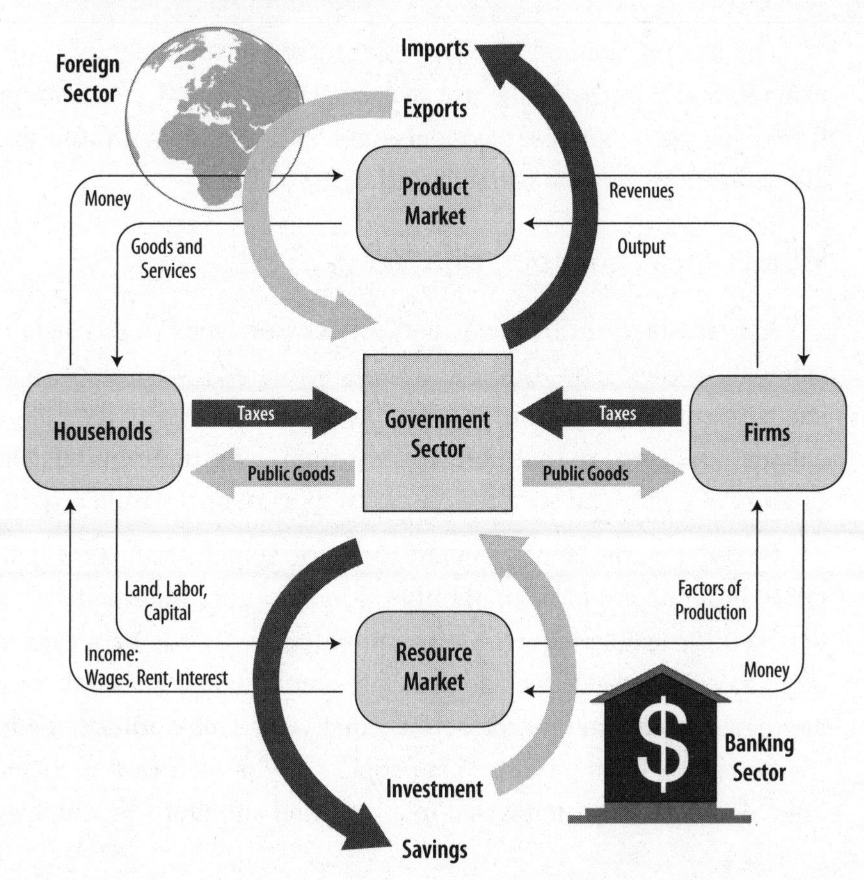

To visualize the expenditure method, see the money flow into the product market represented by consumption. The leakages (income received by households but not spent on domestically produced goods) out of the system such as taxes, purchases of imports, and savings are reintroduced into the product market, either mostly or completely balanced by injections: government purchases, payments received from foreigners who purchase exported goods, and investment. It is also easy to imagine parts of the model disappearing in order to generate a simpler picture. In a **closed economy**, there is presumed to be no international trade, and thus no foreign sector—no imports or exports. A **private economy** does not include taxes or government spending.

TEST TIP

Closed economies and private economies don't exist in the real world, but past AP exam questions have asked about a private, closed economy. If you are faced with this phrasing, remember that it is not designed to trick you, but rather to simplify things so that you don't have to consider the many real-world factors that complicate your life. For example, in a private, closed economy, savings typically equals investment because there are no government deficits (or surpluses), nor are there inflows or outflows of loanable funds.

The income method is even easier to see in the diagram. The payments made by firms to households for the use of land, labor, capital, and entrepreneurial ability are the wages, rents, interest payments, and various types of profit that are the significant elements in the income formula for GDP.

What's in, What's out, and Why?

A few categories of goods and services or types of payments are not included in calculating GDP. You'll need the skills to identify what is or is not included in GDP and to identify the reason why a type of economic activity doesn't count toward the calculation of real output. Recall the formal definition of GDP: the total market value of all final goods and services produced in a country within a specified period of time.

First, let's consider some categories of actual production that are not counted in GDP: in-home production, illicitly sold goods, and intermediate products and services destined for use as inputs in other production. Goods or services that are never sold don't have a market value and therefore aren't counted, even though they are part of the aggregate production for the country that year. This **domestic or in-home production** might include fresh produce that people grow in their own gardens; garments that they knitted and gave to friends and relatives; and situations in which a mechanic works on her own car, a stylist cuts his own children's hair, or a carpenter refinishes a bathroom in her home. These goods and services aren't counted in GDP because, having never been sold, their value would be tough to estimate: Every sale represents at least a moment in time in which two different parties—the buyer and the seller—have agreed on the value of a good. Judging the value of something you made for yourself would be problematic for national income accounting, as would an external judgment of that good's value by a third party that neither produced nor purchased it.

Goods sold around the world each year on **illegal black markets** are estimated to have a higher market value than the annual GDP of any state in the United States, except California, and bigger than all but the ten largest national economies in the world! Predictably, large chunks of this illicit underground economy represent drug and sex trafficking. Larger still, however, is the global trade in counterfeit goods: fake drugs and electronics; knockoff toys, food, and auto parts; and pirated software, movies, music, and video games. These aren't counted in GDP because their production and distribution are hidden and difficult to estimate.

Intermediate goods are excluded from GDP because their value is captured as part of the value of the final good they are used to make. A baker's purchases of flour and yeast are not counted because to do so would result in double counting: The value of the flour has been factored into the price of the loaf of bread because the baker priced the bread to cover his raw material costs. Put another way, when you buy the loaf of bread, part of what you're paying for is the yeast and flour (you're also paying for the labor, electricity, and a small sliver of the rent on the kitchen needed to bake it). To simplify matters when facing a test item, try to think about whether the description of the good suggests that it will be used as an input. Ask yourself, "Will this good be part of the production of another good that will then be sold?" If the answer is yes, then the sale of the good or service should be excluded from GDP calculation.

Second, a few types of economic transactions aren't counted because they don't represent payment for goods and services that were produced. Purely financial transactions, transfer payments, and resale of previously produced goods are three categories of payments that are not counted in a country's aggregate output. **Financial transactions**, such as the purchases of bonds, shares of stock, or mutual funds, are not payments made in exchange for production: No good or service has been made. Bonds represent debt to a government or private firm. They are really fancy pieces of paper that announce, "I can be claimed for a certain amount of money at a given time in the future." If you buy a bond, you have loaned money rather than purchased a good. Similarly, a share of stock is a slice of ownership in a corporation. If that firm earns profit, you may be entitled to a proportional share of it. So purchases of bonds and stocks are excluded, but a couple of tricky spinoff questions could still catch you unaware. The payments for services earned by a bond trader and the commission earned by the stockbroker *are* counted in GDP. Likewise, interest earned on the loan the bond represents and dividends that are paid to a business's shareholders are included. These parts of the transactions do represent a payment for a service and therefore are part of the country's aggregate output.

Transfer payments are also money flows that aren't representative of actual production and are therefore excluded. What are transfer payments? They fall into two categories: public and private. Governments make public transfer payments to private individuals, typically as part of entitlement or income redistribution programs. Social Security deposits into the accounts of elderly Americans and unemployment compensation paid to those looking for work are good examples of transfer payments. Private transfer payments are between individuals. If you've ever received an allowance from your parents or a cash gift from a relative, those are classic cases of private transfer payments. These individuals are not being paid for present work and thus the payments don't factor into our count of national production. No matter how wonderful you are (and the grandparent who slid a crisp $50.00 bill into your last birthday card surely thinks you are even more wonderful), you didn't produce and give marketable goods in exchange for those payments!

Goods that are previously used, when sold again, are excluded from GDP. **Resold goods** have been produced and sold once before. The reason isn't complicated in this case: They should have been counted in the GDP the year when they were first produced, not the year you purchased them at a vintage shop, antique store, or garage sale. Many housing purchases are excluded because most homes sold in a year are not being bought for the first time. As with fees earned on the sale of financial instruments, however, the commissions earned by a real estate agent do count as part of GDP.

Real and Nominal GDP

Because the average level of prices changes as time passes (typically it rises most of the time), comparisons between GDP of a nation across time can become misleading or downright inaccurate unless changing prices are taken into account. For example, if a nation's GDP was $100 billion in 2012 and climbed to $103 billion in 2013, we'd be inclined to say that 3 percent more goods and services were produced in 2013 than in 2012. That may be true, but it could be that all goods were 10 percent more expensive in 2013. In that case, the $103 billion spent on output that year really represents the purchase of *fewer* goods and services. In reality, prices in every economy don't move in lockstep this way: Some goods get more expensive, others get cheaper, and some prices barely move at all.

A price index, or weighted average of prices in an economy for a particular year, is used to convert raw, or nominal, GDP values into real, or inflation-adjusted, values (for more, see the section in this chapter called Price Indices). Nominal GDP for 2012 states the total value of goods and services produced in 2012, with each good valued at the price at which it was sold that year. Nominal GDP for 2013 shows the value of goods and services purchased in 2013 and expressed in 2013 prices. To make more meaningful comparisons, it is necessary to find real GDP values. In this example, to account for inflation (or deflation) that occurred, we want to express 2012's GDP in terms of 2013 prices—raising the value of goods sold in 2012 up to 2013 levels.

Conversely, we could change 2013's GDP back into prices from the prior year, deflating them and ending up with 2013 GDP in 2012 dollars. In that case, we would be using 2012 as the base year and determining what the value of the goods made in 2013 would have been in the year 2012.

You need to do two things: Distinguish real from nominal and convert data between the two. When given information about the output of a country, always consider whether you are given real or nominal data. Most comparisons across large spans of time (or even across short spans of time in highly inflationary circumstances) are meaningless if they are expressed in nominal terms only. As explained later in this chapter, to convert nominal GDP to real GDP, divide by the price index. Multiply by a price index to change values from real to nominal.

Real GDP is a better indicator of economic well-being than nominal GDP. As we've seen, fast inflation can make it seem like a country's output is rising when it isn't. Even when the output is actually rising, we can't tell how many more actual goods and services are being made available to a nation's citizenry unless we can account for inflation.

Per-Capita GDP

Adjusting for wide differences or changes in price level can render unadjusted GDP data more meaningful, and so can accounting for differences or changes in population. Comparing the GDP of one country with a large population (India, about $1.8 trillion in 2011) with a far less populated country (Luxembourg, about $60 billion) suggests that India's economy is about thirty times larger than Luxembourg's. If what we want to do is understand the global flow of goods and services, that figure may be fine. We'd be wrong, however, if we concluded that the average Indian is thirty times as well off as the average Luxembourger. To make conclusions about average economic well being, we need to account for the dramatic difference between populous India and less-populated Luxembourg. In fact, per-capita GDP values, as calculated by the World Bank, are roughly eighty times higher in Luxembourg (about $115,000 per person per year) than India (about $1,500 per person per year).

Cross-time comparisons within a country won't be as dramatically skewed as those presented in this chapter, but they would still be misleading if you didn't keep per-capita values in mind. If a country's population grew faster than its GDP, there would now be more goods and services produced each year, but fewer available for each person living there.

That is not quite the end of the story for India and Luxembourg. Adjusting for *both* differences in population and the average level of prices between the two countries generates an even better comparison of what it is like to be a person in the middle of the socioeconomic spectrum in each nation. We need to adjust per-capita GDP for differences in **purchasing power parity (PPP)**, a term for the varying the cost of living between and among countries. Much like using a price index to compare data from one country across time with different price levels, this adjustment allows more meaningful comparisons between places where goods and services are dramatically cheaper than others. In this case, goods are substantially pricier in Luxembourg than they are in India: Adjusted for PPP, Luxembourg's per-capita GDP is about $90,000. When compared to India's PPP-adjusted $3,600 per capita GDP, we can make a more meaningful conclusion that the typical resident of Luxembourg can purchase something like twenty-five times the real value of goods and services as the typical resident of India can.

GDP's Imperfections

A final word of caution: Even after converting data to PPP-adjusted per-capita values, GDP still has some limitations in terms of giving us a sense of how well the citizens of a country are doing. It doesn't tell us anything about the distribution of wealth or income in a country. There may be plenty of earnings, but they might be highly concentrated among a small group of elites and the masses may be surviving at a subsistence level. GDP also doesn't tell us anything about noneconomic measures of well-being that affect us greatly. Political rights and social freedoms are not measured at all. The overall level of health and the amount of leisure time the people have to enjoy the goods and services they work hard to buy aren't factored in. Crime rates and corruption are not taken into consideration. Also, some expenditures make people better off, others merely fix damages, and some production creates harm in the process. However, GDP treats each dollar spent the same. Accounting for any of these factors would probably be difficult and subject to much debate. GDP has its critics, and many organizations have developed other attempts at measuring overall well-being (economic or otherwise). Nonetheless, warts and all, GDP remains the most commonly referenced measure of macroeconomic health and is certainly one of the concepts you need to know and understand if you are going to do well on the AP exam.

Inflation

Inflation is the general rise in prices in an economy over time, sometimes defined colloquially as too much money chasing too few goods. While most people (and most economists) don't regard it as a welcome phenomenon, it isn't much of a problem if the rate of change of prices is stable, low, and predictable. Often, however, it isn't. Most countries have central banks with the power to take action to keep price levels stable. In some cases, they try to engineer economies with no inflation at all—in practice, a difficult task. Sometimes they aim to have a positive, but low, inflation rate (in recent years the U.S. central bank, the Federal Reserve, has become more open about its goal of 2 percent inflation for the U.S. economy) because they fear the effects of falling prices, or **deflation**, even more than the effects of inflation. You'll need to know different causes and types of inflation, how it is measured, and which groups tend to be helped or harmed by inflation, all of which will be covered below. In Chapter 8, you'll also learn how to show two different types of inflation in graph form. Chapter 10 will provide more coverage of the methods by which central banks try to keep prices relatively stable and some reasons why they tolerate (and sometimes even encourage) a little inflation.

How Inflation Happens

Inflation can develop due to three primary causes. First, **demand-pull inflation** is the rise in prices that develops when more buyers (or richer buyers) desire more goods and pull up the prices by bidding against one another. An unexpected rise in aggregate expenditures is typically the cause. Put another way, buyers are now willing to purchase the same quantity of real output at a higher price level than before. At the initial price level, buyers are willing to buy more goods than are produced; as goods fly off the shelves, sellers order more stock and increase the price tags on the merchandise. Demand-pull inflation is usually correlated with high levels of output, faster growth, and lower unemployment. After all, it takes more work from more producers to try to produce the greater quantities of goods that are demanded. More people are working and fewer are out of work.

Another way that inflation can occur is if the costs of inputs rise and make production more expensive. Firms now need to charge a higher price for any given level of output or produce less output at the same price level. These rising costs of production result in higher prices for final goods in a process known as **cost-push inflation**. Cost-push inflation produces a decrease in overall output while prices rise; the stagnant economy and the inflation have been merged into the term **stagflation**, which you should recognize as connected to cost-push inflation. Stagflation was a persistent and frustrating problem for U.S. macroeconomic policymakers during the 1970s due to rising energy prices.

One of the major schools of twentieth-century economic thought, the monetarists, argued that lack of proper control of the supply of money in an economy was the primary cause of inflation. The fundamental principle is that increasing the amount of money pulsing through the circular flow without a commensurate increase in the productive resources of the economy would only increase prices. Milton Friedman, the most famous of the monetarists, famously said, "Inflation is always and everywhere a monetary phenomenon." Taking the logic a step further, he claimed that all sustained increases in price levels are due to faster growth in money than in production.

Inflation and the expectation of continued inflation can also be causes for prices to continue to rise. When the price level rises and people have reason to believe that it will continue to do so, further inflation can be the result. As buyers anticipate inflation, they purchase more goods before prices jump upward. In doing so, they pull up prices. Similarly, expectations of future inflation lead to faster increases in input costs; in particular, wage rates rise because workers want wages that will purchase the same quantity of real output. Workers believe they need more dollars to accomplish their buying needs. Unions are reluctant to accept wage rates that leave workers feeling poorer; thus, larger cost-of-living increases are built into long-term labor contracts.

DIDYOUKNOW?

Hyperinflation, or out-of-control spirals of rising prices, has caused economies to break down and currencies to be devalued. Governments have unwisely printed currency at a much faster rate than the economy's productive capacity grew in a misguided attempt to avoid taxing or borrowing, or because the regime was at risk of collapse. The most famous case is probably 1923 Germany, in which the inflation rate reached nearly 30,000 percent. In fall 2008, Zimbabwe suffered a peak inflation rate of 79,600,000,000 percent, with prices doubling about once a day.

Price Indices

How are inflation rates calculated? The process starts with the creation of a price index. A **price index** is a weighted average of all the prices in an economy used to measure the **price level**, which can change from year to year, be influenced by governmental policies, or be higher or lower than expected in a given year. Why is a weighted average needed? Because the prices of some goods rise while others fall, it isn't always obvious what is happening to prices in general in an economy. Some categories of goods (energy, for instance) tend to fluctuate far more than others. Some categories of goods (like housing) take up a large portion of a typical household's budget and need to be heavily weighed in the construction of the price index.

TEST TIP

It is likely that you will need to answer a few questions about the way price indices are calculated or about their drawbacks on the AP economics exams. It is also fairly certain that a large number of questions will require that you be comfortable with the concept of the price level and what causes it to change.

All price levels are expressed relative to a **base year**. The base year price level is typically 100 (sometimes 1.00) and is the year into which later or earlier values are converted. Years with lower prices than the base year have price levels below 100; these are typically be years before the base year. A price level of 200 indicates that goods are twice as expensive, on average, than they were in the base year.

There are several price indices that you may see in the news: the consumer price index (CPI), producer price index (PPI), GDP deflator, and personal consumption expenditures (PCE) index are four of the more noteworthy ones. Each has a slightly different formula, sometimes designed to measure a different price trend. The PPI, for instance, tracks changes in wholesale prices in an attempt to anticipate how retail prices will change in the months ahead. The Federal Reserve uses the PCE index to compare core values (which exclude the volatile food and energy sectors) with overall (or headline) values in its forecasts.

The Consumer Price Index

The basic idea of the consumer price index (CPI) is to figure out how much a fixed market basket (an unchanging set of goods that a typical urban household might buy) would cost in a specific year. To calculate CPI, start by figuring out the cost of the market basket in the base year. Then figure out how much that same assortment of goods would cost in another year—the same quantities of the same goods, but at new prices. Divide the new cost of the basket by the old cost of the same basket and multiply by 100 to get a price index for the given year. Let's walk through an example below.

Suppose that in a very simplified economy, citizens buy the following basket of goods each month:

- Four pounds of coffee
- Five dozen eggs
- Thirty pizzas
- One unit of housing (this could be a standard mortgage payment or rent on an apartment)

Below are sample prices for the goods in each of three years:

Year	Coffee	Eggs	Pizza	Housing
1	$5.00/lb.	$2.00/doz.	$10.00	$1,670
2	$7.50/lb.	$2.00/doz.	$12.00	$1,800
3	$12.50/lb.	$3.00/doz.	$15.00	$2,125

First, calculate market basket cost for each year:

Year 1: 4($5.00) + 5($2.00) + 30($10.00) + $1,670 = $2,000

Year 2: 4($7.50) + 5($2.00) + 30($12.00) + $1,800 = $2,200

Year 3: 4($12.50) + 5($3.00) + 30($15.00) + $2,125 = $2,640

Second, find the price index for each year. In this case, using year 1 as the base year:

Year 1: $(2{,}000/2{,}000) \times 100 = 100$

Year 2: $(2{,}200/2{,}000) \times 100 = 110$

Year 3: $(2{,}640/2{,}000) \times 100 = 132$

In general, divide the cost of the market basket in a given year by the cost in the base year and multiply by 100.

Calculating an Inflation Rate

With this information, you are now in a position to calculate the inflation rate from one year to the next. Just like any rate of increase, take the new value, subtract the prior value, divide by the prior value, and express as a percentage.

The inflation rate between year 1 and year 2 is $(110 - 100)/100 = 10\%$

Between year 2 and year 3, prices rose faster $(132 - 110)/110 = 20\%$

If we had used year 3 as the base year, the same inflation rates would have applied, but the price indices would have been different (year 1 would be 75.8 and year 2 would be 83.4). Confirm that these price index numbers generate the same inflation rates. Then try to rework the problem with year 2 as the base year and see if you get the same percentage increase in prices.

TEST TIP

Finding price indices and using them to calculate inflation rates is one of the few areas you need to calculate with precision on the AP exam. It pays to practice this enough so that you feel confident and avoid spending a long time on one question that frustrates you. Remember two key hints: First, since you can't use a calculator on the exam, you won't be expected to crunch lots of nasty numbers. If you get irregular decimals, double-check how you've set up the problem. Second, use your common sense. In the case presented in this chapter, prices rose each year, and we can tell that they rose more between year 2 and year 3 because housing alone increased more than the whole market basket did the prior year. Confirming that the values you reach using the formulas make sense in the context of the problem is a simple way to avoid mistakes.

Nominal and Real Values

A price index is also a basic tool that allows conversion between real and nominal values. To convert real to nominal, multiply by the price index for the given year, and divide by 100. If you are given nominal GDP and a price index for a specific year and you are asked to find real GDP in a base year's dollars, divide by the price level and multiply by 100. You will then be able to make a more meaningful comparison between output levels in two different years. When converting nominal output from years with price levels lower than the base year into real values, your resulting real GDP should be higher than the nominal value you started with. When converting nominal values from a higher-priced year than the base year to real values, your result should be lower—you have "deflated" the value to account for the effects of inflation. Be conscious of whether you are looking at raw unadjusted nominal numbers or inflation-adjusted real numbers in any economic situation, whether it be on the AP exam or in the real world: Many graphics and news bites exaggerate effects by leaving data in nominal terms.

Key Formula

Nominal Value = (Price Level / 100) × Real Value

Real Value = (100 / Price Level) × Nominal Value

DIDYOUKNOW?

In the United States, the hourly minimum wage typically stays fixed in nominal terms for a period of years. During this time, the real value declines as prices rise. When the wage of $0.25 per hour was introduced in 1938, it could buy the equivalent of about $4.00 at 2009 price levels. The wage has been increased three times since 2007 to $7.25 per hour, but is lower in real value than the 1968 federal wage floor of less than $2.00 per hour!

Inflation Creates Losers and Winners

Inflation isn't always obvious when it is happening because prices move up and down and change directions. Inflation is the general trend of the overall average of those prices. The level of inflation is even less clear when you are trying to anticipate the future. The price level often rises by more or less than was expected. When prices rise at a different rate than people in an economy believed that they would, some wealth is transferred between or among groups.

Faster than anticipated inflation is a threat to those living on fixed incomes, savers, and those who loaned money to be repaid at a fixed interest rate. However, borrowers and those with long-term purchase contracts can benefit. From the perspective of a worker with a wage rate that's been negotiated for the next two years or a retiree with a fixed pension, the harm of rising prices is clear: The same number of nominal dollars has less purchasing power and translates into a smaller basket of real output (goods and services). Individuals saving for a large purchase (or retirement) may feel as if they are running toward a receding finish line. Loans with a fixed interest rate have repayment plans with specific fixed monthly payments. The lender, when repaid, receives lower and lower real value with each successive payment in an inflationary climate, and if inflation is more than it was forecast to be, those payments have a lower real value than anticipated when the interest rate was calculated at the time the money was lent.

Borrowers, on the other hand, get to pay back dollars that are less valuable than the ones they borrowed if the price level rises; with fast inflation, the dollars paid at the end of the loan (perhaps five years for a car, as long as thirty for a house) are worth far less than anyone might have anticipated. If the terms of your lease allow you to renew for the same rent, inflation enables you to pay less in real purchasing power for the same apartment.

When inflation is slower than it was expected to be, the opposite effects occur. Borrowers are harmed because they pay back money that was more valuable than they thought it would be. Under this circumstance, savers and lenders come out ahead.

TEST TIP

Think of dollars in times of low inflation or low price levels as being powerful. When the price level rises, your dollars get weaker. Inflation inflates the prices and zaps power away from your dollars. To purchase a gallon of gasoline and a soda, you could still have change to spare from a single powerful dollar of the 1950s. Today, a gallon of gasoline and a soda could cost $5.00 or more!

Unemployment

The unemployment rate is the third major broad indicator for you to master. In general, because unemployment measures people out of work, it is safe to conclude that typically it is inversely related to output and inflation. As more goods and services are produced, more workers are needed for production and sales, and pressure on prices rises. If the economy is sluggish and output is low, fewer workers are needed and there isn't as much spending that normally pushes prices upward most of the time.

Defining and Measuring Unemployment

Unemployed individuals are workers who have not worked in the last week and have been actively looking for work during the last month or are awaiting recall from a layoff. **Employed individuals** have worked for pay, worked at one's own or a family business, or are temporarily absent from a continuing job (because of sickness or vacation leave). Notice that not everyone is either employed or unemployed; many people are not in either category. The **labor force** is made up of people between the ages of 16 and 65 who are willing and able to work. Individuals not counted in the labor force are those who are institutionalized, military personnel, students, homemakers, retirees, the disabled, and "discouraged" workers (to be described in more depth later in the next paragraph). The labor force participation rate is the percentage of the adult civilian noninstitutionalized population who is in the labor force.

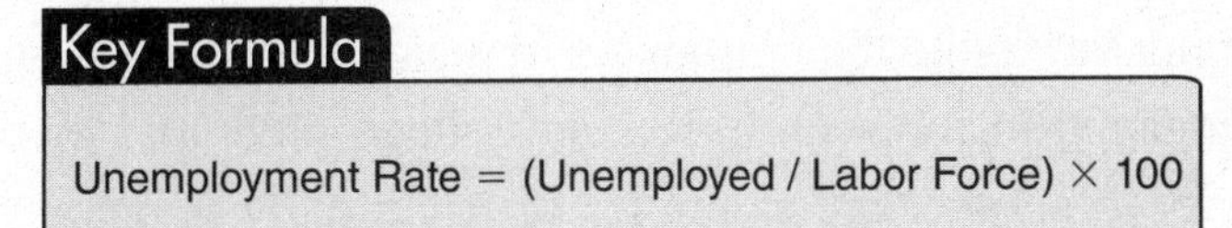

The **unemployment rate** is the percentage of the labor force that is unemployed, expressed as a percentage. If there are 100 people in an economy's workforce and six are unemployed, the unemployment rate is 6 percent. According to the U.S. Bureau of Labor Statistics (BLS), in October 2012 there were 155,641,000 members of the civilian labor force; 12,258,000 were unemployed, for an unemployment rate of 7.9 percent. Because some unemployed workers stop looking for work, they are not counted in the official unemployment rate as calculated by the BLS and are known as **discouraged workers.** They aren't counted because they are technically not part of the labor force.

DIDYOUKNOW?

The official unemployment rate is only one of six rates tracked by the BLS—it is actually called U3. Since 1950, the BLS has calculated the percentage of the workforce unemployed for fifteen weeks or longer, a narrower measure of unemployment known as U1. U4 is broader than the official rate and includes discouraged workers. U6, the broadest measure of all, includes both discouraged workers and those who are working part-time but who are seeking full-time employment.

Types of Unemployment

Unemployed individuals can fall into different categories: structural, frictional, and cyclical unemployment.

Structural unemployment results from workers having skills that are no longer in demand. As technology advances, capital machinery sometimes can accomplish what human labor once did and, over time, buyers' tastes can change. When workers are replaced by computerized robots or production jobs are outsourced, workers become structurally employed. Workers whose job skills are not suited to technological advances are likely to remain unemployed until they acquire skills for in-demand jobs. For this reason, structural unemployment can be long-lasting and particularly painful.

Frictional unemployment describes workers who have skills that are valued in the economy but who have not yet found the employers to match those skills—it is closely related to time spent engaged in job search. Recent college graduates or professionals moving from one city to another are examples of frictionally unemployed people engaged in job searches. These workers usually find work faster than the structurally unemployed; they have marketable skills and therefore don't need to learn new skills in order to be hired.

Cyclical unemployment results from general swings in the business cycle. During recessions, this kind of unemployment rises and spikes when output is farthest below the full employment level. When the economy grows quickly and GDP is higher than usual, cyclical unemployment drops and can even be negative. How? Employers gobble up frictionally and structurally unemployed workers to meet the temporary increase in demand.

In a world with no business cycle in which real output is always at its potential level, there is no cyclical unemployment. **Potential output** (or potential GDP) is the level of real output that an economy can sustain while using all of its productive resources. It is what the output would be were it not subject to the fluctuations of the business cycle.

Natural Rate of Unemployment

When the economy is operating at potential GDP, otherwise known as **full-employment output**, not everyone in the labor force has a job. That much production always comes with some technological innovation, leaving some people structurally unemployed. New opportunities and ambitions always leave some talented, employable people looking for work and thus frictionally unemployed. However, cyclical unemployment would not exist. The amount of residual unemployment (frictional and structural) that remains when an economy is at full-employment output is called the **natural rate of unemployment (NRU)**. Another way to think of NRU is that it is the rate of unemployment that exists when the number of job seekers matches the number of job vacancies. People are still unemployed because some are still transitioning from one job to another and others are in need of acquiring skills to be hired for the available jobs.

While a country's unemployment rate tends to revert back to the NRU, the NRU can change over time due to changes in labor force participation trends or advances in the speed with which frictionally unemployed workers can connect with those who want to hire them. NRU can also vary from one country to the next. Countries with social welfare policies that mitigate the impact of unemployment tend to have higher natural rates of unemployment. The NRU for the U.S. economy is estimated to be 5 to 6 percent, which is a bit lower than Canada and most of western Europe.

Chapter 8

The Aggregate Demand and Aggregate Supply Model

Goal of the Aggregate Demand and Aggregate Supply Model: Income and Price Determination

The most significant and heavily tested graph in macroeconomics is the aggregate demand and aggregate supply (AD-AS) model. The free-response section will almost always require you to reproduce this graph and use it to show the effects of various changes on real output and on the price level. This graph allows you to apply basic demand and supply analysis (covered in Chapter 3) to the overall market for all goods and services. Many of the same principles that governed demand and supply work with aggregate demand and aggregate supply, but often the explanations you use to justify shifts are different.

The fundamental principle is that the point of intersection between aggregate demand and aggregate supply determines the equilibrium level of real output and also therefore national income. The resulting equilibrium price level leads producers to want to sell the same quantity of real output that buyers want to purchase. The different types of inflation are easy to depict with this graph, as are the effects of governmental policies (explained in Chapter 10).

It may be helpful to think of the AD-AS graph as a central hub for your macroeconomics studies: While there are other graphs you need to know, this is the most important one.

The changes you may be asked to show or consider on other graphs usually influence or are caused by changes in the AD-AS picture. Many of the questions that don't explicitly mention this model are easier to figure out by thinking in terms of it. Let's get started!

Aggregate Demand as a Concept

Recall that demand is the relationship between the price of a good and the quantity demanded of that good over a specified period of time. **Aggregate demand** is the inverse relationship between the price level in an economy and the quantity of real gross domestic product (GDP) demanded.

Note that it is the average price level rather than price of a specific good. Aggregate demand is a bit like demand for all goods and services shown as one demand curve. It is a summation of all the buying plans of all the actors in an economy, including households, firms, all the levels of government, and the foreign sector.

Figure 8-1. An Aggregate Demand (AD) Curve

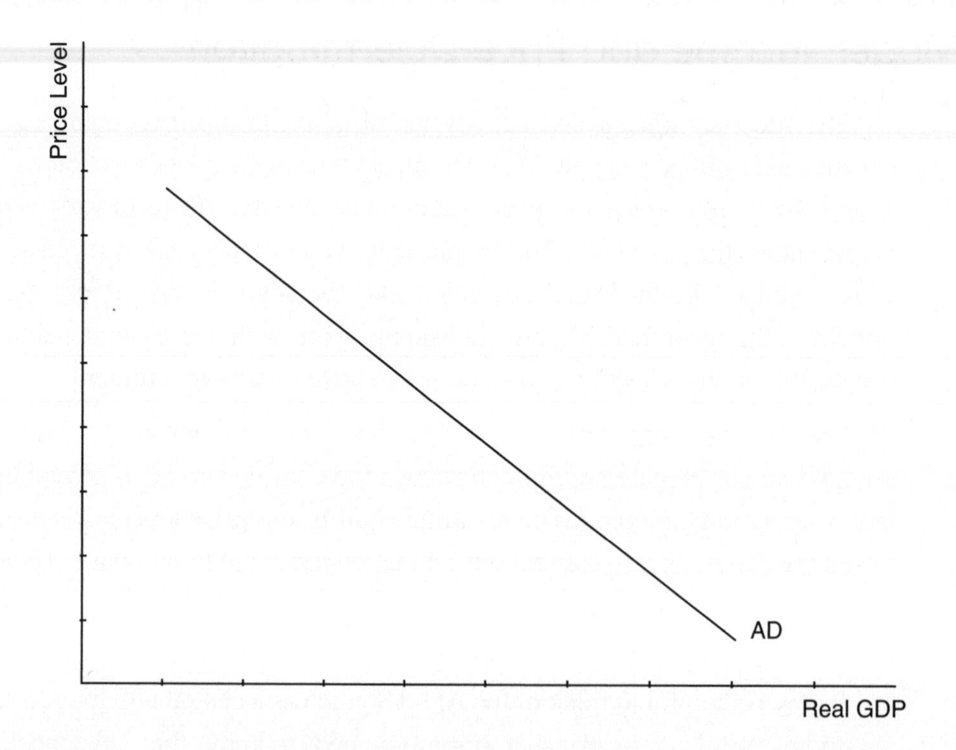

Figure 8-1 shows an aggregate demand curve. While it looks like a demand curve, the axis labels are different, reflecting the fact that AD shows a relationship between different variables than a simple demand function does.

TEST TIP

While AD is drawn in this chapter as a linear curve (straight line), it is really a matter of personal preference whether to put a bit of a bend in it or not—if curved, it is typically shown as convex to the origin (bowed inward). In this book, AD is shown as linear because curvature does not make a significant difference in any items on the AP exam. When it comes to drawing aggregate supply, you will need to pay more attention to slope. Save your worries about curves and slope for AS, not AD.

The Slope of AD

Demand curves slope down for three reasons: diminishing marginal utility, the income effect, and the substitution effect (see Chapter 3). None of these are quite enough explanation for the downward slope of aggregate demand. However, there are three explanations for why a lower price level induces us to want to purchase a higher quantity of real output and why we desire fewer goods and services when overall prices are higher.

Wealth Effect

Why would a higher price level lead people to purchase fewer goods and services? The balances in their savings accounts have not risen. Thus, nominal wealth is the same, but because the price level has risen, real wealth is reduced. The feeling of being less wealthy leads rational buyers to cut back on current purchasing to allocate more income toward savings because the long-term goals toward which we save have become harder to reach. This wealth effect (also called the real-balances effect) causes a lower quantity of real GDP to be demanded at higher price levels.

The reverse is also true: When the price level declines, buyers have more real wealth in their savings; thus, they feel less like saving current income and feel inclined to spend more of their current earnings. This leads to a higher quantity of real GDP demanded.

Interest Rate Effect

As price levels rise, the same amount of nominal money has less purchasing power—its real value is reduced. Because more nominal money (a greater number of dollars) is required in order to purchase needed goods and services, people keep less money in banks and keep more money on hand to perform transactions. Less available funds in banks pushes up real interest rates (see the section in Chapter 10 called The Loanable Funds Market) and therefore reduces the level of private investment. Because investment is a component of GDP, the quantity of output demanded declines.

The effect also works in reverse. At lower price levels, people don't need as much money on hand to make transactions, so more is held in banks. Banks have more to lend and therefore lend at cheaper real interest rates, which encourages investment. Thus, more real GDP is demanded at lower price levels.

Net Export Effect

As prices in an economy rise, domestically produced goods become comparatively less attractive to both buyers within the country and to foreign consumers. The nation's citizens purchase more imported goods and fewer domestic ones. Foreign consumers respond similarly, desiring to purchase fewer of the country's exported goods. Net exports (exports minus imports) therefore decline, reducing the quantity of real output demanded.

The reverse explanation also holds: Lower price levels mean domestic goods and services are cheaper to produce than they used to be compared to foreign goods. Imports are less attractive, and exports gain appeal in foreign markets. Net exports rise, pushing up the level of real GDP demanded.

These three effects reinforce one another, so no graph can show the differences among them. However, Figure 8-2 depicts the effect of an increase in price level on quantity of real GDP demanded.

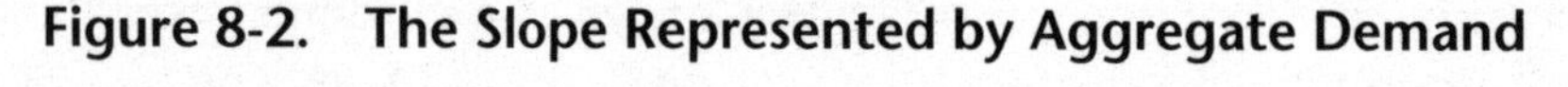

Figure 8-2. The Slope Represented by Aggregate Demand

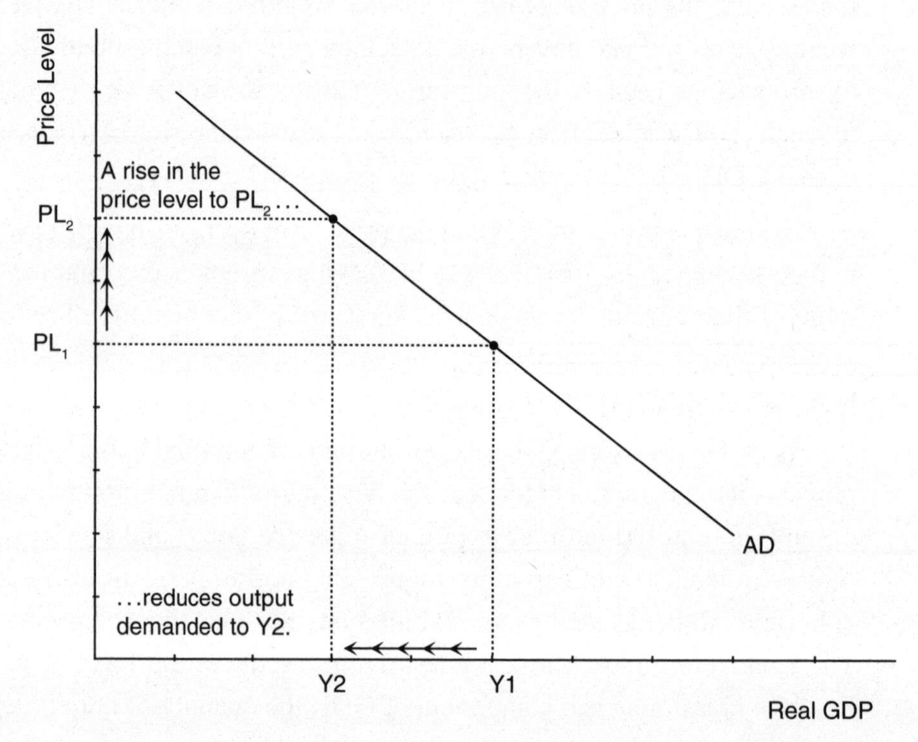

Aggregate Demand's Components and Their Behavior

The components that make up AD and the factors that influence each are absolutely essential to know. Several questions in the multiple-choice section of the AP exam will expect you to know how and why AD shifts, and this topic will often be covered in the free-response section of the test as well. The best way to be sure whether (and in which direction) AD moves and the most solid explanation for why it does so is by referencing the specific component that changes and articulating concisely what caused that component to change.

Fortunately, you already know the components of AD: They are the exact same ones that comprise the expenditure formula for calculating GDP, namely, consumption, investment, government purchases, and net exports. This should not be tough to recall because expenditures logically connect to purchasing and the idea of demand. This chapter explains what causes each of these components to change and therefore the major factors that shift the aggregate demand curve.

Key Formula

AD = C + I + G + (X − M)

Consumption

As explained in Chapter 7, consumption is the total of all expenditures by households and individuals on finished goods and services in the product market. Consumption is the largest share of GDP for many, if not most, countries. In the United States, roughly 70 percent of GDP each year is made up of consumption expenditures, which can include purchases of necessities such as food, haircuts, and fuel as well as larger purchases that might be financed by borrowing, like the purchase of durable goods or vacation spending. Several factors govern households' level of planned consumption: disposable income (DI), the marginal propensity to consume, the level of household wealth, expectations about future prices or income, and the interest rate.

Disposable Income and Consumption

The single best predictor of the level of consumption of an individual household is the amount of income available to it; similarly, national income bears a strong positive correlation with aggregate consumption. A household's disposable income is that which is left over after taxes. A rise in gross (pretax) income or a reduction in taxes, other things equal, would leave households with more take-home pay that can be allocated between consumption of goods and services in the present or savings that can be used to make purchases in the future. **As disposable income rises, the level of consumption rises**. This relationship should be obvious enough that memorizing it won't be necessary: You almost certainly spend more on goods and services when you have more to spend, and that relationship most likely holds true for the people you know. The more people earn, the more they tend to spend. Thus, an increase in disposable income shifts the AD curve to the right.

Consumption and Savings Functions

The consumption function shows the relationship between income and consumption. The savings function shows the relationship between income and savings. The two are related because, at any level of income, savings and consumption, when added together, must equal disposable income. For now, we'll ignore the effects of taxes and assume that all income is disposable. While that isn't true in real life, it often does apply to simplified problems you'll face on the AP exam that are related to savings and consumption. There are only two things you can do with your money: Spend it or save it!

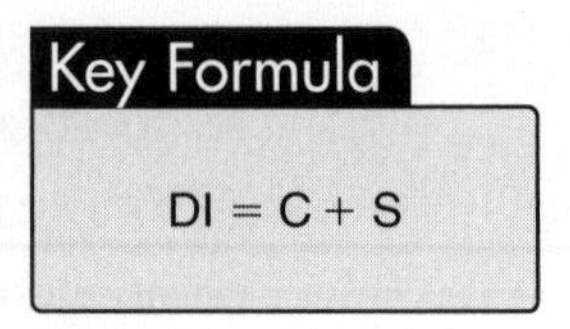

Figure 8-3. The Consumption Function

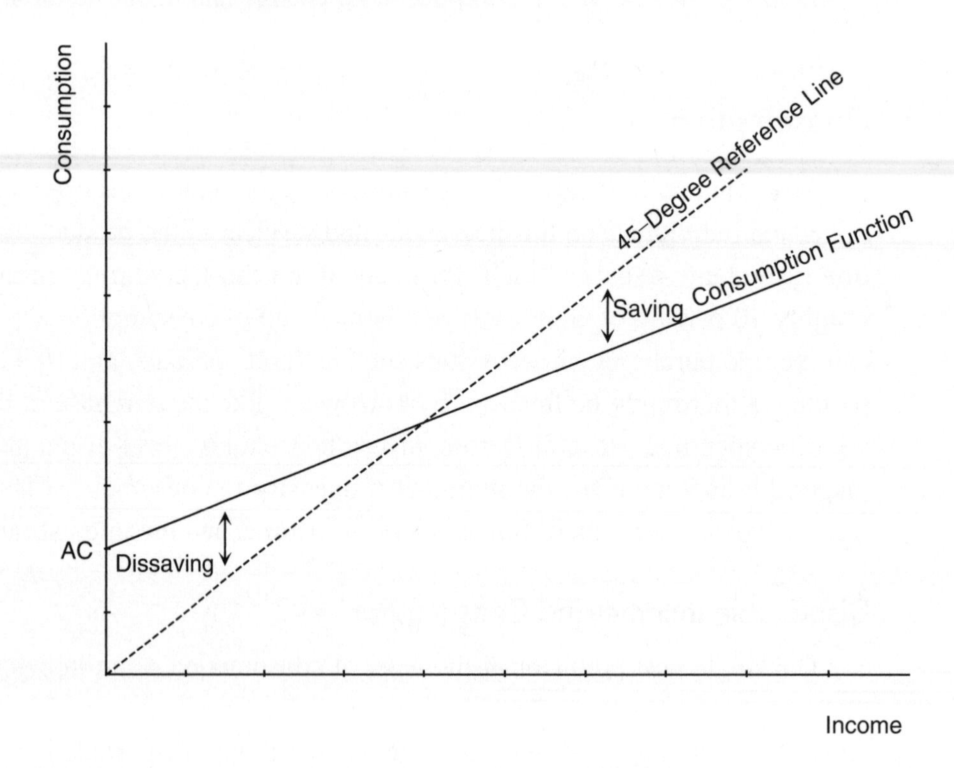

Figure 8-3 shows a consumption function; Figure 8-4 shows a savings function. From earlier analysis, you already know that the consumption function slopes upward. The dotted 45-degree reference line allows easy visual comparison between consumption and income because it is the set of points for which the two are equal. Note that, at low levels of income, consumption exceeds income; as income increases, consumption rises

Figure 8-4. The Savings Function

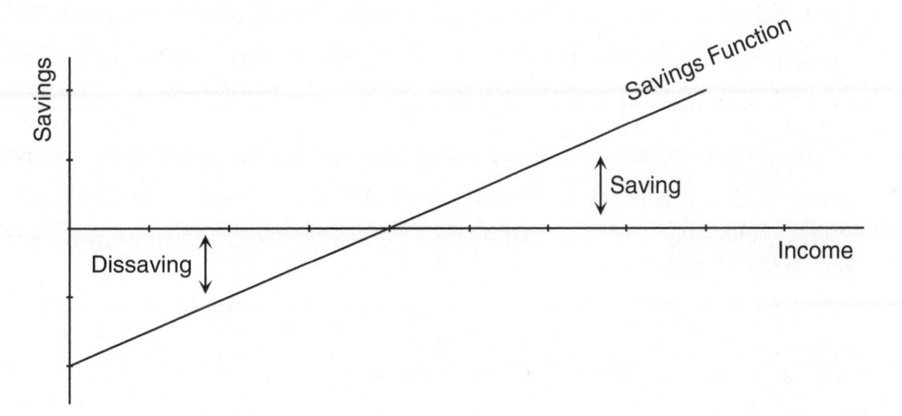

more slowly than income. This is because increases in income lead not only to more consumption but also to more saving. The vertical space between the reference line and the consumption function is the level of saving or dissaving. At very low levels of income, households may dip into prior savings or borrow in order to meet their consumption needs, a process known as **dissaving**. The amount of spending that a household or population will engage in regardless of income earned is called **autonomous consumption (AC)**. The extreme case, with no earned income, is shown as point AC in Figure 8-3. In this case, AC is 2. For any given income level, the amount of consumption is 2 plus however much consumption occurs as a result of earned income, known as **induced consumption**. At high levels of income, savings is positive because consumption is lower than the amount earned.

The savings function shows the gap between consumption and income: the saving or dissaving at each level of income. The most important facts to keep in mind about these two functions are (1) both savings and consumption are positively correlated to the level of income, (2) savings is the difference between income and consumption, and (3) they typically move in opposite directions—one shifting up and the other down—*unless* disposable income changes. In that case, both shift up if DI increases and down if DI decreases.

Marginal Propensities to Save and Consume

Now let's consider the slopes of the two lines that represent the consumption and savings functions. We know that, as income rises, both savings and consumption increase. However, the rate at which they increase is significant. Consider what happens when you have an increase in your paycheck or allowance: Probably you spend most of that increase and save a little of it. Typically, if income increases, consumption increases more than savings does. No matter the degree to which both increase, however, the total of the increase in savings and the increase in consumption is always equal to the increase in disposable income. There really isn't anything else that households can do with the new income except to save it or spend it.

The proportion of an increase in income that is spent on consumption is called the **marginal propensity to consume (MPC)**. It is represented by the slope of the consumption function. For the consumption function shown in Figure 8-3, the MPC is 0.5, which means that each new dollar of income results in a 75-cent increase in consumption.

Key Formula

$MPC = \Delta C / \Delta DI$

The proportion of an increase in income that is saved is called the **marginal propensity to save (MPS)**. It is represented by the slope of the savings function. For the savings function shown in Figure 8-4, the MPS is 0.5. This means that each new dollar of income results in 25 cents of increased savings.

Key Formula

$MPS = \Delta S / \Delta DI$

Note that the value of MPC and MPS total 1. All of the added income is either devoted to increased consumption or increased savings. Remember, income can either be spent or saved, and the same must be true of new income resulting from, for example, a pay raise. If MPC is more than 1, MPS must be negative.

Key Formula

$MPC + MPS = 1$

TEST TIP

MPC and MPS may change for individuals in the real world as their income changes. Perhaps when you're just squeaking by, an extra dollar of income leads to almost a whole dollar of added consumption, but if you have enough disposable income to meet all your needs and already have nearly everything you want, you'd be inclined to save most of an income increase. AP exam problems that specify a value for either MPS or MPC usually make the assumption that those are constant. Thus, if you're told that the MPC is 0.8, assume that everyone in the economy spends 80 percent of every additional dollar they earn. This makes solving these types of problems easier even if it isn't the most accurate representation of how people really behave.

Changes in MPC and MPS result in a change of slope in the consumption and savings functions. This means that any change in income leads to a bigger (if MPC increases) or smaller (if MPC decreases) change in consumption. The section in this chapter called The Multiplier Effect: Magnifying Initial Changes in AD explains this concept in more detail.

Wealth and Consumption

Another factor that governs the quantity of consumption in an economy is the wealth of households. The wealthier consumers are (or feel that they are), the more they will spend; if they feel or are less wealthy, they will spend less. Past AP exams have sometimes had prompts asking for the effect on AD of an increase in the value of stock portfolios or of the value of homes owned by households.

When the value of assets owned rises, individuals are wealthier, and they tend to spend, shifting the consumption function upward and the savings function downward. AD moves to the right, pulling up real GDP and the price level in the process. Conversely, a decrease in household wealth leads families to save more and spend less. This shifts the consumption function downward and the savings function up. As a result, AD decreases, shifting left and resulting in a decrease in real GDP and the price level.

Consumer Confidence and Expectations

As consumers' views and predictions about the future change, so do their buying plans in the present. The most significant expectation for a given consumer is about what will happen to her individual income in the future. Thus, for an entire economy, the key expectation is about the state of the economy in the future. Economic indicators that attempt to measure how confident consumers are about future economic health seek to find out what those beliefs are—the most commonly cited of these is the University of Michigan Consumer Sentiment Index.

If consumers feel hopeful about their future income prospects or the economy as a whole, then they are likely to spend more freely now, increasing the consumption function and aggregate demand. On the other hand, if the outlook among consumers is pessimistic, households are likely to rearrange their budgets to save more for the coming tough times, spending less in the present. The savings function shifts upward, the consumption function shifts downward, and AD decreases, moving leftward and causing a decrease in real GDP and the price level.

Interest Rates and Consumption

Some types of consumption expenditures depend on the interest rate. **Interest-sensitive consumption** refers to the categories of consumption that are influenced by the interest rate. These categories typically include larger, more expensive purchases.

Cars, furniture, appliances, home remodeling, college tuition expenses, and vacations are often paid for over a period of time by borrowing on credit. The lower the interest rate, the cheaper it is to borrow and the more attractive those purchases seem. As a result, interest-sensitive consumption increases and shifts AD rightward. When interest rates are high, borrowing is costly and households are less inclined to make major purchases, instead waiting to do so when conditions are more favorable. So a rise in the interest rate causes interest-sensitive consumption and aggregate demand to decrease.

DIDYOUKNOW?

You will often find the sellers of large items spending more time talking about the low interest rates they offer than the products they are selling. Car dealers are among the most likely to advertise an especially low annual percentage (interest) rate (APR) to increase sales. It seems unlikely that car dealers would focus so heavily on this were it not to influence our collective behavior.

Investment

In Chapter 7, you read that gross private domestic investment is composed mainly of firms acquiring new capital goods, but that it also includes changes in the inventories of businesses and the purchase of newly-constructed homes by households.

Investment is a much smaller share of annual GDP than is consumption for many nations, but it is usually far more volatile than consumption. In the United States, investment often comprises roughly 15 percent of GDP annually; worldwide, the value is slightly over 20 percent. Why is it so volatile? Because it is largely a reflection of businesses' anticipation of demand for their products; small changes in consumption or in consumer confidence are magnified into larger changes in business confidence. The purchase of new capital goods is something businesses can wait to do unless significant depreciation has occurred; businesses are also unlikely to construct new plants or update equipment unless they believe demand for their goods will increase in the near term. Likewise, households often wait to order new homes to be constructed if economic conditions seem to be deteriorating: the last thing most families want is a mortgage payment if the jobs that provide their monthly income are at risk.

DIDYOUKNOW?

Most components of AD increase slightly from year to year in a relatively predictable way. Investment, however, is far more volatile. According to the Bureau of Labor Statistics (BLS), gross private domestic investment increased from just under $1 trillion in 1990 to just under $2 trillion in 2000, but decreased to about $1.7 trillion in 2010 (values in real 2005 dollars). The BLS is projecting that it will increase to nearly $3 trillion by 2020.

What factors influence the level of investment, other than general beliefs about future economic conditions? The primary factor is the interest rate. Think of interest as the price that firms must pay for capital. Firms often borrow in order to purchase new equipment, such as building a new factory. They pay off the loan over a period of time, not only repaying the principal borrowed but interest as well. The higher the interest rate, the more that the firm needs to pay back. Thus, the firm needs to anticipate a higher rate of return in order to justify the higher monthly payments when interest rates are high. If interest rates are low, firms feel that more investment projects are likely to be profitable because the repayment cost will be lower.

What if firms pay for their investment projects with profits they have saved from previous sales? The interest rate is still inversely related to the level of investment; if the firm keeps its earnings in savings, it earns interest. If it spends them on new capital goods, it forgoes the interest earnings. So interest, in this case, serves as the opportunity cost of investing. Of course, a high interest rate is a deterrent to households taking out loans in order to build new homes; a low interest rate encourages that type of planning.

Thus, the investment demand curve is downward-sloping, illustrating the inverse relationship between interest rates and the level of gross private domestic investment. A drop in the interest rate causes an increase in the level of investment demanded, as shown in Figure 8-5; an increase in business confidence about future economic conditions causes a rightward shift in the investment demand curve, as shown in Figure 8-6. Because the quantity of investment is a component of aggregate demand, either effect causes AD to shift right.

Figure 8-5. Investment Demand

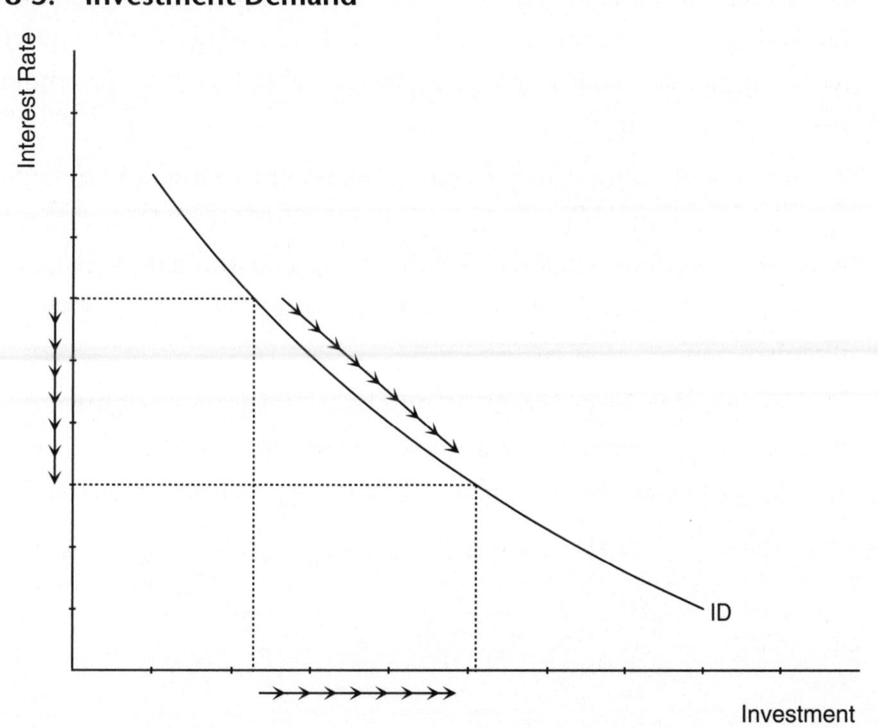

Figure 8-6. An Increase in Investment Demand

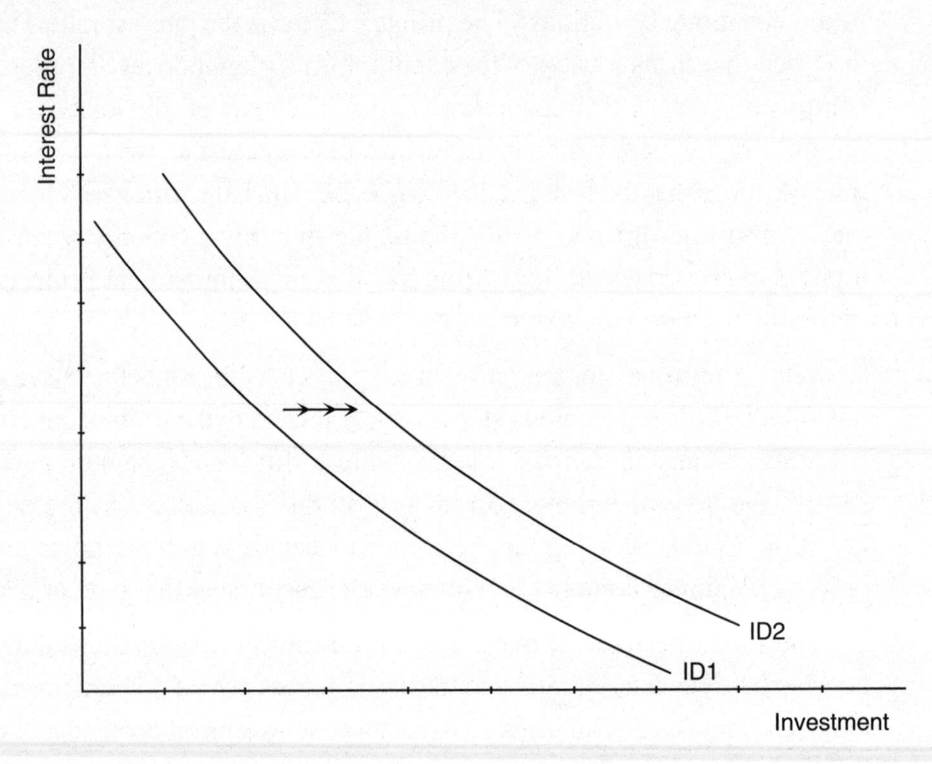

Government Purchases

The budgetary process in Congress determines the level of federal government spending. This includes purchases that count as part of AD and transfer payments that boost disposable income for their recipients, causing those recipients (or households) to spend more on consumption. Likewise, other levels of government make spending decisions via the legislative process.

It is common for governments to respond to economic downturns by increasing spending on transfer payments or direct purchases of goods and services (though many state governments and localities are constrained by balanced budget amendments). Military conflicts also tend to increase spending by governments, as do major disasters.

An increase in government purchases leads to a rightward shift in aggregate demand. If government spending decreases, AD shifts left. The use of government spending and taxes to manipulate AD is known as fiscal policy and is explained further in Chapter 10.

Exports

Exports are goods produced in a country and sold to consumers in other nations. When foreigners are wealthier, their demand for goods and services increases. So the primary determinant of a nation's exports is the national income of its trading partners. If those trading partners have more disposable income, a country's exports increase. Increases in exports cause AD to increase. If trading partners experience economic stagnation or slide into recession, a country can expect demand for its exports to decline and its AD curve to shift left.

Changes in the relative price level or exchange rates can also influence demand for exports. If a country's price level rises (or that of its trading partner declines), then its goods are comparatively more expensive and exports decline.

The stronger the value of a country's currency, the more expensive its goods are in international markets and the lower is the value of its exports. On the other hand, countries with weaker or depreciating currencies can export goods more easily because their goods carry comparatively lower price tags in international markets. (See Chapter 12 for more on currency values and their connection to international trade.)

Imports

Just as a rise in disposable income leads to more consumption spending, it also increases spending on imported goods. Because consumption changes by far more than imports, the effect on imports merely decreases the magnitude of the consumption change.

The AP exam may focus on factors that change imports and exports together, such as exchange rates or relative price levels. If a nation's trade partner experiences a rise in price level, that nation will import fewer goods because foreign products are now more expensive. If a nation's currency rises in value, foreign goods are less expensive and imports rise.

Other things equal, an increase in imports shifts a country's AD curve left. If imports become less attractive, the same amount of consumption leads to a rightward shift of AD at any price level.

The Multiplier Effect: Magnifying Initial Changes in AD

When a component of aggregate demand increases, AD increases more than the initial expenditure change because that new spending becomes income, most of which is respent again and again. This process is known as the multiplier effect and is based on the value of the economy's marginal propensity to consume.

TEST TIP

The multiplier effect can be referenced by several names: the Keynesian multiplier, the spending multiplier, and the fiscal multiplier. All refer to the same concept: the idea that expenditure becomes income, which is then partially respent. Be sure not to confuse this with the banking or money multiplier, which is based on the reserve ratio and the relending of money deposited in banks. More information about the money multiplier can be found in Chapter 9.

As GDP Increases, So Does Income

The increases in real GDP that result from rightward shifts in AD may become greater than the initial changes because money spent in an economy increases national income. Visualizing the circular flow may assist you in understanding why. AD measures aggregate expenditure, but those expenditures are received by households when firms purchase resources from them. Households then spend more because their incomes have risen, and they buy goods and services, which causes firms to purchase even more resources, further increasing household income. While it may seem as if this cycle never ends, there is a finite sum to this seemingly infinite process.

MPC Revisited: How Income Becomes Consumption

Because some of the new income is saved rather than respent, each successive step in the process involves a smaller and smaller increase in expenditures. Recall that the fraction of added income that is saved is the marginal propensity to save and that the fraction of added income that is spent on consumption is the marginal propensity to consume. An initial increase in expenditures of a given amount, say, $1 million, leads national income to rise by the full value of $1 million. However, some of that increase in income is saved. If MPS is 0.2 and MPC is 0.8, then $200,000 is saved and $800,000 is spent. This $800,000 increase in expenditures then results in national income rising by $800,000, of which 80 percent, or $640,000, is spent. Each time, the fraction saved, in this case 20 percent, leaks out of the circular flow and the fraction spent, in this case 80 percent, continues to recycle through the flow.

Key Formula

Spending Multiplier =
1 / MPS or 1 / (1 − MPC)

Mathematically, the series is infinite, but it has a finite sum. The result is that AD shifts right by the amount of the initial increase in spending multiplied by the reciprocal of MPS (also equal to the reciprocal of 1 − MPC). The initial $1 million increase in spending is multiplied by 5 (1/[1 − 0.8] or 1/0.2) to find the final rightward shift of AD: $5 million. Note that smaller values of MPC lead to a smaller multiplier effect and that, as MPC approaches 1, the multiplier effect becomes stronger and stronger.

A reduction in taxes has a similar, but weaker, multiplier effect on AD. Recall that taxes and disposable income are not components of AD. Thus, when income rises due to a tax cut, some of that increase is saved and only part of the new income is spent. Multiply the value of the tax cut by one less than the spending multiplier to find the final increase in AD (or real GDP).

The Multiplier Effect: In Theory and Practice

In reality, the multiplier is usually far weaker than would be predicted by the value of MPC. The values of MPC and MPS actually determine the theoretical maximum that a given increase in expenditure could yield. Why is the multiplier weaker in practice than in theory? Taxes and imports are two primary reasons.

When income rises, households typically owe more in taxes, so they don't have all of that money to allocate between savings and consumption. If a family's income rises by $1,000, but that household faces a marginal tax rate of 30 percent, then disposable income only rises by $700. If MPC is 0.8, then consumption increases by only $560, not $800. Marginal taxes reduce the multiplier because they weaken the link between real GDP and disposable income.

The purchase of imports similarly reduces the multiplier effect in practice. As spending rises, some of the goods purchased are produced abroad; payment for them goes into other economies and does not increase the income of households inside the country. The marginal propensity to import weakens the multiplier just as the marginal tax rate does.

As you prepare for the exam, keep in mind these factors that serve as leakages from the circular flow. The AP test can ask you why the multiplier isn't as strong in practice as in theory or directly inquire about leakages. However, problems that expect you to calculate the multiplier or use it to figure out how much of an eventual increase in real GDP results from an initial increase in spending will often ask you to consider the effect in a simplified economy without trade or taxes. The code phrase to look for is *private closed economy*. When you see that phrase, calculate the multiplier simply based on the value of MPS or MPC that you are given.

Showing Changes in AD

Just as with demand, shifts in aggregate demand are shown by creating a new curve to the right of the old curve if AD increases. The most common causes of this shift, as explained in this chapter, are increases in the following: disposable income, consumer confidence, business confidence, government spending, and/or the wealth or price level of trade partners. AD might also shift to the right because of decrease in the following: interest rate, personal or business taxes, and/or the international value of the country's currency. Figure 8-7 shows an increase in AD.

Figure 8-7. An Increase in AD

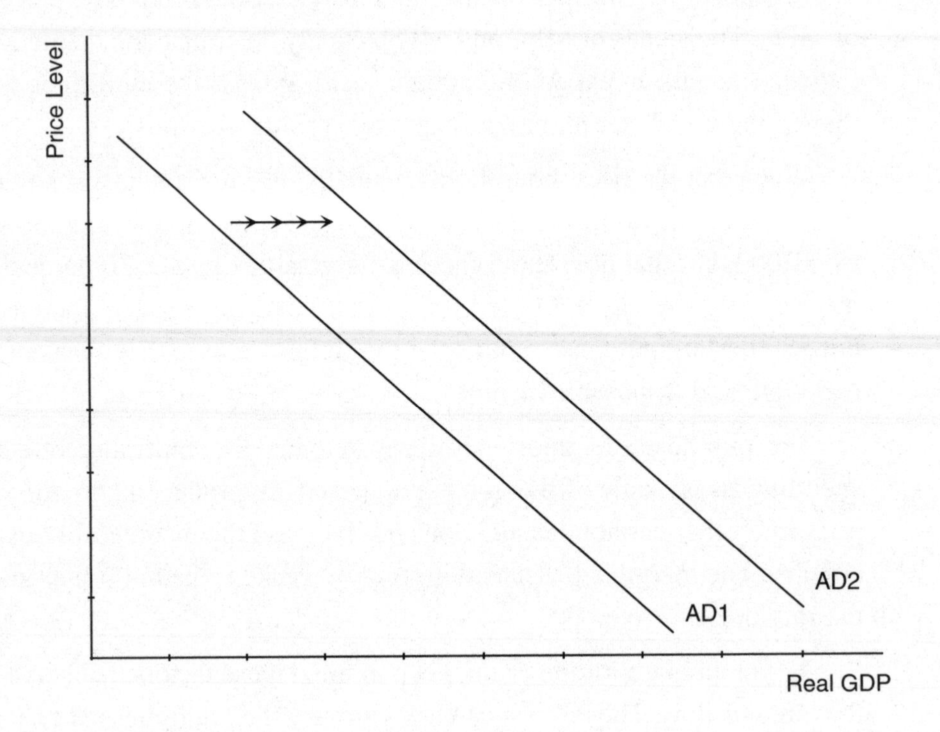

If AD decreases, show a new curve to the left of the old one. This shift can be the result of a decrease in the following: disposable income, consumer confidence, business confidence, government spending, and/or the wealth or price level of a trade partner. Decreases in aggregate demand can also result from increases in the following: interest rate, personal or business taxes, and/or the international value of the country's currency. See Figure 8-8 for a decrease in AD.

Figure 8-8. A Decrease in AD

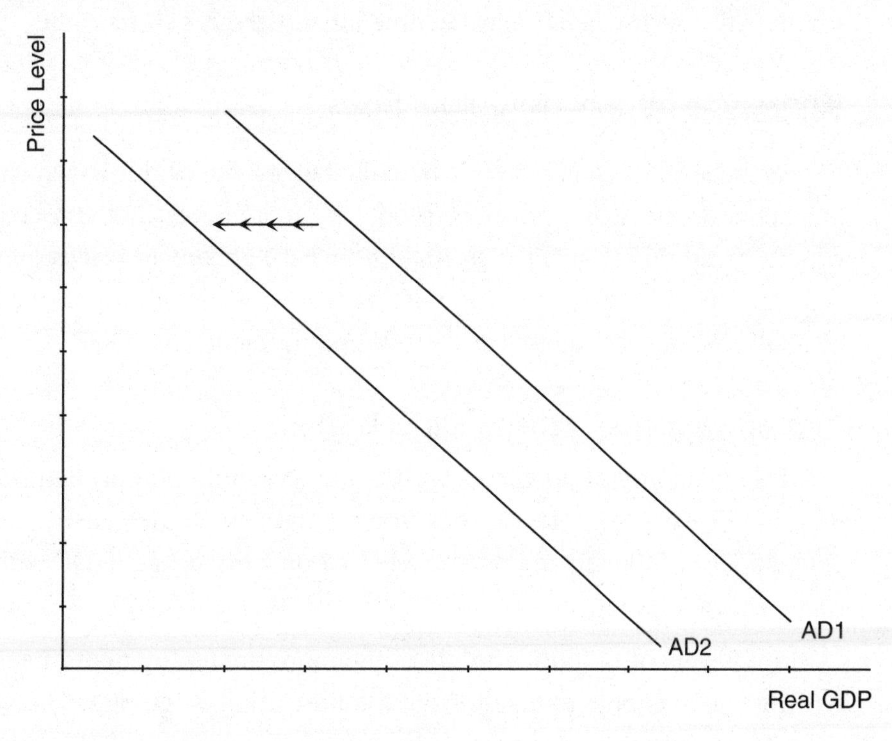

As you might predict (and as you will see later in this chapter, with the addition of aggregate supply to the diagram), a rightward shift of AD has a tendency to increase both real GDP and the price level, at least in the short run. When AD shifts left, real GDP and price level tend to decrease.

Aggregate Supply

Aggregate supply is the relationship between the quantity of real GDP supplied in a given period of time and the price level in an economy. As you might predict, the two are positively correlated: As the price at which suppliers can sell their goods and services rises, producers are willing to supply a higher quantity of real GDP. However, the story is slightly more complicated than it is with aggregate demand.

Aggregate supply does resemble the income method of calculating GDP; however, the relationship is not quite as close as the one between the expenditure method of tallying GDP and the price level. Nonetheless, changes in wages and the costs of other inputs are major factors in the shift of AS. As with supply, when input costs rise, aggregate supply shifts left; when inputs become less costly, AS shifts right.

Aggregate Supply as Output Rises

As the level of an economy's output changes, the degree to which suppliers are able to respond to the higher prices by producing more goods and services changes. The best way to grasp this concept is to imagine what happens to prices as aggregate demand continues to shift right, starting with very low levels of output, then approaching and ultimately surpassing potential (or full-employment) real GDP.

Aggregate Supply When Output Is Low

If an economy is operating well below potential output, then many resources are unused. These resources can be brought into use rather easily, and therefore more demand leads suppliers to produce a higher quantity of real GDP without the price level rising much, if at all.

Low levels of output correlate with a high unemployment rate. Many workers are willing and available to take jobs at the prevailing wage rate. Thus, employers do not need to offer higher wages to induce these laborers to work; unemployed workers, by definition, are interested in working at the current wage rate, but they cannot find work.

Similarly, machinery and factories are operating at well below capacity under these circumstances. Firms typically do not need to bring less efficient production processes into use in order to make more units of the goods they produce. As they increase output, the per-unit costs of production do not rise.

The same applies to raw materials, which are available in greater supply than is being used when output is low. The economy is capable of providing more of all types of resources relatively cheaply under these conditions.

For all these reasons, the lower the level of output, the flatter the AS curve tends to be. Rightward shifts of AD lead to greater production and higher levels of real GDP without upward pressure on prices.

TEST TIP

Some AP exam items may refer to a horizontal range of aggregate supply. Do not be confused. These questions are asking you to think about situations in which the level of output is well below full-employment level and are telling you not to consider the effects of inflation as output rises.

Aggregate Supply as Output Approaches Potential GDP

As the economy heats up and output rises, resources are increasingly scarce. Workers may need higher per-hour pay in order to produce more goods if they are asked to work overtime hours. Firms begin to bid against one another for the services of the most productive workers; other workers require a higher wage in order to join the labor force or to take work that they regard as not suited to their skill sets. Each new worker hired will probably be slightly less productive than those already employed. Another factor that begins to come into play is the diminishing marginal product of labor. Workers are added to factories that may already be somewhat crowded, leading workers to add less and less to the production process. These factors push up the per-unit labor costs of producing additional goods and services.

Capital resources undergo a similar phenomenon. As firms expand production, they must use machinery that is older or less efficient. Because some energy is required to fix machines that jam or break slightly more often and machines are being used that are not as productive as machines already in use, per-unit production costs rise.

These factors lead aggregate supply to take a more predictable upward slope. The rightward shifts in AD not only result in more output produced but also in higher prices. AS slopes up at a steeper and steeper rate the higher output gets.

Aggregate Supply When Output Is Above Potential GDP

At some point, there are no more unused resources for an economy to bring into the productive process, and output has reached its maximum. Every economy has only so much land, labor, capital, and entrepreneurial ability to use in the making of goods and services. Firms bid against one another for the few workers, who take advantage of the situation by asking for higher and higher wages. Machinery is running nearly full-time and cannot do more. Factories may be open and running at full capacity around the clock.

Under these circumstances, rightward shifts of AD do not create any more real output; they merely lead to higher prices and the same real GDP produced. The AS curve is vertical; the economy has reached its upper bound.

Figure 8-9 shows the three ranges of aggregate supply. Rather than depict three distinct curves with separate slopes and corners, this curve shows the three zones blending into one another as resources become scarcer with increases in output.

Figure 8-9. Three Ranges of Aggregate Supply

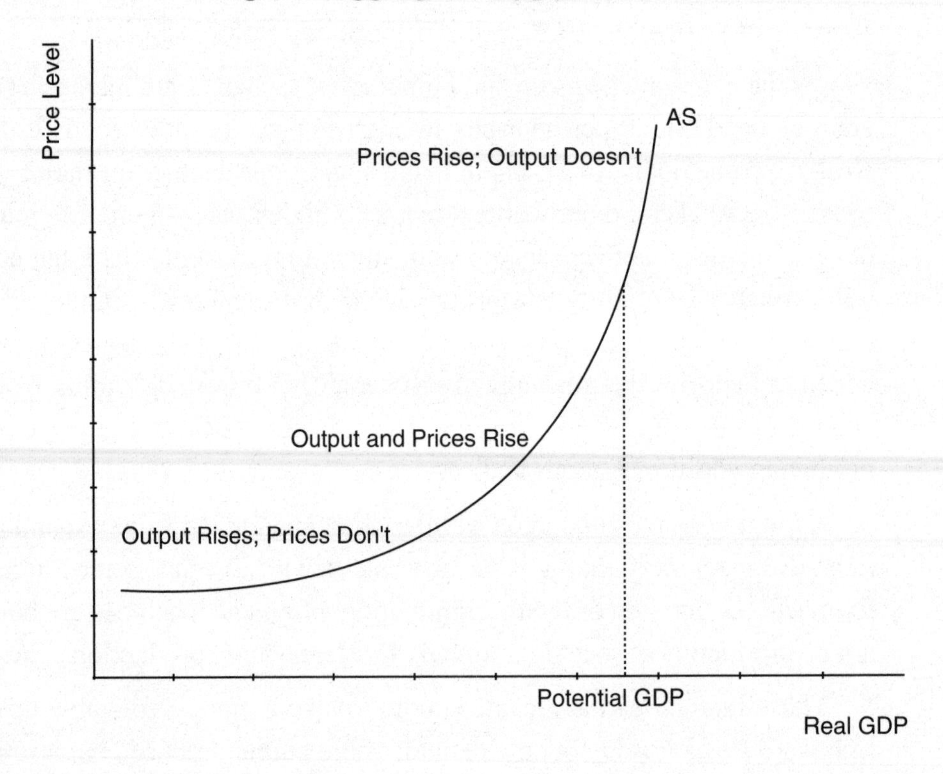

Shifts of the AS Curve

As with supply, aggregate supply shifts right when it is increased, as shown in Figure 8-10. What factors cause AS to shift right? Factors that reduce per-unit production costs result in increases in aggregate supply. These factors include a reduction in wage rates, decreases in energy costs, lower expected inflation rates, and increases in worker productivity.

Figure 8-10. An Increase in Aggregate Supply

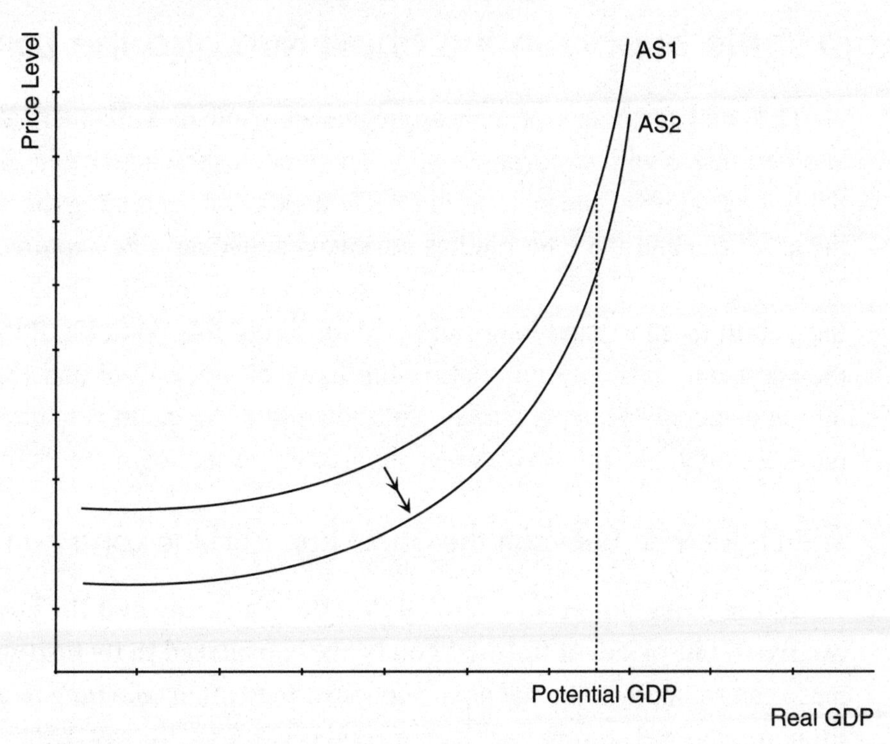

Conversely, when wage rates rise, when oil or other energy prices increase, when producers expect higher prices in the future, or when productivity decreases, AS shifts left. A decrease in aggregate supply is depicted in Figure 8-11.

Figure 8-11. A Decrease in Aggregate Supply

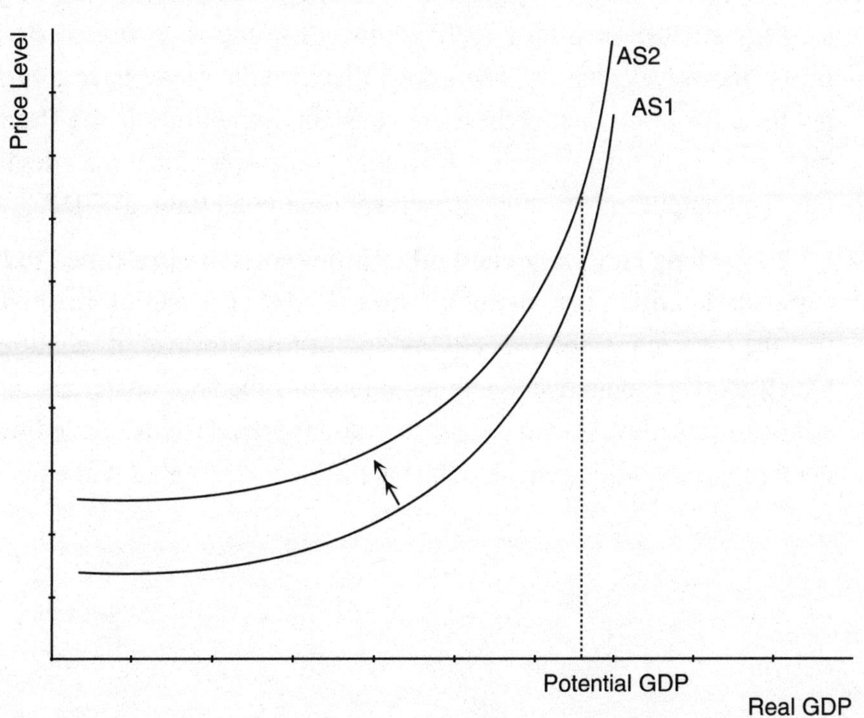

Aggregate Supply in the Short Run and the Long Run

Different textbooks present aggregate demand in a manner very similar to one another; not so with aggregate supply. The model, shown above in Figures 8-9 through 8-11, is certainly adequate to use in AP contexts, but separating the way AS behaves in the short run and the long run has advantages that can't be captured with that model. Your teacher likely has helped you negotiate the complexity of AS, hopefully instructing you in its short- and long-run behavior. From this point on, this text will separate the short-run and long-run relationship between price level and real output supplied into two aggregate supply curves. Your job on the AP exam is made easier if you draw the AD-AS graph with two distinct supply curves and learn the factors that shift each.

The Difference Between the Short Run and the Long Run

In the short run, it is presumed that the wage rate and the costs of other inputs are fixed, but prices of finished goods are considered to be flexible. While in reality these can sometimes change in an economy, they often take time to align with changes in the price level. Firms may have negotiated prices for raw materials that are binding for a period of time. Employment contracts, especially in unionized sectors of the economy, may fix the wage rates of employees for a period of months or even years. It may take time for workers and other actors in the economy to recognize that the overall price level in an economy is changing and to take action in order to adjust prices of labor and other inputs accordingly. This temporary inflexibility in the wage rate is referred to as **wage stickiness**. Sticky, or fixed, wages in the short run create situations in which firms' incentives change: The goods they produce may have a higher or lower price, but the costs of producing them are constant. Sometimes in the short run, prices may be higher or lower than expected. As a result, unemployment may deviate from the natural rate, and output may be higher or lower than potential real GDP.

In the long run, wages and other input costs are presumed to be variable and are expected to adjust proportionally to the level of prices of finished goods. This means that the long run is not a specific period of time. Instead, it identifies the future time at which workers, employers, and suppliers of other raw materials have had a chance to adjust to price-level changes and revalue labor and inputs accordingly. In the long run, unemployment will be equal to the natural rate, and output will equal potential real GDP.

Short-Run Aggregate Supply

Short-run aggregate supply (SRAS) is the relationship between the quantity of real GDP supplied and the price level when the costs of inputs are fixed. To understand why SRAS slopes upward, consider what happens to output when prices of finished goods rise and fall, but wage rates and the costs of other raw materials are constant. If finished goods can be sold for higher prices but are produced at the same old (lower) costs, producers have an incentive to squeeze more output out of the production process. Put another way, for all producers, marginal costs remain the same, but marginal benefit has risen. Just as any other rational economic actor, they'll do more, in this case producing a higher quantity. If, instead, finished good prices fall while wages remain fixed at their old (high) levels, producers feel as if marginal benefit fell, while marginal cost has remained the same. Thus, they have an incentive to produce less, and **SRAS is upward sloping.**

Changes in the price level of finished goods cause changes from one point to another along a given SRAS curve. If costs of production rise or fall, then a new SRAS curve should be drawn; these are factors that result in a shift of SRAS. The most common causes of shifts in SRAS that appear on the AP exam are changes in the wage rate, changes in the costs of oil or energy, and changes in inflationary expectations. Negative (or adverse) aggregate supply shocks result from increases in the wage rate or oil prices or from expectations that inflation will rise faster than previously thought. Positive supply shocks result from a reduction in wages, oil or other energy prices, or in the expected inflation rate.

Long-Run Aggregate Supply

Long-run aggregate supply (LRAS) is the relationship between the quantity of real GDP supplied and the price level when the costs of inputs have adjusted proportionally to the price level of finished goods and services. If prices at which suppliers can sell their goods and the costs of inputs that they need to produce them both rise (or fall) in balance to one another, then producers tend not to change their level of output. Marginal benefit and marginal cost for producers have both changed, but by equal measures and in the same direction, so their incentives to produce have not altered at all. When the price level is as expected, the full-employment level of output is supplied. Producers supply the economy's potential real GDP when unemployment is equal to the natural rate. Thus, the **LRAS is vertical.**

LRAS shifts when potential GDP changes. If the quantity and quality of resources available in an economy change, then either more or fewer goods can be produced when the economy is operating at full employment. Discovery of new productive resources, an increase in the population or labor force, improved production processes, and growth of capital stock are the primary factors that cause LRAS to shift rightward. This is known as (long-run) economic growth. A more detailed explanation of the causes of economic growth can be found in Chapter 11.

If, on the other hand, those factors of production shrink instead of grow, LRAS shifts to the left. While this is not common, it could be the result of a major decrease in the workforce due to disease or destruction of capital equipment during armed conflict.

If LRAS shifts in either direction, SRAS shifts with it. This is in contrast to the factors explained earlier in this chapter that shift SRAS, which typically do not cause a change in LRAS because they result in a level of output different than potential GDP, not a change in the full-employment level of output.

Figure 8-12. Short- and Long-Run Aggregate Supply

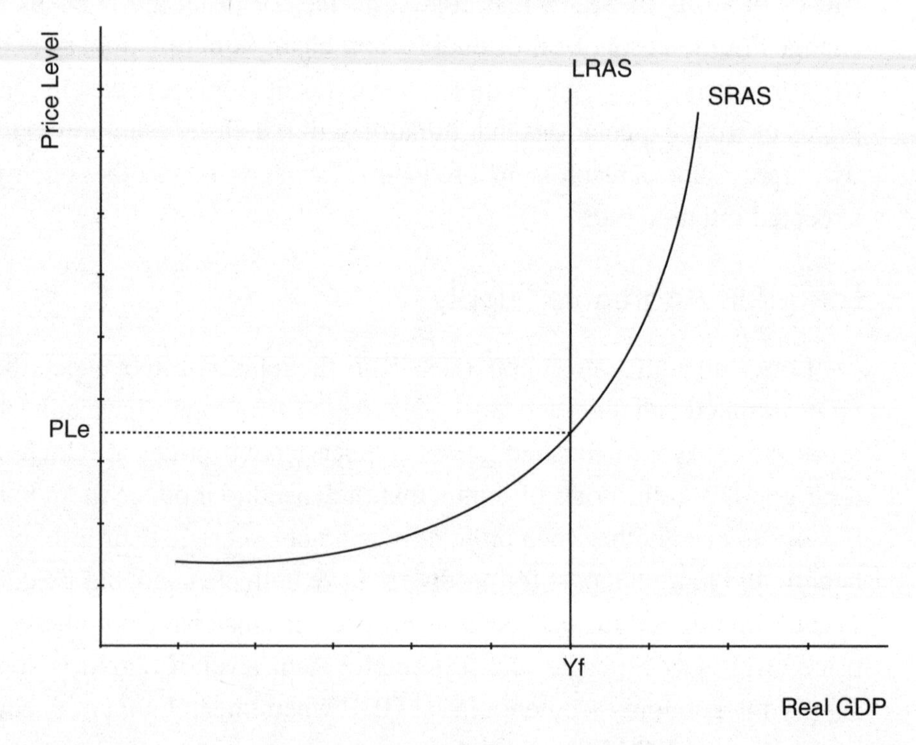

Figure 8-12 shows short- and long-run aggregate supply together on one set of axes. Note that the intersection point is at potential, or full-employment, output (noted as Yf) and the expected price level (PLe). This graph showing two separate supply curves forms the basis for most of the AD-AS analysis that the AP exam will expect of you.

DIDYOUKNOW?

In the eighteenth and nineteenth centuries, classical economists such as Adam Smith and David Ricardo thought that AS would behave as if it were vertical. Say's law, which is no longer widely accepted, suggested that "supply would create its own demand," and therefore there would be fluctuations in the price level, but not in output over time. During the Great Depression, John Maynard Keynes observed that economies could be caught below potential output for long stretches of time and believed that output levels were highly variable, but that the price level was quite sticky. These debates still exist today.

Short- and Long-Run Equilibrium in the AD-AS Model

Putting together the ideas of aggregate demand and aggregate supply allows us to show economies in one of three basic positions: short-run equilibrium when operating below full-employment output, long-run equilibrium at full employment, and short-run equilibrium when operating above full-employment output.

Two Supply Curves, Two Types of Equilibrium

No matter which of the three basic positions the macroeconomy is in, you need to be able to distinguish between short-run and long-run equilibrium. **Short-run equilibrium is found where AD intersects SRAS**. This may be at a level of output that is above or below the level of potential real GDP. These situations are not uncommon, but they are usually considered to be temporary and not ideal. In Chapter 10, you'll learn about how governmental tools (fiscal and monetary policy) can be used to correct them. If none of these tools are used, the economy **self-corrects** if wages are flexible. How long that takes is a matter of much debate.

In contrast, **long-run equilibrium is found where AD intersects LRAS**. This may be the same point as short-run equilibrium, in which case the situation is considered stable and not in need of adjustment. When the economy is in long-run equilibrium, the inflation rate and price level are equal to the expected levels and unemployment is equal to the natural rate of unemployment; there is no cyclical unemployment. Real GDP is equal to potential GDP under these circumstances.

Figure 8-13. An Economy in Long-Run Equilibrium

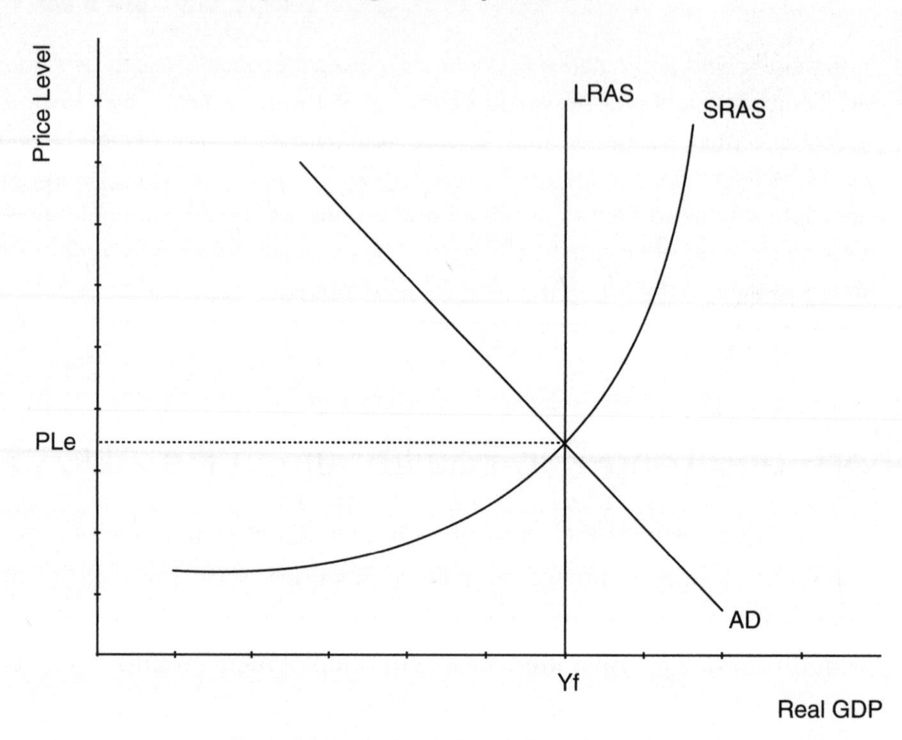

Figure 8-13 shows an economy in long-run equilibrium. Note that AD intersects SRAS and LRAS at the same point. The level of output noted at Yf is both potential real GDP and actual real GDP in this situation. The price level is the same as the expected price level (noted at PLe). There will be no pressure on prices or wages under these conditions until or unless some factor causes a shift in AD or SRAS.

When the Economy Is below Full-Employment Output

If AD is too low, then there is a **recessionary gap**—the level of actual real GDP is below potential real GDP. This situation is shown in Figure 8-14. The current short-run equilibrium is shown at output level Yr, and the price level is shown at PLr. Under these conditions, output is lower than the full-employment level (Yf), and the price level is lower than PLe, the expected level. Unemployment is higher than the natural rate.

Figure 8-14. An Economy Below Full Employment Output

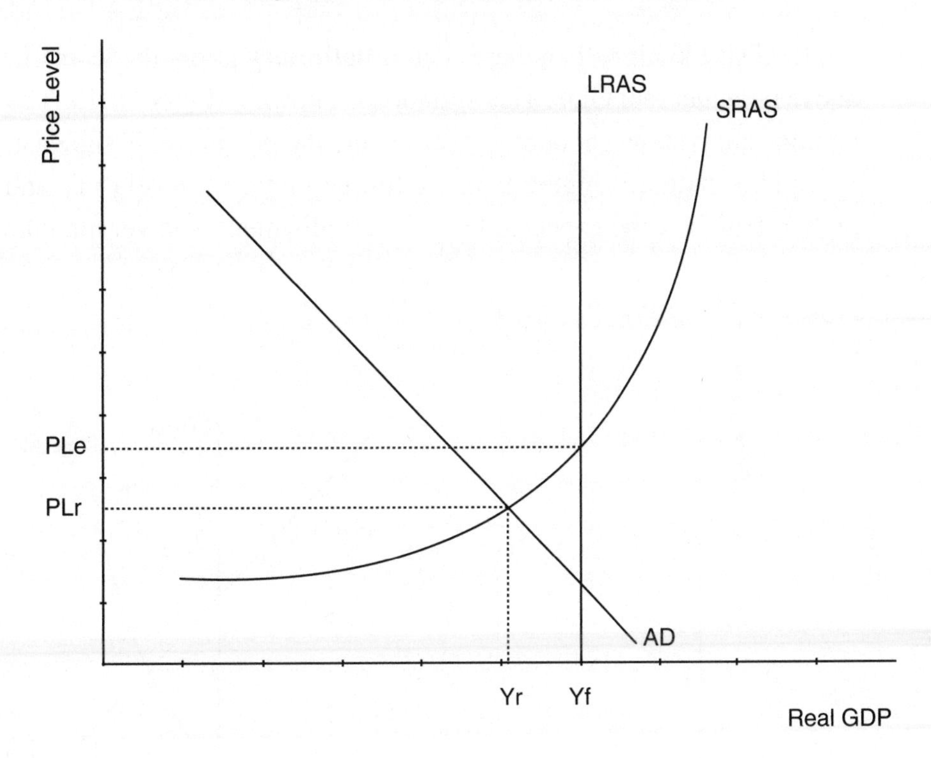

If no action is taken and wages are flexible enough to decrease, the high level of unemployment pushes down wages (remember, there are lots of unemployed workers willing and eager to work at the prevailing wage rate). This process shifts SRAS to the right, correcting the recessionary gap and returning the economy to full employment. Because this is close to what Smith and Ricardo (the classical economists) believed would happen, it is sometimes referred to as **neoclassical self-correction**.

DIDYOUKNOW?

Wages might not move down, even when the economy is in a recessionary gap, for several reasons. Minimum-wage laws, the structure of labor contracts, and a collective belief that we ought to make more than we did the year before all make downward wage flexibility less likely than wage changes in an upward direction. This effect makes recessions less likely to self-correct.

When the Economy Is Above Full-Employment Output

If AD is too high, then there is an **inflationary gap**—the level of actual real GDP is above potential real GDP. This situation is shown in Figure 8-15. The current short-run equilibrium is shown at output level Yi, and the price level is shown at PLi. Under these conditions, output is higher than the full-employment level (Yf), and the price level is higher than PLe, the expected level. Unemployment is lower than the natural rate.

Figure 8-15. An Economy Above Full Employment Output

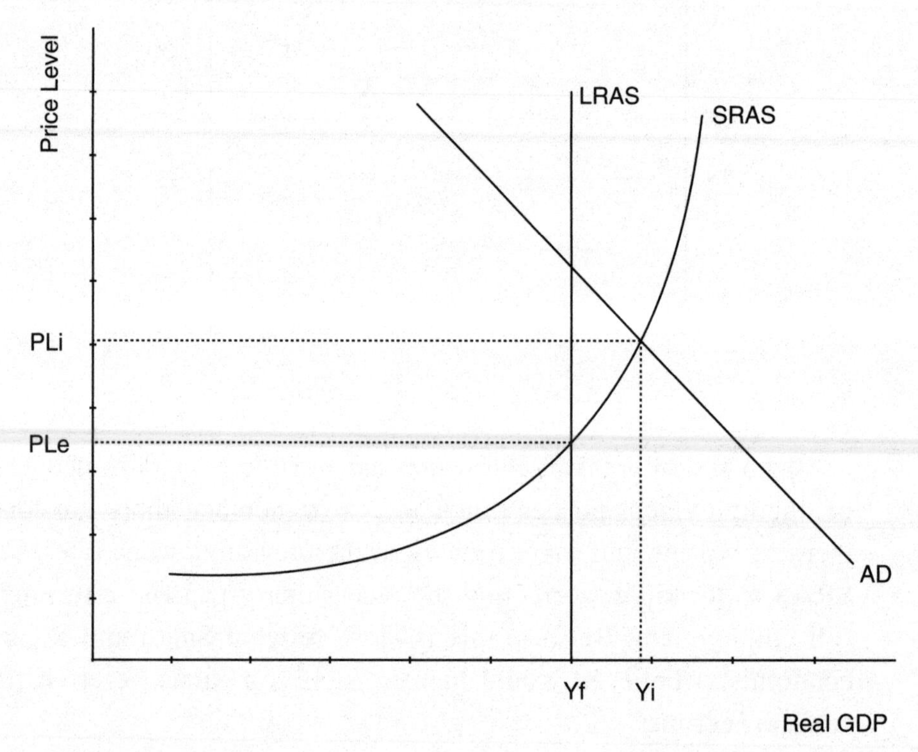

If no action is taken and wages are flexible, the low level of unemployment pushes wages upward (remember, workers are scarce, and therefore their wage rate rises). This process shifts SRAS to the left, correcting the inflationary gap and returning the economy to full employment. This type of self-correction is far less controversial among economists. Given enough time, workers will demand higher wages and firms will need to honor their demands because (1) they have options when other firms are willing to hire talented workers and (2) the cost of living has risen.

TEST TIP

Be especially alert for AP exam items that ask you to consider the effects of fiscal or monetary policy action taken by the government to fix an output gap. If no such indication is present in the question, check for hints that suggest you should think in the long run. Questions related to this self-correction process typically say "assume no policy action is taken" or "in the long run" or "assuming flexible wages." These phrases are synonymous: They all mean that you should think about what the current level of output is, determine whether the unemployment rate is above or below the natural rate of unemployment (NRU), consider whether workers are scarce or plentiful, and then determine the direction in which wages are likely to fluctuate. Then you'll have a strong chance to see the direction in which SRAS would move to take the economy back to long-run equilibrium.

Chapter 9

Banking and the Financial Sector

Money and the Money Supply

Money is not an economic resource; it is not a factor of production from which goods and services can be made. The factors of production are land, labor, capital, and entrepreneurial ability. Nonetheless, the amount of money in circulation is important in determining interest rates and the price level. Money is traded in a market much like other goods and services. If it isn't a resource, what is money?

Types and Purposes of Money

Money is a tool societies have developed to serve three fundamental purposes: as a medium of exchange, as a store of value, and as a unit of account. Because it is universally accepted, money is a **medium of exchange**: a tool used to facilitate trades between people who don't always have exactly what the other wants. Money is a **store of value** because it holds purchasing power over time for use in the future. As a **unit of account**, money serves as a common denominator when adding the value of a group of goods (as in totaling gross domestic product [GDP]) or comparing several goods at once. To work well in these capacities, whatever a society uses as money should be divisible, uniform, widely acceptable, durable, portable, and predictably scarce.

Paper bills are actually a rather recent phenomenon; for most of the time that humans have used money, it took other forms. **Commodity money** is the use of a good that has intrinsic value as money. The most common example was use of a coin made of precious metal that stood for the same value in money as the value of the metal it was made from. Over time, most modern societies evolved away from commodity money and began using **fiat money**. Fiat money involves use of tokens, each of which has far more value than it would as a commodity. This type of money gains legitimacy by government decree, and it maintains that value as long as the public has faith that it will hold its value and be widely accepted in exchange for goods and services.

Money, Stocks, and Bonds

People can choose to hold onto their wealth in many ways: Households may purchase assets such as land or gold, buy ownership of corporations in the form of shares of stock, lend money by purchasing a bond or security, or keep cash. Consider these alternatives in terms of how effectively they serve two of the fundamental purposes of money described in this chapter. **Liquidity** is the ease with which a form of wealth can be spent, or used as a medium of exchange to help satisfy our present want for goods. The most liquid ways to hold wealth, however, do not store value the most effectively for future use. Currency, the most liquid form of money, does not bear any interest and loses value as prices rise. Gold and real estate should retain value as prices rise (at times, they may rise in real value), but both are less liquid because they must be sold to convert wealth back into a readily spendable form. Gold and real estate are therefore better stores of value, but they are less liquid.

Money can exist in many forms, and it can be measured in several ways, as described later in this chapter. You should think of currency and funds deposited into banks as money. It is easy to spend—at most it needs to be withdrawn from a bank in order to use it for purchasing goods, and we can often skip this step these days. Thus, it makes sense to have as much wealth in the form of money as we expect to spend at any given time.

Transferring money into ownership in a corporation by buying stock is a riskier but a potentially more rewarding option if the goal is to store value for future use. Owning stock in a company entitles one to a share of profits the company might distribute, known as dividends. Shares of stock can also be sold. Depending on the change in their value, this can yield profits or losses. Stocks generally gain value in the aggregate over time, but they are less liquid than holding money because shares of stock must be sold in order to obtain spendable currency.

Bonds, or securities, are pieces of paper that represent debt. They are promises by governments or corporations to pay a loan back to the bearer of the bond at a future date. Sovereigns and companies who issue bonds use them as a tool to borrow. A huge range of securities are traded. Some are risky and pay a high interest rate, while others pay lower interest rates, but also carry less risk. For AP purposes, the word *bonds* means government treasury securities in the hands of the public, banks, and the Federal

Reserve. When these are being traded cheaply, they pay relatively high rates of interest. When the price of these bonds is high, the interest yield is low. The inverse relationship between the price of bonds and the interest rate is an important factor in how monetary policy works. Bonds are *not* money; they are an alternative way to save for the future.

Measuring the Money Supply

Because money and many forms of wealth that are close to money can be used to buy goods and services and therefore can cause prices to rise, economic policymakers who need to forecast inflation track changes in these monetary aggregates closely.

M1 is a narrow definition of money and contains the most liquid forms of money: cash in the hands of the public and funds deposited in checking accounts. These checkable deposits (or demand deposits) are considered money because they can be directly spent by writing a check or by using a debit card. Cash held by banks is excluded because it would double-count money in customers' accounts.

Key Formula

M1 = Currency + Checkable Deposits + Traveler's Checks

M2 is a broader concept of money and includes all of M1 plus funds deposited into savings accounts, time deposits under $100,000 (these are small-scale certificates of deposit [CDs]), and funds that households have deposited in money market funds. As savings accounts became easier to access over the past few decades, households chose to hold more funds in interest-bearing savings accounts, knowing that they could move that money into slightly more liquid checking accounts as needed. For this reason, the Federal Reserve began using M2 as its primary tally of the money supply.

Key Formula

M2 = M1 + Savings Deposits + Small-Time Deposits + Household Money Market Funds

Broader definitions have since been used and tracked in recent years, including M3, M4, money zero maturity (MZM), and L, the broadest measure of liquidity. Each represents a slightly different attempt to measure liquid assets that can cause inflationary pressure. As the financial industry continues to develop new near-monies that bear interest for customers and allow them easy access to liquidity, the monetary authorities need to develop new and broader definitions of money in order to track the risk possible future inflation poses.

DIDYOUKNOW?

The authorities don't always get it right when they develop a new money supply definition. In 2006, the Fed stopped tracking M3 after admitting that it gave them no additional information beyond what they knew already when tracking M2.

Balancing the growth of the money supply is important. If the money supply grows too fast, inflation accelerates. If it shrinks or grows too slowly, it limits the expansion of GDP. A country's central bank and its banking system are responsible for the size of the money stock at any given time.

The Banking Process

The Purpose of Banks

The financial sector helps facilitate the circular flow of economic activity by directing savings into consumption and investment. Banks (along with thrifts, credit unions, and other financial intermediaries) allow people and institutions that never meet one another to engage in lending and borrowing. From the point of view of the customer, the bank provides a convenient and secure place to store funds and a possible source of credit when borrowing.

Banks earn profit by lending at higher interest rates than those at which they borrow. Because their earnings stem from lending, banks typically have an incentive to lend all the funds they can as long as they feel the risk of nonrepayment is reasonable. In their role as lenders, banks are vital connectors between the money supply and aggregate demand: As more money is available, banks lend more money, and businesses borrow to increase investment spending while households increase consumption. Conversely, if credit conditions tighten—if banks don't have faith they will be paid back or if there is no demand for loans—then economic activity can grind to a halt. Saved income isn't transferred to those wishing to spend it, and expenditures are less likely to have a multiplied effect on output.

Fractional Reserve Banking: How Banks Create Money

Banks are allowed to create money through lending because of fractional reserve banking. Banks take deposits from customers and are not obligated to hold all of the deposited funds. Instead, banks are required to hold only a fraction on reserve and can loan the remainder. Because the original depositor has money in a checking account and the new borrower has borrowed funds available to spend, the money supply is greater than before. When banks lend, the money supply expands by the amount of the loan. Conversely, repaying loans destroys money.

When a dollar of money is held in currency, it can be only one dollar. Once deposited in a bank, most of that dollar can be lent, spent, and redeposited not only once but several times. The portion of a new deposit that banks are allowed to relend determines the magnitude of the total effects of this process.

Reserve Ratio and the Money Multiplier

The **required reserve ratio**, the percentage of demand deposits that banks must keep in reserve, is set by a country's central bank—in the case of the United States, the Federal Reserve, or the Fed. The Fed has set 10 percent as the amount of a new deposit that banks must retain. Thus, a new deposit of $1,000.00 into a bank permits that bank to lend and therefore create up to $900.00 (the other $100.00 of required reserves may be held as vault cash or deposited at the Federal Reserve Bank). If that $900.00 changes hands and is deposited into another bank, then $90.00 must be held on reserve and $810.00 can be relent. The next bank could expand the money supply by an additional $729.00 while holding $81.00 in reserves. At the conclusion of the process, we have an infinite series with a finite sum: The first bank increased the money supply by $900.00, the next by $810.00, the next by $729.00, the next by $656.10, and so on.

The finite sum of this series can be found by multiplying the initial increase in the money supply of $900.00 by the reciprocal of the required reserve ratio, or 10. This reciprocal, known as the **money multiplier**, is the maximum number of dollars one deposited dollar can become. In our current example, the $1,000 initial deposit can support creation of $9,000; in the end, it can become $10,000. Note that only $9,000 of this is new money because the $1,000 held by the public at the start of the process was part of the money supply. Had the process started with a purchase of $1,000 worth of bonds by the Federal Reserve, the entire $10,000 would be an increase because the Fed made its purchase with newly-created money.

Key Formula

Money Multiplier = 1 / Reserve Ratio

The lower the reserve ratio, the higher the money multiplier. More of each deposit can be lent and redeposited elsewhere in the banking system, and more money can be created from a given deposit. With a higher reserve ratio, the money multiplier is smaller because more deposited funds are held in reserve at each stage of the process, and the same size of deposit leads to less new money creation.

In practice, the total expansion of the money supply that results from a given deposit is smaller than the deposit expansion multiplier would predict. Any time the public holds money in cash form rather than in banks, those dollars cannot expand because they can't be lent. Another factor that weakens the effective money multiplier is if banks hold more reserves than is required by law. In this case, less than 90 percent of the deposits are relent each time.

TEST TIP

When confronted with banking expansion problems, follow these simple steps: First, recall that the reserve ratio is the fraction of demand deposits that must be held on reserve. Second, isolate the excess reserves—those held above the required amount. These can be lent and represent the maximum that a bank can increase the money supply. Third, multiply the excess reserves by the money multiplier if you are asked to determine how much the banking system as a whole can create in new lent money.

Assets, Liabilities, and Balance Sheets

Problems about the reserve ratio, bank lending, and the money multiplier can also be presented in the form of a **T-account** or **balance sheet** showing a bank's assets and liabilities. A balance sheet illustrates the financial position of a bank and allows basic bank transactions to be shown visually. Balance sheets follow some simple rules, which will be explained by referring to the example shown in Table 9-1.

Table 9-1. Balance Sheet of a Sample Bank

Assets		Liabilities and Net Worth	
Reserves	30,000	Checkable deposits	200,000
Government securities	70,000	Borrowed from banks	20,000
Loans to customers	140,000	Net worth	20,000
Total assets	240,000	Total liabilities	240,000

In this simplified example, first note that assets are arranged in one column and liabilities in the other. **Assets** are holdings that have monetary value. Cash in the bank's vault (or deposited in its reserve account at the Fed) can be used to pay debts and is therefore an asset. Bonds are assets because they represent a debt the bank is owed by the government. Loans to customers are assets for a similar reason; those customers owe the bank money as those loans come due, whether the full amount is due at a specific date or the customer repays the bank with monthly payments, such as on a home mortgage or car loan. Funds that the bank had loaned to other commercial banks are also assets. In addition, banks might have physical assets like computers, desks, and chairs and may also own real estate or foreign currency.

On the other side of the chart are **liabilities**, or debts that the bank owes. Funds deposited into accounts by the bank's customers represent liabilities because those depositors can demand that money from the bank or request that some funds be transferred to another bank (this is what writing a check or using a debit card does). Any funds that the bank has borrowed from other banks (or that it borrowed from the Fed) are debts the bank must pay back and therefore are counted as liabilities for the bank.

Note that the total of the bank's assets minus its liabilities must equal its net worth. For a privately owned bank, the net worth would not be a liability. However, many banks have shareholders, each of whom are entitled to a fraction of the net worth of the corporation. Regardless of the type of bank, listing net worth on the liabilities side of the ledger allows easier accounting. The two sides of a balance sheet always balance; this fact can help you reason through how various kinds of transactions affect the bank's financial position.

A second principle related to the balance sheet that you need to know is the reserve requirement. As explained already in this chapter, the reserve requirement is the percentage of deposits that a bank must hold in reserve and therefore cannot lend. In the example shown in Table 9-1, the bank has $200,000 of customers' money and has $30,000 in reserves. If the required reserve ratio is 15 percent, all of the bank's reserves are required. Under these circumstances, the bank is said to be loaned up, meaning it has no excess reserves and cannot lend without receiving more deposits, borrowing from the Fed or another commercial bank, or selling some of its assets.

On the other hand, if the required reserve ratio is only 10 percent, then only $20,000 of reserves are required to support the checkable deposits that are outstanding, and the bank has $10,000 of excess reserves. Under that scenario, this bank could lend, and therefore create, $10,000 of new money. The reserve ratio of 10 percent implies a money multiplier of 10 ($1/0.1 = 10$), so the banking system as a whole could create up to $100,000 worth of new money using those excess reserves.

TEST TIP

Don't be intimidated by balance sheets—often much of the information is extraneous to the questions asked. Items on past AP exams about T-accounts have frequently expected students to calculate excess reserves to determine how much money an individual bank or the banking system can create. Alternatively, the balance sheet given may separate required from excess reserves and then expect you to determine the required reserve ratio. To do that, divide required reserves by the amount of checkable deposits.

Interest Rates, Money Demand, and the Money Market

Interest as the Price of Money

When a lender gives a borrower use of money for a specified period of time, the lender incurs risks and costs. Specifically, the lender may never be repaid, may lose purchasing power to rising prices, or may find herself lacking funds to which she otherwise would have access. These are the bases for the lender requiring that the borrower pay back interest as well as the principal amount borrowed. Interest is the price that must be paid tomorrow in order to use another person's money today.

The interest rate, expressed as a percentage of the principal owed each year of the loan's term, can be seen as the opportunity cost of either borrowing or of holding money that otherwise might be lent. Higher interest rates thus discourage borrowing and spending and encourage saving and lending. Low interest rates make saving and lending less profitable and make borrowing or holding money less costly.

Often economists make the assumption that there is a universal prevailing interest rate in an economy. (This certainly would make some questions easier for you to answer on the AP exam!) In reality, many important interest rates are in effect at any given time. When a bank lends, the interest rate it charges depends on the creditworthiness of the borrower in question. A stable borrower with a high credit rating may pay a relatively low commercial interest rate called the prime rate, whereas a borrower deemed less likely to pay the bank back might have to pay a higher, or subprime, rate in order to borrow. When banks themselves borrow to acquire funds, they may borrow from the Federal Reserve's discount window or from other commercial banks through the federal funds market. The **discount rate** is the interest rate the Fed charges for short-term loans to banks. Loans between banks in the federal funds market are made at the **federal funds rate**. This federal funds rate can be influenced by the Federal Reserve, is widely considered to be an important wholesale price of money, and influences other interest rates in the economy. In general, the prime rate will be about 3 percent higher than these wholesale rates at which banks can obtain funds.

The Demand for Money

People want money for two reasons: to spend it on goods and services or to save it so that it can be spent at a later time. These two motives connect to the functions that money performs: spending money in the present involves using it as a medium of exchange; saving it for the future involves using it as a store of value. These two motives for holding money are called transactions demand and asset demand for money, respectively.

Transactions demand is the relationship between the interest rate and the amount of money people want to hold in order to purchase goods and services. Because most of the money needed to make purchases is not dependent on the interest rate, transactions demand is shown as a vertical line on the money market graph. The two factors considered to be paramount in determining the amount of money demanded for transactional purposes are the level of real GDP and the price level. Changes in real GDP mean changes in the quantity of goods and services we purchase: If we buy more goods, we'll need more money; if we buy fewer goods, we won't need as much money. Likewise, an increase in the price level means that it takes more money to purchase the same number of goods and therefore transactions demand for money rises. Keeping in mind that price level times real GDP is equal to nominal GDP, it follows that transactions demand for money varies directly with nominal output.

Asset demand is the relationship between the quantity of money people desire to hold as a store of value and the interest rate. Why would the interest rate influence how much of their savings people want to hold in money? To begin with, we will assume that those saving for the future would like to have their real purchasing power grow over time so that they'll have more wealth later than they do today. After all, savings is a sacrifice and people want to be rewarded for it. Recall that lending money (and thus holding wealth for the future in the form of a loan or bond) yields interest; therefore, holding wealth as money entails the sacrifice of interest that might be earned. Another way to understand this is to simplify the choices of how to hold wealth for future use to only two: hold wealth as money or as bonds. Money doesn't earn interest, but bonds do. So bonds are more desirable because they give holders the opportunity for wealth to grow. However, they are also risky because there is some chance that they won't be repaid, and they are illiquid because they must be sold to convert the wealth held into a spendable form. If you have an unanticipated need to get new brakes for your car or to fix a leaky roof, it is unlikely that you can pay for the repairs with a stack of bonds! How many bonds and how much money people want to hold in order to preserve wealth into the future depends on the rate of interest the bonds will pay.

TEST TIP

Anything you need to know about bonds for an AP test question can be figured out from these three simple truths:

- Bonds are not money.
- Bonds are pieces of paper that represent debt—a fancy form of an IOU.
- The price of bonds and the interest rate are inversely related.

At high interest rates, bonds are cheaper and more attractive because they represent opportunities to increase wealth quickly. At low interest rates, bonds are more expensive and less attractive because they involve the same sacrifice of liquidity and risk of non-repayment, but they don't offer as much of a benefit in terms of interest earned. From this analysis, we can determine that there is an inverse relationship between the interest rate and the quantity of money people wish to hold as a store of value.

Putting together the vertical transactions demand for money and the down-sloping asset demand for money generates a down-sloping total money demand curve. More money is demanded at lower interest rates and less money is demanded at higher interest rates. The interest rate is therefore the opportunity cost of holding money: it is what you have to pay to borrow money and it is a benefit you forgo if you hold money rather than lending it out.

Money Market Graphical Analysis

The money market shows the quantities of money supplied and demanded at various nominal interest rates. The money market is in equilibrium when the quantity of money demanded equals the quantity supplied. This unique point correlates with the equilibrium nominal interest rate.

Figure 9-1. The Money Market

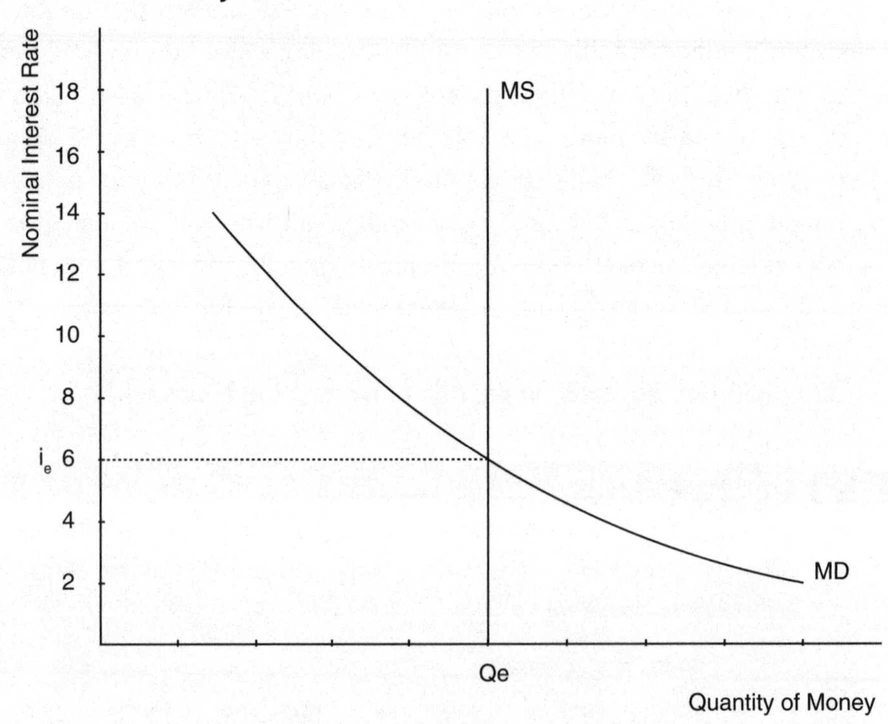

These features of the money market are shown in Figure 9-1. The vertical supply curve is probably the most noteworthy feature. It shows that the quantity of money supplied at any given time is not influenced by the interest rate; instead, the country's central bank (or in some countries, a currency board) determines the money stock in circulation. The money demand curve is down-sloping because high interest rates make holding money costly. The intersection determines the money market's equilibrium position. The equilibrium interest rate, i_e, is shown here at 6 percent.

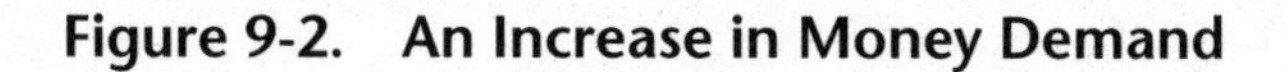

Figure 9-2. An Increase in Money Demand

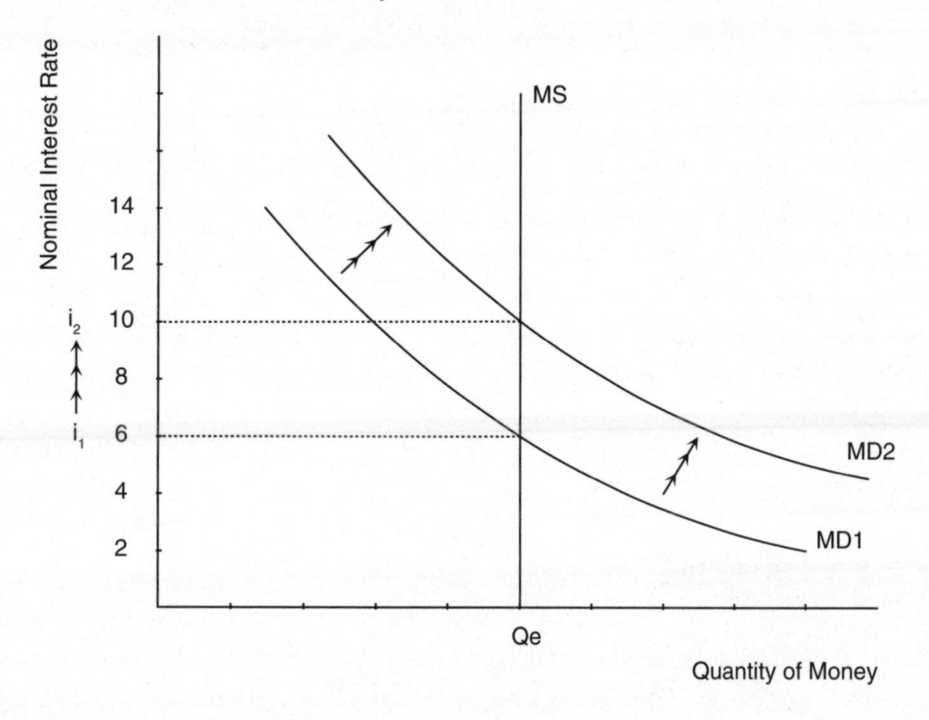

From the previous section in this chapter, you are already familiar with some of the factors that cause money demand to shift. An increase in the price level or in real GDP results in a rightward shift of money demand and pushes up the interest rate, as shown in Figure 9-2. Other prompts asking you to draw or consider this graph might ask about the effects of deficit spending or simply state that stocks and/or bonds became less desirable and holding money became more preferred. Conversely, if holding money became less necessary because the public was purchasing a lower quantity of real GDP or if the price level fell, money demand would shift left, decreasing nominal interest rates.

Most AP test items about the money market will involve shifts in supply rather than demand. Central banks can change the quantity of money in circulation and use this ability to influence interest rates, and therefore investment and consumption, aggregate demand, and, ultimately, output and price level (see the section called Three Major Tools of Monetary Policy in this chapter and Chapter 10 for more information on this important chain of events). Figure 9-3 shows the effects of changes in money supply. Decreasing the money supply from MS1 to MS2 increases the interest rate from 6 percent to 10 percent. An increase in the money supply from MS1 to MS3 results in a new lower equilibrium interest rate of 4 percent.

Figure 9-3. Changes in the Money Supply

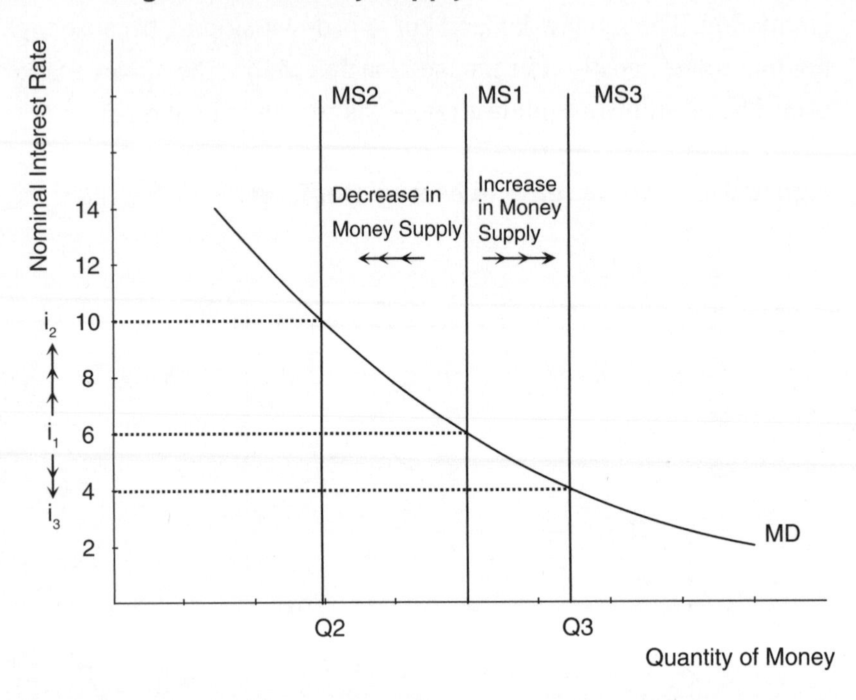

TEST TIP

The money market isn't difficult to learn and it is important to know. In recent years, the free-response section of the AP exam has required students to draw the money market in graph form, and every year the exam includes several multiple-choice questions that are easily solved by sketching a money market graph. Remember the basics: quantity of money on the horizontal axis; nominal interest rate on the vertical axis because interest is the price of money; vertical supply curve because money stock is controlled by the Fed, not interest rates; and down-sloping demand curve because interest is required to get people to part with liquidity and the convenience of holding money. Because of the vertical supply curve, results of shifts won't be familiar, but they can be observed easily on your graph. When in doubt, draw it out!

The Federal Reserve

The Federal Reserve serves as the central bank for the United States. On AP exam questions, you can feel free to treat *Federal Reserve* and *central bank* as synonyms because they will be used interchangeably; you won't be tested on any of the differences between the U.S. central bank and those of other countries.

The Purpose of Central Banks

The use of fiat money (monetary tokens that, by government decree, have more value than they would be worth as commodities) can work only if there is a monetary authority willing to take seriously the task of regulating how scarce those tokens are. At times, governments have produced too much money and devalued the currency of the society so much that runaway inflation was the result. In extreme cases, citizens lost so much trust in the official fiat currency that a foreign currency was used or people reverted to a barter system, trading goods and services directly.

Central banks developed in the seventeenth century. Generally central banks seek to promote economic stability by controlling interest rates and the money supply. Their defining attribute is that they have a monopoly on the issuance of official currency. They often perform other roles, such as acting as a bank for commercial banks or overseeing and regulating the banking sector. In addition, central banks sometimes manage the finances of the government or print currency.

One characteristic that supports effective central banks is political independence. Political branches of government are typically prone to increasing the money supply faster than is ideal. Expanding the stock of money may seem attractive to politicians because it can enable the government to pay off debts and to provide services to the public without raising taxes, or because the effects of lowering unemployment and increasing growth are more immediately visible to the public. However, politicians are rarely trained as economists and therefore may make weaker economic decisions than central bankers (who are almost always economists).

DIDYOUKNOW?

Countries have, from time to time, operated with more or less free banking in which there is no central bank with exclusive authority to regulate the money supply. The mid-nineteenth century was as close as the United States ever got to such a system, but the experiment has also been tried in Sweden, Scotland, Switzerland, and Australia. In such systems, banks can create their own currency in the form of transferrable banknotes that can be redeemed at the issuing bank.

Federal Reserve System Structure and Functions

The United States was relatively late to the game in terms of instituting a central bank—a major financial panic in 1907 served as the impetus to create a system empowered with the authority that characterizes modern central banks. The Federal Reserve Act of 1913 created the Federal Reserve System, a central banking network consisting of a

Board of Governors in Washington, D.C., and twelve regional Federal Reserve Banks spread across the country. The seven governors are political appointees, but they serve staggered fourteen-year terms in order to give them the political independence to do what they deem right for the economy regardless of the short-term popularity of those actions.

DIDYOUKNOW?

Is the Federal Reserve part of the national government? This question does not have a straightforward answer. Because the Fed is owned and partially run by private banks, yet accountable to the public and responsible for types of oversight and enforcement typically associated with governments, it is described as quasi-public and quasi-private.

The main job of the Federal Reserve is to foster maximum employment and price stability, often referred to as a **dual mandate**. Its task is to strike a balance between an economy that grows quickly enough to provide jobs for the labor force yet doesn't grow so fast that prices rise in an undesirable way. As we've seen in prior chapters, these goals (keeping both unemployment and inflation low) can often be in tension. Under normal economic circumstances, the Fed attempts to fulfill its dual mandate by using the three tools described in the next section.

The arm of the Fed most responsible for carrying out monetary policy in furtherance of the dual mandate is the Federal Open Market Committee (FOMC). This group meets at least eight times each year in order to estimate the current state of economic activity relative to its goals (unemployment between 5 percent and 6 percent, with inflation as close to 2 percent as possible) and to determine policy actions that will best help achieve them. The FOMC is made up of nineteen members, the seven governors and the twelve presidents of the regional Federal Reserve banks. Twelve of these nineteen members have a vote in any given year—the seven governors and the president of the New York Fed, along with four other Fed presidents on a rotating annual schedule. The FOMC decides on specific actions that the Fed needs to take, most of which are carried out through the New York Fed's Open Market Desk.

Beyond the dual mandate, other parts of the Federal Reserve perform a variety of functions that help support a strong banking system and a stable economy. Most significantly, the Fed acts as a bank for commercial banks. Just as you may keep money in a bank account for safekeeping, banks can deposit funds to their accounts at the Federal Reserve Bank. A large percentage of a bank's reserves are typically kept on deposit at the Fed. In addition, the Fed sets regulations for banks, supervising them in ways designed to protect the public interest. Banks from different areas of the country use the Fed to settle payments owed from one to another when clearing checks written on one bank's account but cashed or deposited at another bank. The Fed also manages the nation's reserves of foreign currency and much of the gold supply it holds. These functions are not nearly as important for your purposes as the use of the three main tools of monetary policy that the Fed uses. Let's examine those in more detail next.

Three Major Tools of Monetary Policy

Central banks like the Fed typically have at their disposal three approaches to taking monetary policy action, or changing the money supply in order to influence the economy. Each of the tools can be used to either increase or decrease the money supply. When central banks increase the money supply, they are using expansionary policy; they use contractionary policy to decrease it.

Open Market Operations

The most frequently used tool (and most commonly tested on the AP exam) of central banking is the use of open market operations to influence the money supply. This involves the central bank buying bonds from banks to inject their balance sheets with more reserves, or selling bonds to banks to drain reserves from their balance sheets.

To increase the money supply, the Fed can buy government securities from a commercial bank, taking ownership of the bonds from a bank willing to sell them and depositing newly created money into the bank's reserve account as payment for them. Because the bank has the same number of deposits, it has the same number of required reserves. Therefore, the entire amount of the purchase of the bonds becomes excess reserves and that bank may lend them all out, thereby increasing the money supply by the full amount of the purchase. Eventually, the banking system can increase the money supply by the amount of the transaction times the money multiplier. With a reserve ratio of 10 percent, a $1 million purchase of bonds by the Fed could increase the money supply by as much as $10 million.

If, instead, the Fed purchases bonds directly from the public (for example, if a bond trading firm sells the Fed the securities), then the money supply immediately increases by the amount of the purchase because the money is in public circulation. If the bond traders then deposit the funds, the banking system can increase the money supply further via the multiplier effect.

Increasing the money supply lowers the interest rate. Because these transactions involve the purchase of bonds, they tend to drive up the prices at which bonds are traded on the secondary bond market. When prices of bonds increase, the interest rate those bonds yield drops. A second connection comes through the Federal Funds Market. As the Fed injects reserves in the banking system, an increasing number of banks find themselves with more reserves than they need, and fewer banks find themselves in need of more reserves. More banks are willing to lend to other banks, and fewer need to borrow in order to meet short-term reserve requirements. Thus, the federal funds rate decreases. Lower interest rates on bonds and in interbank lending markets tend to push down interest rates across the economy.

A decrease in the money supply works in the opposite way—the Fed offers bonds for sale in an auction, and interested banks bid a price they are willing to pay for them. The Fed accepts the highest offers, and the price of bonds on secondary markets drops, increasing the interest rate on bonds. The Fed gives the bonds to the bank, withdrawing money from that bank's reserve account as payment. That money, now in the hands of the central bank and no longer in circulation, ceases to exist. Because excess reserves have been drained from the banking system, fewer banks have extra reserves; therefore, banks are less interested in lending to one another. They charge other banks a higher federal funds rate. Bonds pay more interest now and banks have to pay more to obtain funds to lend; both factors mean that banks are likely to charge customers higher interest rates for loans they might take out to buy a car, finance a home mortgage, or send a child to college.

DIDYOUKNOW?

During the financial crisis of 2007–2008, the FOMC reduced the target it set for the federal funds rate several times—to historic lows. In December 2008, the target was moved downward as far as it could go—the Fed announced that it would purchase assets from banks in order to keep the federal funds rate between 0 percent and 0.25 percent. In doing so, it entered uncharted waters, inventing new tools to use as part of its zero interest rate policy. On one hand, this extreme injection of liquidity into the banking system may well have prevented a much more severe economic collapse. On the other, the Fed has held rates this low for over four years and promised to do so until 2015, and unemployment has not yet fallen to normal levels.

The main tool that the Fed uses to conduct monetary policy is the purchase or sale of securities on the open market, which injects or drains reserves from the banking system and encourages a lower or higher federal funds rate (FFR). The Fed cannot directly control the rate at which banks lend to one another, but it can set a target range it thinks is appropriate for these loans and then announce that it will use open market operations to keep lending within those parameters, buying bonds if the effective federal funds rate climbs above the Fed's comfort zone and selling bonds if banks begin lending to one another at rates the Fed feels are too low.

Lending to Commercial Banks

The Fed and other central banks also serve as lenders of last resort, meaning that they position themselves as places where commercial banks can go to borrow in order to meet reserve shortages if they cannot find banks willing to lend to them in the interbank lending market. When banks borrow from the Fed directly, they do so at the discount window. These banks then owe the Fed the principal amount of the loan plus the discount interest rate set by the Fed.

When the Fed changes the **discount rate** at which it is willing to lend to member banks directly, it uses a slightly different way to change the wholesale price of money for banks. When the Fed reduces the discount rate, banks can borrow money more cheaply and are, in turn, willing to lend it at lower interest rates. This makes borrowing and lending cheaper and more attractive, increasing the banking system's lending activity. Conversely, a higher discount rate makes money more expensive for banks and therefore they are likely to charge bank customers higher interest rates on loans, thus discouraging borrowing and lending.

Because these interest rate changes make banks more or less likely to lend, they change the supply of money in circulation. Less lending means less expansion of the money supply via the multiplier effect. More lending means the money supply expands.

Usually a change in the target federal funds rate is implemented in conjunction with a similar change in the discount rate. This change stabilizes the spread between the price that banks must pay the Fed to borrow directly from it and the price banks must pay to borrow from other banks.

Changing the Reserve Requirement

Recall that the reserve requirement is the percentage of a checking deposit that a bank must hold rather than lend. The money multiplier is the reciprocal of the reserve ratio. When the Fed (or any other central bank) changes the ratio of checkable deposits that must be held on reserve, the money multiplier changes.

If the reserve requirement is reduced, some of the reserves that had previously been required become excess and therefore can be lent. Every time money is deposited, more of it can be lent because the money multiplier is larger. This increases the money supply and reduces interest rates.

An increase in the reserve requirement decreases the money multiplier, converting some excess reserves into required ones and decreasing the lending potential of the banking system. As a result, the money supply shrinks and interest rates rise.

Changing the reserve requirement is a tool that central banks rarely, if ever, use. Why? A higher reserve requirement functions like a tax on banks, dictating to them that a greater portion of their funds cannot be lent at interest and makes banking less profitable. A reserve rate that is too low makes a run on banks more likely. This problem occurs when so many depositors want to withdraw money and the bank doesn't have sufficient reserves to cover the desired withdrawals. An additional reason that reserve requirements aren't adjusted frequently is because this tool of monetary policy is stronger than the others and its effects are difficult to predict. Despite the tool being seldom used, the AP test will probably ask about the effects of reserve requirement changes, so be comfortable with all three basic monetary policy tools.

Table 9-2. The Effects of Central Banking on the Money Supply

Basic Central Bank Tool	Contractionary Action	Expansionary Action
Open market operations	Sell bonds to increase FFR	Buy bonds to decrease FFR
Discount rate	Increase discount rate	Decrease discount rate
Required reserve ratio	Increase ratio	Decrease ratio
Effect on money supply	**Money supply decreases**	**Money supply increases**

Putting the Fed's Tools in Perspective

Table 9-2 summarizes the two ways each of the three tools explained in this chapter can be used to change the money supply. Note that any of the contractionary actions decrease the money supply and increase prevailing interest rates in the economy. These actions slow economic activity, reducing inflation and output. Likewise, the expansionary tools increase the money supply and reduce interest rates on loans throughout the economy. All of these actions speed up economic activity, leading to increases in both the price level and output.

TEST TIP

It is likely that in the free-response portion of the AP exam, you will need to show the effects of central bank action on the money market graph introduced earlier in this chapter. Even if you don't, several multiple-choice questions will ask you to identify the effects of the changes shown in Table 9-2. The easiest way to do this is to sketch quick graphs of the money market and show the changes that the question is asking about. Drawing a quick graph in the scratch space, even if it isn't labeled formally, will make difficult questions far easier.

Figure 9-4. Expansionary Monetary Policy Decreases the Interest Rate

Nominal Interest Rate
MS1
MS2
Increase in Money Supply
14
12
10
8
i_1 6
4
i_2
2
MD
Q1
Q2
Quantity of Money

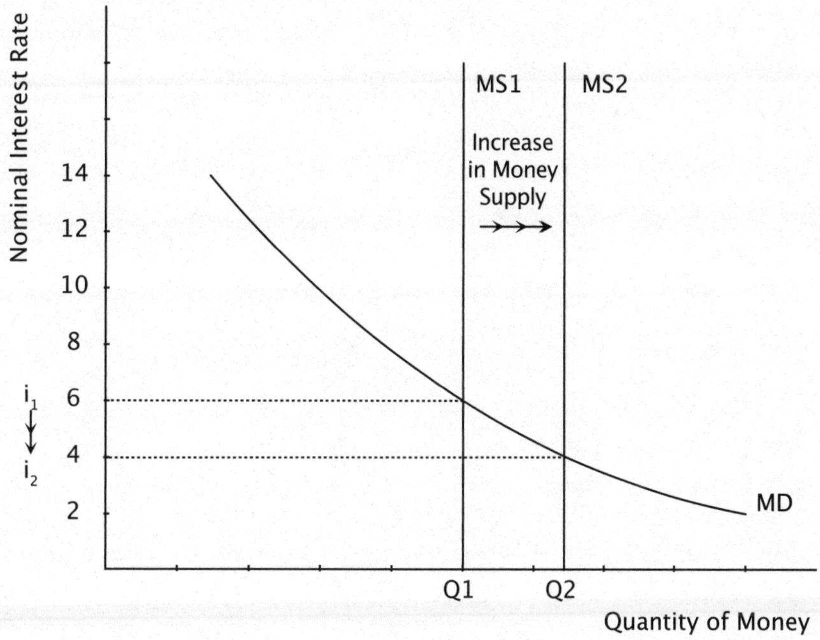

Figure 9-5. Contractionary Monetary Policy Increases the Interest Rate

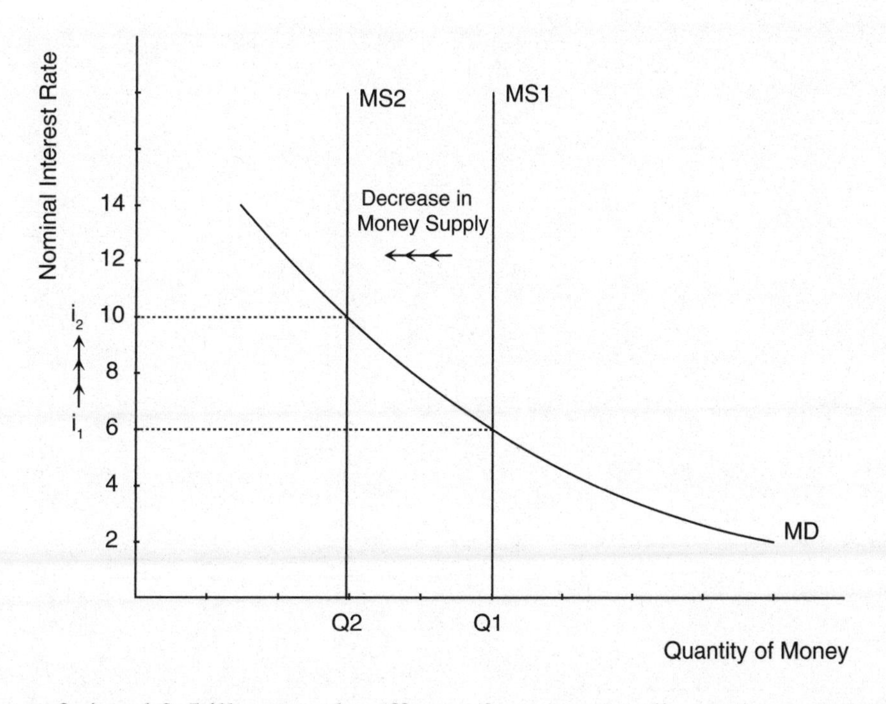

Figures 9-4 and 9-5 illustrate the effects of monetary policy actions on the interest rate. In Figure 9-4, an increase in the money supply from Q1 to Q2 decreases the interest rate from 6 percent to 4 percent, which encourages more borrowing and spending. In Figure 9-5, when the money supply decreases from Q1 to Q2, the interest rate rises from 6 percent to 10 percent, which makes borrowing and spending more costly.

Chapter 10

Fiscal and Monetary Policies in Action

Fiscal Policy Explained

Fiscal policy is the use of the tax code and the budgetary process to manipulate the macroeconomy. Because taxes are taken from income before earners get to spend it, changing taxes alters the amount of disposable income available to households. This causes consumption spending to rise or fall (as explained in Chapter 7), thus influencing GDP.

The federal budget is a set of bills passed by Congress that appropriate money to various departments of the executive branch, authorizing government purchases of goods and services as well as transfer payments. Transfer payments are money payments to individuals. Because they are not payments made in exchange for goods produced or services rendered, these are not directly counted in GDP. Nonetheless, they do influence aggregate demand and GDP because they become disposable income for the recipients of these payments. Government purchases are part of aggregate demand and therefore affect output.

Expansionary and Contractionary Fiscal Policy

Fiscal policy is typically used to shift aggregate demand. If the elective branches of government wish to change employment and output, they may use tax changes and spending decisions as ways to accomplish their goals.

Expansionary Fiscal Policy

To shift aggregate demand to the right, the government uses expansionary fiscal policy. If government purchases of goods and services are increased, aggregate demand (AD) shifts right by the amount of the purchase and may further shift by the multiplier effect. Recall that 1/MPS or 1/(1 − MPC) times the value of the increase in purchases is the maximum amount AD could shift rightward.

Alternatively, the president and Congress might decide to lower taxes, leaving consumers with more disposable income. The increase in disposable income causes an increase in savings and consumption, according to the marginal propensity to save (MPS) and the marginal propensity to consume (MPC), respectively. Taking the amount of the first spending change times the multiplier yields the full amount that AD might shift to the right.

If the government instead increases transfer payments to individuals, then disposable income increases just as it would have with a tax cut. Again, some of the payment amount is saved and some is spent. AD first shifts by MPC times the amount of the payment increase, then will be affected by the multiplier.

Expansionary Fiscal Policy
1. Increase government purchases.
2. Decrease taxes.
3. Increase transfer payments.

Expansionary fiscal policy is so named because it is designed to expand or grow the economy. Predictably, these policies shift AD to the right, causing an increase in output and employment. Often they come at a cost of rising prices.

Contractionary Fiscal Policy

To shift aggregate demand to the left, the government uses contractionary fiscal policy. If government purchases of goods and services decrease, aggregate demand shifts left by the amount of the purchase and may shift further because of the multiplier effect. Recall that 1/MPS or 1/(1 − MPC) times the value of the decrease in purchases is the maximum amount AD can shift leftward.

Alternatively, an increase in taxes leaves consumers with less disposable income. The decrease in disposable income causes a decrease in savings and consumption. AD is affected first by MPC times the value of the tax increase. Taking the amount of the first spending decrease times the multiplier yields the full amount that AD might shift to the left.

If the government instead decreases transfer payments to individuals, then disposable income decreases just as it would have with a tax cut. Again, both savings and consumption decrease. AD first shifts by MPC times the amount of the payment decrease, then is affected by the multiplier.

Contractionary fiscal policy is so named because it is designed to contract the economy. Predictably, these policies shift AD to the left, causing a decrease in output and employment. The benefit is typically a decrease in inflation.

Contractionary Fiscal Policy
1. Decrease government purchases.
2. Increase taxes.
3. Decrease transfer payments.

Automatic and Discretionary Policy

One downside to taking fiscal policy action to stabilize the economy is that it can be slow. There are other drawbacks as well: A partisan political process may not always lead to the best policy formation, and in many countries elected officials are not economists by trade. Because of the complex and contentious process of enacting tax reform or altering various kinds of government spending, this type of discretionary fiscal policy can't do the job by itself.

Fortunately, **automatic stabilizers** are built into the way several categories of government spending are governed. The tax code tends to work in this fashion as well. Together, these can influence aggregate demand, even when elected officials take no policy action, and they provide a slight tug working against any shift in AD.

When AD shifts to the left, employment and output fall. Because some people lose work, more members of the labor force qualify for unemployment benefits (a category of transfer payments), and it is possible that the number enrolled in the Supplemental Nutrition Assistance or Medicaid programs may increase as well. Meanwhile, as national income is declining, tax revenues fall because Americans' taxable incomes have decreased in the aggregate. First, note that these factors take effect without explicit governmental action; they are results of the way the tax code and entitlement programs have been structured. Second, both serve to push AD a little bit back toward the right. Changing economic conditions caused fiscal policy to push back against the leftward movement of aggregate demand.

Under different circumstances, AD might shift right. As the national income rises, more people pay taxes and do so on greater earnings, so tax revenues rise. Fewer people qualify for various need-based government assistance programs (because the unemployment rate is falling, fewer people draw unemployment insurance checks), so government spending drops. Both of these automatic stabilizers nudge AD to the left.

TEST TIP

The automatic stabilizers described in this chapter work against changes in aggregate demand, so they stabilize its movements. These don't usually keep AD where macroeconomic policymakers might want it, but think of them as working to offset part of the multiplier effect. Fortunately, on the AP exam, you won't be asked anything about the degree to which these balance one another.

Fiscal Policy Is Designed to Be Countercyclical

Fiscal policy in general is used to create the same effects as the stabilizers—to move aggregate demand in order that the economy is closer to its long-run equilibrium position. When the aggregate demand curve is too far to the left and employment and output are low, expansionary fiscal policy can be used to boost economic activity. Thus, in recessions or troughs in the business cycle, you might see a tax cut or a stimulus spending bill gain support.

If the economy is in a fast expansion phase or a peak in the business cycle, contractionary policy might be used to slow growth in output and control inflationary pressure. These policies shift AD leftward. Tax increases and spending cuts tend to be less common; both are unpopular. As a result, many governments carve out larger and larger economic roles over time and frequently get into the habit of spending more than they raise in tax revenue.

Automatic fiscal policy is **countercyclical**, and discretionary policy is supposed to work that way as well. They ideally work to push against and even out the movements in aggregate demand that result from the business cycle.

Fiscal Policy and Aggregate Demand

Fiscal policy is a set of tools that can be used to move aggregate demand right or left. The odds are very strong that the AP exam will ask you to show this process in a graph that you draw. Several multiple-choice questions on the same subject will be easy to answer by visualizing fiscal policy's effect on AD in graphical form.

Figure 10-1 shows the effects of fiscal policy properly employed to fix a recessionary gap. As aggregate demand shifts right, real GDP and the price level rise. The short-run equilibrium slides up and along the short-run aggregate supply (SRAS) curve. If effective, the shift leaves the economy in long-run equilibrium on the long-run aggregate supply (LRAS) curve. As a result, unemployment falls while price level rises.

Conversely, Figure 10-2 shows contractionary fiscal policy in action. As AD shifts left, from AD1 to AD2, real output falls from Yi to Yf, and the price level falls from PLi to PLe. If you are asked to draw how fiscal policy should be used to correct an inflationary gap in which GDP was above full-employment level, you should produce a graph like the one in Figure 10-2.

Figure 10-1. Expansionary Fiscal Policy Shifts AD to the Right

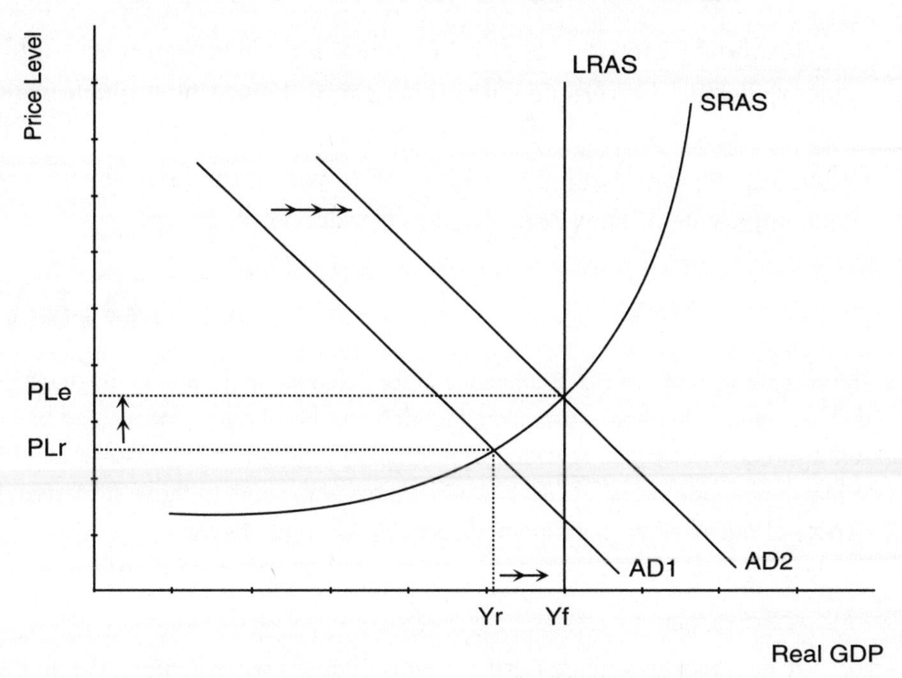

Figure 10-2. Contractionary Fiscal Policy Shifts AD to the Left

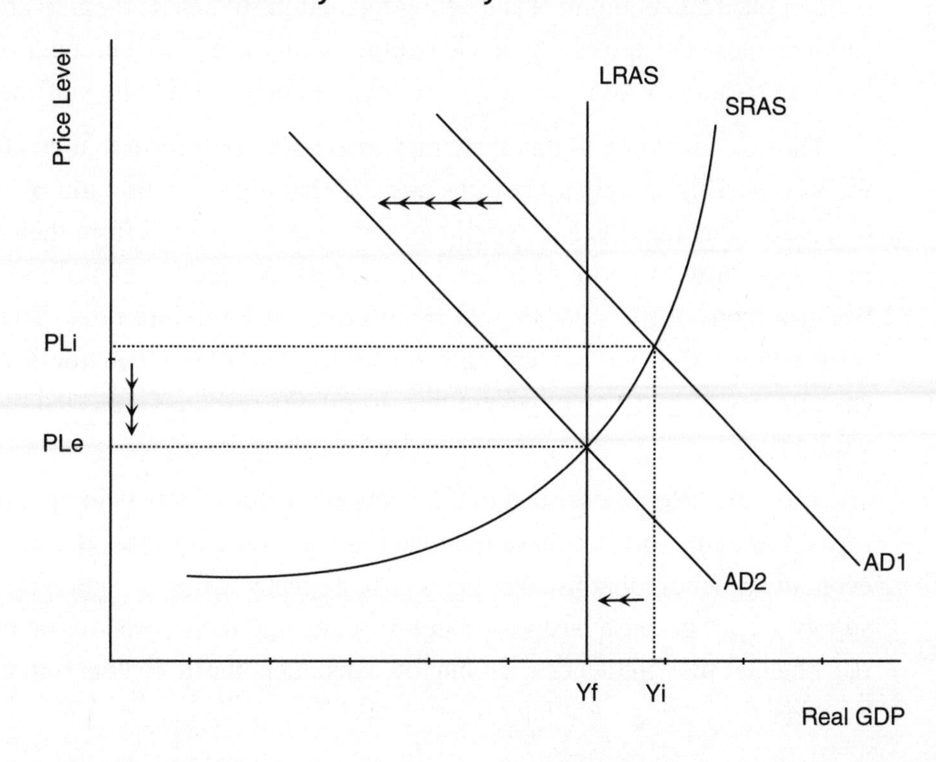

The effects of fiscal policy on aggregate demand are not in much doubt. You can feel confident that a sound knowledge about how expansionary and contractionary policies affect AD will pay off on the test.

Fiscal Policy and Aggregate Supply

Just how various kinds of fiscal policy influence aggregate supply is the subject of intense debate. Governmental actions can influence how much firms want to produce and how much people in the labor force want to work. If successful, these policies shift short-run aggregate supply to the right, lowering the price level while boosting output and employment. How does fiscal policy accomplish this?

DIDYOUKNOW?

The oil embargo of the 1970s influenced macroeconomic theory. In the mid-1970s, Robert Mundell was among the first to articulate the idea that fiscal policy tools could be used to shift short-run aggregate supply to reverse the stagflation problem that was a result of the oil embargo. While the Reagan administration experimented with some of these strategies, there is still some debate about whether these methods are reliable and effective.

If governments make business activity less costly, firms have an incentive to increase production. So supply-side economists favor cutting capital gains taxes to spur investment in plant and equipment and lifting regulations to enable them to produce goods and services more cheaply. In their view, minimum-wage laws and environmental restrictions on business activity increase production costs, artificially shifting SRAS left.

Those subscribing to this view may also seek tax reform that creates motivation to work. Lowering marginal tax rates ensures that a greater fraction of income becomes disposable income. Because employees have less deducted from their paychecks, they may want to work more or at least be willing to accept a slightly lower initial wage because more of their wages will be left over at lower tax rates. The famous economist Arthur Laffer argued that, in some cases, lower tax rates would speed up growth, encouraging so much employment that overall tax revenues collected by the government would rise.

The conclusions described in this section are not widely held by mainstream economists. Generally, tax cuts have led to less government revenue, not more. Demand-side economists believe that fiscal policies have a greater effect on aggregate demand than on supply, in part because businesses and workers base their decisions on many factors. Tax rate changes may influence spending by consumers far more than future work decisions.

TEST TIP

It isn't likely that you will see a lot of questions on the supply-side view of fiscal policy on the AP exam, but remember that cutting taxes on businesses can change SRAS as well as AD. If a multiple-choice item asks about fiscal policy, focus on aggregate demand, unless the question strongly suggests that you consider the supply-side view.

Fiscal Policy and Interest Rates

The connection between fiscal policy and interest rates is a topic that the AP exam almost always covers. Questions asking about real interest rates or their relationship to fiscal policy will be based on your ability to understand the loanable funds market.

The Loanable Funds Market

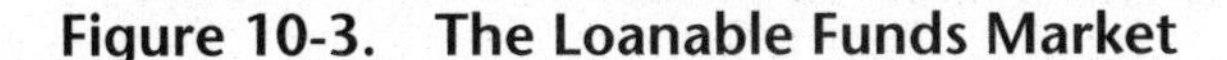

The loanable funds model is an alternative to using the money market model. Instead of showing the nominal interest rate at which overnight loans are made from one commercial bank to another, the loanable funds market shows the real interest rate on long-term loans. The basic principles of demand and supply hold, so there is nothing particularly scary about learning how to do your own loanable funds analysis.

Figure 10-3. The Loanable Funds Market

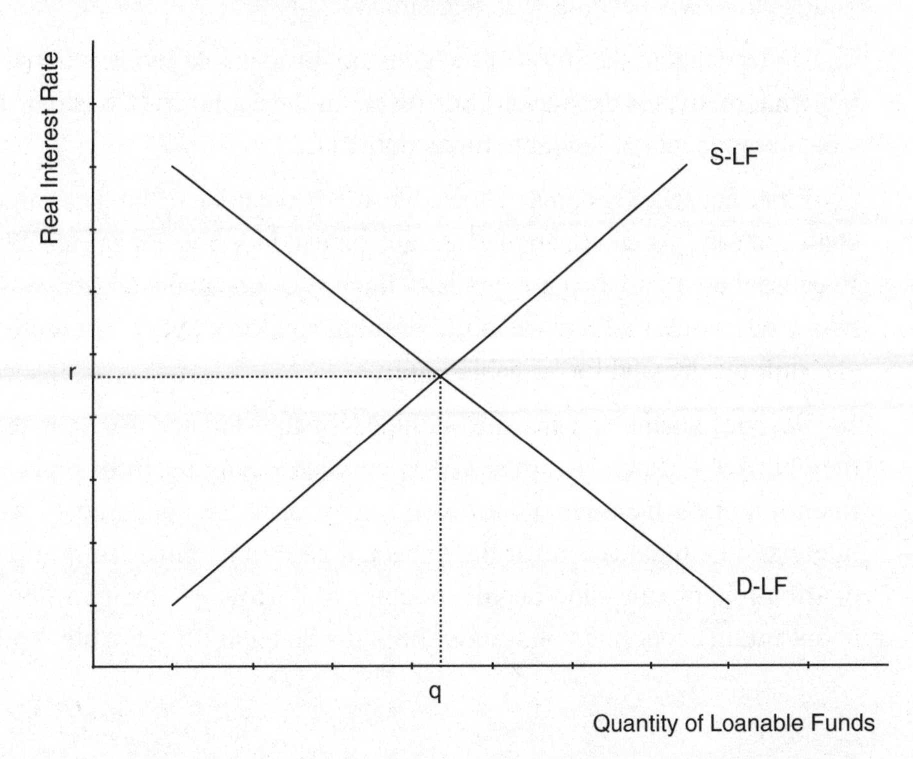

In the loanable funds market, which is shown in Figure 10-3, note that the vertical axis is the real interest rate. This is the actual increase in purchasing power that the lender can expect, or the interest that is repaid adjusted downward for any inflation that may have occurred between the loan and the repayment. Because longer-term loans like five-year car loans, ten-year student loans, and thirty-year home mortgages involve substantial changes in the price level between the loan date and the end of the repayment schedule, lenders and borrowers have to make guesses at the time of the loan about the actual value of the money that will be repaid far in the future. This model assumes that the price of money that long-term lenders and borrowers are concerned with is the real interest rate.

The quantity axis is labeled, quite predictably, as Quantity of Loanable Funds and represents the money that people are trying to lend (or sell) and borrow (or buy) at various values of the real interest rate. And as you might expect, the equilibrium real interest rate and quantity of funds borrowed and lent are determined by the intersection of the demand and supply for loanable funds.

Demand for Loanable Funds

The demand for loanable funds slopes downward, showing the inverse relationship between the quantity of loanable funds demanded and the real interest rate. When interest rates are high, borrowers must promise to pay back more in future purchasing power than when they are low. This serves to discourage borrowing. On the other hand, when interest rates are low, borrowing is encouraged. Not much future wealth will need to be sacrificed in order to repay a loan, so more cars, houses, college educations, and capital goods purchases become wise decisions.

Understanding the shifts of the demand for loanable funds is a matter of understanding what motivates the various borrowers in the economy. Consider the following possible components of loanable funds demand.

First, households demand loanable funds in order to finance large purchases. Purchases of cars, vacations, appliances, and demand for home loans are all interest-sensitive. Because these purchases are typically financed, consumers are responsive to the interest rate. Households that feel wealthier or more confident about the future borrow more and can shift the demand for loanable funds.

Second, business firms are included in the demand for loanable funds because they borrow to finance capital goods purchases ranging from replacement machinery to entirely new factories or stores. Firms balance the added cost (part of which is the interest to be repaid) against the expected gain in revenue from improved production, distribution, or sales and decide whether to borrow. A change in business confidence about future economic conditions shifts the demand for loanable funds.

Third, the foreign sector may borrow. If interest rates are lower in a given country than the interest rates for its neighbors, there might be a high foreign sector demand for loanable funds in that country. Changes in the interest rates of foreign nations can influence the demand for loanable funds.

Fourth, the government might borrow from the loanable funds market in order to finance deficit spending. If tax revenue is smaller than government expenditures, governments must find a way to pay for the difference by borrowing. This increases the demand for loanable funds. This public sector borrowing can cause a crowding-out effect on the borrowing done by private firms and households, as explained in the next section.

Supply of Loanable Funds

Unlike the money supply controlled by the Fed, the supply of loanable funds slopes upward, as you might expect. Loanable funds don't quite measure the same thing, however: The supply of loanable funds represents the relationship between the real interest rate and the amount of money that lenders wish to loan. The better the rate of return, the more they'll lend. At low interest rates or in dire circumstances, lenders may not want to lend funds at all, fearing that the risk of nonrepayment is bad enough to justify holding funds and earning no interest at all.

The supply of loanable funds comes first and foremost from savings. If households and firms save lots of money in banks, those banks have plenty of excess reserves that they are eager to lend to qualified borrowers. Increases in savings lead to rightward shifts of the loanable funds supply curve.

Foreign sectors play a role in many countries' loanable funds supplies. If lenders cannot find borrowers domestically, they may lend money abroad. For many possible lenders, foreign markets represent a chance for more certain repayment, a location of willing borrowers who have a stable stream of future income with which to repay a long-term loan or a safe haven from unpredictable changes in their domestic price levels.

Last, governments can be part of the loanable funds supply if they run surpluses. When governments run surpluses, the gains most often merely offset a small portion of a longer-term governmental debt.

Figure 10-4 shows an increase in the supply of loanable funds, which reduces real interest rates and increases the quantity of funds borrowed and lent. As the real interest rate drops from r1 to r2, private firms find more capital goods purchases to be favorable because the same expected rate of return is now, in many cases, greater than the interest cost, which has decreased. Consumption is also encouraged because terms for consumer loans are more enticing: That new car, television, refrigerator, or vacation can be financed with a lower interest cost.

Figure 10-4. An Increase in the Supply of Loanable Funds

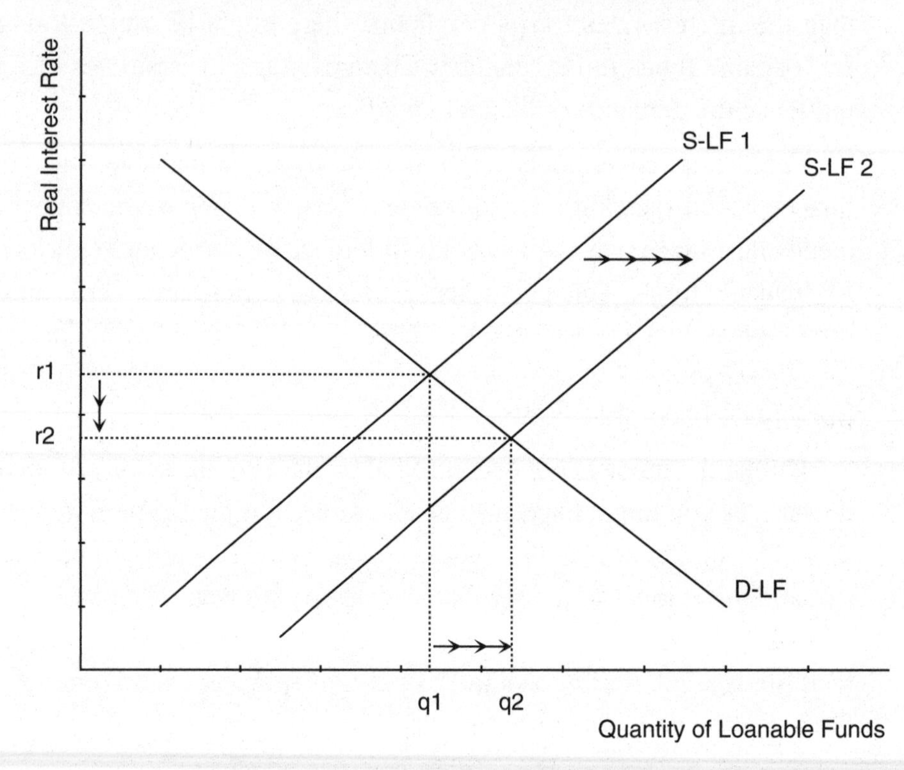

The loanable funds market provides an important connector between interest rates on one hand and national output and price level on the other. Two components of aggregate demand—interest-sensitive consumption and investment—are influenced by actions in the loanable funds market. But investment is also a determinant of future long-run aggregate supply because capital goods acquired today can be used to produce goods in the coming years.

TEST TIP

Most AP exam questions about the loanable funds (LF) market will test your knowledge of the crowding-out concept. However, some free-response and multiple-choice questions have asked students to consider the effects of a shift in the supply of loanable funds or about how an interest rate ceiling or floor might influence the market's operation. Pay close attention to what the question is asking and use the fundamental demand and supply principles you know. Then think about how the changes in the loanable funds market (usually the change in real interest rate) influences the other concepts included in the question. Generally, asking yourself how a given institution or group would behave differently if money were more or less expensive will help you answer unfamiliar loanable funds model questions.

Crowding-Out Effect

Quite often, the AP exam includes a series of questions designed to test your ability to connect deficit spending to loanable funds demand, to the real interest rate, and to the level of private investment, capital stock, and long-term growth. That's quite a chain of events to be responsible for! However, it is not as tough as it initially sounds. In fact, the idea serves as a helpful and intuitive answer to the question about why governments don't use expansionary fiscal policy to increase GDP more often—trying to use the public sector to boost output in the short run can often limit long-run economic growth. To understand how, let's break it into steps using our new tool—the loanable funds market—to illustrate.

The Cause

Imagine that the government uses expansionary fiscal policy to increase aggregate demand and real output. Whether government spending is increased or taxes are reduced or some combination of the two, the government's budget balance is pushed toward deficit. If the government had a balanced budget before, it now must borrow (if it was running a budget deficit before, it is forced to borrow even more). That's the initial cause of the crowding-out concept: An expansionary fiscal policy requires the government to borrow, shifting the demand for loanable funds to the right.

Figure 10-5. The Crowding-Out Effect

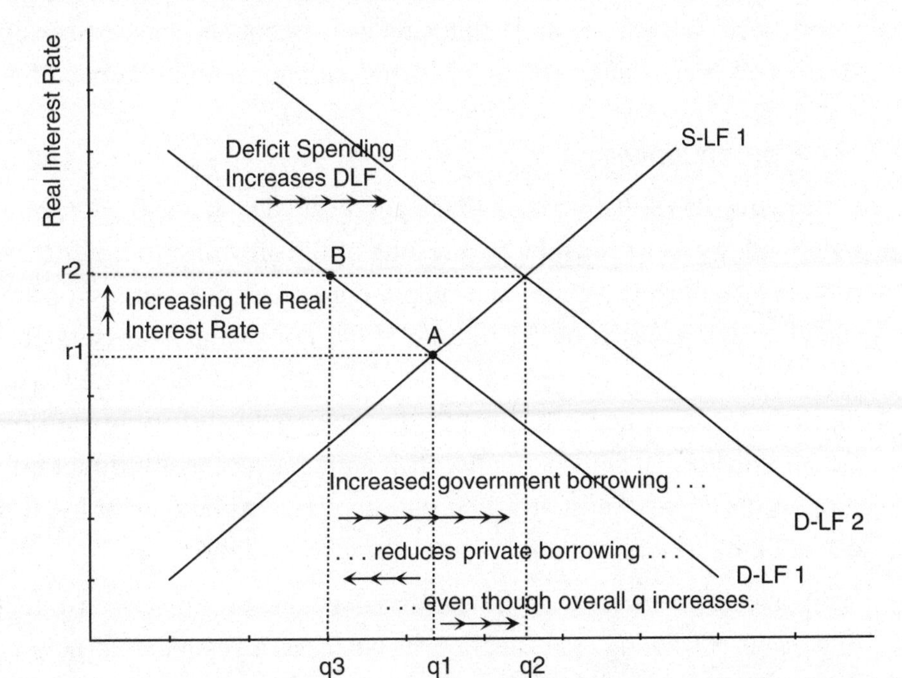

As standard demand-supply analysis suggests, this rightward shift of loanable funds demand pushes up the real interest rate in the loanable funds market. More funds in total are being borrowed and lent as well. Figure 10-5 shows some important steps in the causal chain. Right now, focus on the fact that loanable funds demand shifted right from D-LF 1 to D-LF 2. This results in an increase in real interest rates from r1 to r2 and a greater quantity of funds lent (q2 as opposed to the old q1).

The Effect

Observe that the government's increase in borrowing did not increase overall borrowing anywhere near the full amount of the expansionary policy, which is because of the unintended consequence of higher borrowing costs on private sector borrowers. Firms and households that wanted to take out loans at the lower r1 but not at the new higher prevailing interest rate r2 have been discouraged, squeezed out, or **crowded out** of the market. To see this more clearly, consider that D-LF 1 still represents the borrowing plans of households and businesses. Projects that have large expected gains are shown by points up high to the left on the curve; borrowers are willing to take out loans for these purposes even at high rates. Points lower on the demand curve symbolize projects that have progressively lower anticipated rates of return. Firms are not willing to pay very high interest rates on investments that don't stand to increase their profits much. The section of the demand curve between point A and point B shows the possible planned expenditures that firms and households have now decided not to pursue due to the higher real interest rate. Before, if the government budget was balanced, private actors borrowed and spent q1 funds on investment and interest-sensitive consumption. At the new higher interest rate (r2), firms and households demand fewer loans (q3).

The Consequences

Linking this situation back to the aggregate demand and aggregate supply (AD-AS) model allows us to consider two results of the crowding-out effect. First, in the short-run, AD won't shift right by the full amount predicted. Let's suppose that government spending is increased by $5 billion. If the borrowing necessary for this expenditure raised interest rates enough to crowd out $2 billion of private borrowing and spending (consumption and investment), the AD would shift rightward by only $3 billion. Because the initial shift is smaller than anticipated, the multiplier effect would also be proportionally smaller. Crowding out therefore explains why fiscal policy sometimes doesn't have as large an effect as policymakers might wish.

You are far more likely to be asked about the longer-run effects of the decline in private borrowing. The decline in business investment in new capital equipment decreases the rate at which the nation's capital stock grows (**capital stock** is the set of tools, machines, human know-how, and factories available in an economy at a given time, a kind of national toolbox). Fewer investment projects feel profitable for firms and therefore they add less new capital to the country's collective toolbox.

The growth of capital stock is one of the primary factors driving long-run economic growth (see Chapter 11), our ability to produce more goods and services over time. As the acquisition of new production plants and equipment slows, so does the rate at which the economy grows. This means that long-run supply and the production possibilities curve do not shift right as fast as they otherwise might.

TEST TIP

You are almost certain to be faced with questions over the following series of events in the crowding-out process:

> Expansionary fiscal policy ➔ government borrowing ➔ higher real interest rates ➔ decreased business investment ➔ less added to capital stock ➔ slower long-run growth rate.

Know it well. Be able to show and explain how the relevant steps affect both the loanable funds and AD-AS graphs. Don't worry about applying this process in reverse, or in some sort of "crowding back in" process. This is one of the few causal connections that the AP exam seems to test in one direction only.

The Impact of Deficits and the Public Debt

In any given year, if a government collects less in taxes than it spends, it runs a deficit. Years in which tax revenues exceed expenditures result in annual surpluses. Each year's deficit adds to the national debt; the debt is the total of all the annual deficits minus any annual surpluses. Because many governments have deficits far more often than they run surpluses, large national debts are the norm in many developed economies.

Government deficits occurring over a series of years may lead to higher interest rates and therefore slower growth. They are controversial for other reasons. Many people feel that they show a lack of discipline on the part of politicians to budget properly and result from excessive spending programs; however, voters tend to elect politicians who try to deliver more in government services than they want to tax.

One result of frequent or chronic deficit spending that cannot be denied is that public debt grows. The more debt a country is in, the more it must pay in interest payments, known as debt service. This category of expense, growing in many industrialized countries, represents payments that must be made in the future for goods and services enjoyed in the past or the present. According to the Government Accountability Office (GAO), over the last several decades, between 5 and 15 percent of the federal budget has gone annually toward paying interest (not principal) on prior debts. Some see this situation as a fairness concern: Future generations may pay taxes to pay interest on loans from which they did not (directly) benefit.

Another area of concern regarding high government debts is that they may, at some point, grow beyond the willingness of lenders to loan or that lenders to will worry about governments defaulting on their promises to repay. Willingness to loan to governments can be gauged by looking at the bond market: If people want to buy U.S. government treasury securities or other countries' sovereign bonds, even at low interest rates, that means they are willing to lend those governments money cheaply and must feel confident that they'll be paid back. While there was fear in the summer of 2011 that downgraded U.S. treasury bonds would lose favor among lenders, it seems that the amount of outstanding debt is less of a factor than the inability of Congress to project an image of confidence to markets that they will allow continued borrowing. Some countries whose economies are weaker than the U.S. economy have in fact seen a decreased willingness on the part of lenders to buy their sovereign bonds; these fears show up as lower bond prices, meaning that bond purchasers want a higher rate of return to compensate themselves for the greater likelihood that governments won't be able to pay them back.

The current U.S. government debt, $16,400,000,000,000.00, is a really large number (this is the debt as of January 2013, according to the National Debt Clock), much larger than the tab any other borrower on the planet would be allowed to run up! However, debts are probably best examined by comparing them to national income or annual GDP and comparing them to other historical contexts. Adjusting values to 2010 real dollars, the U.S. national debt is still dramatically higher than at any other time in history, but so is annual real GDP. As a percentage of output, the national debt is close to 100 percent—high, but not as high as it was immediately after World War II. Critics of this comparison will rightfully point out that, at other times in history, when the debt-to-GDP ratio spiked, it was connected to our involvement in wars. Now, however, the rising ratio stems from lack of tax revenue and rising federal entitlement spending. This structural problem was compounded by a deep recession in the late 2000s, with the result that over $1 trillion was added to the national debt each year for four consecutive years!

Real and Nominal Interest Rates

Real interest rates (RIRs) and nominal interest rates (NIRs) are both important for you to understand. You already know that the equilibrium nominal interest rate is determined in the money market and that the real interest rate is determined in the loanable funds market. How do these concepts connect?

Interest, Inflation, and Purchasing Power

When lenders give up money for a period of time, they undertake risks and costs: the inconvenience of having an asset that isn't liquid, the risk of not being paid back by the borrower, and the likelihood that the amount loaned will not be worth as much at the time of repayment because prices will have risen. This last factor is a near-certainty for long-term loans.

The first two factors lead lenders to charge a real rate of interest on loans: The nonrepayment risk and the opportunity cost of illiquidity are costs to the lender, and therefore the lender deserves compensation for those costs in the form of being paid back more purchasing power than was lent. The extra purchasing power that the lender retains after the loan is repaid is called the real interest rate. The third factor justifies charging an inflation premium, in effect raising that real interest rate by the amount that prices are expected to rise during the term of the loan.

The Fisher Equation

The Fisher equation relates inflation and interest rates. It suggests that lenders add the real interest rate and the expected inflation rate to figure the nominal interest rate—the rate that is printed into a contract and actually calculated. At the conclusion of the repayment process, the nominal rate (the rate of interest that was actually charged) minus the actual inflation rate equals the real interest rate that was gained by the lender.

The difference between the two formulations of this Fisher equation is a change from the expected rate of inflation to the actual inflation rate. At the time the loan terms are agreed on, the inflation rate of the next few years (or decades) is not known. All that the borrower and lender can do is forecast what they think inflation will be. They agree to loan terms (in this case, a fixed nominal interest rate) building in that anticipation about how much prices will rise. After the loan is repaid, one can subtract the actual rate at which the price level rose in each of the years involved to find what how much real purchasing power is gained by the lender.

Key Formula

The Fisher Equation—Two Versions
Before loan: NIR = RIR + expected inflation rate
After loan: RIR = NIR − actual inflation rate

Keeping loanable funds and money markets distinct from one another is tough for many students. The Fisher equation can be seen as a way to connect the two or explain their differences. Consider the money market as the market for short-term liquidity, such as overnight loans between banks that are only for the purposes of meeting reserve requirements temporarily. With loans of such a short term, it isn't necessary to adjust for inflation very much—if inflation were 2 percent per year, an overnight loan's nominal interest rate would need to include less than 0.005 percent of an adjustment for inflation!

Using the nominal rate on the vertical axis to explain the behavior of borrowers and lenders is fine. On longer-term loans—such as those the loanable funds market shows—accounting for the inflation rate is essential. With 2 percent inflation, every dollar repaid at the end of a thirty-year mortgage would be worth about half as much as the dollars lent! That is why the motivating factor for borrowers and lenders on long-term loans is the real, rather than the nominal, interest rate.

TEST TIP

Questions on the AP exam will seem easy if you know the two formulations of the Fisher equation. One simple question type will ask you to determine one of the three concepts given values for the other two; these problems are either simple addition or simple subtraction, typically with whole numbers. For example, the question will tell you the nominal rate on a loan is 8 percent and the expected inflation rate is 3 percent, then ask what real interest rate the lender could expect to gain (5 percent). Given values for any two, finding the third is easy. Second, and slightly more challenging, are questions that ask you to take directions of change in two of the factors and speculate about the third. For instance, you might be asked to predict what would happen to real interest rates if the Fed pushed down nominal rates, eventually causing a rising price level (real rates would necessarily fall). Last, you might use the Fisher equation as a concept to help you answer items asking who benefits (or is harmed) if inflation occurs faster (or slower) than expected. A faster-than-anticipated inflation rate causes lenders to earn less real interest than they had thought; more of the interest paid is gobbled up by rising prices than the lender had planned for.

Combinations of Fiscal and Monetary Policy

Perhaps when reading about the crowding-out effect, you thought about why the central bank doesn't just lower the interest rate in order to prevent the decrease in private borrowing? If this question occurred to you, congratulations on making a connection to an idea that is the basis for one of the more challenging topics tested on the AP exam each year: combinations of fiscal and monetary policy.

Sometimes you will be asked on the AP exam how the Federal Reserve might be able to offset or cancel out an action taken by the fiscal policy authorities (or an important effect of an action, such as the increase in interest rates that comes with increased government borrowing). Other times, AP exam questions may describe possible fiscal and monetary actions and ask you to predict the effects. Because there are two types of broad policy types (fiscal and monetary) and two directions in which each can be used (expansionary and contractionary), the basic results can be summarized easily in a 2 × 2 grid, as shown in Table 10-1. Each cell represents a different combination of policies, and within each cell, the effects on interest rates and aggregate demand are the two basic questions you should focus on. All the other results and effects identified come from one or the other of these.

Table 10-1. Fiscal Policy vs. Monetary Policy

	Expansionary Fiscal Policy 1. Increase government spending. 2. Decrease taxes.	Contractionary Fiscal Policy 1. Decrease government spending. 2. Increase taxes.
Expansionary monetary policy 1. Buy bonds to decrease federal funds rate. 2. Decrease discount rate. 3. Decrease required reserve ratio.	AD shifts right, so output and price level increase, while unemployment decreases; the change in interest rates is uncertain.	Change in AD is uncertain; interest rates decrease, so investment increases, capital stock grows faster, and long-run growth accelerates.
Contractionary monetary policy 1. Sell bonds to increase federal funds rate. 2. Increase discount rate. 3. Increase required reserve ratio.	Change in AD is uncertain; interest rates increase, so investment decreases, as do capital stock growth and long-run growth.	AD shifts left, so output and price level decrease, while unemployment increases; change in interest rates is uncertain.

As Table 10-1 shows, in each cell, either the change in interest rate or the change in aggregate demand is known; the other is uncertain and depends on the comparative size and effectiveness of the two policies undertaken. Both types of expansionary policies shift AD rightward, but fiscal and monetary options have opposite effects on interest rates: Monetary policy decreases interest rates via the money market and fiscal policy increases them in the loanable funds market.

Think through the causal effects in each cell for each of the two basic questions (AD and interest rates). Aggregate demand shifts cause changes in real GDP, the price level, and the unemployment rate. Changes in the interest rate are a main cause of investment—the process of adding new capital goods to the capital stock and one of the primary drivers of economic growth.

Unemployment and Inflation: The Phillips Curve

Based on the AD-AS model, we can draw conclusions about unemployment. As output increases, more labor is needed to produce a greater level of real GDP, leading to a decrease in the unemployment rate. You will be able to use this knowledge to support statements about unemployment through inference rather than by seeing it on a graph. The Phillips curve is an attempt to show the unemployment rate directly in comparison to the inflation rate, on the horizontal and vertical axes. Different results occur in the short and the long run, just as occurred with aggregate supply. In fact, you'll see how the Phillips curve and aggregate supply are related to one another quite closely.

The Short Run: A Trade-off

The short run, defined as the period of time in which product prices may fluctuate but wage rates are fixed, shows an inverse relationship between unemployment and inflation.

Definition and Slope of the Short-Run Phillips Curve

The **short-run Phillips curve (SRPC)** shows the connection between the unemployment rate and the inflation rate while the money wage rate is fixed. SRPC slopes downward, showing that, as the unemployment rate decreases, inflation tends to rise. This is due to the higher level of consumer spending combined with firms experiencing increasing marginal costs as they employ more labor. If the wage rate is fixed and product prices are rising, firms want more workers and hiring more workers pushes down unemployment. This change is shown in Figure 10-6, in which the short-run change in inflation and unemployment is represented by a movement along the SRPC from point A to point B. The unemployment rate drops from UE1 (about 5 percent) to UE2 (perhaps 2.9 percent), while the inflation rate rises from the old rate of 2 percent to a new rate of 5 percent. This type of change correlates with an increase in real output because, with a smaller percentage of the labor force unemployed, more goods and services are produced.

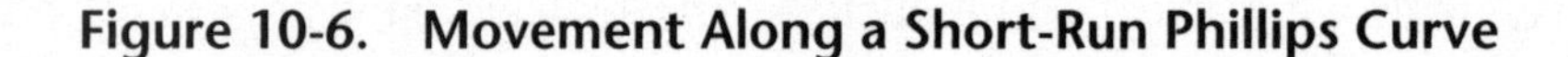

Figure 10-6. Movement Along a Short-Run Phillips Curve

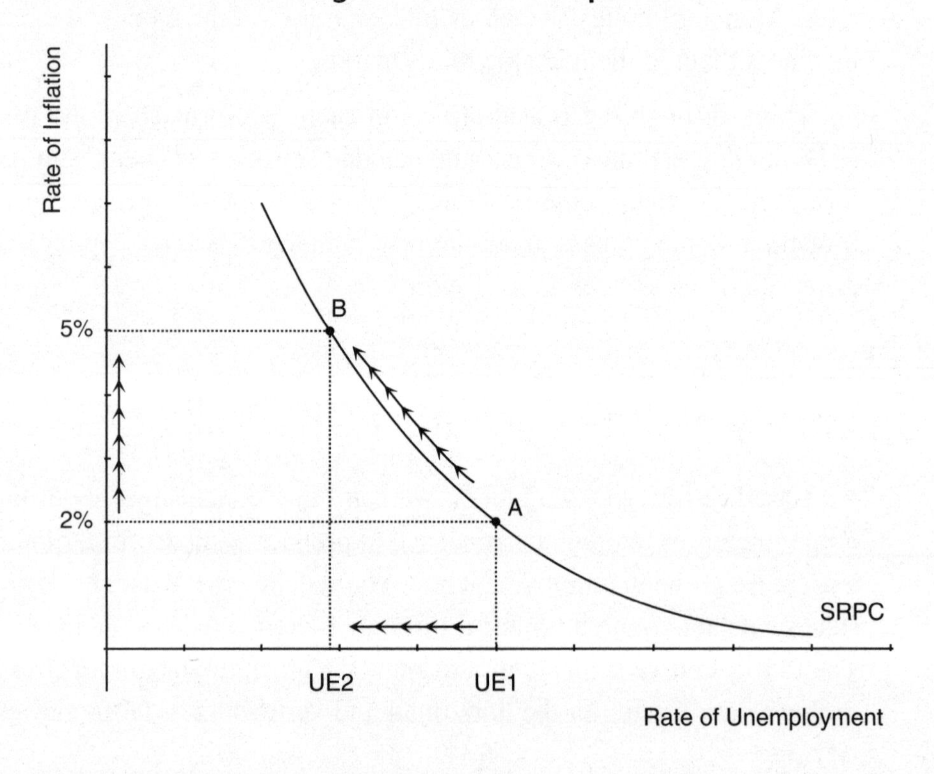

Shifts of the Short-Run Phillips Curve

The SRPC shifts whenever the costs of productive resources change. Per-unit costs of commonly used inputs influence production costs; notable near-universal inputs include labor and energy. If the money wage rate rises, any level of inflation is accompanied by a higher unemployment rate. Firms don't want to hire as many workers if wages are costlier. SRPC shifts to the right in this example, as shown in Figure 10-7. Note that any given inflation rate (say, 2 percent) now correlates with a higher unemployment rate (UE2 of about 7 percent as opposed to UE1 of just under 4 percent). Likewise, any given unemployment rate (like UE1, for example) now correlates with a higher rate of inflation (nearly 5 percent as opposed to 2 percent before).

Figure 10-7. A Rightward Shift of the Short-Run Phillips Curve

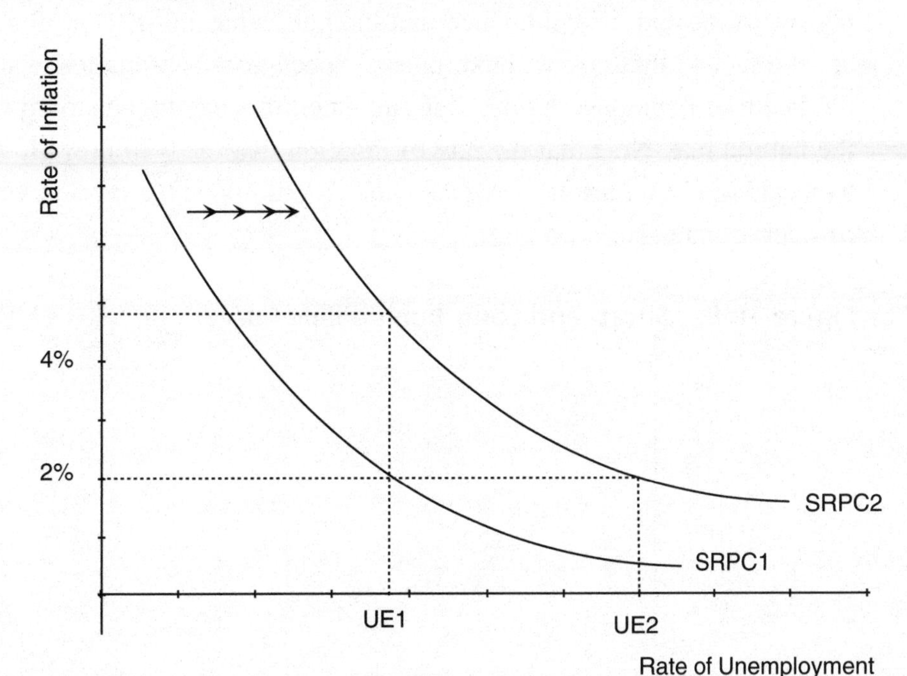

In addition to changes in the money wage rate and changes in the per-unit costs of other inputs such as electricity or oil, changes in the expected rate of inflation can shift SRPC. The short-run Phillips curve shifts to the right when inflationary expectations increase; it shifts left if less inflation is expected.

The Long Run: Natural Rate of Unemployment at Any Inflation Rate

In the long run, let's assume that nominal wages have had time to adjust to changes in the price level of finished goods and services. This is the same assumption we made when analyzing why wages are sticky in the short run and flexible in the long run, and when deriving the slopes of short-run and long-run aggregate supply.

Definition and Slope of the Long-Run Phillips Curve

If the prices of inputs like labor and capital equipment have adjusted to the new price level, then firms no longer have an incentive to employ more workers, as they did in short-run situations when prices were high but wage rates were comparatively cheaper. This is another way of saying that, in the long run, the unemployment rate is the natural rate of unemployment (NRU). The **long-run Phillips curve (LRPC)** shows that the rate of inflation in an economy is unrelated to the rate of unemployment when the economy is in long-run equilibrium. Therefore, it appears as a vertical line at NRU in Figure 10-8. In practice, the actions of the central bank in expanding the money supply over time and the confidence that the public has in the central bank's consistency are the factors that govern inflationary expectations. No matter what rate of inflation the Fed tries to engineer in the long run, unemployment tends to gravitate back toward the natural rate. Note that the rate of inflation that tends to prevail, whether by public expectation or as a result of central bank credibility, is the level at which the two Phillips curves intersect.

Figure 10-8. Short- and Long-Run Phillips Curves

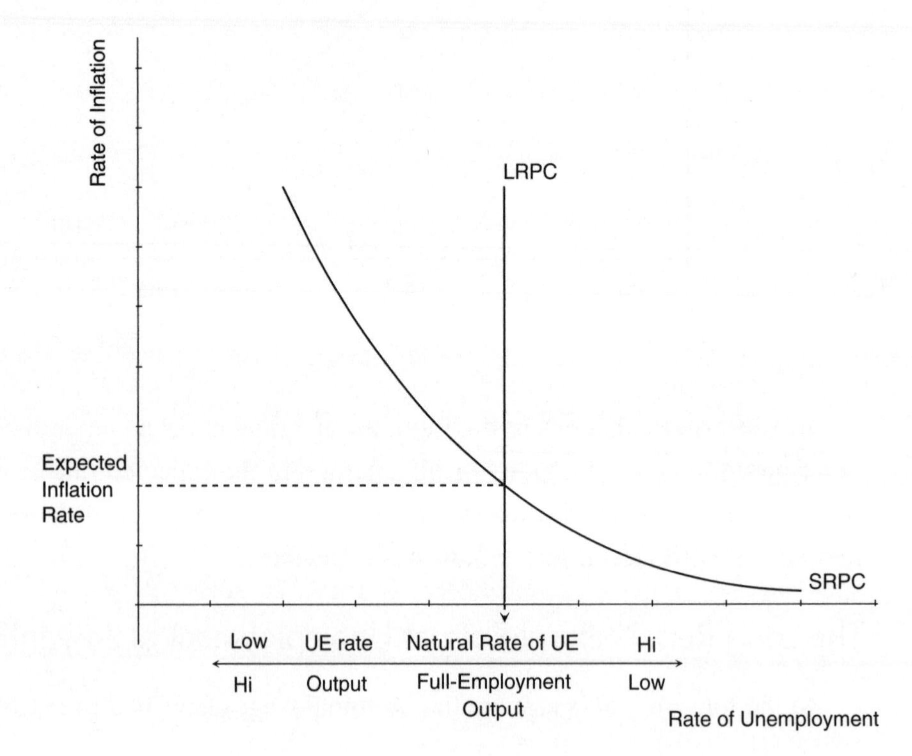

Shifts of the Long-Run Phillips Curve

Because LRPC shows the natural rate of unemployment, it moves when NRU changes. Recall that NRU is the unemployment rate without the effects of the business cycle, or discounting cyclical unemployment. So the amount of structural and frictional unemployment that tend to persist in an economy determines its NRU.

While NRU is considered to be stable for an economy at a given time, it can change slowly over time and does differ between economies. Analyzing the factors that distinguish countries with higher natural rates of unemployment from those with lower rates can help us identify the policy choices and characteristics of the labor force's behavior that can cause NRU to change and shift LRPC.

DIDYOUKNOW?

The natural rate of unemployment in the EU countries tends to be higher than in the United States. EU member states have experienced unemployment rates that seem to average between 8 and 10 percent, whereas the U.S. economy's NRU is estimated to be in the 5 to 6 percent range.

Policies that change the costs or benefits of being unemployed tend to influence the natural rate. The more generous and long-lasting the unemployment insurance benefits that workers who are laid off can collect, the less urgent the job search. An employer-based health insurance system might also keep the natural rate lower than a public system where workers' insurance or healthcare access is independent of work. Enacting either of these would likely cause a country's LRPC curve to shift right. Natural rates of unemployment also depend on cultural factors, such as which groups tend to join (or stay out of) the workforce and beliefs about the value of leisure and work.

Don't judge this too quickly—while higher unemployment may sound like a bad thing because output declines, there might be positive and negative consequences to such policies. A healthier workforce might be more productive even with fewer workers employed. And if employer-based healthcare encourages people to stay in suboptimal jobs because they fear losing healthcare access, increasing frictional unemployment could sometimes be beneficial. Instead of worrying about good and bad, just consider LRPC and the NRU as descriptive characteristics of an economy. If an AP exam question seems to be encouraging you to think about policies that change how costly it is to be unemployed, then probably shifting the LRPC curve is the way to go.

The Phillips Curve and the AD-AS Model: Mirror Images

To understand a helpful trick that enables you to connect the Phillips curve and the AD-AS model, consider another feature of Figure 10-8: the extra labeling underneath the horizontal axis. The high rates of unemployment to the right on the graph correlate with low employment and therefore lower output levels. Points further to the left on the graph mean lower unemployment and therefore higher employment and real output levels. This means that the horizontal axes of the AD-AS graph and the Phillips curve are opposites. The vertical axes, price level, and inflation rate are directly related. Thus, placing the AD-AS graph and Phillips curve graphs side by side enables you to use one model to check your work in the other. If you understand how movements of aggregate demand affect the short-run equilibrium point in the AD-AS model, you will know how to show those same processes in the Phillips curve graph.

TEST TIP

When planning for a free-response problem involving the Phillips curve, always sketch a fast AD-AS graph (aligned side by side) to make sure you've got things straight. Nearly all students are far more comfortable and confident in their understanding of shifts in aggregate demand and supply than they are in movements and shifts on the Phillips curve graph. Just remember that translating between the graphs involves reversing rightward and leftward movement, and keep in mind that SRPC is really just a horizontal mirror image of SRAS.

Demand-Pull and Cost-Push Inflation Shown Graphically

Demand-pull inflation is caused by AD shifting to the right faster than the economy's productive capacity grows. In Figure 10-9(a), note how the short-run equilibrium point moves up and to the right from point A to point B as aggregate demand shifts rightward. On the Phillips curve graph in Figure 10-9(b), the economy moves up and left from point A′ to point B′. Because the equilibrium point slid up along SRAS, it slid up along SRPC as well. Both points B and B′ represent short-run equilibriums in which unemployment is below NRU and output is higher than the full-employment level, but in which the price level has risen or inflation has accelerated. As the situation moves into the long run, if the economy remains at the new higher price level and inflation rate, this will become the expected inflation rate and workers' nominal wages will rise. Why? First, unemployment is low, and firms need to escalate salaries in order to compete with each other for scarce workers. Second, in salary and wage negotiations, both employers and employees expect prices to rise by a greater amount than they have in the past. Now both SRAS and SRPC curves shift up (SRAS moves left, and SRPC moves right). The new long-run equilibrium points are C and C′. Note that, in both graphs, the economy moved back toward the long-run curves (LRAS and LRPC) as wages adjusted to the new unemployment and price level.

Figure 10-9.

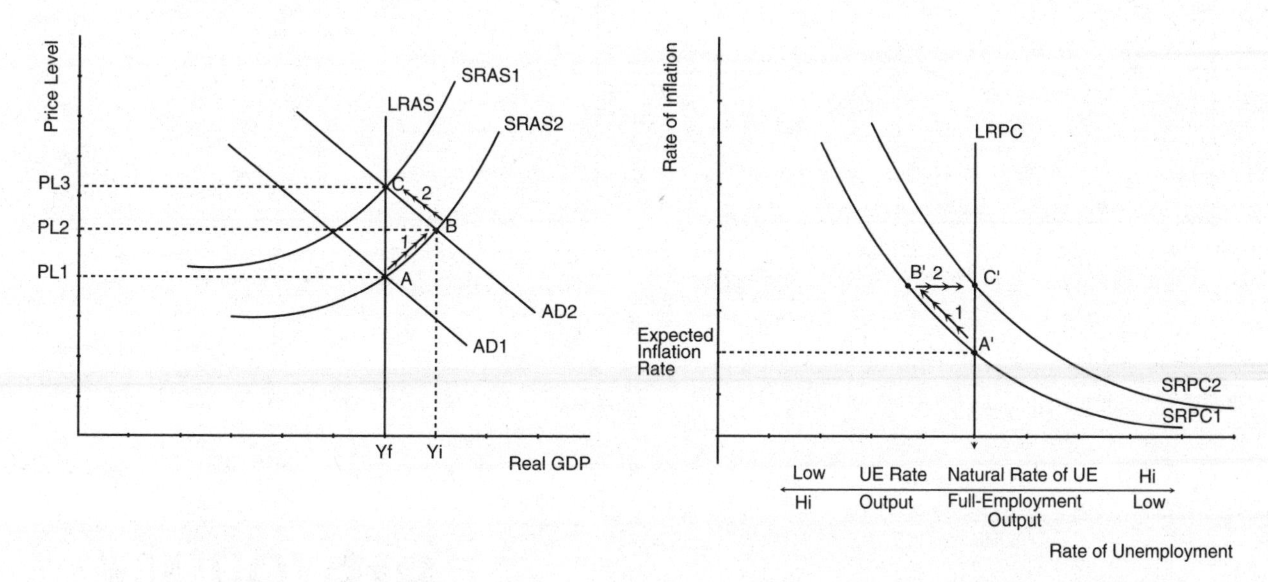

Panel A. Demand-Pull Inflation in the AD-AS Model **Panel B.** Demand-Pull Inflation in the AD-AD Model

Figure 10-10 shows a different kind of problem: stagflation. When costs of inputs rise unexpectedly, as is the case with the price of oil at times, the economy experiences a decrease in output and a rise in unemployment, but with higher than normal inflation, which is not the case during a typical recession caused by a leftward shift of aggregate demand. If you were asked to depict this situation on the Phillips curve, it might seem like a tough question. Starting with what you know about the aggregate demand and aggregate supply model will make answering the problem easier. Begin by remembering that production costs are a factor that shifts SRAS. They've risen, so making goods is more costly, and we need to shift SRAS up and to the left. Your planning graph should look similar to Figure 10-10(a). Then translate to the Phillips model and shift SRPC up but to the right. You should get a result that looks similar to Figure 10-10(b). In both graphical models, the new short-run equilibrium point involves a higher price level and greater unemployment rate than before, but with lower output.

Figure 10-10.

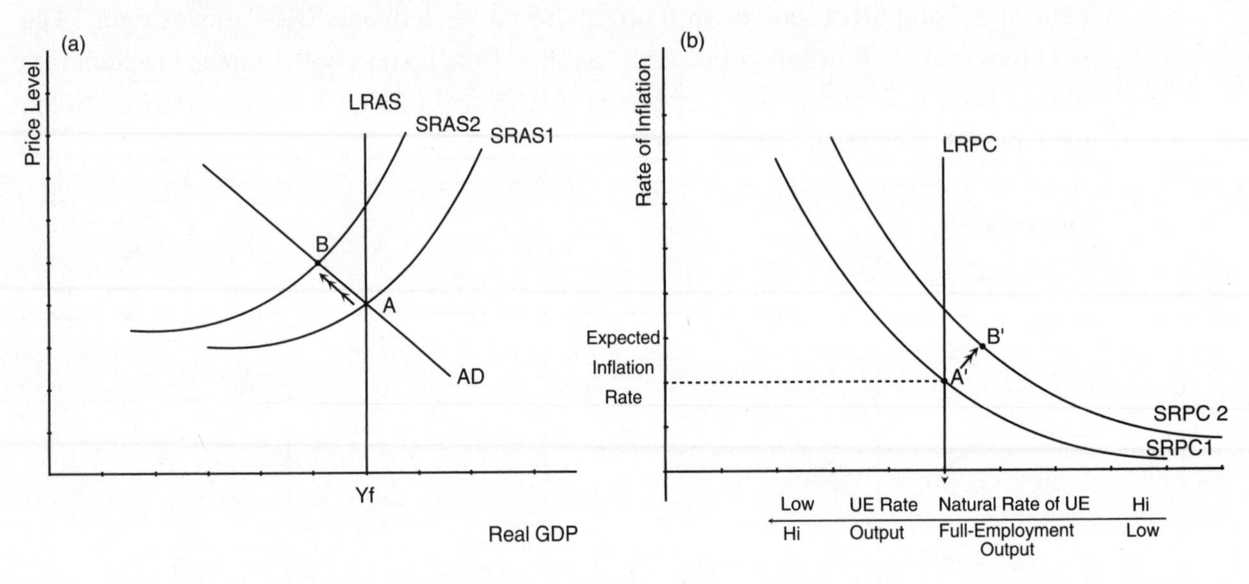

Panel A. Cost-Push Inflation in the AD-AS Model

Panel B. Cost-Push Inflation on the Phillips Curve

DIDYOUKNOW?

Cost-push inflation was not well understood prior to the oil price shocks of the 1970s. Economists were so used to recessions being driven by shifts in demand that the concept of the LRPC had not been developed yet. Stagflation led many economists to abandon the Phillips curve theory. Others figured out that the relationship between inflation and unemployment is different in the short run and in the long run.

Monetary and Fiscal Policy in the Phillips Model

By now, you should have sensed the pattern: When AD moves, the economy's short-run equilibrium point slides along SRAS either up and right or down and left. Those changes involve sliding along SRPC, either up and left or down and right. Because both fiscal and monetary policy options involve movement of AD, they don't cause shifts of either curve on the Phillips graph in the short run.

Sketch the graphs next to one another, matching your starting situations. If the initial equilibrium point is below full-employment output (left of LRAS) on your AD-AS graph, it should be right of the LRPC curve on the Phillips curve graph. On the other hand, inflationary gaps correlate with points to the left of LRPC.

Consider what the fiscal and monetary authorities can do on each graph. On the left (AD-AS), they can push AD to the right or to the left, sliding the economy up and right by using expansionary policy or down and left with contractionary options. On the right panel (Phillips curve), they can slide the economy up and left with expansionary choices and down and right with contractionary ones. A little practice showing different situations on both graphs side by side will help you get comfortable with how they interact.

Changes in Inflationary Expectations

The one circumstance that students often feel is easier to work out on the Phillips curve graph and then translate back to the AD-AS model is a prompt asking you to show how a change in expectations about future inflation affects the economy. To do this, remember that the point where SRPC and LRPC intersect is at the natural rate of unemployment and the expected inflation rate. If people begin to adjust to a new lower norm for inflation, then SRPC shifts down and left, intersecting LRPC at a lower point. Transfer these results into the AD-AS graph, and you'll see an increase in SRAS as the economy moves to a lower price level given this new expectation. Conversely, an increase in inflationary expectations shifts SRPC to the right and SRAS to the left.

Changes in Long-Run Curves

The factors that move short-run curves on both graphs are the same, and they do shift the short-run curves in opposite directions—SRPC moves right when SRAS moves left. It would seem that, because both LRPC and LRAS are vertical lines, both correlate to an economy at full employment, and both correlate with only the natural rate of unemployment, one would always move left when the other shifts right. However, that reverse relationship isn't nearly as strong when it comes to the long-run curves. To see why, let's revisit what each represents briefly.

Recall that LRAS is a vertical line that tells us the level of real output produced when we are at full employment. This level rises if the population grows and if capital stock is added to the economy. In fact, any change in the quantity or quality of resources available to the economy would alter the full-employment level of output (the amount of stuff we can create when our economy is operating normally, to put things bluntly).

LRPC, however, is a vertical line that tells us what the unemployment rate is when the economy is at full employment. Earlier in this chapter, we discussed the reasons for changes in NRU; only a change in NRU leads to a shift in LRPC. Most economies experience a rightward shift of LRAS each year as population grows and technological advancements are made, but frequently the same NRU exists for decades.

Keep in mind, as you consider how LRPC and LRAS are related, that LRAS is a quantity value and LRPC is a rate. This means that their changes are not always correlated. If LRPC shifts, it is likely that LRAS will as well—if we have the same resources but use less of the labor available to us, we tend to produce fewer goods and services. However, many LRAS shifts are not accompanied by movement on the Phillips curve.

Bear in mind this chapter contains many of the most difficult concepts that will appear on the AP Macroeconomics exam and is a synthesis of topics that will probably be covered by the majority of questions on the exam. Be sure you are thoroughly familiar with how monetary and fiscal policy work (both together and separately) and how to show their effects graphically in the money market, loanable funds market, and AD-AS and Phillips models.

Chapter 11

Economic Growth

The Concept of Growth

The basic appeal of economic growth is that we are all happier with more. While that may not always seem true in a philosophical sense, economically if what our society produces are goods, rather than "bads," then it is true for the society as a whole. Economic growth is desirable because it allows us to enjoy greater quantities and varieties of the things we want, either on a societal or per-capita basis.

Definition and Calculation

Long-run economic growth is the increase of productive capacity in an economy over time. Potential real output increases—more goods and services can be produced when the economy is at its full-employment level. It is important to distinguish between economic growth and merely a short-run change in real output. Real output fluctuates up and down in the short run due to the business cycle; growth is the underlying long-run process or trend.

Growth rates can be expressed based on nominal or real data. Real gross domestic product (GDP) growth is a better metric for measuring change over time because it accounts for inflation. GDP growth can also account for an increase in population if it is expressed in per-capita terms.

Calculating economic growth rate is not difficult. Use the same formula for calculating any rate of change, subtracting the first value from the second and dividing by the first. If a country's potential output increased from 2,000 units in year 1 to 2,100 units in year 2, then that country would have experienced a growth rate of 5 percent (2,100 − 2,000)/2,000.

If the values for the two time periods are in nominal terms, the nominal growth rate is the result. As always, beware of nominal values because they don't represent actual quantities of goods and services until they've been adjusted for inflation.

If, instead, the values are per-capita real values (adjusted for inflation and divided by population), then the result is **per-capita real GDP growth rate (rGDP)**. It is found by calculating (per-capita rGDP year 2 − per-capita rGDP year 1) ÷ per-capita rGDP year 1. This value could be positive, showing that, on average, citizens of that country produced and enjoyed more goods and services per person than before. It is also possible for it to be negative, demonstrating that per-person real output had declined.

TEST TIP

It is relatively common for the AP exam to include questions in the multiple-choice section asking you to calculate a growth rate from a table of data or adjust a simple data set from nominal to real values. Thus, it is worth practicing using the formulas. You might be given a table of values and asked about the conclusions that you can draw from it. For example, if given simple data about population, nominal GDP, and price level, you should be able to determine whether real per-person output rose or fell.

Economic Growth in Various Graphical Models

The process of an economy gaining productive capacity over time can be shown in several ways using a variety of diagrams.

The Production Function

A good place to begin with graphical analysis of growth is by thinking about the production function. The goal is to consider how a few key variables affect the amount of goods and services that an economy can make. In particular, total output (Y) is a function of three factors: quantity of labor employed (L), the size of the capital stock (K), and the state of technology (T). Because the capital stock and the level of technological accomplishment of a society are fixed in the short term, Figure 11-1 plots various levels of output against increasing quantities of labor employed. Certainly employing more labor leads to greater levels of output, but the *rate* at which labor yields returns decreases as more and more of it is used. Put another way, there is a diminishing marginal return to labor. Figure 11-1 shows this in the flatter and flatter slope of the function as labor quantity increases.

Figure 11-1. The Production Function

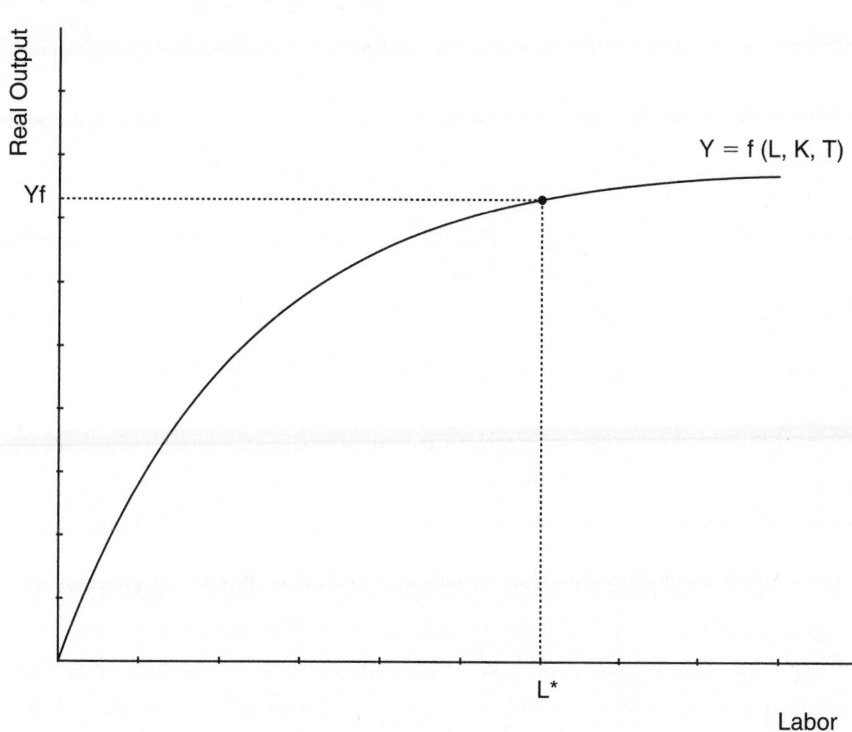

When the economy is at full employment, a given quantity of labor is employed, noted as L* on the horizontal axis. L* represents the number of employed units of labor when unemployment is equal to the natural rate. For example, if there is a 5 percent natural rate of unemployment (NRU), then 95 percent of the number of people in the labor force is the quantity for L*.

Growth, which might be the result of either improvements in technology or an increase in the stock of available capital goods, would be shown in this model as an upward shift of the production function. At any given level of employment (say, L*), a new, higher level of output results. Thus, potential output increases in this case because, with better and more tools, workers become more productive.

The Business Cycle Graph

Figure 11-2 shows a simplified diagram of the business cycle. As actual GDP rises and falls, the economy passes through short-term stages of expansion: peaks, during which there are inflationary gaps; contractions and troughs, during which there are recessionary gaps.

Figure 11-2. The Business Cycle

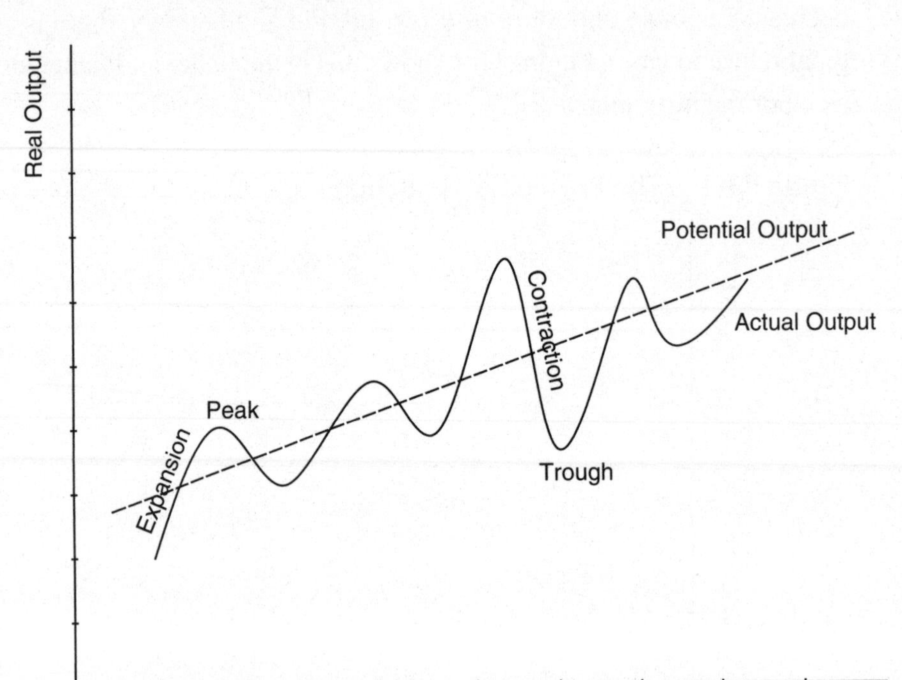

A line of best fit is an approximation of the level of potential output. This is an estimate of what the output would be if the economy was at full employment and the unemployment rate was at its natural level—if there had been no business cycle at all.

The economic growth rate is shown as the upward slope of the line of best fit: in this case, the dashed line labeled Potential Output. A country with a steeper line of best fit would be experiencing a faster growth rate than would a country with a flatter slope.

TEST TIP

The production function graph is not one that the AP exam will likely ask you to draw, but it does help visualize how both short-run changes in employment and long-run changes in technology and capital stock can influence the level of output. The business cycle diagram is not frequently required or even referenced explicitly in questions on the AP exam. Despite this, the principles of the business cycle, depictions of it in other graphical models, and the details of how governments try to tame that boom and bust cycle underlie the majority of questions on every year's AP Macroeconomics exam.

The Production Possibilities Curve

Showing growth on a production possibilities diagram is even easier and even more likely to be asked about on the AP exam. In this case, we might plot production of consumer goods against capital goods, as shown in Figure 11-3. After economic growth, productive capacity has risen; now some combinations of goods are possible that just weren't attainable before. The production possibilities curve's (PPC's) outward shifts represent economic growth.

Figure 11-3. Growth in the Production Possibilities Model

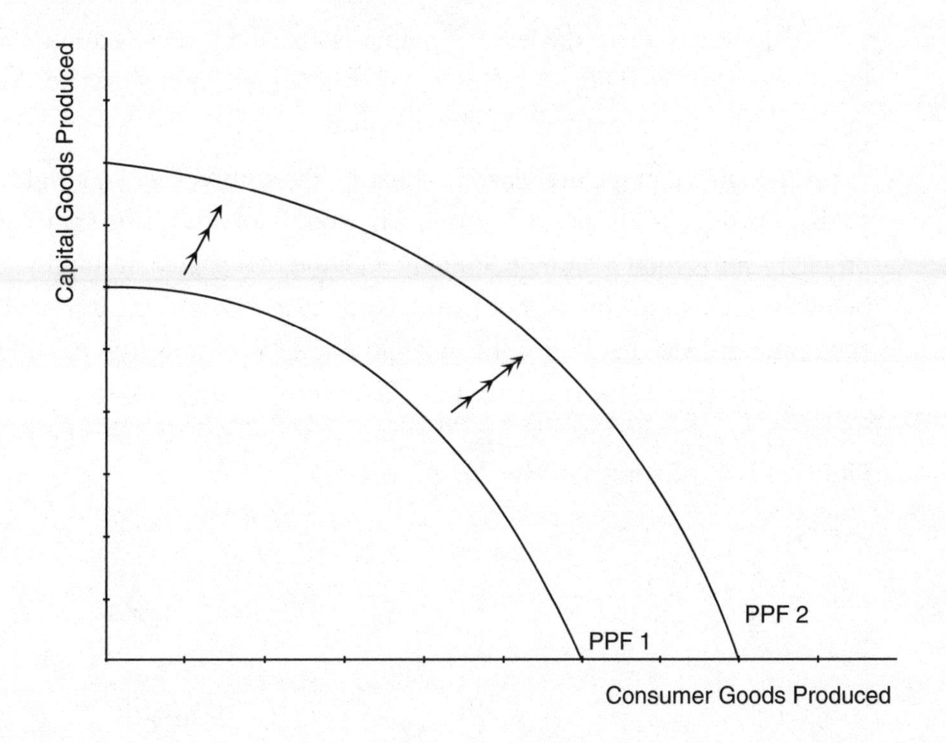

In this model, it is particularly easy to distinguish between long-run growth and short-run changes in real GDP. The curve represents potential output. The point at which the economy is operating (which might be well inside, close to, or really pushing hard at the production possibilities frontier [PPF]) is how short-run GDP is depicted.

Note also, while considering growth and production possibilities, that a faster growth rate will be achieved if a society chooses a point with a greater capital goods production, sacrificing consumer goods today to build more tools instead. These capital goods today become part of the capital stock tomorrow and can be used to produce more goods year after year, shifting the production possibilities frontier outward.

The Aggregate Demand and Aggregate Supply Model

Because growth is the increase in potential output over time, it stands to reason that the simplest way to show growth on the aggregate demand and aggregate supply (AD-AS) graph is to shift long-run aggregate supply (LRAS) to the right. Consider a new long-run equilibrium point to the right of the old one.

The story is not quite as simple as that, however, because LRAS is not the only curve to move. Whatever we've added to our technological progress or accumulated capital can be used to produce goods and services in the short run and in the long run. So the short-run aggregate supply (SRAS) shifts right as well.

AD moves because the level of output is also the level of national income, meaning that workers are paid higher wages and therefore have more to spend. Aggregate demand increases due to the increase in consumption.

Although the graph in Figure 11-4 has all three curves moving rightward just enough so that the price level stays the same, this would not always be the case. Over time, AD probably shifts right a bit more quickly than the two aggregate supply curves do. This is one way to explain why the price level tends to rise over time. It is also possible to have economic growth that leaves the economy at a lower long-run price level than before. This would be the case if LRAS and SRAS moved further to the right than AD did.

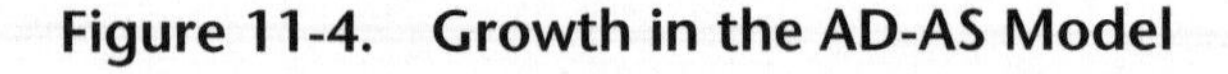

Figure 11-4. Growth in the AD-AS Model

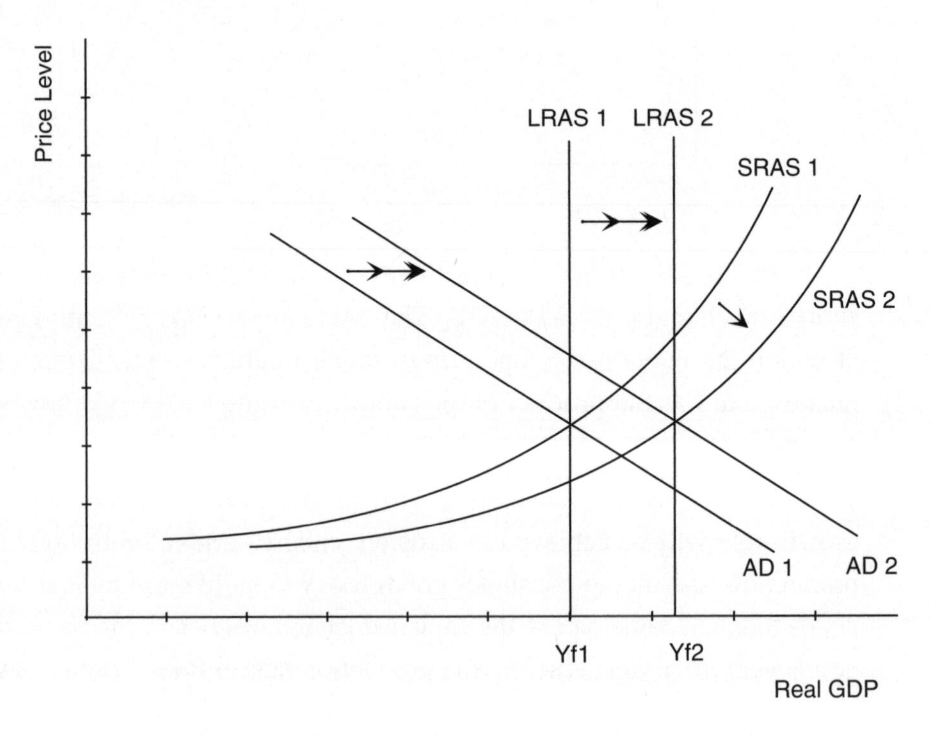

Determinants of Growth

What factors can contribute to the shifts in the AD-AS graph shown in Figure 11-4 and leave us with a higher per-capita real output than we had before? The short answer is that we need more or better resources. Therefore, increases in the quantity or quality of land, labor, capital, or entrepreneurial ability available in an economy are the major causes of economic growth.

Each of the four resources can become more abundant or more useful in producing goods and services, so each can be a source of growth. When more of a type of resource is available, its quantity is contributing to growth. When a resource is improved, its productivity increases, so each unit used helps create more units of output.

Before considering the resource categories individually, think along the lines of the production function graph shown in Figure 11-1 for a moment. Increases in full-employment output (Yf) can come from sliding to a point further up and to the right along a fixed production function curve (as a result of a growing labor force) or from an upward shift of the curve as capital and technology are added (increasing labor productivity). You might think of the quantity of goods we can sustainably produce as being equal to the amount of labor we have times the output that each unit of labor yields. Growing population and addition of new groups to the labor force increase the first factor, labor quantity. Technology; additions to the capital stock; improvements in human capital, such as education and job training; and better allocation of resources in the production process all increase labor productivity, the second factor.

DIDYOUKNOW?

Economists have tried to calculate how much of the growth in the U.S. economy comes from various sources. According to one estimate, two-thirds of the growth between 1930 and 2000 came from an improvement in the productivity of resources and one-third came from an increase in the quantity of labor available when the economy is at full employment.

Land

Throughout history, societies have sought to acquire more land. More land means more raw materials to make the goods and services desired. Whether this is the main cause of war in human history isn't the issue—it is clear that one motive is often the acquisition of more land and, in many cases, the underlying reason has to do with economics.

While it may seem that those types of conflicts are mostly a feature of the past rather than the present, national borders still change from time to time. Remember, however, that land isn't only the number of acres controlled, but also the raw materials and resources that can be harvested from them. Some growth that modern economies experience comes from increased land in the form of resources that weren't previously seen as productive (such as when oil drilling or natural gas extraction became productive and feasible).

Labor

Labor represents the primary input in making lots of goods and is certainly the most universal of the resources. As already explained in this chapter, a significant portion of economic growth comes from increases in the quantity of labor available in an economy. Much of the rest stems from various factors that increase the productivity of labor.

Every time the population of a country expands, its labor force is likely to expand. Sometimes the labor force expands independent of increases in the population. During the early twentieth century, many Western countries experienced a major increase in the percentage of women who wanted or needed to participate in the labor force. The **labor force participation rate** increased. If the natural rate of unemployment is relatively constant, then the number of employed workers when the economy is operating at full employment increases and potential real output grows.

Even when the number of employed individuals doesn't increase, there can be increases in the quantity of labor employed if the average number of hours in a workweek rises. This average is influenced by both the workers' desires and the cultural value placed on work and leisure time—in some economies, more workers want to work part-time or desire to have more vacation time and are willing to accept lower pay in exchange. It may also be affected by employment legislation and norms of the labor market—if employers are required or expected to provide nonsalary benefits like health insurance, pension, or paid vacation time to full-time employees, then many employers may seek to fill their labor needs with several part-time employees rather than a few full-time ones.

Labor productivity, or the average real output per hour of work, is influenced by three major factors: increases in human capital, investment in additional physical capital, and technological progress resulting from research and development (R&D). Each can be seen as an increase in capital or entrepreneurship and will be explained in this chapter.

As labor productivity rises, both aggregate supply curves shift rightward because each unit of work creates more goods and services. And because productive workers are worth more to the firms that employ them, they tend to earn higher real wages. This in turn causes AD to shift right as those higher real wages become more consumption spending. Therefore, increases in both the quantity and efficiency of labor can lead all three curves in the AD-AS model to shift to the right, as shown in Figure 11-4.

Capital

Capital goods, or tools used in the production process, can be broken down into human and physical categories. **Human capital** is the set of skills and know-how that workers collectively possess and that enable them to be more effective in the workplace.

Human capital can be enhanced by better education, a healthier workforce, or by better job training and skills development. An educational system that is effective helps to generate a working population that has critical thinking and problem-solving skills, as well as scientific and mathematical knowledge, and thus is a more productive labor force. If you've heard politicians (or anyone else) talk about improving an education system or helping failing schools so that workers become more competitive, this is what they were talking about.

Public health programs and widespread (if not universal) access to affordable healthcare can also help grow an economy by increasing worker productivity. When workers miss work due to illness, then fewer goods and services are produced—either because someone's job is unoccupied or because a temporary employee replaces that worker who generally doesn't have the experience or specialized skills to accomplish the job as efficiently. Thus, the healthier a population, the more productive its labor force.

A system to help workers develop job skills and add new skills as the economy changes is the last major contributor to human capital. As the pace of economic change accelerates, more jobs become obsolete even faster than they did in the past. This means that many workers will perform several different jobs during their careers. Therefore, for a country to get all that it can out of its workforce, it becomes increasingly necessary for both the public and the private sectors to support systems through which workers can update job skills and acquire training that enables them to be productive members of the ever-changing labor force.

Physical capital is the tools, machinery, and factories that enable large-scale production or make individual workers more powerful than they would be otherwise. Private firms engaging in investment are adding new capital goods to the nation's capital stock, making more tools, robots, and machinery available in the future than is available today. However, government programs can add to physical capital as well. If public sector investment in infrastructure (roads, canals, ports, bridges) increases, there is a greater stock of physical capital available for the firms to use in distributing their products (see the section called Growth Policy later in this chapter).

As you'll recall from reading about investment in Chapter 7, private firms want to purchase more capital goods when interest rates are low, when the economic outlook is good, and their confidence in future consumer demand is high. They also purchase capital goods when new technologies are available and when the tax and regulatory environment is conducive to their ability to profit from the added capital goods.

Additions to both human and physical components of the capital stock are considered part of investment. Because investment is part of aggregate demand and involves the purchasing of goods that will later be used in the production process, increases in investment cause the rightward shift of all three curves on the AD-AS graph, as shown in Figure 11-4. Remember that an increase in AD is not enough to cause economic growth because it increases only real GDP in the short run. Unless potential GDP increases, those changes will likely be offset in the long run as wages rise, shifting SRAS to the left and decreasing real output back to the former level of potential GDP.

Entrepreneurial Ability and Other Factors

Technological advancements can be viewed as providing capital goods that are better than old ones or as providing improvements in the ways that other inputs are mixed together to generate outputs. Some innovations seem to fit better with one interpretation and some with another. The technological rearrangements associated with the introduction of the assembly line are examples of newer, and more productive, entrepreneurship.

Whether you think it seems more connected to capital or to entrepreneurial ability, technological progress still merits brief discussion. Breakthroughs in technology often come at unexpected times, but they are the result of funding research, even if we aren't certain where that research is headed. Public sector research is important—grants and indirect support through state universities are major sources of scientific progress. Spinoff technologies from the military and space programs have created modern conveniences and life-changing tools. Public sector firms also engage in lots of R&D spending to develop new products. Situations in which firms have the greatest likelihood of funding research are ones in which the firm faces some rivals but not so many that it is likely to lose economic profit opportunities because new firms enter.

A few other factors can contribute to growth. The more efficient the production processes, the more we can enjoy as a result of those limited resources. Increasing allocative efficiency means giving us a mix of goods that is more satisfying with the same number of inputs. The concept of entrepreneurial ability can be seen as the skill of getting the most desirable set of goods and services possible out of the resources available to a firm. In that sense, more efficient firm operations can be a source of growth.

Growth Policy

Governments can make various policy choices and take various actions that will help promote long-run increases in potential GDP, a result that every elected politician would love to be able to claim credit for. When growth occurs, governments are better off as well—tax revenue increases and certain kinds of spending fall, giving them more room in their budget processes. Also, unemployment is low and people generally enjoy a rising standard of living. Under those circumstances, citizens are historically likely to reelect politicians.

DIDYOUKNOW?

Long-term growth rates in the United States average between 3 and 4 percent per year. Many of the most recent decades have shown overall average annual growth rates in this general range. When expressed in per-capita terms, the increase in per-person real GDP is slightly over 2 percent. The reason for the difference: the U.S. population has grown over the last half century, but at a slower rate than real output has risen.

Fiscal and Monetary Choices That Promote Growth

Some of the actions that governments can take are within the scope of normal fiscal and monetary policy behaviors. Expansionary monetary policies designed to increase real GDP in the short run can also shift supply because they lower interest rates, an important catalyst for new investment spending. On the other hand, fiscal policies attempting to increase short-run output push interest rates upward, perhaps trading away some chance of growth in the future, in exchange for a boost in output for a short period of time.

Monetary policy set by the central bank can have another role in promoting long-run growth: maintaining the kind of credibility that keeps inflationary expectations low and stable. The less that is known about how prices will increase in the future, the harder it is for lenders and borrowers to lend and borrow with confidence in the loanable funds market and the less likely it is that savings can be channeled smoothly back into consumption and investment.

Perhaps it is a given that governments try to increase output in both the short run and the long run because politicians realize the reelection benefits of lower unemployment in the short run and rising living standards over time. Even so, fiscal policy authorities can make some choices that encourage growth in the long term more than other options.

Spending government funds boosts AD, but sometimes it can have positive effects on aggregate supply as well. Government investment in the educational system, infrastructure, and public health can increase labor productivity and therefore can lead to faster increases in potential output.

Tax cuts that encourage more work or increase the percentage of business earnings that firms can retain are both likely to stimulate some increase in AS. Tax cuts that merely substitute government money for earnings or that don't function as incentives may not be as beneficial.

TEST TIP

The most common line of reasoning that the AP exam will test you on related to growth is the ultimate impact of the crowding-out effect. Remember that, at higher interest rates, investment is more costly for firms, so they buy fewer new capital goods and add less to the capital stock. This process slows down the overall growth rate.

Other Supportive Actions

Governments help promote healthy economic activity by providing a supportive environment conducive to mutually beneficial trade. While we may not typically think of law enforcement and a trustworthy judicial system as economic roles for government, they certainly help economic actors know that contracts and property rights are enforceable. Sanitation and food safety (and even environmental regulations) can ensure that the population stays healthy and productive and trusts the goods in the marketplace. Infrastructure for the provision of water, energy, communication, and garbage collection all allow typical citizens to focus more on production than on timely ways to fend for themselves in acquiring these modern conveniences. In some cases, these goods are provided for everyone in a community and paid for through taxes if governments have reason to believe that the private market won't adequately meet the community's need.

Chapter 12

The International Sector, Trade Accounting, and Exchange Markets

Trade Accounting and Balance of Payments Accounts

Over time, most countries have discovered that international trade is beneficial because it makes new types of goods available in an economy and because making goods where there is a comparative advantage to do so reduces opportunity cost. International trade and comparative advantage allow countries to have more of the goods they enjoy than would be possible with domestic production alone. In addition to trade in goods and services, there is sizeable international trade in financial assets. As finance and production of goods and services have become more globalized, these flows between countries have increased. This chapter reviews the major measurement tools used in international trade and the way rates of exchange between different currencies are determined. The significant connections between exchange rates and other macroeconomic tools are also explored.

International Flows of Goods and Capital

Figure 12-1 is a starting point for thinking about how goods, services, financial assets, and money flow into and out of a given country. We'll use the United States as an example. The figure separates the trade for goods and services from the markets in which financial assets are traded. This is a simplified picture—complexity will be added along the way. This diagram and the one in Figure 12-2 are intended to help you visualize the **balance of payments**, the relationship among three major accounting measurements: the current account, the financial account, and the official reserves account.

Figure 12-1. Net International Inflows and Outflows of the United States

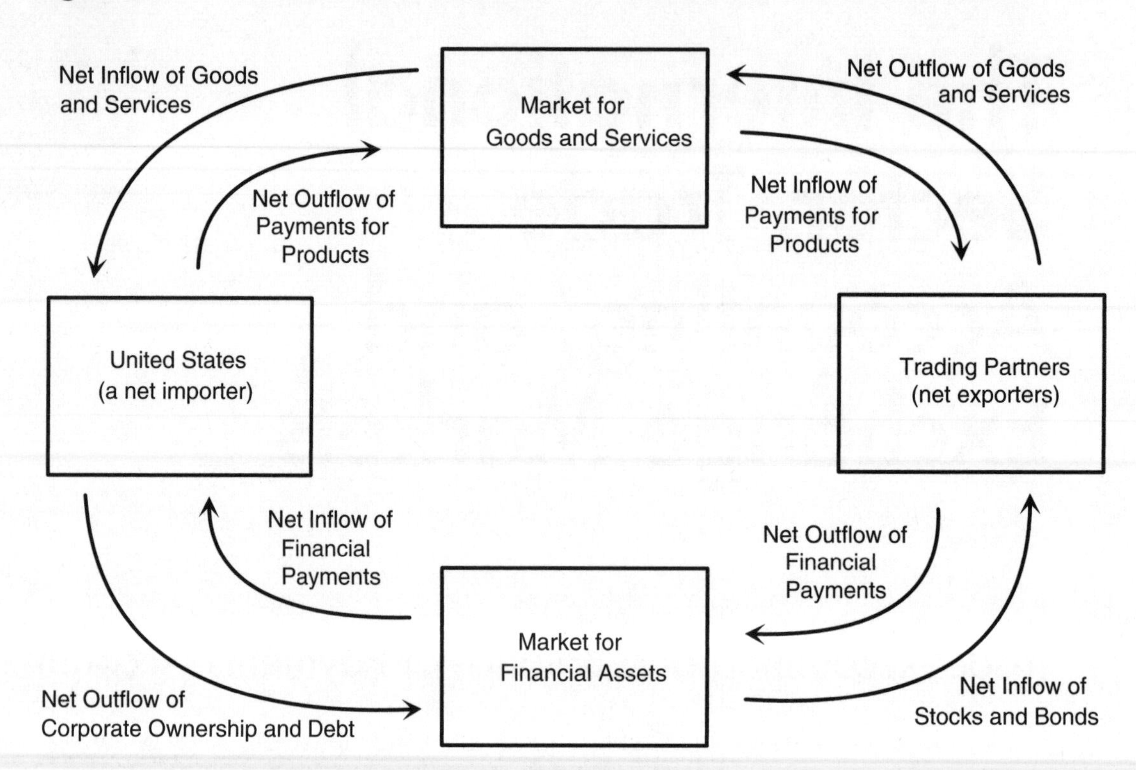

Markets for Goods and Services

First, examine the market for goods and services at the top of figure 12-1. Of course, consumers in the United States purchase goods made in other parts of the world—in fact, no country imports more goods than the United States does annually. At the same time, U.S. exports are sold around the world. Payments for imported goods flow out to the countries in which they were produced; payments that foreign consumers make for U.S. exports flow into the United States to domestic producers. Because imports exceed exports, on balance money flows out and goods flow in. The upper left portion of the diagram simplifies this situation, showing only the net flow of goods and services inward and the net flow of money payments for them outward. When a country imports more than it exports in a given year, it has a **trade deficit**. As a net importer, the United States has a trade deficit; its trade partners therefore together export more to the United States than they import from it.

The Current Account

The major category into which the payments (both inflows and outflows) for internationally traded goods and services fall is called the **current account**. The current account, otherwise referred to as a country's balance of trade, can be either positive or negative over a period of time (such as a month, quarter, or year). A country with a negative current account has a net outflow of payments and therefore a trade deficit. These countries are therefore net importers; some examples are the United States, the United Kingdom, India, and France. Countries with positive current accounts are net exporters; these countries experience larger inflows than outflows in the market for goods and services. Saudi Arabia, Germany, Russia, and China had some of the world's current account surpluses in 2011.

Let's examine what is included in the current account and how it's measured a bit more closely. Four categories of payments are counted: goods, services, income, and transfers. No matter the category, payments flowing into a country are recorded as credits and those flowing out are recorded as debits.

In trade for goods and services, exports are sold abroad and payments for them flow into a country. These are recorded as credits in (and are therefore added to) the current account. Imports are recorded as debits and are subtracted from the current account because payments flow out of the country. Trade in goods and trade in services are categorized separately in international balance of payments accounting, but the difference has little significance for you on the AP exam: goods and services are referenced together on many items on the test each year.

DIDYOUKNOW?

The United States exported nearly $1.5 trillion in products in 2011, more than any country except China or Germany. One of the largest categories of U.S. exports is machinery, including engines, electronics, and vehicles. Oil is the third largest category of exports, but predictably, the largest category of imports: The United States imported over $300 billion more oil than it exported in 2011.

Income balance is the third category of payments that are counted in the current account. If U.S. citizens earn income abroad and send it back to the United States, these are inflows and are recorded as credits, which are added to the current account. Earnings that foreign nationals send home from employment in the United States are recorded as debits and are subtracted from the current account.

Transfers are the fourth category of payments in the current account. Government transfers (such as foreign aid) are known as official transfers; transfer payments made from one citizen to another, such as private gifts or grants, are known as private transfers. The common element between official and private transfers is that both are payment flows that are not made for providing goods or services. Again, flows into the country are added to the current account as credits and outflows are debited from it.

Figure 12-2 shows a more detailed look at flows in both directions. Focus on the left side of the diagram. The darker arrows are debits from the current account; the lighter ones are credits. Those darker arrows represent much larger flows than the lighter ones: quite a bit bigger, given the approximately −\$470 billion current account balance that the United States held in 2011. Refer again to Figure 12-1. The net flows through the market for goods and services are outward. Think of dollars building up in foreign nations that trade with the United States as these imbalances don't even out over the months, quarters, or years. What will foreigners do with those dollars?

Figure 12-2.

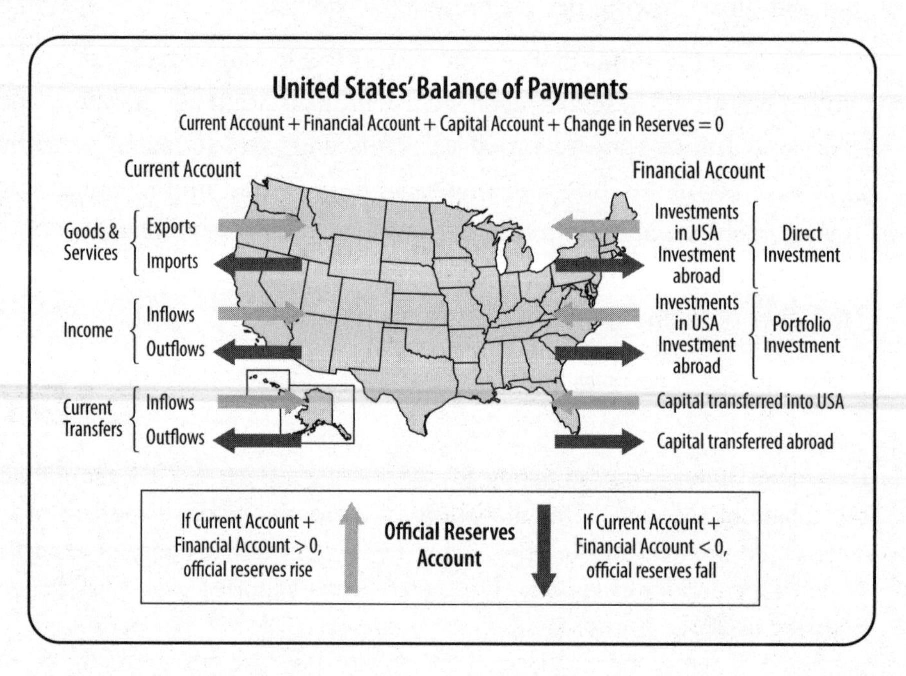

Markets for Financial Assets

The vast majority of those "expatriated" dollars come back as inflows in a different type of market. The lower half of Figure 12-1 and the arrows on the right side of Figure 12-2 show inflows and outflows in the market for financial assets, like stocks and bonds. Similar principles apply to accounting in the financial assets market as in the product market. The key difference is that purchases represent ownership of debt or of corporations in another country—because these payments are trades of ownership and do not represent production, they are not likely to affect the gross domestic product (GDP) of either nation directly.

The Financial Account

A country's total net inflow or outflow of payments in markets for financial assets is its **financial account**, the total of all credits minus all debits. Money flows into and out of the United States every day in markets for real estate, production facilities like offices and factories, debts represented by bonds, and slices of ownership in corporations represented by stock shares. These transactions are reflected in the financial account.

TEST TIP

The financial account is also known as the capital account. Official balance of payments accounts reference both terms, but the term *financial account* is preferred on the AP exams. If you examine past publications or older test items (or if your textbook isn't a recent publication), then you may see this subject described only as the capital account. The terms mean the same thing, but beware: the older term led some students to mistakenly think that purchases of capital goods were recorded there when actually they are counted in the current account because purchase of them is payment for production.

The individual flows that are counted in the financial account are shown in the right portion of Figure 12-2. Foreign direct investment, portfolio investment, and transfers of financial capital are the three categories of payments included. As with the current account, the financial account records as debits all payments made from a country (dark arrows) and as credits the payments made to it (the lighter arrows).

Foreign direct investment is the purchase of 10 percent or more of a foreign business—a significant share of ownership of a firm. U.S. purchases of foreign corporations are counted as debits because they are an outflow of payments. When foreigners purchase U.S. businesses, those transactions are counted as credits in the financial account because money payments flow into the United States. Sales work in reverse: If Americans sell foreign holdings, money flows into the United States and is recorded as a credit.

Portfolio investment is the purchase of smaller amounts of ownership in corporations—less than the 10 percent required to qualify as foreign direct investment. This category includes trade in government securities (remember, these are bonds that represent ownership of sovereign debt). When domestic investors purchase foreign debt or stocks, they make payments that flow abroad, which are debits in the financial account. If Americans sell British shares of equity or redeem British sovereign bonds, money flows into the United States and is recorded as a financial account credit. Chinese purchases of the growing number of U.S. Treasury securities, which represent the U.S.

public debt, would therefore be counted as credits in the United States' financial account and debits in China's financial account.

Transfers of financial capital are the third category of transaction included. Loans made by banks in one country to businesses or individuals in another are the primary example of these transfers. If foreign banks lend to Americans, those loans are credits in the U.S. financial account because money flows into the United States. If Americans pay back those loans, money flows out and is a debit in the financial account. Loans by U.S. banks to foreigners work in reverse: The loan is a debit and the repayment is the credit.

The arrows on the bottom half of Figure 12-1 show that the net flow in the financial account for the United States is positive. Therefore, on balance, money flows inward in the market for financial assets. More U.S. financial assets are purchased by foreigners than the quantity of foreign assets purchased by Americans. That's the story that the inner arrows in the figure tell. The outer arrows show something else: Ownership of U.S. companies is being transferred abroad, and an increasing share of the governmental, corporate, and household debt of Americans is owed to foreign sources.

Official Reserves and the Balance of Payments

The **official reserves account** is the pool of foreign assets held by a country's central bank. These assets, such as foreign currency and foreign governments' sovereign bonds, are assets to the central bank and liabilities against foreign central banks (in the case of currency) or foreign treasuries (in the case of sovereign bonds). The official reserves account can be used by central banks to intervene and thus control the values of their own currency or to sell currency, using the proceeds to finance government activity or pay down debt. The official reserves account is relatively insignificant, and most of the time it changes very little because the financial and current accounts tend to balance with one another.

Current and Financial Accounts Stay in Balance

Every year, for every country, the current account and the financial account have opposite signs. Countries with net outflows in the market for goods and services also have inflows in the market for financial assets. In fact, the two are very nearly opposites of each other, equal in absolute value. The total of financial account and current account and changes in official reserves must equal zero because net inflows are added to the official reserves account and net outflows are paid from it.

For your purposes, think of the financial and current accounts as equal in magnitude and opposite in sign. Looking at Figure 12-1 as a whole can help understand how this is true in the same way that looking at a standard circular flow model can help you see how the income and expenditure methods of tallying GDP must be equal. If the current account outflow on top is bigger than the financial account inflow on the bottom, then dollars build up in the reserve accounts of foreign nations that trade with the United States. At some point, these dollars will return to the United States, either in the market for goods and services, making the net outflow for the United States smaller, or in the financial asset market, making the net inflow for the United States bigger. There is not really anything else sensible for foreigners to do with them.

Effects of a Country's Balance of Trade

It seems that several countries tend to run current account deficits on a regular basis (and therefore nearly always have financial accounts that are in surplus). For example, over the past forty years, all the countries in the Western Hemisphere have run current account deficits the vast majority of the time (the lone exception is Venezuela). Consider what will happen over time if a country persistently runs a current account deficit. Weaker currency values, foreign ownership of debt and assets, and a rise in interest rates are possible effects.

Because the country is importing more than it exports, its currency is supplied more than demanded (the next section will explain supply and demand in the foreign exchange market). Therefore, its value drops. This makes foreign goods feel more expensive in domestic markets and international travel more expensive for citizens of the country. Domestic consumers therefore feel poorer because prices are rising for them. Exporting firms within the country, however, have an easier time selling goods abroad because the same domestic production costs translate into lower prices in foreign markets.

Central banks sometimes feel the need to respond to this inflationary pressure by raising interest rates and making domestic financial assets (like bonds) more appealing (bonds have cheaper prices, thus reflecting the greater rate of interest they earn). In doing so, they decrease the level of private domestic investment and therefore slow growth of the capital stock. So a persistent trade deficit can lead to higher interest rates that slow economic growth.

Because the outflow of payments in the market for goods and services must be balanced in the market for financial assets, countries with long-standing trade deficits have large inflows in the financial markets. Money flowing in means ownership flowing out, so a greater indebtedness to trading partners who now own more of the country's bonds is likely. There is also a corresponding increase in foreign ownership of domestic firms' stock. Put another way, these countries are living slightly beyond their means and paying for it by incurring future debt and by trading away ownership of domestic resources.

If a country is a net exporter that continually runs a trade surplus, there are likely to be pressures in the opposite direction. First, the country's currency is likely to appreciate because the world's demand for its exports outstrips its purchases of imported goods. Net inflows in the market for goods and services require foreigners to demand more of the country's currency, which rises in value. This tends to make foreign goods more affordable, reducing the trade imbalance. Exporters and overall GDP may suffer if currency appreciates because domestic goods carry higher price tags in foreign market.

Second, if the country continues to export more than it imports, trading partners may become irritated. At times, this can lead to protectionist measures—limits on foreign trade designed to curtail imports—being imposed by other countries. Tariffs, quotas placed on imports, and subsidies for domestic goods are three ways in which trade partners may work to make a net exporter's goods less attractive and correct the trade imbalance.

Third, domestic ownership of foreign assets rises, but income may lag behind production. The inflows that come from selling exports are not all spent on imported goods; many are spent purchasing interest-bearing assets in the financial market. In turn, ownership of greater and greater shares of foreign corporations and government debt are likely to result.

Several forces encourage the financial and current accounts to stay close to one another in absolute value. When the desirability of a country's goods compared to that of its trading partners roughly matches the desirability of opportunities to earn returns by purchasing its financial assets compared to domestic opportunities, the system is in rough equilibrium and there is not likely to be significant pressure on currency values.

Foreign Exchange Markets and Exchange Rates

The markets in which currencies are traded are called **foreign exchange (FOREX) markets**. These work similarly to markets for other goods and services, but because they involve trading one type of money for another, they tend to confuse students far more than they should. Pay close attention to the labels and think carefully about what both lines on each graph represent, and you'll be in good shape because you can gain ground on the tough questions about the causes and effects of changes in exchange rates and how to show them graphically.

Exchange Markets: The Basics

A foreign exchange market is the market for units of one country's currency in terms of another country's currency. The basic principles of supply and demand apply to these markets—if you can figure out which curve to move and which direction to move it, coming up with the resulting change in the currency's value will be no problem at all.

Exchange Rates Relate Currency Values Together

An exchange rate can be thought of as the price of a country's currency. But what would you buy it with? The answer is simple if you've ever traveled abroad (or even if you think about how you'd do that): units of another currency. When you exchange currency, you are trading away some units of one kind of money for a certain number of units of another currency. So the rate of exchange tells you how much of one kind you need to purchase a unit of the other kind. If the price of a U.S. dollar (USD) is the exchange rate, that means there is an exchange rate for every currency on the planet: a price of the dollar expressed in pounds sterling, in euros, in Japanese yen, in Australian dollars, and in Thai bhat. Clearly this means it is possible for the dollar to appreciate against one of those currencies but depreciate against another. Fortunately, the AP exam will not expect you to think about this because in any given AP question, there will be only two countries' perspectives to consider.

Examine Figure 12-3 for an example of a foreign exchange market: In this figure, the market for U.S. dollars in terms of the European euro is shown. First, notice the axes are a special version of price and quantity. The horizontal axis shows the quantity of USD traded. The vertical axis shows the euro price of one U.S. dollar; in this example, the market is in equilibrium, with an exchange rate of 80 European cents per 1 U.S. dollar and with a quantity of Q1 USD traded.

Figure 12-3. Foreign Exchange Market for U.S. Dollars

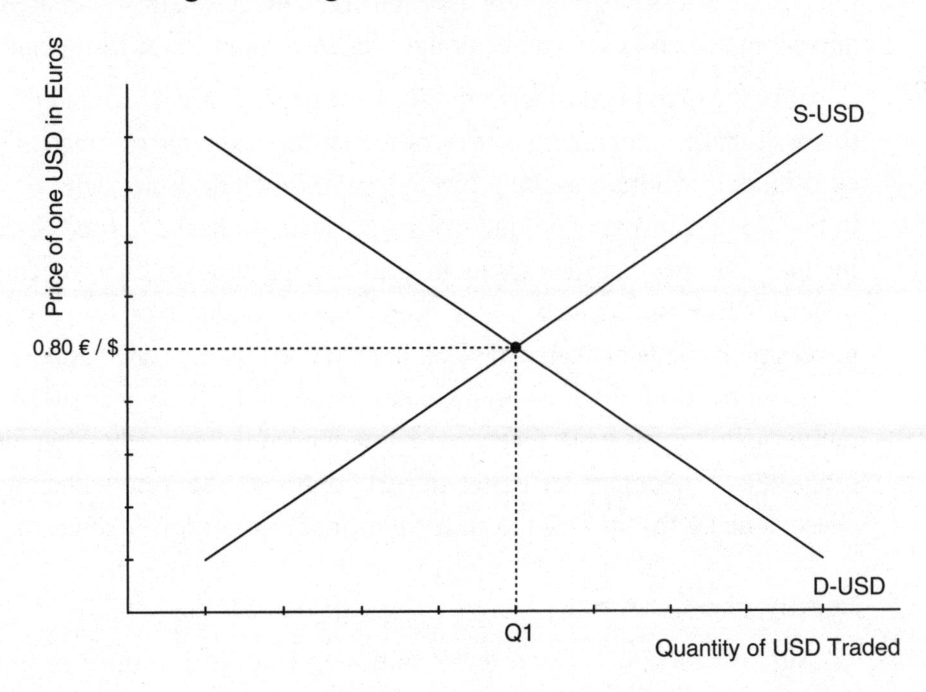

TEST TIP

The FOREX markets present a special confusion we might call the axes of evil, which is the potential, even for well-prepared students, to get quite confused by the axes. Getting the axes right is one of the more challenging parts of mastering this graph. The horizontal axis shows only the quantity of dollars that people want to sell in exchange for euros (in the case of supply) or to buy with euros (in the case of demand). Therefore, the quantities in this market are far smaller than those in the U.S. money or loanable funds market, even though both would be measured as quantities of U.S. dollars. Even more troubling for students is the vertical axis. Keep in mind that, in the market for dollars, we want the price of one dollar. The appropriate unit for this axis is "euros per dollar," just as the shorthand "P" in the banana market would really stand for "price of one banana in dollars" or "dollars per banana." Title your graph "Market for U.S. Dollars," and label the horizontal axis "Quantity of USD." Then give the vertical axis a label with that same currency in the denominator (€/$).

Demand for a Currency

Demand for a country's currency slopes downward, just as you would expect. It represents the people who desire U.S. dollars and have euros for buying those dollars. Because they need to pay more euros for each dollar at higher exchange rates, purchasing dollars is less desirable. As the exchange rate drops, the purchase of dollars is more appealing because each can be bought for fewer and fewer European cents.

Take the time to consider carefully what people are included in this demand curve—this will make recognizing causes of the shifts of the curve much easier to grasp. The euro-holders who are seeking to buy dollars include European consumers who want to buy American-made products or take vacations in the United States. In addition, it includes European businesses looking to buy resources such as machinery or other raw materials from the United States. European individuals or firms wishing to buy U.S. government bonds or shares of stock in U.S. corporations need dollars to complete those transactions. Both the European Central Bank and currency speculators might want to purchase dollars as well. Once you know whose behavior that demand curve for USD represents, it becomes far easier to feel confident about how changing circumstances cause demand for the USD to shift right (increase) or left (decrease).

Supply of a Currency

Supply of a country's currency slopes upward, just as most supply curves do. This line represents the people who want to sell dollars in order to obtain euros. At high exchange rates, they can sell each dollar for more European money, and therefore they are willing to supply more dollars into the market. When the exchange rate is low, selling one dollar yields fewer and fewer European cents, making the quantity supplied low.

Consider the makeup of the supply curve for USD for the same reasons; recognizing prompts that cause a shift in the supply of a currency are far easier if you can think of examples of who are the dollar-sellers and what changes might influence their behavior. First, Americans who want to buy products from Europe or travel there supply dollars in order to obtain euros (when travelling, you have the euros if you use cash; when you are buying British wizardry novels, Belgian chocolate, or Spanish soccer jerseys in an American store, the exchange takes place in a wholesale market you don't see). U.S. firms who need to purchase capital equipment or other raw materials from Europe also want to provide dollars for these transactions. If U.S. savers wish to hold European sovereign bonds denominated in euros, they supply dollars to make their purchases. Speculators who hold dollars and who are betting that the euro will gain value might sell those dollars to buy a foreign currency in the hope that it will appreciate. And if the U.S. government wanted to hold euros as an asset in the Federal Reserve, it would supply dollars in order to obtain them.

Exchange Rate Markets Operate in Pairs

In nearly all AP testing situations, you'll be thinking about FOREX graphs in pairs: the graph for one country's currency in terms of another's and the graph for the other's in terms of the first country's currency. It is handy to orient these graphs side by side and to keep in mind the ways in which they are interrelated. For example, you might place the market for euros in terms of U.S. dollars beside the market for USD in terms of euros.

It is good practice to plan or think with both graphs sketched beside one another, even in a situation in which you are asked to consider or draw only one of the two markets. You'll have one extra chance to catch a silly mistake, and you might just find that hopping over to the other graph and then translating the changes back to the graph you were asked about is easier. *Always* title both graphs so you don't accidentally reverse them.

TEST TIP

To keep the two graphs straight, keep the following in mind. First, the *y*-axes are reciprocals of one another. The price of a dollar in euros and the price of a euro in dollars must move in opposite directions; it is a huge red flag if your analysis leads you to the conclusion that both currencies got stronger relative to the other, because that can't happen! Second, the same people forming the demand in one market are the suppliers in the other. For example, the same U.S. families who supply dollars by buying goods from Europe or visiting Rome are also demanders of euros. When shifting the demand curve on one graph, shift the supply curve on the other graph in the same direction—your double-check mechanism is to see that the exchange rates on the two graphs moved in opposite directions.

In other circumstances, you might be asked about the market for pesos in terms of the U.S. dollar and the market for dollars in terms of pesos. Or perhaps you're asked to graph side by side the market for yen in terms of pounds and pounds in terms of yen. In the end, it doesn't matter; these diagrams work in tandem, and as long as you follow the formula for labeling the graphs and understand what kinds of people each curve represents, you'll do fine, even if you've never heard of the currencies presented in the question. In fact, the AP exam has featured currency markets for fictional countries and mythic currencies before.

Exchange Markets: Changes in Exchange Rates

When graphing changes in side-by-side FOREX markets, the key rule to remember is that the people who have one currency and desire the other are both sellers and buyers, just on different graphs. Supply on one graph is the same set of people as demand on the other; move them both in the same direction at the same time. Euro holders who are dollar seekers are at once both suppliers of euros and demanders of U.S. dollars.

Appreciation and Depreciation

A rise in the price of a currency is called currency appreciation. A currency appreciates if one unit of it can buy more of another currency than before. For example, an appreciation of the U.S. dollar means that one dollar can be purchased for more euros (or European cents) and also that one euro costs fewer U.S. dollars to buy. While the U.S. dollar appreciates, the euro must be depreciating against the dollar. This means that one euro is less expensive than it previously was and that it takes more euros to purchase one dollar.

Think of appreciation of a currency as that currency getting stronger in international value and purchasing power; think of depreciation as that currency getting weaker in international value and purchasing power. For most of the world's major economies, exchange rates are determined in markets where the currency is traded. This means that the currency value sometimes fluctuates in ways that the country's citizens or government may not prefer. More will be explained about this later in the chapter, but for now, think of appreciation as causing more debits and fewer credits in both the current and capital account (more outflows) and depreciation causing an increase in the number and size of inflows in both accounts.

DIDYOUKNOW?

Fixed rather than floating exchange rates were the norm for a long time in currency markets. Prior to the late nineteenth century, currencies were pegged, or fixed, to a specific value of both gold and silver in a system known as bimetallism. The decades leading up to World War I featured most countries switching to a gold standard, meaning the amount of currency in circulation was tied to the national gold reserves. A modified fixed rate regime known as the Bretton Woods System governed currency values for about twenty-five years after World War II before the system collapsed in 1972. The recent trend is for countries to forgo having a stable exchange rate, with most preferring to have independence to conduct domestic monetary policy as they see fit to adjust their own internal economies. Because they do have flexibility over the money supply, central banks can intervene in foreign exchange markets to influence the value of currency.

Causes of Shifts in Foreign Exchange Markets

Exchange rates are determined in FOREX markets and are the price of a currency. Changes in supply of and demand for a currency cause its value to change. Tastes and preferences, national income, relative price level, and relative real interest rates are the four major factors that cause shifts in supply and demand. In real life, speculation plays a role as well, though the AP exam tends not to ask questions about it. Let's take the four major causes included on the AP exam one at a time. Each time, keep in mind the main reasons people might want currency of a country: to purchase its goods and services or to purchase its financial assets.

First, changes in tastes and preferences can cause shifts in foreign exchange markets. If U.S. goods and services become more attractive to the European buying public, Europeans supply more euros and demand more U.S. dollars. If Americans find European goods less appealing, the supply of U.S. dollars shifts left and demand for euros shifts left. Either of these situations would result in the U.S. dollar appreciating against the euro and the euro becoming weaker against the dollar. If, conversely, U.S. goods become less popular or European goods become more popular, then the result would be appreciation of the euro and a decrease in the international value of the dollar. Countries with popular goods tend to experience appreciation.

Second, national income or real GDP is a factor that influences exchange rates. As a country's total income rises, more goods and services, many of which are imports, are purchased. Buying these imports involves supplying currency, depreciating the value of the country's currency. Its trading partners, however, experience appreciating currencies—demand increases for their currencies because demand for their goods has increased. Countries with richer trade partners tend to experience appreciation.

Third, relative price levels or rates of inflation influence the demand and supply of currencies because consumers prefer to buy cheaper goods. A decrease in the U.S. price level would cause more Europeans to buy imports from the United States. In doing so, they supply euros, demanding U.S. dollars in order to purchase U.S. goods. At the same time, Americans find European goods less appealing when compared to the newly cheaper domestic alternatives. Therefore, the supply of dollars decreases and demand for euros decreases. A rise in the European price level works the same way: U.S. consumers are less interested in buying goods from Europe, and European consumers are encouraged to purchase even more from the United States. The U.S. dollar appreciates against the euro. A country with comparatively cheaper goods and services finds them in demand and therefore experiences an increase in the value of its currency.

Fourth, relative real interest rates influence supply and demand for currencies because interest rates represent the anticipated gain from assets purchased. If European real interest rates drop compared to those in the United States, European sovereign bonds would seem less attractive to U.S. savers and investors. (Recall that bonds are more expensive when interest rates on them are lower.) Americans need fewer euros because they seek to purchase fewer European bonds. The supply of dollars shifts left, and the demand for euros shifts left. At the same time, European savers and investors might realize that U.S. bonds are a better value given their lower prices and better interest yields when compared to those issued by European governments. As a result, they'll supply more Euros, demanding dollars in order to purchase U.S. financial assets. Higher real interest rates compared to a country's trade partners is likely to cause appreciation of its currency.

Main causes of currency appreciation
1. More popular goods and services
2. A trade partner's national income rises
3. A lower relative price level or inflation rate
4. A higher relative real interest rate

Figure 12-4 shows a change in the exchange rates in the markets for dollars and euros. Initially, both markets are in equilibrium, with currencies trading at a rate of 80 European cents to one U.S. dollar. The market for dollars in Figure 12-4(a), which follows, shows a decrease in demand for the dollar, and the dollar depreciates as a result—its value drops to 75 European cents. Simultaneously in Figure 12-4(b), which is the market for euros, supply shifts left, pushing up the price of one euro, from $1.25 to $1.34. Note that before and after the change, the exchange rates are reciprocals of one another: When one moves up, the other must move down proportionally.

Figure 12-4.

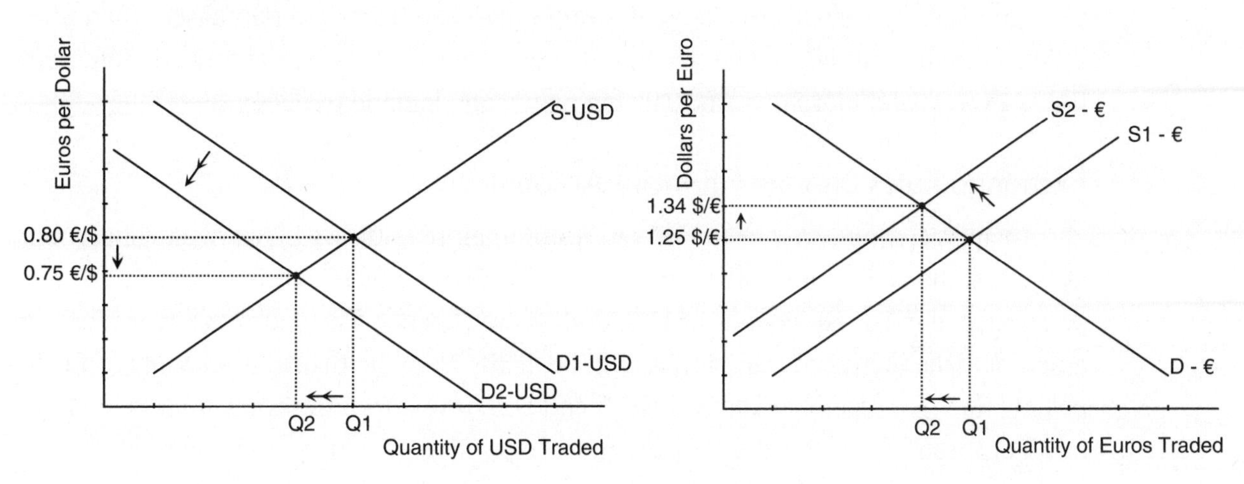

Panel A. A Decrease in the Demand for U.S. Dollars

Panel B. A Decrease in the Supply of Euros

The process shown in Figure 12-4(a) and (b) can be caused by several factors. Check your knowledge by confirming that you can draw that pair of graphs if given any of the following prompts:

1. U.S. goods fall out of fashion and became less desirable to European buyers.
2. European countries experience an economic downturn, with a noticeable drop in consumer confidence.
3. Production costs rise for U.S. heavy industry, reflecting a higher U.S. price level.
4. Bond trading firms in Germany take note of new lower interest rates in the United States.

Exchange Rates and the Current Account

The current account of a country, which shows exports minus imports (or net exports), is altered by changes in the value of the country's currency. A weaker currency makes goods and services produced in a country seem cheaper to foreigners, thus increasing exports. Imports also decrease because the country's citizens face higher price tags on imports in stores within that country. Because exports increase and imports decrease, net exports rise. The country's balance of trade moves toward surplus (or smaller deficit), and its aggregate demand (AD) curve shifts right.

Stronger currencies tend to push the current account toward deficit. If the U.S. dollar appreciates, the result is that Americans have more purchasing power when buying imported goods and services than they used to and respond by purchasing more imports, which results in outflows and reduces the current account balance. Exports from the United States are harder to sell abroad because it takes more units of foreign currency to pay a price that covers the production costs in appreciated American dollars. Because U.S. goods carry higher price tags in foreign markets, fewer are purchased; therefore, inflows (credits) in the current account decrease. This increases the trade deficit, with fewer exports and more imports, causing aggregate demand to decrease.

Exchange Rates and the Financial Account

An appreciating currency is likely to result in more outflows in the financial account as well. If the euro gains value abroad, then European savers and investors find assets denominated in British pounds or U.S. dollars are cheaper. They purchase more foreign assets, and the increased transactions will be debits from the financial accounts of European Union (EU) member states. British and U.S. investors and savers are less likely to buy European bonds because they are more expensive given the pricier euro.

On the other hand, if a country's currency depreciates, its financial account moves toward the positive, recording more credits and representing financial inflows. The cheaper currency lures foreign direct and portfolio investment because domestic assets are cheaper to foreigners. The inflows that result shift the country's financial account toward the positive.

Taken together, you can see how flexible exchange rates reinforce the idea that the current account and the financial account are nearly exactly opposite one another in value. If the net of the two is above zero, there are more inflows than outflows and the currency is likely to appreciate, reducing the inflows. If together they total a negative value, it means outflows outnumber inflows. This desire to trade away the currency lowers its value and encourages more inflows. The fluctuations in the exchange rates serve as a negative feedback loop, cutting off or rebalancing the factor that caused the change in the first place.

Capital Flight

Sometimes this process doesn't cancel itself out and instead forms a dangerous spiral. If concerns about the stability of the economy or government are serious enough, a phenomenon known as **capital flight** can occur. In the market for loanable funds, supply shifts sharply upward to the left because lenders fear the prospects of not being repaid, therefore demanding far higher real interest rates in order to lend. In many cases, the goal is merely to take funds out of the country as fast as possible—this act increases the supply of the currency in the foreign exchange market and therefore depreciates it. The resulting high interest rates can further cripple the budgetary situations of countries in debt because interest payments are higher for "risky" governments than for stable ones. Another effect of high interest rates is that they discourage investment, meaning aggregate demand shifts left in the short run and economic growth slows in the long run because capital stock is accumulated more slowly. In 2012, Greece and Spain suffered from capital flight: At one point, Greece was hemorrhaging $4 billion per week, and Spain lost more than a $1 billion per day during the first quarter that year. Borrowing costs rose for both governments, and unemployment rates elevated sharply in both economies.

Macroeconomic Policy and Exchange Rates

Macroeconomic policy decisions can also influence developments in the FOREX markets; one option is for policymakers to use the reserves in the official account to intervene directly in exchange markets. Because fiscal and monetary tools influence price level, real interest rates, and the level of national income, they can also have indirect effects on the international value of a country's currency.

Direct Intervention in FOREX Markets Using Reserves

The simplest way in which governmental authorities can manipulate exchange rates is to use their official reserves account to purchase or sell currency to create the desired effect on the exchange rate. If the Chinese government, for example, wishes to keep its currency, the renminbi yuan, weaker than its market value, the government can use direct FOREX market intervention to accomplish this goal. To devalue (or intentionally cause a currency to depreciate) the yuan, the government would sell yuan and buy dollars. The same action can be shown in either the graph for yuan in terms of dollars or in the graph for dollars in terms of yuan. No matter which graph we use to show this devaluation, it has the effect of weakening the yuan and strengthening the dollar. Figure 12-5 depicts this action in two ways.

Figure 12-5.

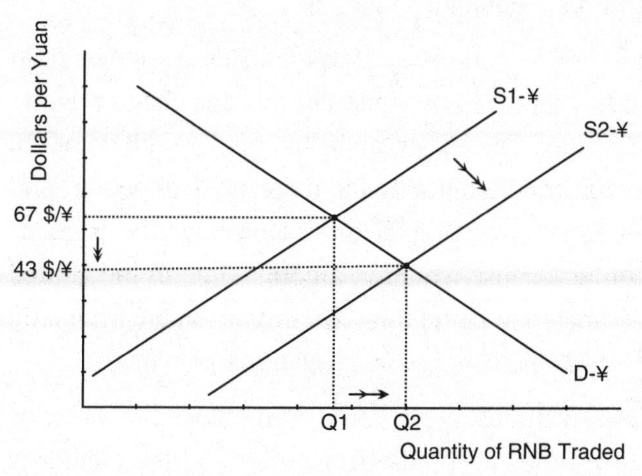

Panel A. The Market for Renminbi Yuan

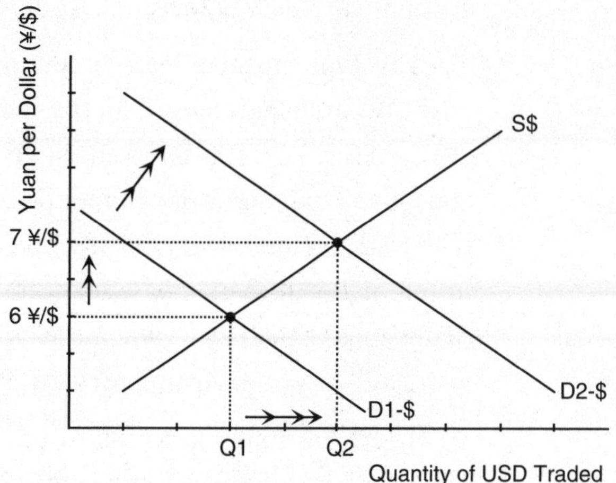

Panel B. The Market for U.S. Dollars

Examine Figure 12-5(a) on the prior page, which illustrates the market for renminbi yuan (RNB or ¥). By selling yuan in order to increase its supply, the government drives down the price of each unit of its currency. The supply of yuan increases and the dollar price of one yuan decreases, from 16.7 cents to 14.3 cents. Examining the same transaction's effects in the market for dollars in Figure 12-5(b) to the right reveals that the Chinese government purchased dollars, increasing demand for them and driving up the price of one dollar, from 6 yuan to 7 yuan.

Why might governments want to weaken their currencies? Weaker currencies enable exporting firms within a country to sell more goods abroad; in this example, it would be easier for a Chinese corporation that can produce its output for, say, 20 yuan each to sell its goods in U.S. markets because the price tag on such goods will drop from $3.33 apiece (the dollar value of 20 yuan when yuan are traded 6 to the dollar) to $2.85 (the dollar value of 20 yuan now that yuan are traded 7 to the dollar). At the same time, Chinese consumers find U.S. goods more expensive and therefore buy fewer imports. Countries might want to increase their net exports to please producers wishing to sell more exports or because it can shift aggregate demand to the right.

Revaluing a currency (intentionally causing it to appreciate) through direct intervention in the exchange market works in a similar manner. The government can purchase its own currency, spending down some of the reserves of a foreign currency that it holds. This shifts supply of the foreign currency to the right, decreasing its value, and shifts demand for the country's home currency to the right, causing it to appreciate or increase in value. Countries sometimes desire stronger currencies because domestic households and firms have an easier time purchasing consumer or capital goods from trade partners, or because they wish to use a stronger currency as a tool to decrease a large current account surplus and therefore shift aggregate demand to the left.

This type of direct intervention in FOREX markets can have a faster or more certain effect on exchange rates than the indirect methods described later in this chapter. However, overuse of direct intervention to devalue a currency may be unpopular with domestic consumers (who now pay higher prices for imported goods and therefore feel poorer) and with trade partners (who may feel the country is creating an unfair advantage for its goods in international markets). China did, in fact, cause irritation among some in the United States in 2009 and 2010 when it was estimated to be holding its currency at an artificially low level—by some estimates as much as 37 percent below its true market value!

There are inherent limits to the use of direct intervention to increase the value of a currency: At some point the official reserves account will run dry and the country's government will have no way of holding the value at artificially high levels. This happened to the United Kingdom in the fall of 1992. The British government spent £27 million trying to hold up the pound's value within the band of values prescribed by the exchange rate mechanism (ERM). When it became clear on September 16, 1992, that the government would not be able to continue to prop up the currency's value, Britain withdrew from the ERM and allowed the pound's value to fall. In the end, the failed attempt to keep the pound's value higher than its equilibrium value cost British taxpayers and firms over £3 billion.

Monetary Policy and Exchange Rates

Monetary policy tools can be used by a country's central bank to intervene indirectly in foreign exchange markets. Because relative interest rates guide decisions about which country's financial assets (like bonds) to purchase, monetary policy can have a strong effect on exchange rates. To devalue the domestic currency, a central bank can use expansionary monetary policy (for example, buying bonds on the open market) to drive down interest rates. At the new lower interest rate, domestic bonds are more expensive and less desirable. Because foreign investors find those bonds less desirable, demand for the currency in which they are denominated decreases. The result is that the currency should depreciate. To achieve the opposite result, a central bank uses contractionary policies to decrease the money supply, pushing interest rates up and making domestic financial assets more attractive to foreign investors. This causes an increase in the demand for the currency and thus causes it to appreciate. In this way, actions in a country's money market affect the processes in the foreign exchange market for its currency.

Two other effects of monetary policy can influence the FOREX market as well: the changes it causes in price level and in real output. Expansionary monetary policy undertaken by a central bank therefore causes depreciation for three reasons. First, it increases national income, causing more imports to be purchased and outflows to increase. Second, it increases the price level, making domestic goods less attractive when compared to foreign goods in markets both at home and abroad. Third, it reduces interest rates, thus decreasing the quantity of the country's financial assets that are demanded. These three causal connections between monetary policy and exchange rates are mutually reinforcing.

Fiscal Policy and Exchange Rates

The connections between fiscal policy and exchange rates are tougher to analyze and probably will be less emphasized on the AP Macroeconomics exam. Fiscal policy influences interest rates, price level, and national income as well. However, the effects that changes in spending and taxing have on these three factors don't end up pushing exchange rates in the same direction as they do for monetary policy actions. Therefore, it is essential that, when you are asked about these changes, you pay careful attention to the exact cause of currency value changes that the question asks you to analyze.

The first way that a fiscal policy action can influence exchange rates is by affecting the interest rate. Expansionary fiscal policies increase the need for government borrowing and therefore increase the demand for loanable funds, pushing up real interest rates. This makes bonds more attractive because they have lower prices and therefore a higher interest yield. An increased quantity of bonds demanded means an increase in the demand for the currency in which they are denominated and appreciation of that currency. For example, if the U.S. Congress and president agree on a sizable tax cut, the government's budget deficit grows. More borrowing means a higher demand for loanable funds and a higher real interest rate. The higher interest rate encourages investors to purchase U.S. securities and doing so requires having U.S. dollars. Both demand for the dollar and its value increase. A contractionary fiscal policy eases the need for government borrowing and tends to bring real interest rates down, causing the currency to depreciate.

Expansionary fiscal policies tend to increase both output and the price level. When output rises, so does national income. Thus, the citizens of a country are richer and are purchasing more goods and services, including imports. This increases outflows in the current account, meaning that the supply of the currency increases, causing it to depreciate. A rising price level means that domestically produced goods are more expensive—more domestic consumers are lured to purchase the comparatively cheaper imported goods, and fewer foreigners want to buy the country's exports. Supply of the currency increases, while demand for it decreases, causing depreciation.

Contractionary fiscal policy decreases both price level and national income. With a lower level of national income, a country's citizens are likely to purchase fewer imports, meaning that supply of the currency shifts left, causing it to appreciate.

The second and third ways that fiscal policy can influence exchange rates (price level and national income) work in opposition to the path that leads through interest rates and the loanable funds market. Expansionary fiscal policy tends to increase the value of a currency (think about the interest rate connection) but tends to decrease the currency's value (think about the price level or national income connection). This can create confusion because the net effect of these three forces isn't entirely clear. For this reason, the test creators recognize that it isn't fair to ask you questions like, "On balance, what will an expansionary fiscal policy do to the value of a country's currency?" Instead, you'll first be asked (either in a previous part of a free-response question or as part of a lead-in to, or prior column of, a multiple-choice item) something more like, "Based on the change that an expansionary fiscal policy taken by Japan is likely to have on the demand for loanable funds, how is the value of the yen likely to be affected by such a policy?" or "Given the change in price level you identified in part (b), indicate whether the currency is likely to appreciate or depreciate." Both of these phrasings make clear to you a specific line of reasoning that you are supposed to follow.

TEST TIP

Foreign exchange is one of the more abstract topics you'll need to be ready for, and the questions on this material will be challenging. Because there are so many causal connections, you are likely to overthink some questions and reason your way out of the correct response. To avoid this, look carefully for clues in the question, which should lay out a causal chain of events to follow. Take the most direct path from cause to effect. For example, if you are asked how a rising price level in a country influences its current account balance, you might struggle between two possible explanations: (1) Higher prices cause consumers to be more attracted to imports and make domestic goods tougher to sell abroad, decreasing exports and therefore making net exports decrease, pushing the current account toward deficit *or* (2) a higher price level causes a currency to depreciate, making imports less affordable in domestic markets and exports cheaper in foreign stores, thus increasing net exports and moving the current account toward surplus. Because it is more direct, the first line of reasoning is the preferred one to follow in this situation unless there is a specific indication in the question that you are supposed to think about the changing value of the currency. The AP exam is unlikely to ask for secondary effects, so give the immediate change based on the cause the question specifies.

Take Mini-Test 2

on Chapters 7–12

Go to the REA Study Center

(www.rea.com/studycenter)

AP Microeconomics Practice Exam

Also available at the REA Study Center *(www.rea.com/studycenter)*

This practice exam is available at the REA Study Center. Although AP exams are administered in paper-and-pencil format, we recommend that you take the online version of the practice exam for the benefits of:

- Instant scoring
- Enforced time conditions
- Detailed score report of your strengths and weaknesses

AP Microeconomics Practice Exam
Section I

(Answer sheets appear in the back of the book.)

TIME: 70 Minutes
Number of Questions—60

Directions: Each of the questions or incomplete statements below is followed by five suggested answers or completions. Select the one that is best in each case and then fill in the corresponding oval on the answer sheet.

1. Which of the following are basic questions that all societies' economic systems must address?

   I. Which goods to produce
   II. Who in society should receive the goods
   III. How the goods will be produced

   (A) I only
   (B) I and II only
   (C) I and III only
   (D) II and III only
   (E) I, II, and III

2. The primary difference between capital and consumer goods is best expressed in which statement below?

   (A) Consumer goods are useful in making our lives easier, but capital goods are the ones we really need.
   (B) Consumer goods are intrinsically desirable and capital goods are useful as a means of production.
   (C) Consumer goods are generally cheap and poorly crafted and capital goods are made to last.
   (D) Capital goods lose their value with time far faster than consumer goods.
   (E) Consumer goods lose their value with time far faster than capital goods.

3. Market economies are characterized by

(A) the rate of long-term economic growth they achieve

(B) shared decision making about the production process

(C) centralized decision making about the allocation of goods

(D) generally low levels of income inequality and productivity

(E) private individuals owning the productive economic resources

4. Which of the following would be most likely to cause an increase in the supply of tires?

(A) An decrease in the price of tennis balls, which are alternative products that can be made from rubber

(B) An increase in the demand for tennis balls, which are alternative products that can be made from rubber

(C) An increase in the number of people who walk, bike, or take the bus rather than driving

(D) A law that strictly limits the emissions of tire manufacturing plants

(E) An increase in the price of the rubber and steel used in the production of tires

Use the graph below to respond to Questions 5–6.

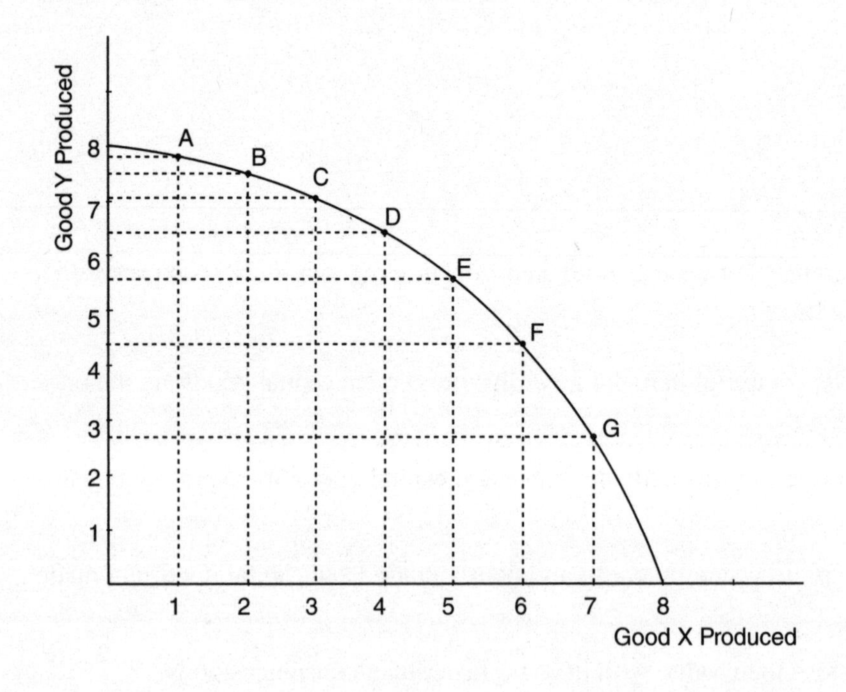

5. Producing the eighth unit of Good X entails a sacrifice of

(A) ½ unit of Good X

(B) 1½ units of Good X

(C) 2¾ units of Good Y

(D) 4¼ units of Good X

(E) 8 units of Good Y

6. Assume Good X represents factory machinery and Good Y represents foodstuffs. From this, one can conclude that

(A) points A, B, and C are not productively efficient alternatives for this society.

(B) producing at point F places more priority on satisfying future wants than producing at point D does.

(C) Good X is subject to the principle of increasing opportunity cost, but Good Y is not subject to the principle.

(D) points F and G are not allocatively efficient alternatives for this society.

(E) Good Y is subject to the principle of increasing opportunity cost, but Good X is not subject to the principle.

7. Which of the following correctly states and depicts the likely effects of a technological breakthrough leading to increased soybean yields?

(A) An increase in supply of soybeans:

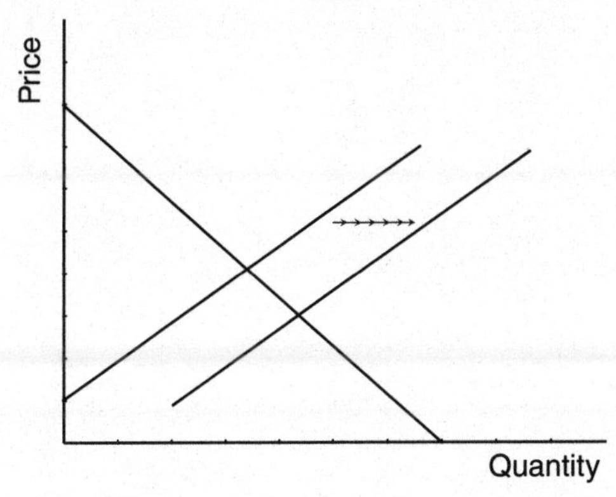

(B) An increase in supply of soybeans:

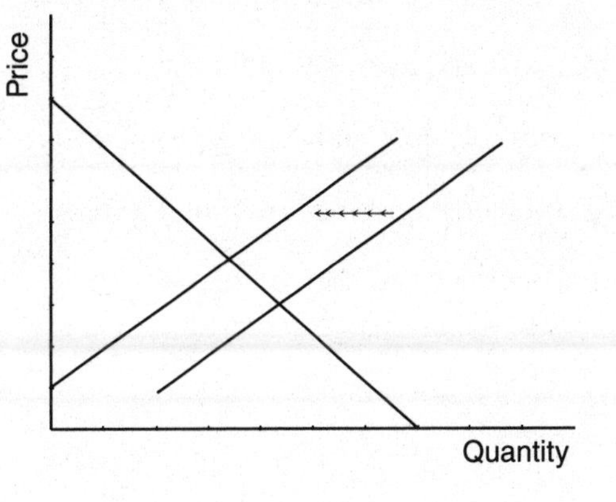

(C) A decrease in supply of soybeans:

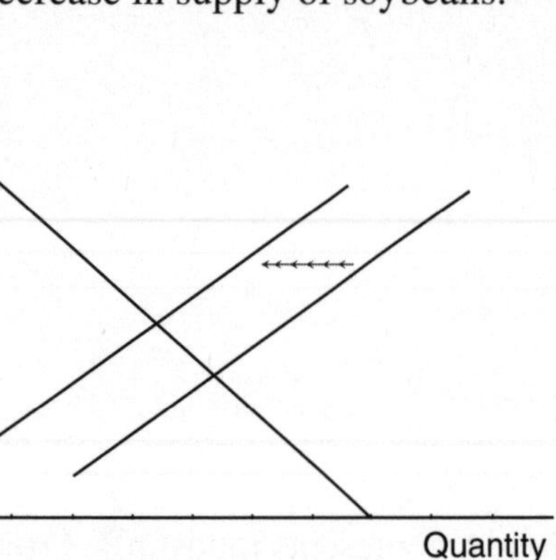

(D) A decrease in supply of soybeans:

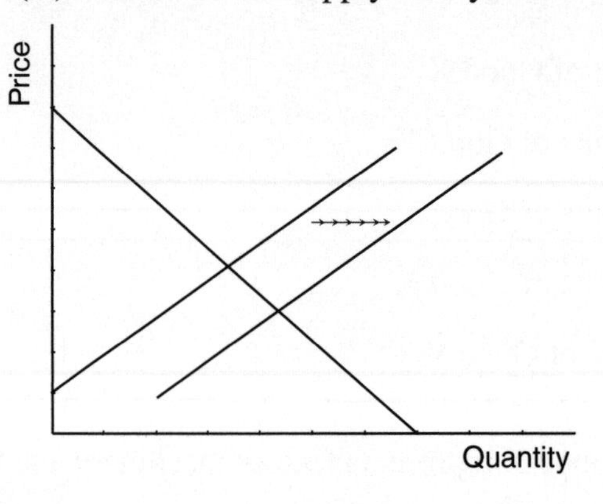

(E) An increase in supply of soybeans:

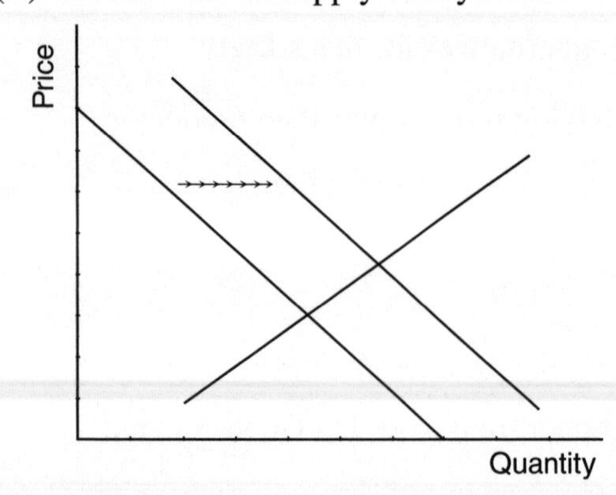

8. Average fixed cost can be inferred even if not drawn on a graph because it is the distance between

(A) marginal cost and average variable cost

(B) marginal cost and average total cost

(C) average variable cost and average total cost

(D) average total cost and the horizontal axis

(E) marginal cost and the horizontal axis

9. If a large rightward shift of the demand curve for cars only increases the equilibrium price slightly, then it can be concluded that

(A) demand for cars is price elastic

(B) supply of cars is price inelastic

(C) demand for cars is price inelastic

(D) supply of cars is price elastic

(E) demand for cars is unit elastic

10. A firm's short-run marginal cost curve generally will increase beyond some level of output because of

(A) more efficient production

(B) economies of scale

(C) diseconomies of scale

(D) diminishing marginal returns

(E) increasing marginal returns

11. Which of the following is true of normal profits?

(A) They are not an economic cost of production.

(B) They act as signals to attract new firms to enter an industry.

(C) They are not really profits, since they don't represent real money.

(D) Economists don't prefer to count them as costs, but accountants do.

(E) They can be seen as the cost of entrepreneurial ability because they represent the opportunity cost of running the firm for the entrepreneur.

12. A sharp rise in the price of gasoline and technological advances in the hybrid engine production process will have what effects on the price and quantity traded in the market for hybrid vehicles?

	Quantity	Price
(A)	Increase	Increase
(B)	Increase	Decrease
(C)	Uncertain	Increase
(D)	Decrease	Uncertain
(E)	Increase	Uncertain

13. In the graph below, at a price of P1,

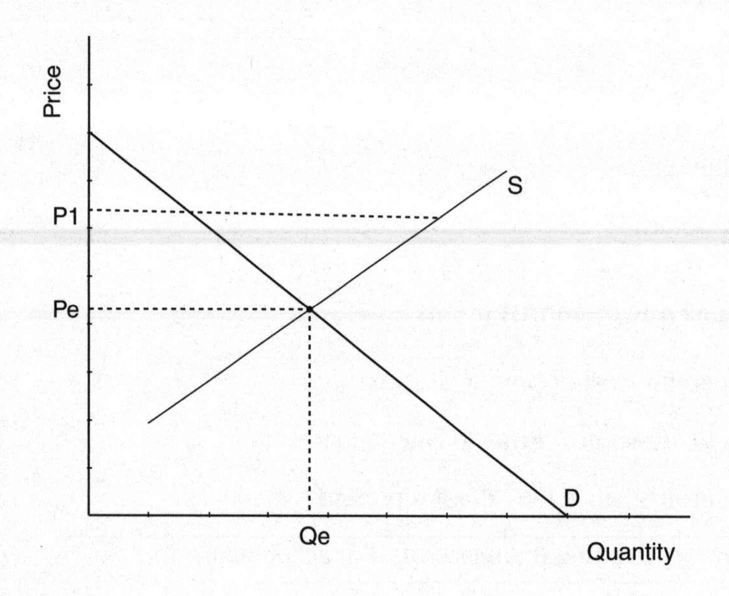

(A) suppliers are not willing to provide enough good to the market

(B) some consumers who are willing to pay the market price will not be able to obtain the good

(C) market forces will lead quantity demanded to decrease as price falls to equilibrium level

(D) the resulting surplus will lead to a drop in the market price

(E) the market will be allocatively efficient in its output

14. How will an effective price ceiling likely affect the quantity traded, price, area of deadweight loss, and area of producer surplus?

Quantity	Price	Deadweight Loss	Producer Surplus
(A) Decrease	Increase	No change	No change
(B) Decrease	Decrease	Increase	Decrease
(C) No change	Decrease	Increase	Increase
(D) Decrease	Decrease	Decrease	Decrease
(E) Increase	Increase	Decrease	Increase

15. Advancements in the extraction of natural gas and increased availability of wind power should lead to

(A) a decrease in both the price and quantity of wind power traded

(B) a decrease in the price of natural gas and an increase in the quantity of natural gas traded

(C) an uncertain effect on the price of natural gas and an increase in the quantity of natural gas traded

(D) a decrease in the price of natural gas and an uncertain effect on the quantity of natural gas traded

(E) an increase in the price of wind power and a decrease in the quantity demanded of natural gas.

Use the graph below to answer Questions 16–19.

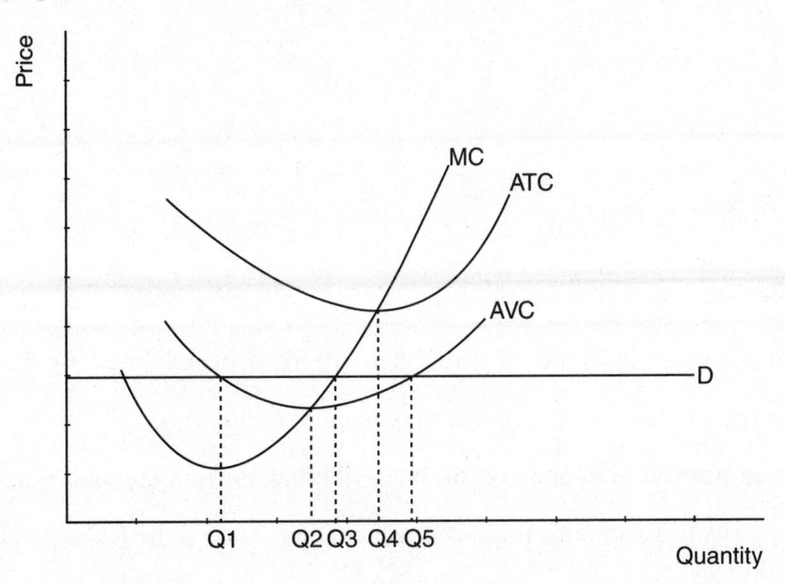

16. The firm shown in the graph is likely to choose to produce which quantity in the short run?

(A) Q1

(B) Q2

(C) Q3

(D) Q4

(E) Q5

17. The firm shown in the graph is likely to choose to produce which quantity in the long run?

(A) Q1

(B) Q2

(C) Q3

(D) Q4

(E) Q5

18. Which of the following statements is true of the firm shown in the graph?

I. The firm will be productively efficient, but only in the long run.
II. The firm's level of output will create deadweight loss.
III. The firm competes with a large number of rivals who sell the same good.

(A) I only

(B) III only

(C) I and III only

(D) II and III only

(E) I, II, and III are all true

19. Which statement best describes the firm's ability to earn economic profits?

(A) This firm is earning a negative economic profit, but will break even in the long run.

(B) This firm is breaking even and will continue to do so in the long run.

(C) This firm is earning positive economic profit, but will break even in the long run.

(D) This firm is earning positive economic profit and will continue to do so in the long run.

(E) This firm is earning negative economic profit and will continue to do so in the long run.

20. The principle of diminishing marginal utility could be used to explain all of the following examples EXCEPT

(A) Maggie notices after studying for a history test for an hour and a half that she's not learning much new because she knows her flash cards well.

(B) Luke likes the 2-for-1 special on candy bars, but buys just four because he can only take so much chocolate at once.

(C) Lillie does believe there's such a thing as too much makeup, even if she has a different sense of how much is really too much.

(D) Caitlin is excited for basketball practice every day, but she was relieved to have a day off when school was cancelled after the snow.

(E) Lucy finds that the longer she sits at the piano to practice, the faster she can learn new songs and the more she enjoys practicing.

21. When a good becomes less expensive, more is demanded because purchasing one unit of it entails a smaller sacrifice of other goods a consumer might purchase. This explanation most correctly defines the

(A) substitution effect

(B) low-hanging fruit principle

(C) law of increasing opportunity cost

(D) principle of diminishing marginal utility

(E) income effect

22. A firm produces 10,000 doorknobs in a year. Its total variable costs were €50,000 and its average fixed costs were €2.00. The total costs for the year were

(A) €50,000

(B) €60,000

(C) €70,000

(D) €80,000

(E) Impossible to determine from the information given

Consider the following table in responding to Questions 23–25.

Fish Caught	Utility Experienced
1	3
2	8
3	12
4	15
5	17
6	18

23. The marginal utility of the fourth fish is

(A) 3 utils

(B) 4 utils

(C) 3¾ utils

(D) 15 utils

(E) 17 utils

24. When four fish are caught, average utility is

(A) 3 utils

(B) 4 utils

(C) 3¾ utils

(D) 15 utils

(E) 17 utils

25. If the first three fish come at a cost of 2 utils and the next three are tougher to catch, costing 4 utils, how many is the optimal number of fish to catch?

(A) 2

(B) 3

(C) 4

(D) 5

(E) 6

26. Marginal revenue product of labor can be found by

(A) multiplying the marginal resource cost by the marginal product of labor

(B) dividing the change in total revenue by the additional number of units produced when one more worker is hired

(C) multiplying the price of the product by the marginal revenue associated with producing one more unit of the good

(D) finding out how much a firm's total revenue increases when one more unit of labor is employed

(E) dividing the profit-maximizing quantity by the number of workers employed

Use the graph below to answer Questions 27–28.

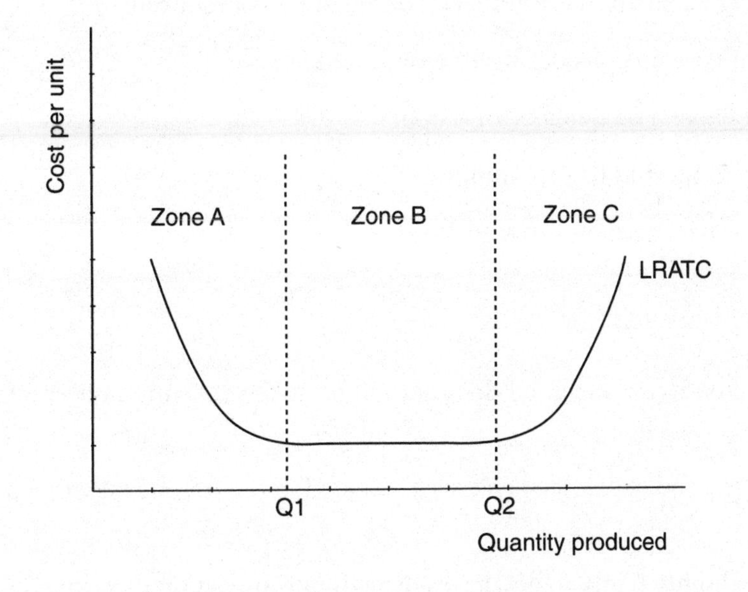

27. The zones A, B, and C respectively represent

(A) economies of scale, constant returns to scale, and diseconomies of scale

(B) diseconomies of scale, constant returns to scale, and economies of scale

(C) maximum efficient scale, constant returns to scale, and minimum efficient scale

(D) diseconomies of scale, economies of scale, and constant returns to scale

(E) increasing returns to scale, diseconomies of scale, and natural monopoly

28. Which of the following predictions about this industry is the most accurate in the long run?

(A) Only extremely large and extremely small firms will be able to compete in the industry.

(B) There will be one extremely large firm that produces all the units that are traded in the market.

(C) There will be a large number of firms, each producing no more than Q1 units.

(D) There will be a few large firms, each producing at least Q2 units.

(E) Firms will vary in size, with each firm producing a quantity between Q1 and Q2.

29. Sunk costs are

(A) marginal costs that eventually rise after a certain quantity is produced

(B) the most important costs in considering economic decisions

(C) variable costs that depend on quantity of output

(D) average costs that you would like to minimize

(E) fixed costs that are spent and not recoverable

30. Rival consumption suggests that

(A) one person's consumption of the good does not influence the consumption of other buyers

(B) a particular unit of a good or service is not easily shared; more for one buyer means less for others

(C) market failures are highly likely to occur, resulting in misallocation of resources

(D) people who are not able to pay the price for the good can still reap some of the utility from units others purchase

(E) the market demand curve will be lower than the socially optimal level of demand

31. For a firm making decisions, the main difference between short- and long-run is that

(A) the law of diminishing returns applies in the long run, but not in the short run

(B) in the long run all resources are variable, but in the short run at least one is fixed

(C) fixed costs are more important to decisions in the long run than in the short run

(D) in the short run all resources are fixed, while in the long run all of them are variable

(E) economic profits are only possible in the short run, not in the long run

32. Which of the following best articulates why an increase in demand for the product a firm produces causes the firm to produce a greater quantity?

(A) Marginal revenue rises, increasing the quantity at which marginal revenue equals marginal cost.

(B) Marginal cost rises, increasing the quantity at which marginal revenue equals marginal cost.

(C) Average total cost decreases, meaning the firm can make more units to increase profit.

(D) Average revenue rises, increasing the profit a firm can make at its current level of output.

(E) The firm purchases more fixed inputs because price increases when demand shifts right.

33. The further a country's Lorenz Curve dips beneath the 45-degree reference line, the

(A) more equally allocated its wealth is

(B) stronger its labor force's training is likely to be

(C) more goods it has a comparative advantage to produce

(D) greater the percentage of goods its government provides publicly

(E) greater its gap between rich and poor will be

34. A monopolistically competitive firm in long-run equilibrium is most likely to earn

(A) positive economic profit, but be neither allocatively nor productively efficient

(B) no economic profit, but be both allocatively and productively efficient

(C) no economic profit and be neither allocatively nor productively efficient

(D) positive economic profit and be allocatively, but not productively, efficient

(E) no economic profit and be productively, but not allocatively, efficient

35. If a firm finds that at its current level of output, average total cost is $400, marginal cost is $400, average variable cost is $235, and price is $450, then

(A) the firm must be selling its good in a perfectly competitive product market

(B) the firm has produced too large a quantity of output

(C) the firm has underallocated resources to the production of the good

(D) the firm is maximizing its profit because price exceeds average total cost

(E) It is impossible to determine whether any of the statements above are true without additional information.

36. Assume imported shoes become more widely available and affordable. Which of the following is the most likely result in the market for domestically-produced shoes?

(A) Demand shifts to the left because imported shoes and domestic shoes are complementary goods.

(B) Demand shifts to the left because imported shoes and domestic shoes are substitute goods.

(C) Demand shifts to the right because imported shoes and domestic shoes are complementary goods.

(D) Demand shifts to the right because imported shoes and domestic shoes are substitute goods.

(E) Demand shifts to the left because domestic shoes, for most customers, are inferior goods.

37. If a few firms strategically weigh their output and pricing decisions based on those of their rivals,

(A) demand will typically shift to the right after the resulting price war between firms

(B) each firm will display allocative efficiency in both the short and long run

(C) the industry will function as an oligopoly and be allocatively inefficient

(D) firms are likely to be able to freely enter and exit the industry

(E) firms will not be able to earn positive economic profit in the long run

Questions 38–40 are based on the firm shown in the graph below.

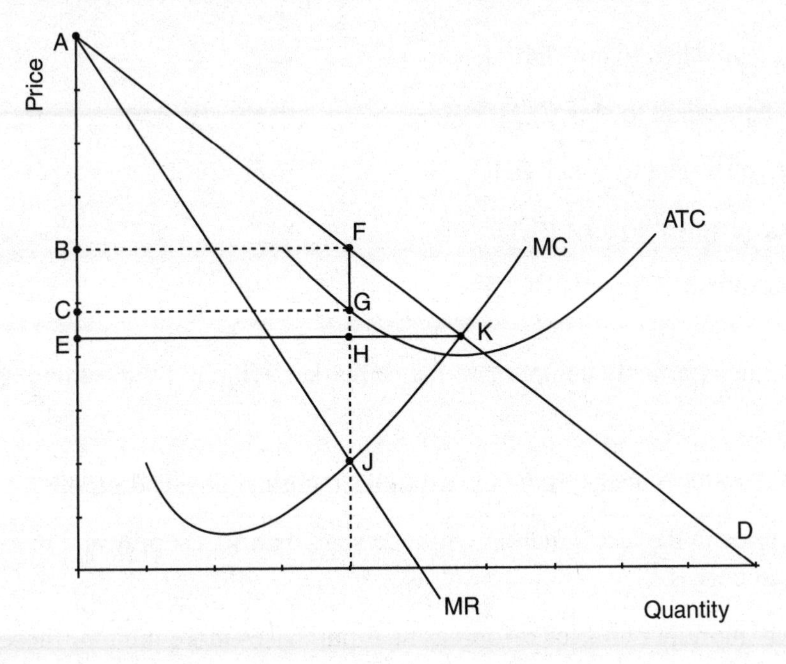

38. The consumer surplus is represented by area

(A) FJK

(B) ABF

(C) ACG

(D) BCGF

(E) CEHG

39. The firm's profit-maximizing output-price combination is at point

(A) F

(B) G

(C) K

(D) J

(E) Impossible to determine from the information present in the graph.

40. This firm is earning

(A) economic profits equivalent to area BEHF

(B) economic losses equivalent to area CEHG

(C) economic profits equivalent to area CEHG

(D) economic losses equivalent to area BCGF

(E) economic profits equivalent to area BCGF

41. For a firm purchasing in a perfectly competitive factor market, which of the following is necessarily true?

(A) Marginal revenue product equals product price times marginal physical product.

(B) The equilibrium price in the factor market will represent the firm's supply and marginal resource cost curves.

(C) The firm must pay more per unit for resources as it purchases more units of those resources.

(D) Marginal resource cost will lie above the supply of the resource.

(E) Marginal resource cost will lie below the supply of the resource.

42. Jean and William have secured a beach vacation package including flights and lodging for $1,000 per person. They estimate that they'll spend $250 on food for the week, the same as they would have at home. If they had stayed at home working, Jean would have earned $1,500 for the extra week of work, whereas William would have earned $1,000 in pay for working that week. The total opportunity cost for them to go on the trip is

(A) $1,000

(B) $2,000

(C) $2,250

(D) $4,500

(E) $4,750

43. Which claim best decscribes the allocative efficiency of a pure monopolist?

(A) A monopolist will be allocatively efficient because it will produce at the unit elastic point on the demand curve it faces.

(B) A monopolist will be allocatively efficient despite charging a high price because deadweight loss will exist in the market.

(C) A monopolist will produce fewer than the allocatively efficient quantity because it will earn economic profit.

(D) A monopolist will produce fewer than the allocatively efficient quantity because marginal revenue will exceed marginal cost.

(E) A monopolist will produce fewer than the allocatively efficienty quantity unless it can perfectly price discriminate.

44. Which of the following conditions are needed for a firm to price discriminate?

I. Price-setting power

II. Ability to segregate buyers by reservation price

III. Ability to discourage buyers from reselling the product

IV. A perfectly elastic demand curve

(A) I only

(B) IV only

(C) I and II only

(D) I, II and III only

(E) I, II, III, and IV

45. The existence of excess capacity indicates that

(A) monopolists are unlikely to be allocatively efficient in the long run

(B) perfectly competitive firms are unlikely to be allocatively efficient in the short run

(C) monopolistically competitive firms are unlikely to be allocatively efficient in the long run

(D) monopolistically competitive firms are certain to be productively inefficient in the long run

(E) monopolists are certain to be productively inefficient in the short run

The following chart shows the daily profits to each of two firms in an industry given the combinations of pricing strategies each might employ. Assume that both firms A and B know the information in the chart. Use the information in it to respond to Questions 46–48.

	Firm B chooses high price	Firm B chooses low price
Firm A chooses high price	Firm A: $200 Firm B: $250	Firm A: $75 Firm B: $325
Firm A chooses low price	Firm A: $175 Firm B: $175	Firm A: $125 Firm B: $200

46. The most likely result if the firms do not cooperate in setting their prices is that

(A) Firm A will earn more profit than Firm B

(B) Firms A and B will each earn $175 per day

(C) Firms A and B will both earn fewer profits than if they had cooperated

(D) Firms A and B will earn the same profits as if they had cooperated

(E) Firms A and B will both earn the maximum profit possible

47. Which of the following statements describes the firms' choices most correctly?

(A) Choosing a low price is a dominant strategy for both firms.

(B) Choosing a high price is a dominant strategy for both firms.

(C) Choosing a low price is a dominant strategy for firm A, but not firm B.

(D) Choosing a high price is a dominant strategy for firm B, but not firm A.

(E) Firm A does not have a dominant strategy, but firm B does.

48. This particular situation can be used to help illustrate all of the following concepts EXCEPT

(A) economies of scale

(B) prisoner's dilemma

(C) Nash Equilibrium

(D) interdependent decision making

(E) the instability of cartels

Consult the table below in order to answer Questions 49–51 about Marcy's Parsleys, an herb stand that produces bundles of herbs to sell at the local farmer's market using labor only as a variable resource.

Number of workers employed	Bundles of fresh herbs sold
1	14
2	30
3	47
4	60
5	71
6	80
7	79

49. If the herb bundles sell for $4 apiece,

(A) the marginal revenue product of the fourth worker is $240

(B) Marcy should never pay the fifth worker a wage rate exceeding $30

(C) the third worker contributes marginal physical product of 47 units

(D) average physical product is 15 when 5 units of labor are employed

(E) hiring the seventh worker would decrease profit at any wage rate

50. If the herb bundles are priced at $5 no matter how many the firm produces, what is the marginal revenue product of the sixth worker?

(A) 9 herb bundles

(B) 45 herb bundles

(C) $45

(D) $80

(E) 80 herb bundles

51. At a constant herb bundle price of $3 each, how many workers will the firm hire in order to maximize profit when the market wage rate is $30?

(A) 4 workers

(B) 5 workers

(C) 6 workers

(D) 7 workers

(E) Impossible to determine given the information provided.

52. How will an effective minimum wage change the quantity of labor employed by a firm hiring in a perfectly competitive market and a monopsonist?

	Perfectly Competitive Firm	Monopsonist
(A)	Indeterminate change	Increase
(B)	Decrease	Decrease
(C)	Indeterminate change	Indeterminate change
(D)	Decrease	Indeterminate change
(E)	Decrease	Increase

53. Which of the following statements help to explain why the short-run per-unit cost curves of a typical firm may slope downward at very low quantities?

I. Firms take advantage of specialization as they hire more workers.

II. Adding more units of all the inputs the firm uses allows the firm to benefit from economies of scale.

III. Average fixed costs decrease sharply as the firm increases output.

(A) I only

(B) III only

(C) I and II only

(D) I and III only

(E) II and III only

54. A firm can ensure it creates the profit-maximizing quantity of its output at the lowest possible cost by

(A) setting the marginal revenue product of each input equal to its marginal factor cost

(B) ensuring that the ratios of marginal factor cost to marginal revenue product for all inputs used are equal to one another

(C) producing at the minimum point on its average variable cost curve

(D) ensuring that the average physical products of all inputs used are equal to each other

(E) ensuring that ratios of average revenue product to average factor cost for all inputs used are equal to one

55. Which of the following statements is correct with respect to regulation of a natural monopolist?

(A) The socially optimal price, though allocatively efficient, may cause the monopolist to leave the industry.

(B) The socially optimal price, though productively efficient, may cause the monopoly to leave the industry.

(C) The fair return price, though allocatively efficient, may cause the monopolist to leave the industry.

(D) The fair return price, though productively efficient, completely eliminates deadweight loss.

(E) The socially optimal price does not eliminate all of the deadweight loss associated with the monopoly's inefficiency.

Use the graph below to answer Questions 56–59.

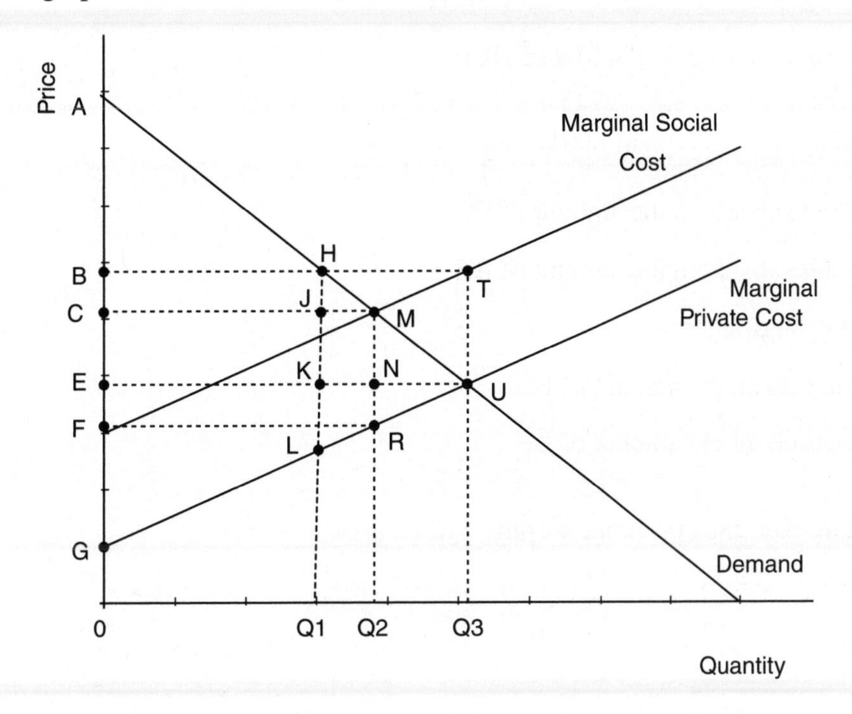

56. In the graph above, the allocatively efficient market price and quantity is

(A) quantity of Q1 and price of B

(B) quantity of Q2 and price of C

(C) quantity of Q2 and price of F

(D) quantity of Q3 and price of B

(E) quantity of Q3 and price of E

57. The externality shown is

(A) negative, resulting in a deadweight loss of area MTU

(B) negative, resulting in a deadweight loss of area MRU

(C) negative, resulting in a deadweight loss of BEUT

(D) positive, resulting in a deadweight loss of CFRM

(E) positive, resulting in a deadweight loss of HLU

58. One effective remedy for this type of market failure would be to

(A) provide a per-unit subsidy in the amount of EF

(B) provide a per-unit subsidy in the amount of BE

(C) set a price ceiling at price B

(D) impose a per-unit tax in the amount of FG

(E) impose a per-unit tax in the amount of BF

59. In an unregulated market, the consumer surplus will be area

(A) ABH

(B) ACM

(C) AEU

(D) AMRF

(E) AMNE

60. Which of the following statements is accurate with respect to pure public goods?

I. Pure public goods are suited to being provided by government, with tax revenue used to pay the costs of production.

II. Pure public goods are likely to be associated with the free rider problem if sold as market goods.

III. Production of pure public goods typically involves negative externalities.

(A) I only

(B) II only

(C) I and II only

(D) II and III only

(E) I, II, and III are all true

Section II

Planning Time: 10 minutes
Writing Time: 50 minutes
Number of Questions—3

Directions: You have 10 minutes to read all three of the questions in this section, to make notes, and to plan your answers. You will then have 50 minutes to answer all three of the following questions. It is suggested that you spend approximately half your time on the first question and divide the remaining time equally between the next two questions. In answering the questions, you should emphasize the line of reasoning that generated your results; it is not enough to list the results of your analysis. Include correctly labeled diagrams, if useful or required, in explaining your answers. A correctly labeled diagram must have all axes and curves clearly labeled and must show directional changes. Use a pen with black or dark blue ink.

1. A rational monopolist is making a profit in the short run.
   a. Graph this firm's situation, showing
      i. Demand and marginal revenue
      ii. Marginal and Average Total Cost
      iii. The price (P*) and quantity (Q*) the firm will choose to produce in order to maximize profit.
      iv. The socially optimal quantity (Q_{so})
   b. If the monopolist chose to produce a smaller quantity than you identified in (a-iii), explain how that would change each of the following:
      i. Total revenue
      ii. Amount of profit
      iii. Area of consumer surplus
   c. Identify one government policy that could be taken to influence the monopolist to produce the socially optimal quantity you identified in (a-iv). Explain how this policy would change the monopolist's incentives.

2. Gwen's Pizzeria sells pizzas for $10 each and can sell as many pizzas as it wants at that price.
   a. How does Gwen calculate the Marginal Revenue Product of the workers she hires?
   b. Assuming that Gwen hires from a labor market for pizza delivery drivers and pizza cooks that is perfectly competitive, draw side-by-side graphs of the labor market and Gwen's Pizzeria, showing
      i. The wage rate.
      ii. The quantity of labor Gwen will hire.
   c. Define Marginal Factor Cost.
   d. Assume now that Gwen hires her labor in a monopsony market. State how this change from the conditions in part (b) would influence each of the following:
      i. The labor supply curve Gwen's faces.
      ii. Marginal Factor Cost. Explain.
      iii. Wage Gwen pays her employees.

3. Two soccer teams, City Blue and Unite Red, compete against one another for the loyalty of fans in a major textile-manufacturing city. They are rivals on the field and also at the box office. Their price and payroll strategy determines their ticket sales and profits at the concession stands at each stadium. Each team can charge high prices for tickets and purchase major stars from populous, but less developed nations, or sell tickets cheaply and put a slightly inferior team of home grown talent on the field. In the grid below, the monthly profits are listed and the information in the grid is known to both teams' management. Analyze the strategic game and then respond to the questions that follow.

	Unite Red pays stars, charges lots for tickets	**Unite Red runs team frugally, sells cheap seats**
City Blue pays stars, charges lots for tickets	City Blue: £25,000 Unite Red: £45,000	City Blue: £41,000 Unite Red: £15,000
City Blue runs team frugally, sells cheap seats	City Blue: £32,000 Unite Red: £60,000	City Blue: £26,000 Unite Red: £30,000

   a. If Unite Red runs its team frugally, which strategy is best for City Blue?
   b. Is there a dominant strategy for Unite Red? Explain.
   c. Define Nash Equilibrium.
   d. If each team chooses its strategy without coordinating with the other, how much monthly profit will each earn? Justify your response, relating back to your response in part (c).

Answer Key

Section I

1. (E)	16. (C)	31. (B)	46. (C)
2. (B)	17. (D)	32. (A)	47. (E)
3. (E)	18. (C)	33. (E)	48. (A)
4. (A)	19. (A)	34. (C)	49. (E)
5. (C)	20. (E)	35. (E)	50. (C)
6. (B)	21. (A)	36. (B)	51. (B)
7. (A)	22. (C)	37. (C)	52. (D)
8. (C)	23. (A)	38. (B)	53. (D)
9. (D)	24. (C)	39. (A)	54. (A)
10. (D)	25. (B)	40. (E)	55. (A)
11. (E)	26. (D)	41. (B)	56. (B)
12. (E)	27. (A)	42. (D)	57. (A)
13. (D)	28. (E)	43. (E)	58. (D)
14. (B)	29. (E)	44. (D)	59. (C)
15. (D)	30. (B)	45. (D)	60. (C)

Detailed Explanations of Answers

Section I

1. (E)

These are all results of the principle of scarcity—an inability to meet all the needs and wants of all the people in the society at once.

2. (B)

Capital goods are tools used to produce other goods. Consumer goods meet our wants and needs by providing utility to us directly. Because they don't directly meet our wants and needs, capital goods are only valuable insofar as they can help make consumer goods (or produce other capital goods that help make consumer goods). Option (A) reverses the basic difference between the two types of goods. The wide variety of quality levels of both consumer and capital goods render choices (C), (D), and (E) false.

3. (E)

Private ownership of property, including factors of production, is at the core of the market system and capitalism. Command economies feature centralized decision making (C) and traditional ones might sometimes work along shared decision making lines (B). While market economies can sustain growth over time (A), this is not the defining characteristic of them. That growth often comes with more, not less, inequality of income (D).

4. (A)

The tennis balls are a substitute in production. As they become less expensive, more rubber would be diverted toward the production of tires. Option (B) reverses the causation. Choices (D) and (E) cause decreases in supply of tires and choice (C) would shift demand for tires left, decreasing quantity supplied.

5. (C)

The eighth unit of good X entails moving from point G to the intercept with the X-axis. This movement to the right (to get another unit of X) entails a movement downward of between 2 and 3 units; this movement represents the marginal sacrifice of units of Y and therefore the opportunity cost of the eighth X.

6. (B)

Future wants can be better satisfied if more capital goods are produced now. Point F involves more production of factory machinery (a capital good) than point D does. Choice (A) is flawed because all points on the production possibilities frontier are productively efficient. Choices (C) and (E) are both incorrect: the bowed shape of this concave PPF shows an increasing opportunity cost for each of the goods. Choice (D) is indeterminate because allocative efficiency depends on the desirability of the goods to the population.

7. (A)

The prompt suggests an increase in supply because production became cheaper, ruling out choices (C) and (D), which state that supply decreases. Choice (A) shows an increase in supply correctly. The graph in (B) is wrong because supply decreases and the one in choice (E) shows an increase in demand rather than supply.

8. (C)

Average Fixed Cost is the space between Average Total Cost and Average Variable Cost because costs are either fixed or variable. The distances in choices (A) and (B) are not meaningful ones. Those in choices (D) and (E) are simply ATC and MC, respectively.

9. (D)

The slope of supply would be relatively flat, enabling a large increase in quantity with price increasing only slightly. The slope of demand (choices (A), (C), and (E)) is irrelevant if demand is the curve shifting. A steeper, more inelastic supply curve (choice (B)) would lead to a large price increase for even a relatively small shift of demand.

10. (D)

After the firm enjoys the benefit of specialization, as it employs more of a variable resource it will begin to overtax fixed inputs, meaning that each successive unit of the resource added will increase output by smaller and smaller increments. This is the principle of diminishing marginal returns. Production is actually becoming costlier for each unit after this point, disproving choice (A). Economies and diseconomies of scale (choices (B) and (C)) apply to long-run changes in firm size. Choice (E) is the opposite of the correct answer and would describe the range of quantities for which specialization was causing marginal cost to decline.

11. (E)

Normal profit refers to the level of accounting profit that encourages neither entry of new firms (B) nor exit of existing firms from an industry. It is therefore equal to the level of profit that could have been earned elsewhere. To economists these do represent costs (A), but to accountants they don't (D). They represent real money earned (C) that compensates business owners for use of their own resources.

12. (E)

The stem refers to two changes: an increase in demand that results from a substitute good becoming more expensive and an increase in supply that results from improved production technology. The certain result is that quantity traded will increase as both demand and supply of hybrid cars increase, ruling out choices (C) and (D). Both (A) and (B) are possible, but (E) is the superior choice because the relative magnitudes of the shifts in supply and demand will determine if price changes and in which direction.

13. (D)

Quantity supplied exceeds quantity demanded at prices higher than equilibrium, so there is a surplus. This provides a cue to buyers and sellers to decrease price toward equilibrium level, Pe. Choices (A) and (B) suggest a shortage rather than a surplus. Choice (C) is wrong because quantity demanded will increase as price falls, and choice (E) is incorrect because at present less than the equilibrium quantity is sold and total economic surplus has not been maximized.

14. (B)

An effective price ceiling is placed below the equilibrium price and decreases quantity supplied, therefore decreasing quantity traded. Price falls to the level of the legal maximum. Because quantity is less than equilibrium there is a deadweight loss that comes from underproduction. Producer surplus decreases because suppliers sell fewer units and receive a lower price.

15. (D)

The stem suggests that supply for natural gas will increase due to extraction advancements and demand for it will decrease because wind power, a substitute, becomes cheaper. The result is that equilibrium price in the market for natural gas will decline, but the relative size of the shifts of demand and supply will determine the effect on the quantity traded. Choice (A) incorrectly predicts a decrease in the quantity of wind power traded—the effect is uncertain in this case. Choices (B), (C), and (E) either have incorrect conclusions or fail to recognize the uncertain change in the quantity traded in the natural gas market.

16. (C)

This firm should produce the quantity at which marginal cost intersects marginal revenue, or Q3 units. Marginal revenue, while not labeled on this graph, always equals demand when demand is perfectly elastic.

17. (D)

In the long run, this firm, because it operates in a perfectly competitive market, will break even and produce at its productively efficient point where ATC meets MC. Exit of firms taking economic losses will bring the D = MR curve up to be tangent to ATC at this point in the long run.

18. (C)

Statement II is false because perfectly competitive firms produce the allocatively efficient level of output (where P = MC) and therefore create no deadweight loss. The other statements accurately characterize perfectly competitive markets: they do feature a very large number of firms selling homogenous products and the long-run ability of firms to enter and exit ensures that production will eventually be at minimum ATC.

19. (A)

The firm in the graph is taking an economic loss in the short run because the demand curve never intersects ATC, meaning that total cost will exceed total revenue for all production quantities. However, in the long run, firms can exit the industry and this firm will experience an increase in demand as market supply shifts left. This will erase losses for individual firms as the industry drifts toward long-run equilibrium. Choices (B), (C), and (D) fail to recognize that the firm is taking a short-run loss. Choice (E) ignores the tendency of perfectly competitive firms to break even in the long run.

20. (E)

Lucy's increased pace of learning is not consistent with the principle of diminishing utility. All the other statements show a decline in the added enjoyment or usefulness of additional time spent on an activity or more units of a good being consumed.

21. (A)

The substitution effect helps explain why demand curves slope downward, and the question stem describes that concept. Choices (B) and (C) are the same principle which helps explain the slope of supply curves. Choices (D) and (E) are other reasons why demand curves tend to have a downward slope.

22. (C)

The firm spent 70,000 € during the year. Total cost is fixed cost plus variable cost. Variable cost is 50,000 and fixed costs were 20,000 (average fixed cost of 2 times quantity of 10,000).

23. (A)

The fourth fish increases total utility from 12 to 15 utils. Marginal utility is the change in total utility; in this case 3 utils are gained from catching the fourth fish.

24. (C)

Average utility is total utility (15 utils) divided by quantity consumed (4 fish). 3.75 utils are gained on average for each fish when quantity is 4.

25. (B)

The first three fish are good decisions to catch because each has a higher marginal utility (added benefit) than marginal cost. The third fish, for example, costs 2 utils to obtain, but adds 4 utils to total satisfaction. The fourth fish is not a good expenditure of effort, costing 4 utils but only increasing total satisfaction by 3 utils. Optimally, consumers would pursue all deals that have higher marginal benefit than cost and would never pursue ones entailing a higher marginal benefit than cost.

26. (D)

The change in total revenue divided by the change in labor is the correct way to calculate MRP. Marginal resource cost (choice (A)) is related to supply more than demand in factor markets. Choice (B) yields marginal revenue, not marginal revenue product. Choice (C) does not have an economic significance and choice (E) results in average product rather than marginal revenue product.

27. (A)

On the long-run average total cost curve shown, the left portion slopes downward, meaning that firms become more productively efficient as they grow. This is known as increasing returns to scale or economies of scale. The flat section in zone B indicates that firms get neither more nor less productively efficient as they grow, suggesting that returns to changes in scale are constant for this range of firm size. An upsloping LRATC, such as in zone C, indicates diseconomies of scale, also known as decreasing returns to scale.

28. (E)

Quantity 1 is minimum efficient scale and Quantity 2 is maximum efficient scale. Firms larger or smaller than this range will incur higher per-unit costs, making their goods less competitive in the market and encouraging them to grow or shrink in order to become more productively efficient. Choices (B) and (D) ignore the effects of zone C, which discourage firm growth beyond Q2. Choice (C) ignores zone A, which would discourage production quantities smaller than Q1 and zone B, all of which is equally cost effective as Q1. Choice (A) reverses the correct conclusion that mid-sized firms have a cost advantage in this industry.

29. (E)

Sunk costs are associated with fixed costs because neither is considered avoidable in the short term and are, therefore, irrelevant when making many production decisions (B). Marginal (A) and variable (C) costs can be controlled because they vary with output. Choice (D) fails to distinguish between fixed and variable costs at all.

30. (B)

Rival consumption describes a situation in which units of a good consumed by one person cannot be enjoyed by others at the same time. Choice (A) describes non-rival goods, which often do lead to misallocation of resources (C). Choice (D) describes non-excludable goods and choice (E) would mostly be true of non-excludable or non-rival goods.

31. (B)

In the short run, one or more inputs is variable: the firm chooses its level of output by adding more of these inputs, often labor. However, at least one resource (often capital) is fixed—the firm cannot change how much it uses of the fixed input(s) in the short run. Choice (A) is backward as to when the law of diminishing marginal returns applies. In the long run, no costs are fixed (C). If all resources were fixed in the short run, the firm could not change its output quantity from day to day (D). Economic profits are possible in the long run for firms that produce goods sold in industries that do not allow new firms to enter (E).

32. (A)

Firms seek to maximize profit, and therefore produce at the quantity where marginal cost equals marginal revenue. Choice (B) is incorrect because demand is linked to marginal revenue rather than marginal cost. Choices (C), (D), and (E) fail to account for the marginal aspect of a firm's output determination.

33. (E)

The Lorenz Curve measures income or wealth inequality; the further it lies from the line of perfect equality, the bigger the disparity in income (or wealth) between the richest and poorest of its citizens. Choice (A) is the opposite of the correct conclusion; the other incorrect options ((B), (C), and (D)) do not speak to income inequality at all.

34. (C)

In long-run equilibrium, a monopolistic competitor will face a demand curve that is tangent to ATC, meaning it will break even with no economic profit. It will be allocatively inefficient because price will exceed marginal cost and be productively inefficient because it will have excess capacity, producing a quantity that does not minimize ATC. Choices (A) and (D) incorrectly state the firm's profit-loss situation. Choices (B) and (E) fail to account for one or both kinds of inefficiency.

35. (E)

None of the statements are certain, mostly because marginal revenue is not included in the values given. Choice (A) cannot be concluded because no information about the slope of demand or the value of marginal revenue is available. Choices (B), (C), and (D) are indeterminate without information enabling comparison between marginal revenue and marginal cost.

36. (B)

Imported and domestically produced shoes are substitute goods: both can be used to cover one's feet. When a good becomes cheaper or more widely available, demand decreases for goods that can be used as substitutes for it. Choice (D) reverses this cause. Complementary goods ((A) and (C)) are enjoyed together, not instead of one another. The sale of inferior goods (E) is determined by the way consumers' buying plans change when income rises or falls, which is not indicated in this problem.

37. (C)

Oligopolies feature a small number of interdependent firms. While price wars sometimes occur in oligopoly, they do not lead demand curves to shift (A). Firms are not allocatively efficient (B) because marginal revenue lies below demand in imperfectly competitive markets. Entry and exit is difficult in oligopoly (D) and because new firms cannot enter the market, the firms that do exist often carry profits into the long run (E).

38. (B)

Consumer surplus is found below demand, above the price that buyers pay, and to the left of the quantity purchased. In this case, area ABF matches those criteria.

39. (A)

The firm produces the quantity at which marginal cost equals marginal revenue and seeks out the market price on the demand curve corresponding with that quantity at point F.

40. (E)

At the firm's profit-maximizing quantity, demand is higher than average total cost, meaning it can bring in more total revenue than it incurs in total cost. The vertical distance between points F and G represents the per-unit profit. When multiplied by the number of units produced, this yields the area BCGF, which is total profit. Choice (D) is the correct area, but misinterprets the area as economic losses rather than profits.

41. (B)

In perfectly competitive factor markets, the market determines the factor's price and each firm then takes this as its supply and marginal resource cost curves. These firms, if hiring units of labor, are called wage-takers. Choice (A) is true for firms that sell their output in perfectly competitive product markets—it isn't true if the firm is a monopolist, oligopolist, or monopolistic competitor. Choice (C) is wrong because these firms can purchase more units without increasing the price paid for the resource: the supply curve each faces is perfectly elastic. Choice (D) is true of monopsonistic firms. Choice (E) does not make sense; marginal resource cost will always be at least as high as the wage rate.

42. (D)

To calculate opportunity cost, include both explicit costs ($1,000 for each traveler, or $2,000 total) and implicit costs (the total of the lost wages, which in this case is $2,500). Choices (A), (B), and (C) ignore one or more of these components. Choice (E) includes the $250 for food, which is not a cost of the trip since the two would have incurred these costs regardless of travel.

43. (E)

A monopoly is not allocatively efficient because it creates deadweight loss. This results from the firm's inability to price discriminate, which causes a monopolist to face a marginal revenue curve below demand and therefore produce fewer units than the level of output where MC = D. Choices (A) and (B) wrongly state that a monopoly will be allocatively efficient. Choices (C) and (D) are correct about the inefficiency, but incorrect about the explanation: profit is independent of efficiency.

44. (D)

Price discrimination involves charging different prices to different consumers for units of the same good. The ability to choose market price is clearly a precondition for this behavior, making statement I true and statement IV false. Additionally, a firm must be able to figure out who is willing to pay a high price from those who have a lower perceived value of the good, so statement II is true. If those who purchase the good cheaply can resell it to those who would otherwise be subject to the high price, the firm's efforts will be for naught, so statement III is true as well.

45. (D)

Excess capacity is associated with monopolistic competition, making choices (A) and (E) inferior. Because excess capacity is concerned with comparing ATC at the quantity produced with minimum ATC, it is related to productive efficiency rather than allocative efficiency, rendering choices (B) and (C) incorrect.

46. (C)

This situation reaches Nash Equilibrium when both firms choose a low price, which entails each earning less profit than if they had both chosen a high price. Firm B earns $200 while firm A only earns $125, making choices (A), (B), and (E) incorrect. Choice (D) is incorrect because cooperation would lead both firms to choose the high price strategy.

47. (E)

Firm A's best choice depends on firm B's decision, so firm A has no dominant strategy. Therefore, choices (A), (B), and (C) are incorrect. Firm B has a dominant strategy, but it is choosing the low price, not the high one, making choice (D) wrong.

48. (A)

Economies of scale relate to how cost functions of a firm change in the long run as it expands or contracts and is separate from game theory. This situation does pose a dilemma for the firms because the Nash Equilibrium results in lower profits than if both had made opposite choices ((B) and (C)). Their decisions are interdependent since each affects the other's ability to profit (D). While a collusive agreement to set high prices would benefit both firms, firm B would have an incentive to cheat on such an agreement, making choice (E) relevant to the situation.

49. (E)

A firm should never hire a worker who would decrease total product; the seventh worker has a negative marginal physical product and, therefore, is a detriment to the firm even if no wage were needed to induce him to work. The fourth worker's MRP is $52, not $240, assuming the price of herbs is independent of output (A). The fifth worker would increase Marcy's profit at any wage rate up to $44 (B). The third worker's total product is 47, but his marginal product is only 17 herb bundles (C). Average product of labor is 14.2, not 15, if the firm chooses to hire 5 workers (D).

50. (C)

The sixth worker adds 9 herb bundles to output, each of which is worth $5, so that worker's MRP is $45. Any choice ((A), (B), or (E)) that is not expressed in dollars is not correctly formatted for MRP: marginal physical product is a measure of output, but marginal revenue product is a measure of revenue and should be expressed in dollars. (D) is incorrect because the sixth worker does not add $80 to the firm's revenue.

51. (B)

Workers 1–5 all add more than 10 units of output to production and, therefore, are worth more than $30 to the firm. However, the sixth worker only gains the firm 9 herb bundles worth $3 each and therefore has an MRP of $27. When MRP is less than the wage rate, the firm will lose money hiring the worker. Therefore, the first five workers add to profit and those thereafter decrease it.

52. (D)

A minimum wage set above equilibrium will cause firms hiring in a perfectly competitive industry to decrease the quantity of labor hired because they will find MRP exceeds MFC for a smaller number of workers. For monopsonists, the minimum wage turns them into wage-takers at low quantities. They will hire until the set wage intersects either MRP or the old labor supply curve, whichever comes first. Depending on how high the minimum wage is set, this may mean the firm hires fewer, more, or even the same number of workers.

53. (D)

Statement I is true and explains why marginal and average variable cost curves slope downward. Statement II is false because at least one resource is fixed in the short run; the amount of each fixed resource that a firm uses cannot be changed in the short run. Statement III is true because average fixed cost declines as output rises; the same fixed costs are spread over a larger and larger quantity. At low quantities, AFC declines sharply, pulling ATC downward, since AFC is a component of it.

54. (A)

When MRP = MFC for each input, the ratio of MRP to MFC is equal to 1 for every input used. This means that each resource needed to create the product is employed optimally. Choice (B) ensures that the quantity produced is done at the cheapest possible cost, but not that the profit-maximizing quantity is made. Choices (C), (D), and (E) focus on average, rather than marginal, values.

55. (A)

Because a natural monopolist's ATC curve is above marginal cost for the entire range of quantities in the market, operating where D = MC (the allocatively efficient quantity) will involve taking an economic loss. A firm facing a regulated price that required a loss would be likely to leave the industry in the long run. Choice (B) confuses allocative and productive efficiency. Choices (C) and (D) are incorrect because the fair return price is not allocatively or productively efficient. Choice (E) is wrong because socially optimal and allocatively efficient are synonyms—there cannot be any deadweight loss if a firm produces the socially optimal (or allocatively efficient) quantity.

56. (B)

The socially optimal output-price combination is found where marginal social cost equals marginal social benefit, which in this case is the same as the demand curve. The other options incorrectly state either the output or the price.

57. (A)

Because marginal social cost is above marginal private cost, some of the costs of producing the good are borne by society rather than the seller. Therefore the externality is negative, ruling out choices (D) and (E). The market will produce Q3 units if unregulated, which is greater than the socially optimal output of Q2. Therefore, the area MTU reflects the social losses associated with overproduction. Choices (B) and (C) incorrectly state the area of deadweight loss.

58. (D)

Because the good is overproduced by the private market, a policy can only correct the misallocation if it reduces output. Subsidies, such as choices (A) and (B), increase output. A price ceiling at price B (choice (C)) would not take effect because it is a legal maximum price set above equilibrium. Choice (E) is incorrect because the per-unit tax needs to be equal to the external cost, or the vertical space between MPC and MSC.

59. (C)

AEU is the triangle of consumer surplus when the market is unregulated and functions with a price of E and an output of Q3. Consumer surplus is found above price paid, below demand, and to the left of the quantity purchased. The other responses are incorrect because they misstate where the consumer surplus can be found.

60. (C)

Statements I and II are true—they describe goods that will be underproduced in private markets because their benefits cannot be denied to non-payers ("free-riders") and are non-rival in consumption. Statement III is false because public goods typically are those that involve positive rather than negative externalities—they have social benefit rather than cost.

Detailed Explanations of Answers

Section II

Question 1
Sample Response

A.

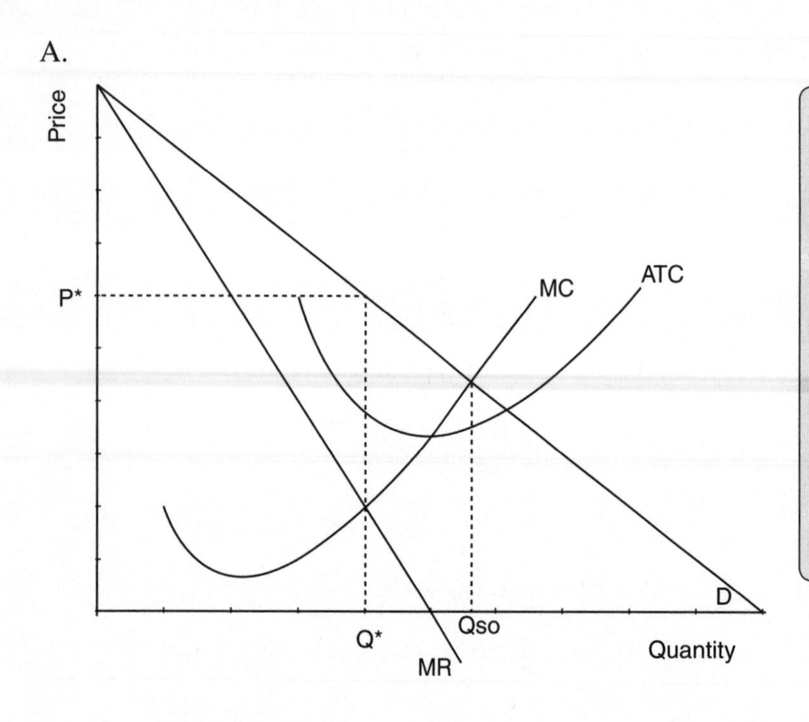

This "long question" didn't have very many parts but there were four explanations required. The graph from part A can be referenced to confirm the ideas in part B, but does not have distracting labeling on it that isn't required for part A.

B. i. Total revenue would decrease because the firm would be moving away from the unit elastic point on its demand curve.

ii. The firm's profit would decrease because it would have chosen not to produce some units for which marginal cost would be lower than marginal revenue.

iii. The area of consumer surplus would shrink because price would be higher and quantity sold would be lower.

C. In order to make them produce more, the government could provide a per-unit subsidy. This would increase the firm's marginal revenue, encouraging them to produce more units.

Scoring Criteria

12 points—Monopolist

- Part a: 4 points
    - Correctly labeled graph with downsloping D with MR below and U-shaped ATC that crosses swoosh-shaped MC at min ATC
    - Q* from MC = MR
    - P* above at Demand
    - Q_{so} below point where MC = D
- Part b: 6 points
    - Total revenue would decrease
    - TR connected to elastic region of demand, MR positive
    - Profit would decrease
    - Profit decreases because the firm would have failed to make some units for which MR was greater than MC, or explanation based on TC and TR including rate of change
    - Consumer surplus decreases
    - CS decreases because Q sold decreases and P increases; existing consumers get smaller surpluses, and some consumers who used to reap surplus no longer will.
- Part c: 2 points
    - One for identifying a policy (subsidy, price ceiling)
    - One for linkage of policy to monopolist incentives. Per-unit subsidy can be explained as decreasing MC or increasing MR. Price ceiling set at socially optimal level transforms the firm into a price taker, making MR horizontal, crossing MC at Q_{so}

Question 2
Sample Response

Notice how the graphs have wage levels that match!

A: MRP of labor is marginal product times $10.

B:

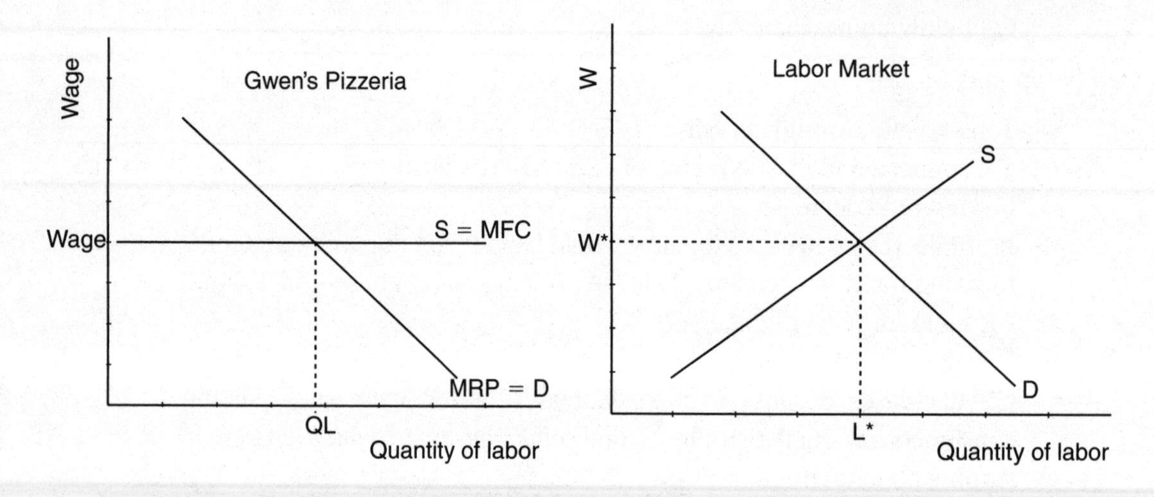

C: MFC is the change in total cost the firm incurs when one additional unit of that factor of production is purchased.

D: i. The labor supply curve would slope up rather than being horizontal.
ii. MFC would be above supply and steeper than it.
iii. Gwen would pay a lower wage.

Scoring Criteria

8 points—Gwen's Pizzeria

- Part a: 1 point
    - MRP is the change in total revenue that results from one more worker being hired OR
    - MRP is the marginal physical product (MP or MPP) of each worker times the price of output ($10)

- Part b: 3 points
  - Side-by-side correctly labeled graphs with labor market having upsloping S curve and downsloping D curve, correct W and L
  - Firm graph has horizontal W = MFC = S curve and downsloping D = MRP curve
  - Correct W*, taken from market graph and QL taken from intersection of MFC and MRP
- Part c: 1 point
  - MFC is the change in total cost when one more worker is hired
- Part d: 3 points
  - Labor supply would be upsloping rather than horizontal.
  - MFC would lie above supply because firm cannot wage discriminate.
  - Wage would be lower than when Gwen was a wage taker.

Question 2
Sample Response

A: City Blue should pay the stars if Unite Red doesn't.

B: Unite Red is always better off paying stars whether City runs frugally or pays stars. Unite Red should have high ticket prices no matter what City chooses. Because Red is better off paying stars regardless of City's choices, that strategic choice dominates the other option.

C: Nash Equilibrium is the combination of strategies where both teams feel they don't want to change their choice because they are making the best response to the choice the other picked.

D: Unite Red will pay stars no matter what. City Blue is better off responding to a "pay stars" choice by selling cheap seats. City Blue will make £32,000 and Unite Red will earn £60,000. This is the same as the Nash Equilibrium solution.

Scoring Criteria

6 points—Soccer Team Strategy

- Part a: 1 point
    - Paying stars is better for City Blue under these circumstances (£41,000 > £26,000).
- Part b: 2 points
    - Yes, Unite Red has a dominant strategy—to pay the stars.
    - Because no matter what City Blue chooses, paying the stars yields a better payoff for Unite Red than running the team frugally would (£45,000 > £15,000 and £60,000 > £30,000).
- Part c: 1 point
    - Nash Equilibrium is a situation in which neither team has an incentive to change its strategic choice given the choice of the other team; it is an outcome that, once reached, will be chosen again.
- Part d: 2 points
    - City Blue will earn £32,000 and Unite Red will earn £60,000.
    - Unite Red will pursue its dominant strategy and City Blue will choose its best response to that option.

AP Macroeconomics Practice Exam

Also available at the REA Study Center *(www.rea.com/studycenter)*

This practice exam is available at the REA Study Center. Although AP exams are administered in paper-and-pencil format, we recommend that you take the online version of the practice exam for the benefits of:

- Instant scoring
- Enforced time conditions
- Detailed score report of your strengths and weaknesses

AP Macroeconomics Practice Exam
Section I

(Answer sheets appear in the back of the book.)

TIME: 70 Minutes
60 Questions

Directions: Each of the questions or incomplete statements below is followed by five suggested answers or completions. Select the one that is best in each case and then fill in the corresponding oval on the answer sheet.

1. The term "economic resources" means

(A) factors used in production

(B) finished consumer goods

(C) assembly line technology

(D) venture capital funding

(E) mined ores and fossil fuels

2. In its most basic sense, economics is a study of

(A) free will

(B) prices

(C) money

(D) scarcity

(E) efficiency

3. The circular flow diagram can be used to show all of the following EXCEPT

   (A) why the income method and expenditure method of calculating GDP should have equal totals

   (B) that households are the sellers in resource markets

   (C) ways in which government interacts in various markets

   (D) how comparative advantage is determined

   (E) the logic behind the simple spending multiplier

4. Gross National Product and Gross Domestic Product are distinguished by

   (A) net foreign factor income

   (B) changes in business inventories

   (C) net exports

   (D) changes in central bank holdings of official foreign reserves

   (E) the marginal propensity to consume

Questions 5–7

The chart below shows the length of time it takes Alison and Eleanor to complete two production tasks.

	Time to make a gadget	Time to make a doodad
Alison	10 minutes	30 minutes
Eleanor	5 minutes	25 minutes

5. Which of the following is an accurate statement with regard to Alison and Eleanor?

   (A) Alison has an absolute advantage in the production of both gadgets and doodads, whereas Eleanor has a comparative advantage in the production of gadgets.

   (B) Eleanor has an absolute advantage in the production of both gadgets and doodads, whereas Alison has a comparative advantage in the production of gadgets.

   (C) Eleanor has an absolute advantage in the production of both gadgets and doodads, whereas Alison has a comparative advantage in the production of both gadgets and doodads.

   (D) Alison has an absolute advantage in the production of both gadgets and doodads, whereas Eleanor has a comparative advantage in the production of doodads.

   (E) Eleanor has an absolute advantage in the production of gadgets, whereas Alison has a comparative advantage in the production of doodads.

6. Which of the following correctly states the opportunity cost of a doodad for each of the producers?

	Alison	Eleanor
(A)	5 doodads	3 doodads
(B)	10 gadgets	5 gadgets
(C)	3 gadgets	5 gadgets
(D)	30 doodads	25 doodads
(E)	1/3 gadget	1/5 gadget

7. At which terms of trade or trading ratio can both Alison and Eleanor benefit?

   (A) 1 gadget can be traded for 0.25 doodads

   (B) 1 gadget can be traded for 0.5 doodads

   (C) 1 gadget can be traded for 2 doodads

   (D) 1 gadget can be traded for 4 doodads

   (E) There is no mutually beneficial trading ratio.

8. Which of the following best articulates the reason(s) for the slope of most supply curves?

   (A) Supply curves have a negative slope because of the law of diminishing marginal returns.

   (B) Supply curves have a vertical slope because there are limited scarce resources.

   (C) Supply curves have a positive slope because of the law of increasing opportunity cost.

   (D) Supply curves tend to slope downward because of the wealth or real-balances effect.

   (E) Supply curves tend to slope upward because of the net export effect and the interest rate effect.

9. An increase in government deficit spending due to expansionary fiscal policy is most likely to have what effect on interest rates, investment and the growth rate of capital stock?

	Interest Rates	Investment	Growth of Capital Stock
(A)	Increases	Increases	Slows
(B)	Increases	Decreases	Slows
(C)	No change	Increases	Accelerates
(D)	Decreases	No change	No change
(E)	Increases	Decreases	Accelerates

10. In an aggregate demand–aggregate supply diagram, equal increases in government spending and taxes will

(A) shift the AD curve to the right

(B) decrease the equilibrium GDP

(C) not affect the AD curve

(D) shift the AD curve to the left

(E) shift the AS curve upward

11. Countercyclical discretionary fiscal policy calls for

(A) surpluses during recessions and deficits during periods of demand-pull inflation

(B) deficits during recessions and surpluses during times of demand-pull inflation

(C) surpluses during both recessions and periods of demand-pull inflation

(D) deficits during both recessions and periods of demand-pull inflation

(E) balanced budgets at all times

12. Which of the following combinations of monetary policy actions would definitely cause a decrease in aggregate demand?

	Discount Rate	Open Market Operations	Reserve Ratio
(A)	Decrease	Buy Bonds	Decrease
(B)	Decrease	Sell Bonds	Decrease
(C)	Increase	Buy Bonds	Increase
(D)	Increase	Sell Bonds	Decrease
(E)	Increase	Sell Bonds	Increase

13. The real interest rate can be found by

(A) subtracting the nominal interest rate from the inflation rate

(B) subtracting the unemployment rate from the inflation rate

(C) multiplying the nominal interest rate by the price level

(D) dividing the nominal interest rate by the price level

(E) subtracting the inflation rate from the nominal interest rate

14. To reduce unemployment, the Federal Reserve could

(A) expand the money supply in order to raise interest rates, which increases investment

(B) expand the money supply in order to lower interest rates, which increases investment

(C) contract the money supply in order to lower interest rates, which increases investment

(D) contract the money supply in order to raise interest rates, which decreases investment

(E) sell bonds and increase the discount rate to encourage borrowing

15. All of the following would likely change the demand for a good EXCEPT

(A) a shift in consumers' attitudes about what is fashionable

(B) a rise in disposable income

(C) an increase in the price of a complementary good

(D) a belief that the good will become more difficult to purchase in the future

(E) an invention that makes the good cheaper to produce

16. Which of the following is included in the calculation of the United States' GDP?

(A) Roasted beans purchased by a coffee shop in Manhattan

(B) American citizens' purchases of imported automobiles

(C) The estimated value of illegal drug transactions conducted in the U.S.

(D) A Kentucky homeowner's purchase of fertilizer for her flower garden

(E) The value of stocks and bonds bought by Americans

Questions 17–18 are based on the data in the table below.

Measurement	Value
Government purchases	$653
Total government expenditures	$792
Consumer spending	$1,782
Wages, salaries, and tips	$1,628
Interest, rents, and royalties received	$102
Unemployment rate	2.3%
Net exports	$-56
Corporate profit and proprietor's earnings	$770
Rate of increase in price level	25%

17. National income for the sample economy above is

(A) $2,444

(B) $2,500

(C) $3,153

(D) $3,292

(E) $4,216

18. This country's real output, using the prior year as a base year would be closest to

(A) $2,700

(B) $2,000

(C) $1,875

(D) $1,700

(E) Impossible to determine without additional information.

19. Which of the following most correctly describes the fundamental goal of calculating Gross Domestic Product?

(A) Its total can determine the wealth of the average citizen in a country.

(B) It measures the total value of the production in a country in a year.

(C) Its total can determine whether a country is experiencing an inflationary gap.

(D) It represents the total number of resources available for use in an economy in a given year.

(E) It measures the wealth accumulated by an economy over time.

20. If a government stimulus plan entails a substantial amount of deficit spending, it is likely that the multiplier effect will be partially offset by

(A) a stronger currency

(B) a decrease in household savings

(C) decreases in investment due to higher costs of borrowing

(D) contractionary actions taken by the monetary policy authorities

(E) the marginal propensity to consume

21. Which of the following are true of Gross Domestic Product?

I. Its largest component if using the income method is wages and salaries.
II. It includes goods made in a country and sold abroad.
III. It excludes payments made when buying stocks and bonds

(A) II only

(B) III only

(C) I and III only

(D) II and III only

(E) I, II, and III are all true of GDP

22. The components of aggregate demand are

(A) wages and salaries, investment, rents, and profit

(B) consumer spending, investment, government purchases, and net exports

(C) consumer spending, interest income, rents and royalties, and net exports

(D) investment, interest, inflation, and imports

(E) wages and salaries, interest payments, rents and royalties, and profits

23. Given the statistics about the simplified economy below, the unemployment rate is:

Total Working-Age Population	**400**
Institutionalized	10
Employed	323
Voluntarily not working	33
Have abandoned the job search	17
Actively seeking work, have no job	17

(A) 4.25%

(B) 5.0%

(C) 9.52%

(D) 4.76%

(E) 8.5%

24. Which of the following best describes aggregate supply?

(A) The amount buyers plan to spend on output

(B) A schedule or graph showing the relationship between inputs and outputs

(C) A schedule or graph showing the trade-off between inflation and unemployment

(D) A schedule or graph indicating the level of real output that will be purchased at each possible price level

(E) A schedule or graph indicating the level of real output that will be produced at each possible price level

25. If TD's disposable income increases from $800 per month to $900 per month and his consumption expenditures increase from $660 to $720 as a result, one could conclude that his marginal propensity to

(A) consume is 0.4

(B) consume is 0.8

(C) save is 0.4

(D) save is 0.6

(E) save is 0.8

26. Long-run economic growth could be caused by all of the following EXCEPT

(A) a lower equilibrium real interest rate

(B) a decrease in the number of inputs needed to produce a unit of output

(C) an increased pace of depreciation of capital stock

(D) an influx of immigrant labor

(E) an increase in the quality of education and job training

27. Recessions are most likely to self-correct under which of the following circumstances?

(A) Trade partners suffer simultaneous slowdowns in economic activity.

(B) Consumers increase personal savings.

(C) There are strong minimum wage laws present in the country.

(D) Wages decrease quickly as unemployment rises.

(E) Most labor contracts in the country are long-term deals.

28. If the MPC is 0.9 and investment increases by $3 billion, then gross output could increase by up to

(A) $2.7 billion

(B) $3.9 billion

(C) $9 billion

(D) $27 billion

(E) $30 billion

29. The production function shifts upward when which of the following increases

I. interest rates

II. capital stock

III. technological advancements

IV. resource costs

(A) I and II only

(B) II and III only

(C) I, II, and III only

(D) I, III, and IV only

(E) II, III, and IV only

30. If the MPS is 0.5 and taxes increase by $50 million, expenditures could

(A) decrease by up to $250 million

(B) decrease by up to $100 million

(C) decrease by up to $50 million

(D) increase by up to $25 million

(E) increase by up to $100 million

31. Which of the following would be recorded as a credit toward a country's financial account?

(A) Citizens of the country increase their holdings of foreign bonds.

(B) Firms in the country purchase capital equipment produced in other countries.

(C) Foreign nationals working in the country send earnings back home to their families.

(D) Foreign investors purchase increased quantities of the country's governmental debt.

(E) Firms in the country sell more of their output in foreign nations.

32. Unexpected inflation would most likely aid

(A) fixed wage workers

(B) pensioners and retirees

(C) creditors who are owed future payments

(D) debtors who owe large sums

(E) those earning minimum wage

33. The supply curve in the money market is

(A) vertical, reflecting the central bank's control of the quantity of money in circulation

(B) upsloping, reflecting the tendency of households to save more at higher rates of interest

(C) vertical, reflecting the tendency of the economy to return to full employment in the long run

(D) upsloping, reflecting the central bank's control of the quantity of money in circulation

(E) vertical, reflecting the inelasticity of household savings with respect to the interest rate

34. Absent policy action, how will the economy shown below adjust into long-run equilibrium?

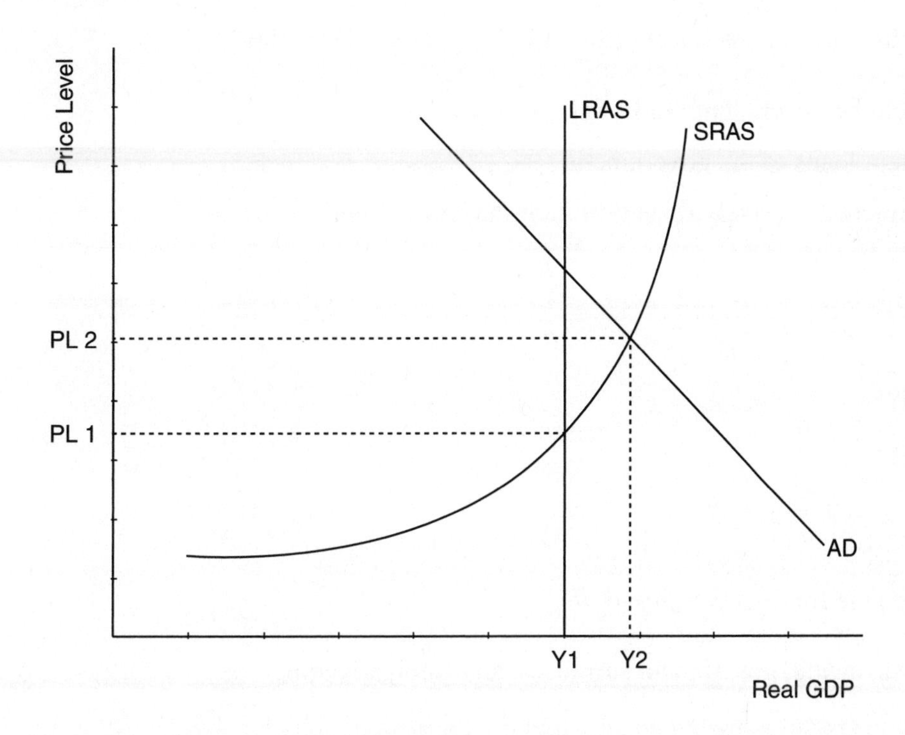

(A) Wages will decline.

(B) Unemployment will begin to fall.

(C) Input costs will rise.

(D) The trade deficit will decrease.

(E) Aggregate demand will decrease.

35. A commercial bank holds $200,000 in demand deposit liabilities and $80,000 in reserves. If the required reserve ratio is 20 percent, then the maximum amount that this bank and the banking system as a whole can increase loans is

	Single Bank	Banking System
(A)	$18,000	$72,000
(B)	$40,000	$160,000
(C)	$40,000	$200,000
(D)	$60,000	$300,000
(E)	$120,000	$500,000

36. Which of the following statements are true of U.S. Treasury securities?

I. They are included in M2, but not in M1.
II. They represent loans to the government.
III. They yield interest inversely related to their current prices.

(A) I only
(B) II only
(C) I and III only
(D) II and III only
(E) I, II, and III are all true

37. Demand for loanable funds is composed of

(A) household borrowing, government surpluses, and foreign lending
(B) household savings, investment demand, and government deficits
(C) government deficits, household borrowing, and investment demand
(D) foreign borrowing, tax credits, and excess reserves
(E) household savings, investment demand, and foreign borrowing

38. Overnight loans from one bank to another for reserve purposes come at a cost of the

(A) prime rate

(B) discount rate

(C) federal funds rate

(D) subprime rate

(E) treasury bill rate

39. The Phillips Curve shows the relationship between

(A) unemployment rate and economic growth rate

(B) unemployment rate and full employment output level

(C) inflation rate and level of private investment

(D) inflation rate and unemployment rate

(E) inflation rate and real interest rates

Use the following information about the Werner bank to answer Question 40.

	Assets	Liabilities
Checkable deposits		$50,000
Cash Reserves in vault	$8,000	
Reserves deposited at Fed	$2,000	
Loans to customers	$23,000	
Physical assets	$7,000	
Securities held	$10,000	

40. Assuming that the Werner bank has only required reserves, a new deposit of $100 into the bank will allow the banking system to expand loans by a total of

(A) $80

(B) $90

(C) $400

(D) $500

(E) $1000

41. Asset demand for money is best expressed in which of the following statements?

(A) Alternative ways to hold wealth are more attractive at high interest rates, making holding money more costly.

(B) Money is an asset and the higher the interest rate the more is demanded because it is more expensive to borrow.

(C) High interest rates require more money to make loan payments and therefore decrease aggregate demand.

(D) Velocity of money is higher when interest rates are lower and therefore less money is demanded.

(E) Velocity of money is higher when interest rates are higher and therefore more money is demanded.

42. Which of the following causes an immediate decrease in Japan's current account?

(A) Japanese tourists take fewer trips to Europe.

(B) Europeans visit Japan in record numbers.

(C) Japanese workers save more by purchasing Japanese bonds.

(D) European firms purchase raw materials from Japan.

(E) Japan imports greater amounts of fossil fuels.

43. How will expansionary fiscal policy taken by Canada's policymakers influence the Canadian price level and the level of Canada's exports and imports, assuming no change in the value of the Canadian dollar?

	Price Level	Canadian Exports	Canadian Imports
(A)	Decrease	Increase	Increase
(B)	Increase	Decrease	Increase
(C)	Increase	Increase	Decrease
(D)	Decrease	Decrease	Increase
(E)	Increase	Decrease	Decrease

44. Which statement distinguishes the money market and the loanable funds market correctly?

(A) The loanable funds market is for longer-term lending and borrowing and determines the real interest rate.

(B) The money market is for longer-term lending and borrowing and determines the real interest rate.

(C) The money market determines the interest rate and the loanable funds market determines the inflation rate.

(D) The loanable funds market determines the interest rate and the money market determines the exchange rate.

(E) The loanable funds market determines excess reserves and the money market determines the price level.

45. Assume the reserve ratio is 10% and Federal Reserve banks buy $4 million worth of U.S. securities from the public, which deposits this amount into checking accounts. As a result of these transactions, the supply of money is

(A) not directly affected, but the money creating potential of the commercial banking system is increased by $40 million

(B) directly increased by $4 million and the money creating potential of the commercial banking system is increased by an additional $40 million

(C) directly reduced by $4 million and the money creating potential of the commercial banking system is decreased by an additional $36 million

(D) directly increased by $4 million and the money creating potential of the commercial banking system is increased by an additional $36 million

(E) not affected directly and the money creating potential of the banking system also remains unchanged

46. To foster growth in the long run without changing the price level in the short run, which combinations of changes would be most effective?

(A) Increase personal income taxes and decrease the federal funds rate

(B) Decrease personal income taxes and increase the discount rate

(C) Increase government spending and decrease the reserve ratio

(D) Decrease government spending and increase the federal funds rate

(E) Decrease corporate taxes and increase the discount rate

47. The equilibrium in the money market determines the

(A) international value of a country's currency

(B) real interest rate in a country's economy

(C) aggregate output of a country's economy

(D) money velocity in a country's economy

(E) nominal interest rate in a country's economy

48. Which of the following explains a reason why inflation can increase?

I. Decrease in aggregate demand

II. Increase in aggregate supply

III. Increase in the rate of money supply growth

(A) I only

(B) II only

(C) III only

(D) I and II only

(E) I, II, and III

49. The CPI in an economy is increasing at 7.5% annually, producer prices are rising 1% each month, the unemployment rate is 3.1%, and wage rates are rising faster than worker productivity. Given these conditions, which of the following changes in the tax rate, government spending, and the target federal funds rate would improve the health of the economy the most?

(A) Increase taxes, increase spending, increase the federal funds rate

(B) Increase taxes, decrease spending, increase the federal funds rate

(C) Increase taxes, decrease spending, decrease the federal funds rate

(D) Decrease taxes, increase spending, decrease the federal funds rate

(E) Decrease taxes, decrease spending, decrease the federal funds rate

50. If the value of one pound sterling was $2 initially and then increased to $3, then

(A) the U.S. dollar appreciated against the pound

(B) American exports to the UK are likely to decline

(C) the pound depreciated against the U.S. dollar

(D) American goods will feel less expensive to British consumers

(E) American savers will purchase more British bonds

51. Suppose that real interest rates increase in India relative to those in neighboring countries. What is the most likely effect on the desirability of Indian government securities, the value of India's currency (called the rupee) and Indian net exports?

	Desirability of Securities	Value of Rupee	Indian Net Exports
(A)	Increase	Increase	Increase
(B)	Increase	Decrease	Increase
(C)	Increase	Increase	Decrease
(D)	Decrease	Decrease	Increase
(E)	Decrease	Decrease	Decrease

52. If the government increases spending without a tax increase and simultaneously no monetary policy changes are made, then

(A) income would not rise at all because no new money is available for increased consumer spending

(B) the rise in income may be greater than the multiplier would predict because the higher interest rates will stimulate private firms' investment spending

(C) the rise in incomes may be smaller than the multiplier would predict because the higher interest rates will discourage private firms' investment spending

(D) income will go up by exactly the amount of the new government spending since this acts as a direct injection to the income stream; the multiplier does not apply

(E) income will not go up unless taxes are cut as well

53. Phillips Curve analysis suggests that the long-run effects of combining a central bank bond purchase program and a tax cut would be

	Inflation Rate	Unemployment Rate
(A)	Increase	No change
(B)	Increase	Increase
(C)	Decrease	No change
(D)	Decrease	Increase
(E)	Increase	Decrease

54. Which of these statements regarding the financial account, the current account, and the official reserves account are true?

I. The financial account and the current account tend to be positive for most developed economies.

II. The official reserves account is small compared to the financial and current accounts, which generally offset one another.

III. Net exporters have positive financial accounts, representing net inflows in international asset trade.

(A) II only

(B) III only

(C) I and II only

(D) I and III only

(E) II and III only

55. Increases in the money wage rate can cause which of the following effects on short-run aggregate supply (SRAS), the short-run Phillips Curve (SRPC), and the long-run Phillips Curve (LRPC)?

	SRAS	SRPC	LRPC
(A)	Decrease	Shift right	Shift right
(B)	Increase	Shift left	No change
(C)	Decrease	Shift left	Shift left
(D)	Increase	Shift right	Shift left
(E)	Decrease	Shift right	No change

56. Which of the following policy recommendations would a supply-side economist be most likely to make during times when an economy was facing cost-push inflation?

(A) Increase military spending and cut personal income taxes.

(B) Cut payroll and capital gains taxes and repeal regulations on producers.

(C) Tax energy usage and increase the legal minimum wage.

(D) Buy bonds, increase the discount rate, and decrease the reserve ratio.

(E) Impose a legal restriction on allowable increases in product prices.

57. Suppose the price level increases in the United Kingdom relative to the price levels in countries with which it trades. What is the most likely effect on British imports, exports, and the value of the Pound Sterling?

Imports	Exports	Value of the Pound
(A) Decrease	Increase	Decrease
(B) Increase	Decrease	Increase
(C) Decrease	Increase	Increase
(D) Increase	Decrease	Decrease
(E) Decrease	Decrease	Decrease

58. Built-in, or automatic, stabilizers mean that

(A) an annually balanced budget will offset the pro-cyclical tendencies created by state and local finance and thereby stabilize the economy

(B) with given tax rates and expenditures laws, a rise in domestic income will reduce a budget deficit or produce a budget surplus while a decline in income will result in a deficit or a lower surplus

(C) Congress will automatically act to change the tax structure and expenditure laws to correct upswings and downswings in the business cycle

(D) government expenditures and tax receipts automatically balance over the business cycle, though they may be out of balance in any single year

(E) budget deficits should increase automatically during peaks in the business cycle and should decrease automatically during troughs

59. A combination of expansionary fiscal policy and contractionary monetary policy taken by a country that has a trade deficit are likely to cause

(A) interest rates to rise, the demand for the country's currency to rise, and the trade deficit to increase

(B) interest rates to fall, the demand for the country's currency to rise, and the trade deficit to increase

(C) interest rates to rise, the demand for the country's currency to rise, and the trade deficit to decrease

(D) an indeterminate change in interest rates, the demand for the country's currency to rise, and the trade deficit to decrease

(E) interest rates to rise, the demand for the country's currency to fall, and the trade deficit to decrease

60. Which of the following correctly states how economic growth would affect the production possibilities curve, long-run aggregate supply, and the long-run Phillips Curve?

PPC	LRAS	LRPC
(A) Point moves toward curve	Shifts right	Shifts right
(B) Point moves toward curve	Shifts right	Shifts left
(C) Point moves along curve	No change	Shifts left
(D) Entire curve shifts up and right	Shifts right	Shifts left
(E) Entire curve shifts up and right	Shifts right	No change

Section II

Planning Time: 10 minutes
Writing Time: 50 minutes
Number of Questions—3

Directions: You have 10 minutes to read all three of the questions in this section, to make notes, and to plan your answers. You will then have 50 minutes to answer all three of the following questions. It is suggested that you spend approximately half your time on the first question and divide the remaining time equally between the next two questions. In answering the questions, you should emphasize the line of reasoning that generated your results; it is not enough to list the results of your analysis. Include correctly labeled diagrams, if useful or required, in explaining your answers. A correctly labeled diagram must have all axes and curves clearly labeled and must show directional changes. Use a pen with black or dark blue ink.

1. Assume the U.S. economy is operating at full employment.

   a. On a correctly labeled aggregate demand–aggregate supply graph, show

      i. current price level
      ii. current output

   Assume that a major financial crisis strikes, resulting in a substantially depressed housing market and markedly reducing the values of stocks and mutual fund portfolios held by American households.

   b. On your graph from part (a), show the effects of this crisis on price level and output.

   c. Assume that the Federal Reserve decides to take action to attempt to reverse the effects you showed in part (b). What open market operation would be most logical for it to undertake?

   d. Using a correctly labeled graph of the money market, show the effects of the open market operation on the nominal interest rate.

   e. Indicate how the change in interest rates you identified in part (d) would influence each of the following

      i. Investment in plant and equipment
      ii. Aggregate demand. Explain.

f. Identify a way each of the following institutions could limit the effectiveness of the Fed's efforts

   i. Commercial banks
   ii. Private firms

2. Assume that the government of Canada reforms its tax structure by incentivizing savings.

   a. Using a correctly labeled graph of the loanable funds market for Canada, show how this policy action would influence the real interest rate.

   b. Indicate how the change in the real interest rate you identified in part (a) would affect each of the following in Canada:

      i. Aggregate demand
      ii. Real output
      iii. The price level

   c. Based on the change in the price level you identified in part (b-iii), what will happen to the international value of the Canadian dollar? Explain.

3. Unemployment is a major concern to policymakers trying to maintain a healthy economy and to officials seeking election or re-election.

   a. By what formula is the unemployment rate calculated?

   b. Define the following

      i. Cyclical unemployment
      ii. Frictional unemployment
      iii. Structural unemployment
      iv. the Natural Rate of Unemployment (NRU)

   c. Identify a governmental policy change that would alter a country's Natural Rate of Unemployment.

   d. Using a correctly labeled graph, show how the change you identified in part (c) would affect the country's long-run Phillips Curve.

Answer Key

Section I

1. (A)
2. (D)
3. (D)
4. (A)
5. (E)
6. (C)
7. (A)
8. (C)
9. (B)
10. (A)
11. (B)
12. (E)
13. (E)
14. (B)
15. (E)
16. (D)
17. (B)
18. (B)
19. (B)
20. (C)
21. (E)
22. (B)
23. (B)
24. (E)
25. (C)
26. (C)
27. (D)
28. (E)
29. (B)
30. (C)
31. (D)
32. (D)
33. (A)
34. (C)
35. (C)
36. (D)
37. (C)
38. (C)
39. (D)
40. (C)
41. (A)
42. (E)
43. (B)
44. (A)
45. (D)
46. (A)
47. (E)
48. (C)
49. (B)
50. (D)
51. (C)
52. (C)
53. (A)
54. (A)
55. (E)
56. (B)
57. (D)
58. (B)
59. (A)
60. (E)

Detailed Explanations of Answers

Section I

1. (A)

Economic resources or factors of production are land, labor, capital, and entrepreneurial ability. They are distinguished from consumer goods (B). Money is not considered a resource but rather a medium that facilitates the exchange of resources and goods (D). Both (C) and (E) are examples of resources, but do not define the term.

2. (D)

Scarcity is the fundamental problem that leads to the discipline of economics. Prices and money are tools that societies find useful in allocating scarce resources. Efficiency is an analytical tool developed by economists to measure how well societies are doing at allocating those factors of production. Free will is involved in the study of choices, but economists are more interested in the analysis of choice-making that emphasizes incentives.

3. (D)

The production possibilities frontier would be more appropriate to help determine comparative advantage between people or societies that potentially would trade for mutual benefit. Choices (B) and (C) are directly shown and visible with a quick look at a circular flow diagram. Choice (E) might be the toughest to spot, but the idea that one person's expenditure becomes another's income and is then re-spent is the central concept behind choice (A) and is visible in the diagram by following the payment arrows.

4. (A)

Income earned by a country's citizens who are living and working abroad is excluded from GDP but included in GNP. Likewise, foreign nationals working in the country contribute to GDP but not GNP. The difference between the value of goods and services produced **by** a country (GNP) and the value produced **in** a country (GDP) is called "net foreign factor income." Changes in business inventories are part of investment. This and net exports are part of the expenditure method of GDP calculation and are also included in GNP. Choices (D) and (E) are measurements that don't count in either tally of national production.

5. (E)

Eleanor has an absolute advantage in the production of both goods: she can produce a gadget in less time (5<10 min) and a doodad in less time (25<30 min). This eliminates choices (A) and (D). Once the data is converted to opportunity cost, we find that when Alison makes a doodad, she sacrifices only 3 gadgets. Eleanor gives up 5 gadgets to make a doodad, so Alison has the comparative advantage in doodad production, making choice (E) superior to option (B). Choice (C) is flawed from the start; it is impossible for one person or country to have comparative advantage in both goods because a country's opportunity costs are reciprocals for the two goods.

6. (C)

When taking 25 minutes to make one doodad, Eleanor would have been able to make 5 gadgets, each taking 5 minutes. Instead of taking 30 minutes to make one doodad, Alison could have devoted 10 minutes each to the production of 3 gadgets. Choices (A) and (D) should never be selected because the opportunity cost of a doodad would never be in doodads: opportunity cost is the units of one good sacrificed when a unit of the other good is produced.

7. (A)

The terms of trade that benefit both producers occur in between the opportunity costs for each. Expressing opportunity cost per gadget, we see that Alison gives up 1/3 doodad per gadget and Eleanor gives up 1/5. One-quarter doodad per gadget (or 0.25 doodads per gadget) is between 1/3 and 1/5. This would allow Eleanor to obtain doodads for a lower cost and Alison to obtain gadgets for a lower cost than either otherwise would be able to.

8. (C)

The law of increasing opportunity cost suggests that production of successive units of a good will require sacrifice of more and more. This implies that producers will face higher and higher marginal costs of making more units and therefore will need a higher price in order to make these levels of output profitable. Choices (A) and (D) incorrectly state the slope of supply curves in all but the most unusual situations; (B) is atypical, though there are situations in which supply is (almost) vertical. Choice (E) identifies the typical supply slope accurately, but gives two reasons that are usually cited for aggregate demand sloping downward.

9. (B)

Expansionary fiscal policy is increasing spending or decreasing taxes. Either way, the government needs to borrow more than it did before, increasing the demand for loanable funds and driving up the real interest rate. Interest rates are inversely linked to the level of investment, and investment is the purchase of new capital goods that become part of the capital stock (or base of production tools a country has at its disposal). Less investment in this case means fewer goods are added to the capital stock, slowing its growth and overall economic growth. This process is known as the crowding-out effect.

10. (A)

Because the spending multiplier is greater than the tax multiplier, AD will shift rightward. Government spending is part of AD, shifting it right initially and then causing further shifts due to subsequent increases in income that lead to more consumption spending. Tax increases first reduce disposable income, inducing a lower level of consumption but consumption doesn't decrease by the full amount of the tax increase—some of the additional tax payments come from savings. As a result, (C) is incorrect.

11. (B)

The idea is to counteract the effects of the business cycle. When AD is too low (recessionary gaps), government spending should inject more into the circular flow than is pulled out in taxes. When inflation occurs, the net effect desired from government action is to decrease spending, so it should extract more in taxes than it injects through governmental spending under these circumstances. The purpose of any countercyclical policy is to push real output toward potential output.

12. (E)

To decrease aggregate demand, contractionary policies that decrease the money supply are needed. Raising the discount rate and selling bonds on the open market (to push up the federal funds rate) both discourage borrowing because they make its cost higher. Increasing the reserve ratio would also reduce the amount of excess reserves in the banking system and therefore reduce lending and decrease the overall money supply.

13. (E)

The Fisher equation relates together nominal and real interest rates. Nominal interest rates paid yield real rates of return that are usually lower due to rising prices. The rate of inflation is the degree to which purchasing power of the dollars repaid at the end of the loan is lower than the purchasing power of dollars lent at the start. Choice (A) is closest to correct of the wrong options, but reverses the subtraction process.

14. (B)

Federal Reserve actions can decrease unemployment if they increase spending. Expansionary policies inject reserves into the banking system and shift the money supply curve to the right in order to reduce interest rates and encourage more borrowing and spending, especially investment spending which is influenced by the interest rate. Contracting the money supply (C, D, and E) will increase interest rates and discourage borrowing. Choice (A) mistakenly suggests that interest rates and investment are positively correlated.

15. (E)

The costs incurred in producing a good are related to supply; choice (E) would shift supply to the right. The other options are all examples of TIMER factors that shift demand: tastes and preferences, income, market size, expectations of buyers, and related good prices. Choice (C) shifts demand left and choice (D) shifts it to the right. Choices (A) and (B) are indeterminate; for normal goods, choice (B) will increase demand.

16. (D)

The fertilizer will be counted in consumption spending. (A) is excluded because it represents an intermediate good—its value will be captured within the price of the cups of coffee the shop sells. Choice (C) is black market activity that is not officially counted and even if counted would be imports that are excluded from GDP. Imported goods (B) are excluded: they get counted as part of consumption and then subtracted out in the net export category.

17. (B)

To calculate NI, add wages, rents, interest income, and profits. 1,628 + 102 + 770 = 2,500.

18. (B)

The prior year (because it is the base year) will have a price level of 100. The price level increased 25% in the last year, so it is 125 this year. To find real output, divide nominal output by price level and multiply by 100. 2,500/125 = 20 and 20 × 100 = 2,000.

19. (B)

Gross Domestic Product is a measure of total output produced within a country in a specified period of time, typically one year. Choice (E) is a stock of accumulated wealth, not the wealth added in a year; GDP is a flow rather than a stock measure.

Choice (D) is correlated with the potential output, but isn't the purpose of calculating GDP. Choice (C) is one possible application of GDP, as is choice (A).

20. (C)

The crowding-out effect describes the consequence that comes from higher interest rates. As government borrowing increases, demand for loanable funds shifts right, increasing interest rates and decreasing the private sector's quantity of funds demanded. This decreases investment and interest sensitive consumption and reduces the overall effect that expansionary fiscal policy will have on aggregate output. The value of each unit of the currency (A) will likely decrease as the price level rises. Household savings (B) will probably increase as income increases. Contractionary monetary policy (D) is not likely to be caused by the stimulus plan. The MPC determines the multiplier and would not offset its effects; MPC is the reason why there is a multiplier effect in the first place.

21. (E)

All of these are true statements of GDP. The income method adds wages and salaries, rents, interest income, and profits. Wages typically account for over 60% of the total of GDP if using the income method. Exports are included in the value of goods produced in a country and are added into the expenditure GDP formula. Payments for stocks and bonds are excluded because these money flows are in exchange for ownership but do not reflect current production of goods and services. Commissions on financial transactions do count, however.

22. (B)

AD is composed of the expenditure formula components and shifts when any of those change. Each of the incorrect options includes one or more measures that are not part of this formula. Choice (A) lists wages, rents, and profit from the income method. Choice (C) lists interest and rents from the income approach. Choice (D) lists imports and inflation, which are not included in adding to nominal GDP. Choice (E) lists correctly the components of national income, which is more closely associated with aggregate supply than aggregate demand.

23. (B)

The unemployment rate is calculated by dividing the number of unemployed individuals by the total number of workers in the labor force. In this case, the number of unemployed individuals is 17 (exclude the 17 discouraged workers and the 33 who are not seeking a job at all) and the number in the labor force is 340 (323 employed and 17 unemployed) for a rate of 5%.

24. (E)

Supply is a relationship between quantity supplied and the price of a good. (A) is planned aggregate consumption. (B) describes production or cost curves. (C) articulates the Phillips Curve. (D) is closest, but is a correct description of the concept of demand.

25. (C)

To find marginal propensities, divide the change in consumption (or savings) by the change in income. In this case, spending increases by $60 when income rises by $100. This implies an MPC of 0.6 and, therefore, an MPS of 0.4.

26. (C)

When capital stock depreciates faster, it is more difficult to increase productive capacity of an economy. Lower interest rates (A) lead to more investment and the capital stock grows more quickly. Productivity (B) is among the most significant causes of growth. New influxes of labor can increase the work force, giving an economy a larger pool of resources with which to produce goods. Choice (E) represents human capital, which is an important contributor to productivity growth.

27. (D)

Decreasing wages cause self-correction because they lead to increased employment and a lower price level. This shifts short-run aggregate supply to the right. Slowdowns in other trade partner nations (A) will decrease exports and worsen a recession. Increases in savings, while good for individual consumers, are bad for an economy, a dilemma named the "paradox of thrift" (B). Minimum wage laws (C) and long-term labor contracts (E) prevent the kind of wage flexibility that the classical economists' relied upon when arguing that recessions would be short-lived and would not require governmental intervention.

28. (E)

An MPC of 0.9 implies a spending multiplier of 10 because the multiplier is the reciprocal of the MPS (0.1). This means that an increase in one of the autonomous components of aggregate expenditure, such as investment, will create ten times the increase in total expenditures because spending becomes income, 90% of which is re-spent.

29. (B)

Capital stock and technology are two of the three components that influence the production function (quantity of labor used is the third). Increases in interest rates make capital stock more expensive to accumulate and increases in resource costs shift short-run aggregate supply left, making output decrease in the short run, but typically not changing the level of output an economy can sustain over time.

30. (C)

In this example, the tax increase will decrease disposable income by $50 million. Consumers will spend $25 million less and save $25 million less as well. The decrease in spending will be doubled because of the multiplier effect. A decrease in governmental spending of $50 million would lead to a $100 million decrease in expenditures, but the multiplier's effect on taxes is weaker than on spending changes. Choice (A) dramatically overstates the effects of the multiplier given an MPC of only 0.5 and choices (D) and (E) reverse the direction of change.

31. (D)

The financial account would be debited in choice (A). Choice (B) would be a debit from the current account. Choices (C) and (E) are credits to the current, rather than the financial account. In choice (D), foreigners are purchasing bonds and therefore creating inflows of funds to the country in the market for financial assets.

32. (D)

Those who owe money will benefit because the dollars they pay back in the future will be worth less than they were expected to be at the time of the loan. Choice (C), creditors, would be harmed for the very same reason: future dollars paid to them will have a lower purchasing power than anticipated. This is also the basis for why choices (A) and (B) are incorrect. Choice (E) is less determinate, but inflation erodes the value of the minimum wage amount and usually does so in a significant way before governmental authorities are inclined to raise the nominal legal wage to keep up.

33. (A)

The money supply curve is vertical. The quantity of money stock in circulation at any given time is determined by the central bank's decisions (purchases and sales of bonds and setting of reserve requirements that govern banks' money-creating powers). Choice (B) explains the supply of loanable funds. Choice (C) explains why LRAS is vertical.

34. (C)

The diagram shows an inflationary gap with short-run output Y2 above the full-employment level Y1. At high output levels, firms bid against each other for scarce resources, driving up their per-unit prices. An increase in wages and other input prices is likely to shift SRAS to the left and restore full-employment output. The decline of wages (A) is the way in which recessionary gaps can self-correct. In this case, unemployment rises as the economy self-corrects. The trade deficit is not directly related to this process, but as the price level increases a trade deficit would increase rather than decrease. Aggregate demand does not change during the self-correction process and the words "absent policy action" suggest that the correct response does not involve shifting AD.

35. (C)

The first task here is to find the excess reserves; that is, how much this bank can lend. If there are $200,000 in demand deposits, the bank must hold $40,000 (20%) of those in reserve. Since actual reserves are $80,000, $40,000 of them are excess. Given the reserve ratio of 20%, one can calculate the money multiplier (5). Taking the excess reserves times the money multiplier yields the total amount of money that the banking system can create through increased loaning.

36. (D)

Statement I is false because securities, more commonly known as bonds, are not part of the money supply at all. However, both other statements are true: the treasury borrows by issuing bonds, which are representative of those loans. The cheaper a bond is on a secondary market, the faster the principal lent will grow, for a higher effective interest rate.

37. (C)

This choice correctly states major long-term borrowers for a typical economy. Choice (A) identifies government surpluses and foreign lending, which are components of the supply of loanable funds. Likewise, choices (B) and (E) identify household savings, another component of loanable funds supply. Choice (D) identifies tax credits, which are not particularly relevant to the loanable funds model, and excess reserves, which if relevant influence supply rather than demand.

38. (C)

The federal funds rate is the prevailing interbank interest rate in the United States The prime rate (A) is the lowest rate that bank's customers are able to secure. The discount rate (B) is the rate at which the Federal Reserve lends to banks. Subprime rates (D) are higher than prime rates and typically charged to customers with poor credit histories. The rate of interest paid on treasuries (E) usually is dependent on the fundamental rate in the economy, but is distinct from the rate paid by banks when borrowing from one another.

39. (D)

The Phillips Curve is designed to show the relationship between inflation rate and unemployment rate. Choice (E) identifies two variables connected with the Fisher equation. The other choices do not correctly pair two variables that are commonly set in opposition to one another on economics graphs.

40. (C)

First, find the reserve ratio. The bank has $10,000 of total reserves and $50,000 of demand deposits, so the reserve ratio is 20%. Thus, a new deposit of $100 will require $20 in reserves and the Werner bank can lend $80. This $80 times the money multiplier of 5 (1/0.2) yields a total possible increase of $400.

41. (A)

When interest rates are high, the opportunity cost of holding money is high and people will be more likely to sacrifice liquidity in order to gain interest through lending. Choice (B) assumes that interest rates are positively related to money demand. Choice (C) relates aggregate demand rather than money demand to interest rates. Choices (D) and (E) mistakenly invoke money velocity, which is not determined by the interest rate.

42. (E)

Japan's current account decreases when Japan imports more goods and services. Choice (A) would increase its current account, as would choices (B) and (D). Choice (C) is a domestic transaction and is therefore not part of the international balance of payments accounting process.

43. (B)

When expansionary fiscal policy is undertaken, AD shifts rightward, pulling up the price level. This makes exports decline because Canadian goods are more expensive to produce. Likewise, imports increase because Canadian consumers seek out alternatives to their more expensive domestically produced goods.

44. (A)

The money market is where overnight lending between banks determines the federal funds rate. Loanable funds analysis uses real interest rates because they are more important when lending over a long-time horizon during which the price level is likely to change a great deal. Choice (B) states the fundamental difference between loanable funds and money markets backward. Exchange rates and changes in the price level (which constitute inflation) are determined in other markets, rendering choices (C), (D), and (E) incorrect.

45. (D)

When the central bank purchases bonds from the public, the full amount is directly injected into the money supply because bonds, which are not money, are traded for money, which does count towards M1. The 10% reserve ratio determines the money multiplier (10). When the $4 million is deposited in the bank, $3.6 million is excess reserves and can lead to an expansion of the money supply of ten times its value.

46. (A)

Two clues in this challenging question should draw your attention. The first is the goal: long-run growth. This is encouraged by low interest rates, which make investment less costly. The second clue is "without changing the price level" and might lead you to recognize that the desired solution will be one that does not result in a shift of AD. This means that you should avoid choices that push up interest rates ((B), (D), and (E)) and ones that include two expansionary policies (C). The remaining option (A) reduces interest rates in order to encourage investment in new capital and offsets the expansionary monetary policy with a contractionary fiscal one.

47. (E)

The money market's vertical axis is nominal interest rate. (A), currency value, is determined in foreign exchange markets. (B), real interest rate, is found on the vertical axis in the loanable funds market. (C), the aggregate output, is on the horizontal axis of the AD-AS graph. Choice (D), money velocity, could be found by dividing nominal output by the money stock.

48. (C)

Of the options given, only increasing the money supply, or the speed of its growth, will contribute to higher price levels over time. Aggregate demand-aggregate supply analysis suggests that either a rightward shift of SRAS or a leftward shift of AD would lead to lower rather than higher price levels.

49. (B)

This inflation rate should seem high. Coupled with an indication that prices are set to continue to rise in the future and a low unemployment rate, this suggests that the economy is experiencing an inflationary gap. Contractionary policies are needed. Fiscally, this means increasing taxes and reducing spending, eliminating choices (A), (D), and (E). Monetarily, this means raising interest rates, further eliminating choice (C). Choice (B) remains and is the only option without any expansionary policy actions listed.

50. (D)

The dollar price of the pound has increased, therefore it has appreciated against the dollar. This eliminates choices (A) and (C) directly. Choices (B) and (E) further can be proved false because Americans would have less purchasing power when buying British bonds and consumers in the UK are more able to afford American goods. For strategy's sake, note that options (A) and (C) mean the same thing, rendering it impossible for one to be correct and the other wrong. Similarly, choices (B) and (D) are opposite in meaning, making it likely that one is correct.

51. (C)

When Indian interest rates increase, prices on Indian bonds are lower and therefore more attractive. As a result, savers will want more rupee-denominated assets that bear this higher real interest yield. Demand for rupees will increase, leading the rupee to appreciate. This makes Indian goods feel more expensive to foreign consumers and imports feel cheaper in Indian markets. As a result, net exports decline.

52. (C)

The expansionary fiscal policy necessitates more government borrowing. This increases interest rates and decreases investment, offsetting part of the increase in AD that would otherwise result from an increase in government spending. Choice (A) is too strongly phrased. Choice (B) suggests that government borrowing encourages private sector investment rather that discouraging it. Choice (D) neglects the multiplier effect entirely. Choice (E) mistakenly suggests that fiscal policies cannot have influence individually.

53. (A)

The long-run Phillips Curve is vertical at the Natural Rate of Unemployment. This suggests that in the long run the unemployment rate will be independent of the inflation rate. Increases in AD caused by the policies mentioned will lead to higher rates of price level increase but will be matched over time by increases in the wage rate, leading to faster inflation with the same prevailing unemployment rate.

54. (A)

Statement I is necessarily false because statement II's claim that financial and current account offset one another is true. Net exporters have positive current accounts and therefore tend to have negative financial accounts (China serves as a clear example of this). Statement II is the only true one, thus the correct answer is (A).

55. (E)

Increases in resource costs, including the wage rate, would cause decreases in SRAS because at the same price level producers are able to supply a smaller quantity of aggregate output. Short-run Phillips Curve acts as a mirror image of SRAS and, therefore, shifts up and right. The economy's NRU, however, is unaffected and, therefore, LRPC does not shift.

56. (B)

This answer choice identifies three components of the supply-side economic strategy favored by advisors to President Reagan in the early 1980s when stagflation was prevalent. Choice (A) would worsen inflation. Choice (C) would increase the recessionary gap. Choice (D) is inconsistent use of monetary policy, lacking a clear effect on the economy. Choice (E), the price ceiling approach, leads to persistent shortages in goods without addressing the underlying causes of the inflation.

57. (D)

When the UK's price level increases, its goods become more expensive to produce—because of this they carry higher price tags. Domestic consumers, therefore, look increasingly to imports and British exports are costlier in foreign markets. The supply of pounds will shift right due to the increases in imports flowing into the UK. At the same time, demand for pounds will decrease as foreigners desire fewer of the higher priced British goods. These two factors push down the value of the pound in foreign exchange markets.

58. (B)

Automatic stabilizers result in increased spending when AD declines (for example, more people are eligible for welfare programs and unemployment insurance) and lower tax receipts (because taxes are calculated as a percentage of income and incomes decline). Choice (A) is misguided: balancing the budget annually would not stabilize the business cycle at all. Choice (C) implies discretionary rather than automatic policy. Choice (D) might be true, but is far from certain: it would fail to balance out in any cycle in which the economy spent unequal amounts of time above and below full employment. Choice (E) reverses the idea of countercyclical policy.

59. (A)

The two suggested actions both push interest rates upward. An increase in interest rates will drive down the price of bonds, making them more attractive. This increases demand for the country's currency, causing appreciation. With an appreciating currency, exports decrease and imports increase, pushing the current account more into the negative.

60. (E)

When economic growth occurs, the production possibilities curve shifts outward to show that combinations of goods that weren't possible to produce before can now be made. Long-run supply is the value of the real potential output a nation can produce, which increases with growth as well. The long-run Phillips Curve is not likely to move, as substantial growth can and frequently does occur without the Natural Rate of Unemployment changing. In the United States, for example, potential GDP has risen substantially over the last few decades, yet the NRU has remained in the range of 4-6%.

Detailed Explanations of Answers

Section II

Question 1
Sample Response

A/B.

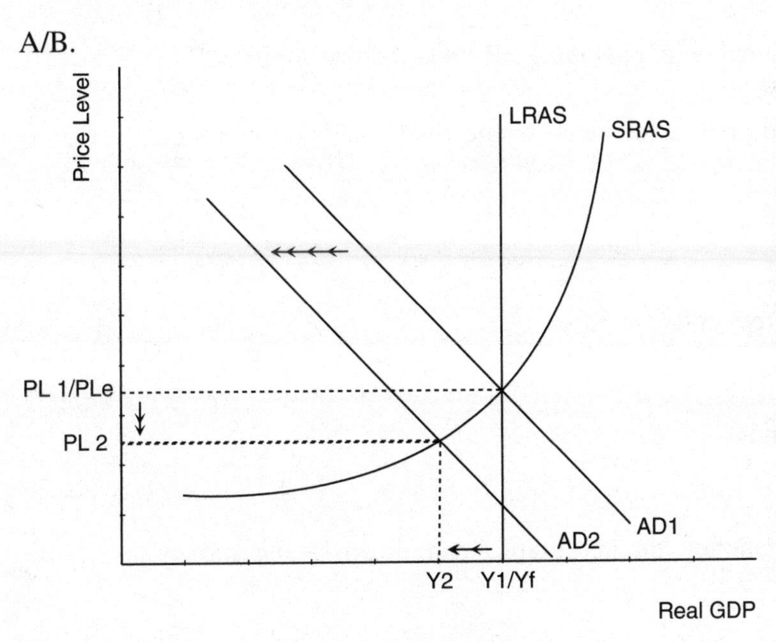

Note that both graphs are completely labeled. Each uses arrows to show direction of change and numbers the before-and-after curves so that changes are easy for graders to spot! The values on the axes are labeled and shown with dotted lines extended from intersection points.

C. Purchase bonds on the open market.

D.

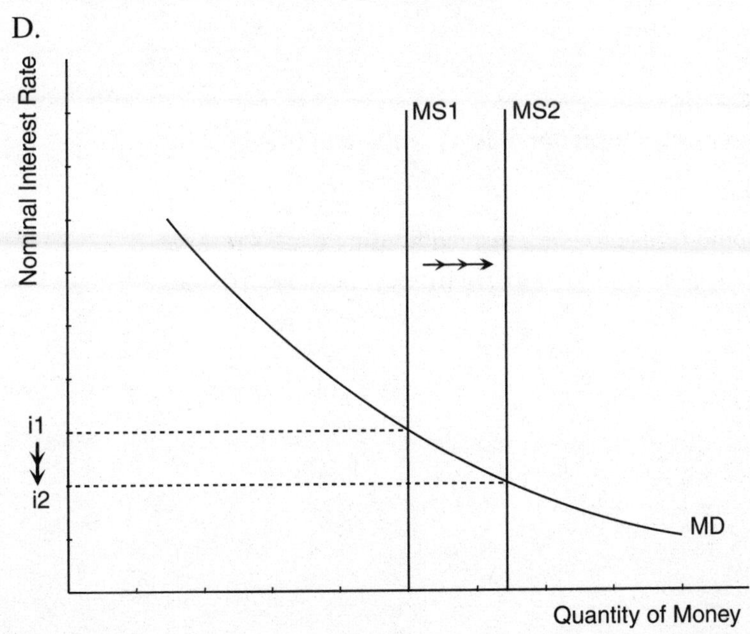

The response follows the structure of the question and leaves no doubt where the answer to a particular sub-part will be found.

E. i. The decrease in interest rate would stimulate more investment.
ii. Because investment is a component of AD, AD will increase.

F. i. Commercial banks might hold excess reserves rather than lending more.
ii. Private firms might decide not to take out loans.

Scoring Criteria

13 points—Financial Crisis

- Part a: 3 points
    - Correctly labeled graph with upsloping SRAS and downsloping AD
    - Vertical LRAS at Yf
    - Current output and price level found where SRAS and AD intersect, output is at Yf
- Part b: 2 points
    - AD shifts left
    - Price level and output both decrease
- Part c: 1 point
    - Buy securities (bonds)
- Part d: 3 points
    - Correctly labeled money market graph with downsloping money demand curve
    - Vertical MS curve
    - MS shifts right, reducing the nominal interest rate
- Part e: 2 points
    - Investment would increase
    - AD would shift right because investment is a component of AD
- Part f: 2 points
    - Commercial banks could refuse to lend, instead holding excess reserves
    - Private firms might decide not to borrow money because business confidence is low

Question 2
Sample Response

A.

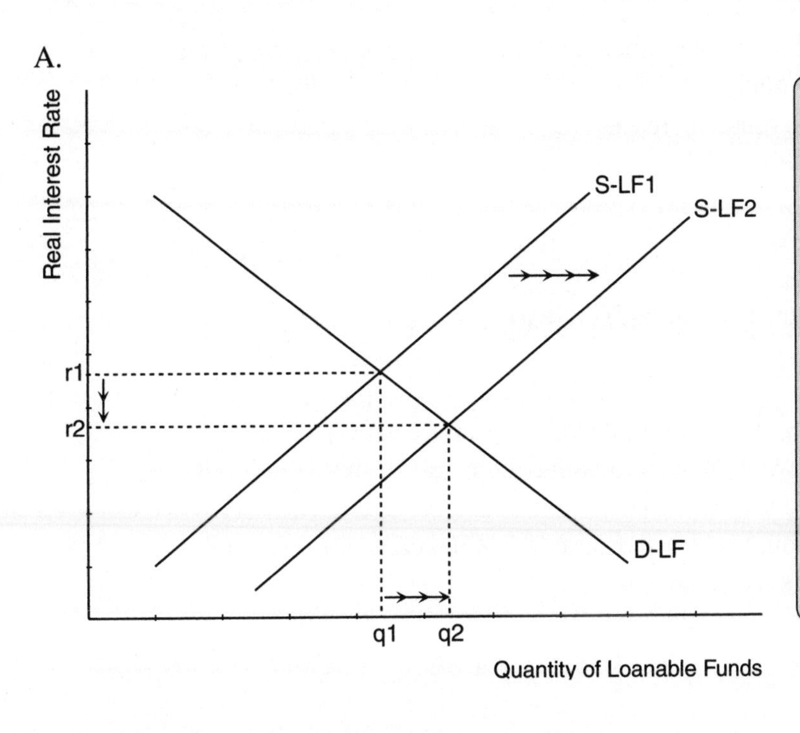

This response features another graph that is fully labeled with arrows and numbers to indicate direction of change clearly. Responses to part B are direct. Part C includes the reasoning needed to earn full credit when the question calls for an explanation.

B. i. Aggregate demand would shift to the right
ii. Real output would increase
iii. The price level would rise

C. The Canadian dollar's value will decline because the rising price level will make Canadian goods more expensive both in Canada and in foreign markets. Canadians will supply more Canadian dollars and foreigners will demand fewer Canadian dollars, both of which will cause the Canadian dollar to depreciate.

Scoring Criteria

7 points—Canada's tax reform

- Part a: 3 points
  - Correctly labeled loanable funds market with upsloping SLF and downsloping DLF curve
  - Supply of loanable funds increases
  - Real interest rate falls
- Part b: 2 points
  - AD would increase
  - Output and price level would both increase
- Part c: 2 points
  - The Canadian dollar's value will decrease or depreciate
  - Higher price level would make Canadian goods less desirable in foreign markets so demand for the Canadian dollar decreases OR
  - Imported goods would be more desirable in Canadian stores so supply of Canadian dollars would increase.

Question 3
Sample Response

A. UE rate = Number of unemployed divided by the number in the labor force, expressed as a percentage.

B. i. Cyclical unemployment arises due to the business cycle and consists of workers laid off during recessions.

ii. Frictional unemployment is short-term unemployment of workers who have the skills they need to get good jobs but haven't yet found that job. Recent college graduates are often frictionally unemployed.

iii. Structural unemployment is longer-term unemployment of workers who no longer have skills that are in demand, such as workers whose jobs have been permanently shipped overseas or replaced by machines.

iv. NRU is the level of unemployment that an economy will return to in the long run. It includes structural and frictional unemployment only because it tries to correct for the effects of the business cycle.

C. Getting rid of unemployment insurance would decrease the NRU.

D.

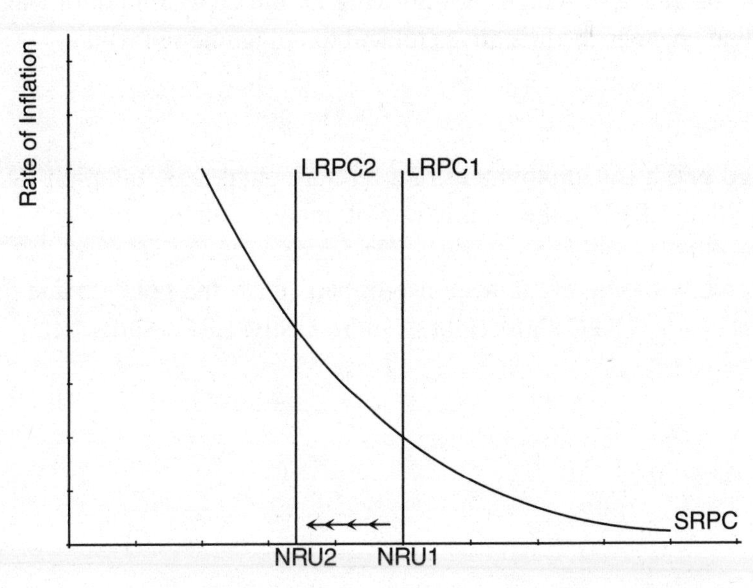

Scoring Criteria

8 points—Unemployment

- Part a: 1 point
    - $\frac{(\text{Number unemployed})}{(\text{Number in labor force})} \times 100$
- Part b: 4 points
    - Cyclical unemployment changes with business confidence and is due to the fluctuations of the business cycle.
    - Frictional unemployment is the short-term unemployment of people with skills that are in demand and is due to the time it takes for employers and qualified workers to find one another.
    - Structural unemployment is the longer-term unemployment of workers who have skills that are no longer in demand; they must be retrained to become employable.
    - The NRU is the structural and frictional components, OR the NRU is the rate of unemployment that remains when output is at full-employment level, OR the NRU is unemployment absent the effects of the business cycle.

- Part c: 1 point
    - Increasing or decreasing unemployment insurance or food stamp benefits, providing universal health insurance coverage, or removing an effective minimum wage or another policy that changes the incentives related to being unemployed
- Part d: 2 points
    - Correctly labeled graph (unemployment rate on horizontal axis, inflation rate on vertical) with vertical LRPC at the natural rate of unemployment.
    - LRPC shifts correctly based on the response in part (c). If the policy made being unemployed less costly, LRPC shifts right; if more costly, LRPC shifts left.

Answer Sheet

AP Microeconomics

1. Ⓐ Ⓑ Ⓒ Ⓓ Ⓔ	21. Ⓐ Ⓑ Ⓒ Ⓓ Ⓔ	41. Ⓐ Ⓑ Ⓒ Ⓓ Ⓔ
2. Ⓐ Ⓑ Ⓒ Ⓓ Ⓔ	22. Ⓐ Ⓑ Ⓒ Ⓓ Ⓔ	42. Ⓐ Ⓑ Ⓒ Ⓓ Ⓔ
3. Ⓐ Ⓑ Ⓒ Ⓓ Ⓔ	23. Ⓐ Ⓑ Ⓒ Ⓓ Ⓔ	43. Ⓐ Ⓑ Ⓒ Ⓓ Ⓔ
4. Ⓐ Ⓑ Ⓒ Ⓓ Ⓔ	24. Ⓐ Ⓑ Ⓒ Ⓓ Ⓔ	44. Ⓐ Ⓑ Ⓒ Ⓓ Ⓔ
5. Ⓐ Ⓑ Ⓒ Ⓓ Ⓔ	25. Ⓐ Ⓑ Ⓒ Ⓓ Ⓔ	45. Ⓐ Ⓑ Ⓒ Ⓓ Ⓔ
6. Ⓐ Ⓑ Ⓒ Ⓓ Ⓔ	26. Ⓐ Ⓑ Ⓒ Ⓓ Ⓔ	46. Ⓐ Ⓑ Ⓒ Ⓓ Ⓔ
7. Ⓐ Ⓑ Ⓒ Ⓓ Ⓔ	27. Ⓐ Ⓑ Ⓒ Ⓓ Ⓔ	47. Ⓐ Ⓑ Ⓒ Ⓓ Ⓔ
8. Ⓐ Ⓑ Ⓒ Ⓓ Ⓔ	28. Ⓐ Ⓑ Ⓒ Ⓓ Ⓔ	48. Ⓐ Ⓑ Ⓒ Ⓓ Ⓔ
9. Ⓐ Ⓑ Ⓒ Ⓓ Ⓔ	29. Ⓐ Ⓑ Ⓒ Ⓓ Ⓔ	49. Ⓐ Ⓑ Ⓒ Ⓓ Ⓔ
10. Ⓐ Ⓑ Ⓒ Ⓓ Ⓔ	30. Ⓐ Ⓑ Ⓒ Ⓓ Ⓔ	50. Ⓐ Ⓑ Ⓒ Ⓓ Ⓔ
11. Ⓐ Ⓑ Ⓒ Ⓓ Ⓔ	31. Ⓐ Ⓑ Ⓒ Ⓓ Ⓔ	51. Ⓐ Ⓑ Ⓒ Ⓓ Ⓔ
12. Ⓐ Ⓑ Ⓒ Ⓓ Ⓔ	32. Ⓐ Ⓑ Ⓒ Ⓓ Ⓔ	52. Ⓐ Ⓑ Ⓒ Ⓓ Ⓔ
13. Ⓐ Ⓑ Ⓒ Ⓓ Ⓔ	33. Ⓐ Ⓑ Ⓒ Ⓓ Ⓔ	53. Ⓐ Ⓑ Ⓒ Ⓓ Ⓔ
14. Ⓐ Ⓑ Ⓒ Ⓓ Ⓔ	34. Ⓐ Ⓑ Ⓒ Ⓓ Ⓔ	54. Ⓐ Ⓑ Ⓒ Ⓓ Ⓔ
15. Ⓐ Ⓑ Ⓒ Ⓓ Ⓔ	35. Ⓐ Ⓑ Ⓒ Ⓓ Ⓔ	55. Ⓐ Ⓑ Ⓒ Ⓓ Ⓔ
16. Ⓐ Ⓑ Ⓒ Ⓓ Ⓔ	36. Ⓐ Ⓑ Ⓒ Ⓓ Ⓔ	56. Ⓐ Ⓑ Ⓒ Ⓓ Ⓔ
17. Ⓐ Ⓑ Ⓒ Ⓓ Ⓔ	37. Ⓐ Ⓑ Ⓒ Ⓓ Ⓔ	57. Ⓐ Ⓑ Ⓒ Ⓓ Ⓔ
18. Ⓐ Ⓑ Ⓒ Ⓓ Ⓔ	38. Ⓐ Ⓑ Ⓒ Ⓓ Ⓔ	58. Ⓐ Ⓑ Ⓒ Ⓓ Ⓔ
19. Ⓐ Ⓑ Ⓒ Ⓓ Ⓔ	39. Ⓐ Ⓑ Ⓒ Ⓓ Ⓔ	59. Ⓐ Ⓑ Ⓒ Ⓓ Ⓔ
20. Ⓐ Ⓑ Ⓒ Ⓓ Ⓔ	40. Ⓐ Ⓑ Ⓒ Ⓓ Ⓔ	60. Ⓐ Ⓑ Ⓒ Ⓓ Ⓔ

FREE-RESPONSE ANSWER SHEET

For the free-response section, write your answers on sheets of blank paper.

Answer Sheet

AP Macroeconomics

1. Ⓐ Ⓑ Ⓒ Ⓓ Ⓔ	21. Ⓐ Ⓑ Ⓒ Ⓓ Ⓔ	41. Ⓐ Ⓑ Ⓒ Ⓓ Ⓔ
2. Ⓐ Ⓑ Ⓒ Ⓓ Ⓔ	22. Ⓐ Ⓑ Ⓒ Ⓓ Ⓔ	42. Ⓐ Ⓑ Ⓒ Ⓓ Ⓔ
3. Ⓐ Ⓑ Ⓒ Ⓓ Ⓔ	23. Ⓐ Ⓑ Ⓒ Ⓓ Ⓔ	43. Ⓐ Ⓑ Ⓒ Ⓓ Ⓔ
4. Ⓐ Ⓑ Ⓒ Ⓓ Ⓔ	24. Ⓐ Ⓑ Ⓒ Ⓓ Ⓔ	44. Ⓐ Ⓑ Ⓒ Ⓓ Ⓔ
5. Ⓐ Ⓑ Ⓒ Ⓓ Ⓔ	25. Ⓐ Ⓑ Ⓒ Ⓓ Ⓔ	45. Ⓐ Ⓑ Ⓒ Ⓓ Ⓔ
6. Ⓐ Ⓑ Ⓒ Ⓓ Ⓔ	26. Ⓐ Ⓑ Ⓒ Ⓓ Ⓔ	46. Ⓐ Ⓑ Ⓒ Ⓓ Ⓔ
7. Ⓐ Ⓑ Ⓒ Ⓓ Ⓔ	27. Ⓐ Ⓑ Ⓒ Ⓓ Ⓔ	47. Ⓐ Ⓑ Ⓒ Ⓓ Ⓔ
8. Ⓐ Ⓑ Ⓒ Ⓓ Ⓔ	28. Ⓐ Ⓑ Ⓒ Ⓓ Ⓔ	48. Ⓐ Ⓑ Ⓒ Ⓓ Ⓔ
9. Ⓐ Ⓑ Ⓒ Ⓓ Ⓔ	29. Ⓐ Ⓑ Ⓒ Ⓓ Ⓔ	49. Ⓐ Ⓑ Ⓒ Ⓓ Ⓔ
10. Ⓐ Ⓑ Ⓒ Ⓓ Ⓔ	30. Ⓐ Ⓑ Ⓒ Ⓓ Ⓔ	50. Ⓐ Ⓑ Ⓒ Ⓓ Ⓔ
11. Ⓐ Ⓑ Ⓒ Ⓓ Ⓔ	31. Ⓐ Ⓑ Ⓒ Ⓓ Ⓔ	51. Ⓐ Ⓑ Ⓒ Ⓓ Ⓔ
12. Ⓐ Ⓑ Ⓒ Ⓓ Ⓔ	32. Ⓐ Ⓑ Ⓒ Ⓓ Ⓔ	52. Ⓐ Ⓑ Ⓒ Ⓓ Ⓔ
13. Ⓐ Ⓑ Ⓒ Ⓓ Ⓔ	33. Ⓐ Ⓑ Ⓒ Ⓓ Ⓔ	53. Ⓐ Ⓑ Ⓒ Ⓓ Ⓔ
14. Ⓐ Ⓑ Ⓒ Ⓓ Ⓔ	34. Ⓐ Ⓑ Ⓒ Ⓓ Ⓔ	54. Ⓐ Ⓑ Ⓒ Ⓓ Ⓔ
15. Ⓐ Ⓑ Ⓒ Ⓓ Ⓔ	35. Ⓐ Ⓑ Ⓒ Ⓓ Ⓔ	55. Ⓐ Ⓑ Ⓒ Ⓓ Ⓔ
16. Ⓐ Ⓑ Ⓒ Ⓓ Ⓔ	36. Ⓐ Ⓑ Ⓒ Ⓓ Ⓔ	56. Ⓐ Ⓑ Ⓒ Ⓓ Ⓔ
17. Ⓐ Ⓑ Ⓒ Ⓓ Ⓔ	37. Ⓐ Ⓑ Ⓒ Ⓓ Ⓔ	57. Ⓐ Ⓑ Ⓒ Ⓓ Ⓔ
18. Ⓐ Ⓑ Ⓒ Ⓓ Ⓔ	38. Ⓐ Ⓑ Ⓒ Ⓓ Ⓔ	58. Ⓐ Ⓑ Ⓒ Ⓓ Ⓔ
19. Ⓐ Ⓑ Ⓒ Ⓓ Ⓔ	39. Ⓐ Ⓑ Ⓒ Ⓓ Ⓔ	59. Ⓐ Ⓑ Ⓒ Ⓓ Ⓔ
20. Ⓐ Ⓑ Ⓒ Ⓓ Ⓔ	40. Ⓐ Ⓑ Ⓒ Ⓓ Ⓔ	60. Ⓐ Ⓑ Ⓒ Ⓓ Ⓔ

FREE-RESPONSE ANSWER SHEET

For the free-response section, write your answers on sheets of blank paper.

Appendices

25 Key Graphs

Some of the following graphs will likely be tested on the AP economics exams. A brief list of the tasks you should be able to perform is provided here for your reference. Can you create all of these pictures?

Key Graphs for Microeconomics and Macroeconomics

1. Production Possibilities Curve or Frontier (See Figure 3-3.)

   Interpret slope as opportunity cost—constant or increasing; understand factors that cause PPC to shift over time and points significance of points inside, on, and outside of the curve; relate to comparative advantage problems

2. Demand, Supply, and Equilibrium (See Figures 3-9–3-15.)

   Demonstrate how prices converge to equilibrium from shortages and surpluses; understand factors that shift demand and supply and effects on equilibrium price and quantity from those shifts

Key Graphs for Microeconomics

3. Producer and Consumer Surplus (See Figure 4-5.)

   Find areas of consumer and producer surplus; show how over- and under-production can lead to less total economic surplus and deadweight loss; graph and explain how areas change when supply and/or demand shift

4. Price Floor (See Figure 4-7.)

   Show how an effective price floor affects quantity and price; find areas of consumer and producer surplus and deadweight loss before and after the floor is imposed

5. Price Ceiling (See Figure 4-6.)

   Show how an effective price ceiling affects quantity and price; find areas of consumer and producer surplus and deadweight loss before and after the floor is imposed

6. Elasticity Along a Demand Curve (See Figure 4-4.)

   Find elastic and inelastic ranges of a demand curve; locate unit elastic point; relate elasticity to marginal and total revenue; recognize demand curves that are perfectly elastic and perfectly inelastic

7. Short Run Cost Curves (See Figure 4-10.)

   Draw and explain reasons for the shape of marginal cost, average fixed cost, average variable cost, and average total cost curves; recognize the shape of total cost, variable cost, and fixed cost curves

8. Long Run Costs (See Figure 4-11.)

   Understand connections between short- and long-run costs; how shape of long-run average total cost influences firm size and market structure; identify areas of economies and diseconomies of scale

9. Perfect Competition: Firm and Market (See Figures 4-12 – 4-18.)

   Create side-by-side graphs showing profit, loss, or break-even situation; show how changes in industry demand or cost structure can influence market price, firm and market output, and profit/loss situation; show how changes in number of firms in the industry brings it back to long-run equilibrium

10. Monopoly (See Figure 4-23.)

    Graph a monopolist maximizing profit or minimizing loss; contrast profit-maximizing quantity with unit elastic and socially optimal quantities; show area of deadweight loss; find consumer surplus and area of economic profit or loss; depict how a change in demand or costs would influence the firm's decision making; identify how price ceiling can be used to increase the firm's output to efficient level

11. Natural and Regulated Monopoly (See Figure 4-24.)

    Graph natural monopoly, showing deadweight loss and area of profit; contrast socially optimal, fair return, and unregulated levels of output and the efficiency loss of each

12. Monopolistic Competition (See Figures 4-25 – 4-27.)

    Show monopolistic competitor in profit and loss situations; practice graph of long-run equilibrium in which firm is breaking even; explain and show how entry and exit of firms results in long-run situation and how product differentiation influences the adjustment into long-run

13. Competitive Factor Market (See Figure 5-4.)

    Construct side-by-side graphs of a factor market (like labor) and an individual firm (such as a wage-taker) purchasing resources in it; find the profit-maximizing amount of a resource to purchase; understand factors that influence market supply and demand and factors that shift a firm's labor demand (marginal revenue product) curve; be able to show effects of those changes on graphs

14. Monopsony Factor Market (See Figure 5-5.)

    Show and explain the reasons for the upsloping supply and marginal factor cost curves the firm faces; find the profit-maximizing quantity of labor for the firm to hire and wage rate they will pay; state the effects of various levels of minimum wage on quantity and wage

15. Negative Externality (See Figure 6-1.)

    Show marginal private and marginal social cost; identify both private market and socially optimal price and quantity traded; find area of deadweight loss; show how various forms of government regulation (floor, ceiling, tax) could correct the externality's inefficiency

16. Positive Externality (See Figure 6-2.)

    Show marginal private and marginal social benefit; identify both private market and socially optimal price and quantity traded; find area of deadweight loss; show how a per-unit subsidy could correct the externality's inefficiency

17. Effects of a Per-Unit Tax (See Figures 6-5 – 6-8.)

    Show how a tax shifts marginal cost or supply, reduces quantity, and decreases the area of consumer and producer surplus; find the area that represents tax revenue; assess the incidence of tax on consumers and producers based on the relative elasticities of demand and supply

18. Lorenz Curve (See Figures 6-9 – 6-11.)

    Be able to read points from a Lorenz curve and draw conclusions about two different societies (or one society over time) based on movement of the curve; identify policies that could decrease inequality and move the curve toward the line of perfect equality

Key Graphs for Macroeconomics

19. Business Cycle (See Figure 11-2.)

    Identify four stages in the business cycle and describe them with appropriate terminology; make predictions about major macroeconomic indicators in those stages; interpret slope of regression line as long-run growth rate

20. Aggregate Demand-Aggregate Supply (See Figures 8-13 – 8-15.)

    Explain slopes of all three curves; recognize reasons why they shift; show recessionary and inflationary gaps; depict cost-push and demand-pull inflation; graph the effects of monetary and fiscal policy on output and price level; understand conditions under which economy adjusts to long-run equilibrium; show long-run economic growth

21. Money Market (See Figures 9-1 – 9-5.)

    Explain why money supply is vertical; know components of money demand; show how shifts in money demand and supply influence nominal interest rates; understand linkage between monetary policy and money market

22. T-Account (See Table 9-1.)

    Recognize types of assets and liabilities; use required ratio to calculate excess reserves; track expansions in the money supply due to lending; use money multiplier

23. Loanable Funds Market (See Figures 10-3 – 10-5.)

    Know shape and components of demand and supply of loanable funds; show how government borrowing can lead to crowding out effect; connect changes in real interest rate to interest-sensitive components of aggregate demand

24. Phillips Curve (See Figures 10-6 – 10-10.)

    Show relationship between inflation and unemployment directly; distinguish movements along from shifts of the short-run Phillips curve; translate changes in the aggregate demand-aggregate supply model to Phillips curve graph; connect natural rate of unemployment to long-run Phillips curve

25. Foreign Exchange Markets (See Figures 12-4 – 12-5.)

    Use side-by-side graphs to show how exchange rates are determined for any pair of countries' currencies; know factors that shift demand and supply of a country's currency and how to relate movement on one graph to the other

Skills Related to Graphing for Economics

Get in the habit of drawing these graphs rather than just examining them in the book—you'll take the test with your hands, not just your eyes. The graphs in many cases will be simpler looking than the ones you've studied in class, but they often have several layers of meaning, ways they change and explanations that you will need to recall quickly. The best scores on AP exams are earned by students who have the deeper meanings understood, rather than those who've simply memorized what each graph looks like. For each key graph use the acronym **DRESSER** to help you recall what you need to do:

D-Draw: Graph the axes and lines with labels

R-Relationships: Each curve is a representation of (tells a story about) two related variables' behavior. The axes are the characters in the story—know the characters and what story each curve is telling about them!

E-Explain: Practice giving a 1- to 2-sentence explanation for everything. What do you need to explain in particular? Slopes, Shifts, and Effects!

S-Slopes: Know and explain why each line slopes as it does: vertical, horizontal, upsloping, downsloping, increasing slope, decreasing slope.

S-Shifts: Know and explain why each line might shift. Lots of free-response problems require you to show and explain shifts, and many multiple-choice items ask about how changed circumstances affect graphs.

E-Effects: Understand and predict what you might be asked about the effects of the shifts you learned in the last step.

R-Recheck: Scan your work to be certain you labeled everything, used arrows to show changes, and left your work looking neat and complete!

25 Key Formulae

From time to time you'll need to perform simple calculations or predict whether a value will increase or decrease. Each formula on this list is helpful for one or both of the AP economics exams.

Key Formulae for Microeconomics and Macroeconomics

1. Opportunity Cost (e.g., for comparative advantage)

$$OC_A = \frac{\text{units of B sacrificed}}{\text{units of A obtained}}$$

2. Marginal Analysis

   MB = MC yields the optimal amount

   Individuals purchase until MB = P

   Firms produce until MR = MC

   Firms hire until MRP = MFC

   Socially optimal (or allocatively efficient) amount is where D = MC or where MSB = MSC

Key Formulae for Microeconomics

3. Utility Maximizing Rule

   Purchase units of A and B such that $\frac{MU_A}{P_A} = \frac{MU_B}{P_B}$

4. Four Kinds of Elasticity

   - Price Elasticity of Demand $= \frac{\%\Delta Q_d}{\%\Delta P}$ (connect to MR and TR) — Drop the negative sign, then compare to 1
   - Income Elasticity of Demand $= \frac{\%\Delta Q_d}{\%\Delta \text{Income}}$ (Normal and inferior goods) — Positive or negative?
   - Cross-Price Elasticity of Demand $= \frac{\%\Delta Q_{Dx}}{\%\Delta P_y}$ (Substitutes and complements) — Positive or negative?
   - Price Elasticity of Supply $= \frac{\%\Delta Q_S}{\%\Delta P}$ — Compare to 1

5. Total, Average, and Marginal (Physical) Product

$$TP = Q \qquad AP = \frac{TP}{L} \qquad MP \text{ or } MPP = \frac{\Delta TP}{\Delta L}$$

6. Costs of the Firm

$$TC = FC + VC \qquad ATC = \frac{TC}{Q} \qquad AVC = \frac{VC}{Q} \qquad MC = \frac{\Delta TC}{\Delta Q}$$

$$AFC = \frac{FC}{Q}$$

7. Total, Average, and Marginal Revenue

$$TR = P \times Q \qquad AR = P = \frac{TR}{Q} \qquad MR = \frac{\Delta TR}{\Delta Q}$$

For price-takers only, $MR = P = AR = D$

8. Three Kinds of Profit

Accounting Profit = Total Revenue − Explicit Costs

Economic Profit = Total Revenue − (Explicit + Implicit Costs)

Economic Profit = Accounting Profit − Normal Profit

Normal Profit = Implicit Cost

9. Least Cost Rule and Profit Maximizing Rule

To make a given number of units at the least cost,

ensure that $\frac{MRP_{labor}}{MFC_{labor}} = \frac{MRP_{capital}}{MFC_{capital}} = \frac{MRP_{land}}{MFC_{land}}$

To maximize profit, those fractions should not only equal each other; each should also equal 1

10. Marginal Revenue Product

$$MRP_L = \frac{\Delta TR}{\Delta L}$$

If the firm is a price-taker, then $MRP_L = MPP_L \times$ product price

11. Marginal Factor Cost (also called Marginal Resource Cost)

$$MFC_L = \frac{\Delta TC}{\Delta L}$$

If the firm is a wage-taker, then MFC_L = wage rate = labor supply

Key Formulae for Macroeconomics

12. GDP: Expenditure Method

GDP = Consumption + Investment + Government Purchases + Exports − Imports

The expenditure method connects very closely to Aggregate Demand

13. GDP: Income Method

GDP = Wages + Rents + Interest + Profits + Adjustments (for indirect business taxes, depreciation, and undistributed corporate profits)

Without these adjustments, the total is called National Income. The income approach is less exact and connects loosely with aggregate supply

14. GDP Growth Rate

$$\frac{GDP_{year\,2} - GDP_{year1}}{GDP_{year1}}$$

15. Real and Nominal GDP

$$\text{Real GDP} = \frac{\text{Nominal GDP}}{\text{Price Index}} \text{ (multiply by 100 if base year index is 100)}$$

Nominal GDP = Real GDP × Price Index (divide by 100 if base year index is 100)

16. CPI Calculation

$$CPI_{year\,2} = \frac{\text{Market Basket Price}_{year\,2}}{\text{Market Basket Price}_{year\,1}} \times 100$$

17. Inflation Rate

$$\frac{\text{Price Index}_{year\,2} - \text{Price Index}_{year\,1}}{\text{Price Index}_{year\,1}}$$

18. Unemployment Rate

$$\frac{\text{Number unemployed}}{\text{Number in labor force}}$$

Labor force is composed of those working for pay and those actively seeking paid employment

19. Labor Force Participation Rate

$$\frac{\text{Number in labor force}}{\text{Working age population}}$$

Working age population is civilians aged 16–65 who are not institutionalized.

20. Marginal Propensity to Save and Consume

$$MPC = \frac{\Delta C}{\Delta DI} \qquad MPC = \frac{\Delta S}{\Delta DI} \qquad MPC + MPS = 1$$

where C, S, and DI stand for consumption, savings, and disposable income

21. Keynesian (or Spending or Investment) Multiplier

When an autonomous component of AD increases, use the spending multiplier

$$\frac{1}{MPS} = \frac{1}{(1 - MPC)}$$

22. Tax Multiplier

When a tax cut increases disposable income, but does not directly influence a component of AD, use the tax multiplier

$$\frac{-MPC}{MPS}$$

23. Money Multiplier

Find the excess reserves to determine how much a bank can lend. To determine how much all banks (or the banking system) can create, take the excess reserves times the money multiplier

$$\frac{1}{\text{required reserve ratio}}$$

24. Monetary Equation of Exchange

$$MV = PQ = \text{Nominal GDP}$$

where M is the money supply, V is money velocity, P is the price level, and Q is real output

As Q approaches and even exceeds potential output, increases in M only result in inflation. This equation is closely linked to monetarism and is sometimes referred to as the quantity theory of money.

25. Fisher Equation

The Fisher Equation relates real and nominal interest rates to one another via the rate of inflation, either expected or actual.

Before a loan, to calculate nominal interest rate:

$$NIR = RIR + \text{Expected Inflation Rate}$$

After a loan is repaid, to calculate real interest rate:

$$RIR = NIR - \text{Actual Inflation Rate}$$

Glossary of Key Economic Terms

absolute advantage The ability to produce more of a good or service than another person or society with the same number of inputs. Alternatively, it means one person or society can make a unit of output with fewer units of input than its counterpart.

accounting profit Total revenue a firm receives minus its explicit costs. Economic profit plus normal profit.

aggregate demand (AD) A schedule or curve that shows the total quantity demanded for all goods and services of a nation at various price levels in a given period of time.

aggregate supply (AS) The total amount of goods and services that all the firms in all the industries in a country will produce at various price levels in a given period of time.

allocative efficiency The amount of production that benefits society the most; distribution of productive resources to achieve the most desirable combination of goods. It is achieved when the marginal benefit of production equals the marginal cost. Also known as the socially optimal level of output. A society is allocatively efficient when it is choosing to make the mix of goods that best satisfy the wants of its population. Firms are allocatively efficient if charge a price equal to marginal cost.

appreciation An increase in the value of one currency relative to another, resulting from an increase in demand for or a decrease in supply of the currency on the foreign exchange market.

average fixed cost (AFC) Fixed cost divided by a firm's quantity of output. Decreases at a decreasing rate as output rises.

asset An item of worth that can be spent or sold; a way to carry wealth from the present into the future. Bonds, land, stocks, and money are all assets.

automatic stabilizers Built-in mechanisms in the tax code and transfer payment programs that increase government spending and reduce tax revenue automatically when aggregate demand decreases. They reduce spending and collect more in tax revenues when aggregate demand increases.

average product (AP) The total product of a firm divided by the amount of a particular input used to produce the total product. Meets marginal product at its maximum point.

average total cost (ATC) The sum of average fixed cost and average variable cost: total cost divided by output. Generally forms a U-shape, meeting marginal cost at its minimum point.

average variable cost (AVC) Variable cost divided by the quantity of a firm's output. Generally forms a U-shape, meeting marginal cost at its minimum point.

balance of payments Measures all the monetary exchanges between one nation and all other nations. Includes the current account, the financial account, and the official reserves account.

balance of trade See Current Account and Net Exports.

balance sheet Also known as a T-account, this table shows the assets and liabilities of a financial institution, such as a commercial bank.

barriers to entry Anything that prohibits or discourages new firms from entering into a market. Perfect competition and monopolistic competition are assumed to have no significant barriers to the entry of new firms or the exit of existing firms from the industry in the long run. Entry can be blocked, as it is in monopolies, by legal barriers, control of an input necessary to production of a good, or extreme economies of scale.

bonds Bonds are not money. Bonds are pieces of paper that represent debt owed by the issuer (corporation or government) to the holder (investor or saver). The price of bonds on secondary markets is inversely related to the interest rate.

breakeven point Output at which a firm's total cost and total revenue are equal (TR = TC); an output at which a firm has neither an economic profit nor a loss, at which it earns only a normal profit.

budget deficit When a government spends more than it collects in tax revenues in a given year.

budget surplus When a government collects more in tax revenues than it spends in a given year.

business cycle A model showing the short-run periods of contraction and expansion in output experienced by an economy over a period of time.

capital The tools, machines, factories, and buildings used to produce goods and services. Includes physical capital, which ranges from hammers to industrial robots and human capital, which is "know-how" or specialized skills that get fused to labor through education and training.

capital account See Financial Account.

capitalism Economic system based largely on markets as the main mechanism for allocating scarce resources that are privately owned by individuals.

cartel A group of producers in an industry who collude in order to function as a monopoly. Cartels are illegal in many countries and tend to be rare and unstable due to the incentives their member firms often have to cheat on agreed prices and/or quantities.

central bank Institution in a country that controls the money supply and conducts monetary policy. Central banks alter money supply to influence interest rates in most modern economies. Some of the most well-known and important central banks are the Bank of England, the Bank of Japan, the European Central Bank, and the Federal Reserve.

ceteris paribus "Other things being equal." The assumption that all variables remain constant except for those being studied by the economist. Ceteris paribus allows economists to understand the relationship between economic variables. As in science, economists like to try to isolate one factor that may be changing at a given time to better understand cause and effect.

circular flow A model or diagram showing how households and firms interact in product and resource markets. Circular flow models help visualize how expenditures become income and how market types relate to one another. Complex versions of the circular flow can include activities of government in regulating or participating in various markets and/or international trade.

classical economic theory The view that an economy will self-correct from periods of economic shock if left alone. Also known as "laissez-faire" and derived from the thinking of Adam Smith, Thomas Malthus, and David Ricardo. Neoclassical theories are up-to-date versions of similar belief systems.

collusion Agreement by producers in an industry to cooperate and set prices instead of competing with one another. Considered an unethical or illegal practice, collusion makes oligopolies function more like monopolies.

command economy An economic system in which government planners make most of the choices for the economy and answer the basic questions of what to produce, how to produce, and for whom to produce. Often contrasted with market economy because these are the two basic extremes; societies can choose strategies for managing the scarcity problem that place them along the spectrum between these two extremes.

comparative advantage The ability to produce a good or service at a lower opportunity cost than someone else. Comparative advantage is the basis of mutually beneficial specialization and trade for societies and individuals.

complementary goods Goods that are consumed together, such as cars and gasoline or peanut butter and jelly. Complementary goods have a negative cross-price elasticity of demand.

concentration ratio Sum total of the percentage market shares of the largest firms in an industry. For example, the four-firm concentration ratio would be the total market share of each of the four biggest firms. Gives an indication of the pricing power firms have and therefore of the market structure in which the product is sold.

constant returns to scale This exists when a firm's long-run average total cost remains constant as the firm's size increases. Between minimum and maximum efficient scale, a firm neither experiences economies nor diseconomies of scale as it grows.

consumer(s) People who buy goods and services. Often a household is considered to be a fundamental unit of consumption.

consumer price index (CPI) An index that measures the price of a fixed market basket of consumer goods bought by a typical consumer. The CPI is used to calculate the inflation rate in a nation.

consumer surplus The difference between the equilibrium price in the market and the price consumers are actually willing to pay for a good or service. The economic gain consumers experience by purchasing in the market. On a graph, consumer surplus is represented as the area beneath the demand curve, above the price paid, and to the left of the quantity purchased.

consumption (C) A component of a nation's aggregate demand; measures the total spending by domestic households on goods and services.

contractionary fiscal policy A demand-side policy whereby government increases taxes or decreases its expenditures in order to reduce aggregate demand. Could be used in a period of high inflation to bring down the inflation rate.

contractionary monetary policy A demand-side policy whereby the central bank reduces the supply of money, increasing interest rates and reducing aggregate demand. Could be used to bring down high inflation rates.

copyright The government protection of someone's intellectual property from being taken or sold by another. Serves as a barrier to entry of new firms, giving the owner of the copyright monopoly power.

cost-push inflation Inflation resulting from a decrease in AS (from higher wage rates and raw material prices, such as the price of oil) and accompanied by a decrease in real output and employment. Also referred to as "stagflation" or "adverse aggregate supply shock."

cross-price elasticity of demand The percentage change in the quantity demanded for one good divided by the percentage change in the price of a related good. Cross-price elasticity determines whether goods are complements (if negative) or substitutes (if positive).

crowding-out effect The rise in interest rates and the resulting decrease in investment spending in the economy caused by increased government borrowing in the loanable funds market. Seen as a disadvantageous side effect of expansionary fiscal policy.

current account Measures the balance of trade in goods and services and the flow of income between one nation and all other nations. It also records monetary gifts or grants that flow into or out of a country. Equal to a country's net exports, or its exports minus its imports.

cyclical unemployment Unemployment caused by the business cycle. Not included in the natural rate of unemployment. When a nation is in a recession or below full-employment output, there will be cyclical unemployment.

deadweight loss The loss of consumer and producer surplus that occurs when a quantity other than the equilibrium quantity prevails in the market. Deadweight loss results from over- or underproduction of a good and is associated with allocative inefficiency.

deflation A decrease in the average price level of a nation's output over time.

demand The relationship between quantity of a good that consumers wish to purchase in a given time period and the price of the good. This inverse relationship can be expressed as a graphical curve or a tabular schedule or as a function in terms of P and Qd.

demand curve A downward-sloping curve showing the inverse relationship between quantity demanded and price.

demand deposit A deposit in a commercial bank against which checks may be written. Also known as a "checkable deposit."

demand-pull inflation Inflation resulting from an increase in AD without a corresponding increase in AS.

depreciation A decrease in the value of one currency relative to another, resulting from a decrease in demand for or an increase in the supply of the currency on the foreign exchange market.

derived demand Demand for goods and services which creates a demand for the factors of production used to produce those goods and services. Thus, demand for resources is derived from (and changes with) the demand for the products those resources make.

determinants of demand The factors that cause demand to either increase or decrease. The determinants of demand include: tastes and preferences, income, market size, prices of related goods, and expectations of future price, availability, or income.

determinants of supply The factors that cause supply to either increase or decrease. The determinants of supply include: technology, input prices, government taxes and subsidies, seller expectations, related prices, and number of suppliers.

devaluation When a government intervenes in the market for its own currency to weaken it relative to another currency. Usually achieved through direct intervention in the foreign exchange (FOREX) market or through the use of monetary policy that affects interest rates, and thereby affects international demand for the currency.

diminishing marginal returns This happens when marginal product is decreasing as an input is added to the production process. Overuse of fixed inputs causes extra units of a variable input to add less and less to production. This principle explains the slope of marginal product and marginal cost curves.

diminishing marginal utility Each additional unit of a good or service that is consumed gives less additional satisfaction or utility than the previous unit that was consumed. One of the reasons why price and quantity demanded have an inverse relationship.

discount rate One of the three tools of monetary policy, it is the interest rate that the federal government charges on the loans it makes to commercial banks.

diseconomies of scale This exists when a firm's long-run average total cost increases as the firm's size increases. The firm becomes less productively efficient as output rises in the long run. Also known as decreasing returns to scale.

disposable income The portion of income that an individual can choose to spend or save; after-tax income. Disposable income is the main factor that drives both spending and savings decisions.

dissaving Negative savings, as might be done at very low levels of income. Dissaving is accomplished either through drawing down prior accumulated wealth or by borrowing.

dominant strategy In game theory, a strategy in which a player always chooses independent of the other player's choice. For a choice to be a dominant strategy, it must be the best response a player could choose for every one of the choices available to the other player.

economic growth An increase in the potential output of goods and services in a nation over time.

economic profit Profits earned by a firm over and above normal profit. Areas of profit shown on economics graphs are economic profit and encourage new firms to join industries in which they can expect to earn more than normal profit. Economic losses similarly lead firms to leave an industry.

economic rent Amount paid to a factor of production in excess of the amount needed to encourage that quantity to be provided. Associated with perfectly inelastic supply, such as of land or individual and unique talents.

economic resources Land, labor, capital, and entrepreneurial ability that are used in the production of goods and services. They are "economic" resources because they are scarce (limited in supply and desired). Also known as "factors of production."

economics The study of the choices that presumptively rational people make to get what they need and want given the condition of scarcity. This field of inquiry is divided into macroeconomics—which concerns itself with how societies manage scarcity—and microeconomics—which primarily focuses on how firms and households make choices based on incentives to achieve their objectives.

economies of scale This exists when a firm's long-run average total cost declines as the firm's size increases. The firm becomes more productively efficient as output rises in the long run. Also known as increasing returns to scale.

elastic Describes a rate of change in quantity that is greater (in percentage terms) than the rate of change in price. The upper halves of linear demand curves are elastic, corresponding with the quantities at which marginal revenue is positive.

elasticity The sensitivity or responsiveness of quantity changes relative to changes in other factors, often prices.

entrepreneur An individual who possesses the factor of production called entrepreneurship. Entrepreneurs run firms that attempt to maximize profit.

entrepreneurial ability The ability of individuals to take risks and combine land, labor, and capital in new ways in order to make profits by providing a good or service instead of selling their labor to an employer.

equilibrium The condition that exists in the market when a single price and quantity result from the intersection of supply and demand. The unique price-quantity combination at which neither a shortage nor a surplus exists.

estate tax A tax assessed on the total value of a person's private property after he/she dies; often assessed only on large estates. Estate taxes are used to decrease income inequality.

excess capacity The difference in the long run between the quantity produced by a monopolistically competitive firm and the quantity that would minimize its ATC curve. Underutilization of the factories or productive capabilities of each firm; amount by which a firm would increase production in order to be productively efficient.

excess reserves The amount by which a bank's actual reserves exceed its required reserves. Banks can lend excess reserves; when they do, they expand the money supply. The amount of excess reserves in the banking system determines the equilibrium interest rate.

exchange rate The price of one currency in terms of another currency, determined in the FOREX market.

excise tax A per-unit tax on the production of a good or service. Excise taxes tend to reduce supply, decreasing quantity of a good that is sold and increasing the price that buyers pay.

expansionary fiscal policy A demand-side policy whereby government decreases taxes or increases its expenditures in order to increase aggregate demand. Could be used in a period of high unemployment to increase output.

expansionary monetary policy A demand-side policy whereby the central bank increases the supply of money, decreasing interest rates and increasing aggregate demand. Could be used to bring down high unemployment rates.

explicit cost Costs that a business' owners pay out to others. Accounting profit factors only explicit costs. Implicit costs, or normal profit, are the other nonmonetary costs.

exports (X) The spending by foreigners on domestically produced goods and services. Counts as an injection into a nation's circular flow of income.

externality A positive or negative side effect of market activity; spillover cost or benefit. Costs incurred by those who do not produce the product and benefits that accrue to those who are not the purchasers are both examples of externalities.

factor markets The markets in which the factors of production are bought by firms and sold by households. Factor markets are sometimes called resource markets.

factors of production The resources used to produce goods and services. These include land, labor, capital, and entrepreneurial ability.

federal funds rate (FFR) The interest rate banks charge one another on overnight loans made out of their excess reserves. The FFR is the interest rate targeted by the Fed through its open-market operations.

Federal Open Market Committee Federal Reserve governors and bank presidents, serving together, are responsible for setting the direction of monetary policy. The FOMC meets at least eight times each year and sets the target for the Federal Funds Rate, a benchmark interest rate in the economy.

federal reserve The United States' central banking system. The Fed is composed of a Board of Governors in Washington, D.C., and twelve regional banks. The Fed serves as the main agent of monetary policy, acts as a bank for member banks, and regulates the banking sector.

financial account Measures the flow of funds for investment in real assets (such as factories or office buildings) or financial assets (such as stocks and bonds) between a nation and the rest of the world. Foreign direct investment and portfolio investment are two components of the financial account. Formerly known as the Capital Account.

firm An organization that produces a good or service in order to make a profit for its owner or owners. Many people refer to a firm as a business. A fundamental assumption of economics is that firms seek to maximize profit.

fiscal policy Changes in government spending and tax collections implemented by government with the aim of either increasing or decreasing aggregate demand to achieve the macroeconomic objectives of full employment and price-level stability.

fixed cost A short-run cost that does not change as a firm's production changes. Fixed costs are incurred prior to producing even the first unit.

fixed exchange rate system When a government or central bank takes action to manage or fix the value of its currency relative to another currency on the FOREX market.

floating exchange rate system When a currency's exchange rate is determined by the free interaction of supply and demand in international FOREX markets.

FOREX market (foreign exchange market) The market in which international buyers and sellers exchange foreign currencies for one another to buy and sell goods, services, and assets from various countries. It is where a currency's exchange rate relative to other currencies is determined.

fractional reserve banking A banking system in which banks hold only a fraction of deposits as required reserves and can lend some of the money deposited by their customers to other borrowers.

frictional unemployment Unemployment of workers who have employable skills, such as those who are voluntarily moving between jobs or recent graduates who are looking for their first job.

full employment When an economy is producing at a level of output at which almost all the nation's resources are employed. The unemployment rate when an economy is at full employment equals the natural rate, and includes only frictional and structural unemployment. Full-employment output is also referred to as "potential output."

game theory The study of strategic decision-making used in economics and many other disciplines in which analysis of interdependent choices is performed. To an economist, a game is a situation in which a discrete number of players can be identified, each has specific strategies or choices, and the payoffs to each player can be quantified (or approximated) for strategic analysis. Oligopoly's few firms and interdependent pricing and output decisions involve the same strategy present in many games.

GDP See Gross Domestic Product.

GDP deflator The price index for all final goods and services used to adjust the nominal GDP into real GDP.

gift tax A tax placed on gifts received from another person; often applied only to large monetary gifts. Gift taxes are used to decrease income inequality.

Gini coefficient The ratio of the area above the Lorenz curve to the total area below the line of equality. Gini coefficients range between zero and one. Societies with higher Gini coefficients have more unequally distributed wealth or income.

gross domestic product (GDP) The total market value of all final goods and services produced during a given time period within a country's borders. Equal to the total income of the nation's households or the total expenditures on the nation's output.

homogenous products Products that are identical or so similar that consumers can't or don't distinguish between the products made by various firms. Perfectly competitive industries are assumed to feature many firms producing goods that cannot be distinguished from one another and therefore are perfectly substitutable for one another.

human capital The value skills integrated into labor through education, training, knowledge, and health. An important determinant of aggregate supply and the level of economic growth in a nation.

implicit cost See Normal Profit.

imports (M) Spending on goods and services produced in foreign nations. Counts as a leakage from a nation's circular flow of income.

income effect Consumers' buying power changes inversely to changes in price. This is one reason for the inverse relationship expressed in the law of demand. Consumers buy fewer units at higher prices because their same nominal income has less purchasing power.

income elasticity of demand The percentage change in the quantity demanded divided by the percentage change in consumers' income. Measures whether and how much buying increases (typically) or decreases (in unusual cases of less-desirable goods) when income rises. Income elasticity of demand determines whether goods are normal (if positive) or inferior (if negative).

increasing marginal returns This happens when both total and marginal product increase as an input is added to the production process. This principle explains why marginal product initially slopes up and why marginal cost initially slopes down.

inelastic Describes a rate of change in quantity that is less (in percentage terms) than the rate of change in price. The lower halves of linear demand curves are inelastic, corresponding to quantities at which marginal revenue is negative.

inferior good A good whose demand varies inversely with consumers' incomes.

inflation A rise in the average level of prices in the economy over time (percentage change in the CPI).

inflationary gap The difference between a nation's equilibrium level of output and its full employment level of output when the nation is overheating (producing beyond its full employment level).

inflationary spiral The rapid increase in average price level resulting from demand-pull inflation leading to higher wages, causing cost-push inflation.

interdependence The condition in which the decisions of producers are based on the possible decisions of other producers. Oligopolies feature interdependence because firms must take into consideration the actions of other firms when determining their optimal price and quantity.

interest rate The opportunity cost of money. Either the cost of borrowing money or the cost of spending money (e.g., the interest rate is what would be given up by not saving money). Conversely, this is the price a lender is paid for allowing someone else to use money for a time.

inventory The stock of merchandise a firm has produced but not yet sold. Changes in inventory are considered part of investment for the purposes of calculating GDP.

investment (I) A component of aggregate demand, it includes all spending on capital equipment, inventories, and technology by firms. This does not include financial investment, which is the purchase of financial assets (stocks and bonds). Also includes household purchasing of newly constructed residences.

Keynesian economics Economic theory based on the ideas of John Maynard Keynes, who argued that periods of low employment and output would not self-correct quickly and that government action to stimulate aggregate demand was useful in these times.

kinked demand model Type of oligopoly in which firms act to ignore competitor price increases but match competitor price decreases.

labor People's mental and/or physical effort and skill used in producing goods and services.

land Natural resources used in producing goods and services. An economist's definition of land includes land area and the minerals, oil, timber, and other useful bounty that the land provides. Sometimes it is even used so broadly as to be nearly synonymous with raw materials.

law of demand The price and quantity demanded of a good are inversely related because of income effect, substitution effect, and diminishing marginal utility.

law of increasing marginal cost The cost of producing each additional unit of a good or service incurs a greater cost than the previous unit. Results from the need to use resources that are less and less well-suited to production of that good as quantity produced increases.

law of increasing opportunity cost As the production of one good increases, producers must sacrifice ever-increasing amounts of the other goods because factors of production are not perfectly interchangeable between the production of both goods. Explains production possibilities frontiers that are concave to the origin.

law of supply The price and quantity supplied of a good are directly related. Higher prices induce increased production quantities.

liability A debt with a monetary value.

liquidity The property of being easily spent on goods and services. Assets are more liquid the more easily spent they are; money is the most liquid of all assets, whereas real estate is not a liquid way to hold wealth.

loanable funds market The market in which the demand for private investment and the supply of household savings intersect to determine the equilibrium real interest rate.

long run In microeconomics, the production period in which all of a firm's inputs can be varied and in which firms can enter or exit various industries. In macroeconomics, the time period in which GDP will equal potential GDP, wages will be flexible, and unemployment will gravitate back to the natural rate.

long run aggregate supply (LRAS) The level of output to which an economy will always return in the long run. The LRAS curve intersects the horizontal axis at the full employment or potential level of output.

long run average total cost (LRATC) A graph which shows a firm's average total cost as it varies its size and displays economies of scale (if downward sloping), constant returns to scale (if horizontal), or diseconomies of scale (if upward sloping).

lorenz curve A graph that shows the relative equality of the income or wealth distribution in a society.

M1 A measure of the money supply including currency and checkable deposits.

M2 A more broadly defined component of the money supply. Equal to M1 plus savings deposits, money-market deposits, mutual funds, and small-time deposits.

M3 and MZM Broader yet measures of the money supply including more near monies than M2. MZM stands for "money zero maturity."

macroeconomic equilibrium The level of output at which a nation is producing at any particular period of time. May be below its full employment level (if the economy is in recession) or beyond its full employment level (if the economy is overheating).

macroeconomics The study of entire nations' economies and the interactions between households, firms, government, and foreigners.

managed exchange rate See Fixed Exchange Rate.

marginal analysis Decision-making which involves a comparison of marginal (extra) benefits and marginal costs.

marginal benefit The additional benefit of doing one more bit of something, such as consuming one more unit of a good or service. The rate of change or slope of total benefit.

marginal cost (MC) The additional cost of doing one more bit of something, such as producing one extra unit of a good or service; change in total cost divided by change in output. The slope of the total cost and variable cost curves.

marginal factor cost (MFC) The cost of employing one additional unit of a factor; change in total cost divided by change in quantity of the factor in question (often labor). Bears a close relationship to labor supply. Also called Marginal Resource Cost (MRC).

marginal private benefit (MPB) The private benefit of consuming an additional unit of a good or service; benefit obtained by the consumer only.

marginal private cost (MPC) The private cost of producing an additional unit of output; costs incurred by the producer/seller only.

marginal product (MP) The additional output which is produced when an additional unit of input, often labor, is added to the production process. Also referred to as Marginal Physical Product (MPP).

marginal propensity to consume (MPC) The fraction of any change in income spent on domestically produced goods and services; equal to the change in consumption divided by the change in disposable income.

marginal propensity to save (MPS) The fraction of any change in income that is saved; equal to the change in savings divided by the change in disposable income.

marginal resource cost (MRC) See Marginal Factor Cost.

marginal revenue (MR) The change in total revenue that results from the firm producing and selling one more unit of a good. Positive marginal revenue correlates with the elastic region of a demand curve.

marginal revenue product (MRP) The added revenue a firm gains when employing an additional unit of a factor. Change in total revenue divided by change in the quantity of the factor in question (often labor). Bears a close relationship to labor demand.

marginal social benefit (MSB) The benefit to society of consuming an additional unit of a good or service. This includes marginal private benefit and the external benefits that are captured by non-buyers.

marginal social cost (MSC) The cost to society of producing an additional unit of output. This includes marginal private costs and those external costs that are incurred by third parties.

marginal utility The additional satisfaction or usefulness a consumer gets from consuming an additional unit of a good or service; change in total utility divided by change in quantity consumed.

market A forum for interactions between demanders wishing to make purchases and suppliers wishing to make sales. Markets exist wherever buyers and sellers meet to exchange goods, services, or the factors of production.

market economy An economic system that relies on individuals pursuing their own self-interest in the market in order to cope with scarcity. In market systems, prices are used to guide production decisions in a decentralized manner. Buyers "vote" with their spending dollars, making those goods more expensive, thereby encouraging producers to make more of goods that are more desired and useful. Contrasted with command economy in which production decisions are made centrally.

market failure The failure of a market to provide a good/service or to allocate goods/services in a socially optimal manner. Market failure may result from inadequate competition, from externalities, from informational advantages on the part of the buyer or seller, or high transaction costs.

microeconomics The study of the interactions between consumers and producers in markets for individual products.

monetarism The macroeconomic view that the main cause of changes in aggregate output and the price level are fluctuations in the money supply.

monetary policy The central bank's manipulation of the supply of money aimed at raising or lowering interest rates to stimulate or contract the level of aggregate demand to promote the macroeconomic objectives of price-level stability and full employment.

money Any object that can be used to facilitate the exchange of goods and services in a market.

money demand The sum of the transaction demand and the asset demand for money. Inversely related to the nominal interest rate.

money market The market where the supply of money is set by the central bank; includes the downward-sloping money-demand curve and a vertical money-supply curve. The "price" of money is the nominal interest rate.

money supply The vertical curve representing the total supply of excess reserves in a nation's banking system. Determined by the monetary policy actions of the central bank.

monopolistic competition A relatively competitive market structure in which many firms compete, each having a limited ability to set prices and earn economic profits because of product differentiation. Because there are no barriers to entry of new firms, in the long run each firm earns only normal profit.

monopoly A market with one seller. Monopolies face the entire market demand curve and therefore a steeper MR that lies below demand. No other companies make close substitute goods for the monopolist's and entry in the market is blocked, making long-run profits possible.

monopsony A market dominated by a single consumer. The monopsony model is used to show why in labor markets with only one large firm hiring all the labor in an area, wages and employment will be lower than if there were several firms bidding for labor resources. Monopsonies often give rise to union formation.

multiplier effect The increase in total spending in an economy resulting from an initial injection of new spending. The size of the multiplier effect depends upon the spending multiplier.

Nash equilibrium Situation in game theory that once reached is likely to remain stable. In a Nash equilibrium, neither player has an incentive to deviate from his or her strategic choice given the choice(s) of his or her rivals.

natural monopoly A market condition in which a firm is able to prevent competition because its economy of scale allows it to produce at a lower average total cost than any smaller competitor could.

natural rate of unemployment (NRU) The level of unemployment that prevails in an economy that is producing at its full employment level of output. Includes structural and frictional unemployment. While countries' NRUs can vary, the NRU in the United States tends to be close to 5 percent.

negative externality A side effect of production or consumption which places a cost on someone other than the consumer or producer of the good or service. These unpaid costs to society lead goods of this type to be overproduced in unregulated markets.

net exports (NX or X_N) A component of aggregate demand that equals the income earned from the sale of exports to the rest of the world minus expenditures by domestic consumers on imports.

nominal Unadjusted for inflation. Nominal values may be inflation adjusted into real values. Nominal GDP is converted to real GDP by using a price index. Nominal interest rates are converted into real rates by way of the Fisher equation.

non-excludable good A good that provides benefits which cannot be denied to non-payers. Non-excludability often leads to the free rider problem in which people who would otherwise buy a good choose not to and end up receiving most or all of the benefit anyway.

non-rival good A good that lends itself to shared consumption; one person's consumption of the good or service does not prevent another person from consuming the exact same unit of the good or service.

normal good A good whose demand varies directly with consumers' incomes.

normal profit Fair market value of the resources owned by the entrepreneur that the firm uses. In particular, this includes the wages or salary that the entrepreneur could have earned working for another firm. Can be referred to as implicit cost, because these are nonmonetary costs incurred by the firm.

official reserves To balance the two accounts in the balance of payments (current and financial accounts), a country's official foreign exchange reserves measures the net effect of all the money flows from the other accounts.

oligopoly A market structure in which a few firms dominate and behave interdependently. Entry of new firms is often quite difficult because of the size of existing firms, meaning that firms may be able to earn positive economic profit in the long run.

open-market operations The central bank's buying and selling of government bonds on the open market from commercial banks and the public. This is aimed at increasing or decreasing the level of reserves in the banking system and thereby affects the interest rate and the level of aggregate demand.

opportunity cost That which is given up when a choice is made about the use of a scarce resource. Opportunity cost includes explicit costs (money payments made) and implicit costs (nonmonetary costs or sacrifices).

patent A government-granted license to be the sole producer of a new good or service. Similar in function to a copyright because it is a source of monopoly power for the sole legal producer.

payoff matrix A grid that shows the outcomes of decisions made by producers in a game. Based on a payoff matrix, dominant strategies can be determined.

perfect competition A market condition in which sellers are so numerous that each has no influence over price. Firms trade in homogenous goods and are unable to place barriers to entry or exit from the market so they only earn normal profit in the long run.

perfect price discrimination The ability of a monopolist to charge each individual consumer the highest price the consumer would willingly pay for a good or service. Because each buyer pays his or her reservation price, there is no consumer surplus if a firm perfectly price discriminates.

Phillips curve (long run) A vertical curve at the natural rate of unemployment showing that in the long run there is no trade-off between the price level and the level of unemployment in an economy.

Phillips curve (short run) A downward-sloping curve showing the short-run inverse relationship between the level of inflation and the level of unemployment.

positive externality A side effect of production or consumption which provides a benefit to someone other than the consumer or the producer of the good or service. Positive externalities tend to result in underproduction of the good or service in question.

price ceiling A price ceiling is a legal maximum price and is effective if set below the equilibrium price. This results in the quantity demanded exceeding the quantity supplied at the ceiling price. Hence a shortage exists in the market.

price discrimination The ability of some producers to charge consumers different prices for the same good or service. When firms price discriminate they sell some units at high prices and other units at lower prices, usually on the basis of different customers' willingness to pay.

price elasticity of demand The responsiveness of quantity changes relative to price changes; the percentage change of quantity demanded divided by the percentage change in price.

price elasticity of supply The percentage change in quantity supplied divided by the percentage change in the price of a good or service.

price floor A price floor is a legal minimum price set above the equilibrium price. This results in the quantity supplied exceeding the quantity demanded at the floor price. Hence a surplus exists in the market.

price leadership model Type of oligopoly in which one firm functionally sets the price for the industry. Other firms defer to the price leader either due to its size or traditional role as the anchor firm in the industry.

price taker Firms in perfect competition are price takers because they cannot control the market price for the good they sell. Due to the number of sellers of homogenous goods, each seller can sell any quantity it wants at the market price. Above this price, they would sell zero units. This means they face demand curves which are horizontal or perfectly elastic.

producer(s) People who make and sell goods and services; suppliers.

producer surplus The difference between the market equilibrium price and the lowest price producers would willingly accept for a good or service. On a graph, producer surplus is represented by the area beneath the price received, above the supply (or marginal cost) curve, and to the left of quantity sold.

product differentiation The efforts by firms to make their products appear different from those of their competitors. Also known as non-price competition, this involves firms making all sorts of claims about the relative quality of their product or service. Location, reliability, friendly employees, community tradition, social responsibility, popularity with the masses, and an air of exclusivity related to the product are all types of claims firms make to differentiate their products and justify higher prices without losing much market share.

production function The amount of output varies as inputs are added in production. Typically, output increases as inputs are added, but often at a decreasing rate.

production possibilities curve An economic model that shows all of the possible combinations of two goods that could be produced using scarce factors of production and available technology.

production possibilities frontier See Production Possibilities Curve.

productive efficiency The condition that exists when the least amount of waste happens in producing as much output as possible. When a society is using all its resources to produce goods and services, it is productively efficient. Firms are productively efficient if they produce the quantity that minimizes average total cost.

productivity The output per unit of input of a resource. An important determinant of the level of aggregate supply in a nation; strongly correlated with real wages.

profit The revenue a firm has remaining after paying all of its costs. See Economic, Normal, and Accounting Profit.

progressive tax A tax which takes a greater percentage of income from households with high income than households with low income. The United States income tax is set up in a progressive manner, with higher-income earners in higher tax brackets than low income earners.

proportional tax A tax which takes the same percentage of income from all households.

protectionism The use of tariffs, quotas, or subsidies to give domestic producers a competitive advantage over foreign producers.

Meant to protect domestic production and employment from foreign competition.

public good A good or service that is provided by the government. Goods tend to work best as public goods if they are non-rival and non-excludable. Public goods are financed by tax revenue and provided in the socially optimal quantity.

quantity demanded The amount of a good or service that consumers are willing and able to buy at a given price in a specified period of time.

quantity supplied The amount of a good or service that producers are willing and able to sell at a given price in a specified period of time.

rational expectations theory The hypothesis that business firms and households expect monetary and fiscal policies to have certain effects on the economy and take, in pursuit of their own self-interests, actions which make these policies ineffective at changing real output and only result in changes in the price level.

recession A contraction in total output of goods and services in a nation. Could be caused by a decrease in aggregate demand or in aggregate supply.

recessionary gap The difference between an economy's equilibrium level of output and its full employment level of output when an economy is below full-employment.

regressive tax A tax which takes a greater percentage of income from households with low income than households with high income.

required reserves The proportion of a bank's total deposits it is required to keep in reserve with the central bank. Determined by the required reserve ratio.

rival The condition in which one person's consumption of a good or service prevents another person from consuming the exact same unit of the good or service.

scarcity The fundamental problem of economics. The condition that exists because people's wants and needs are greater than the available resources to meet those wants and needs.

self-correction The idea that an economy producing at an equilibrium level of output that is below or above its full employment will return on its own to its full employment level if left to its own devices. Requires flexible wages and prices and is associated with classical economic views.

short run In microeconomics, the period of production time in which at least one input is constant. In macroeconomics, the period of time in which wages are presumed to be sticky, therefore output may stray from potential and unemployment may vary from the natural rate.

short run aggregate supply (SRAS) Positive relationship between the aggregate amount of GDP produced and the price level in an economy in the short run, when it is presumed that prices of goods are flexible but wage rates are fixed.

shortage The condition that exists when the quantity demanded exceeds the quantity supplied. Indication of price being lower than equilibrium level.

socially optimal The market condition that is met when the marginal social benefit equals the marginal social cost. Also known as the allocatively efficient level of output. Socially optimal levels of output incur no deadweight loss.

specialization A person or society's decision to focus production on a particular good or service, leading it to trade with others for remaining goods it needs. To achieve maximum benefit, the person or society should specialize according to their comparative advantage.

spillover See Externality. For Spillover Benefits, also see Positive Externality; for Spillover Costs, also see Negative Externality.

stagflation A macroeconomic situation in which both inflation and unemployment increase. Caused by a negative supply shock.

sticky wage and price model The short-run Aggregate-Supply Curve is sometimes referred to as the "sticky wage and price model," because workers' wage demands take time to adjust to changes in the overall price level, and therefore, in the short run an economy may produce well below or beyond its full employment level of output.

stock Ownership of a corporation is divided into shares of stock. Each share represents ownership of a small percentage of the firm, and often entitles the owner to participate in the governance of the firm and to earn shares of the firm's profits, called dividends.

structural unemployment Unemployment caused by changes in the structure of demand for goods and in technology; workers who are unemployed because they do not match what is in demand by producers in the economy or whose skills have been left behind by economic advancement.

subsidy A payment from the government that is made to either a consumer or producer of a good/service. Subsidies function like a negative tax: they encourage production and/or consumption of a good by reducing the cost of production.

substitute goods Goods which are used in place of each other. For example, margarine is a substitute for butter.

substitution effect The tendency of consumers to substitute lower-priced items for higher-priced items. A reason why the law of demand is true; consumers purchase fewer units at higher prices because substitutes (whose prices are unchanged) seem relatively cheaper.

supply The willingness and ability of producers to offer a good or service for sale at the various prices which exist in the market within a certain time frame. The positive or direct relationship between quantity supplied and price that is often displayed on a graphical curve or in a tabular schedule or as a function in terms of P and Qs.

supply curve An upward-sloping curve that illustrates producers' willingness and ability to bring units of a good or service to market during a particular time period.

supply side economics Theory that changes in business taxes, regulations, and work incentives can be an effective form of fiscal policy to shift the SRAS curve as opposed to traditional Keynesian policies focused on shifting demand. Gained popularity in response to stagflation of the 1970s.

supply shock Anything that leads to a sudden, unexpected change in aggregate supply. Can be negative (decreases AS) or positive (increases AS). May include a change in energy prices, wages, or business taxes, or may result from a natural disaster or a new discovery of important resources.

surplus The condition that exists when the quantity supplied exceeds the quantity demanded. Indication of price being higher than equilibrium level.

tariff A tax on imported goods. Imposing a tariff increases the price of imports relative to domestic goods, therefore is a form of trade protectionism.

terms of trade The rate at which people trade two goods. The ratio or "real price" for which a unit of one good can be purchased for units of another good. Mutually advantageous terms of trade are found between the opportunity costs of the two people or societies trading.

total cost The sum of fixed and variable costs. Economists include implicit costs (normal profits) as costs. Total cost increases at a decreasing and then increasing rate after the firm experiences the point of diminishing marginal returns.

total product All of a firm's output created by its inputs; synonym for quantity produced.

total revenue The price of a good or service multiplied by the quantity sold. Total receipts a firm takes in from selling its finished goods and services.

total revenue test A test for price elasticity of demand. If price changes vary directly with total revenue, then the demand is inelastic. If price changes vary inversely with total revenue, then the demand is elastic. If price changes do not cause a change in total revenue, then demand is unit elastic.

trade deficit When a country's total spending on imported goods and services exceeds its total revenues from the sale of exports to the rest of the world. Synonymous with a deficit in the current account of the balance of payments and with a negative net export component of GDP.

trade surplus When a country's sale of exports exceeds its spending on imports. Synonymous with a surplus in the current account of the balance of payments.

trade-off An alternative use for scarce factors of production. Trade-offs are a result of scarcity and inherently connected to the making of choices. A trade-off is an opportunity cost.

transfer payment A payment made when no good or service is exchanged. Allowances are private transfer payments; social security checks are governmental transfer payments. Transfer payments are not included in GDP because they do not represent production.

unions Organizations of workers who seek to increase the wage rates, working conditions, and number of jobs available in their industries. Unions can be of various types and may seek to include all workers in a sector or make membership more exclusive in a particular craft.

unit elastic Describes percentage change in quantity that is equal to percentage change in price.

utility The want-satisfying power that goods and services provide. The amount of usefulness or satisfaction that a consumer gets from consuming a good or service.

utility maximization Economists assume that consumers always try to maximize their total utility. With a budget, consumers seek combinations of the goods they buy which yield the greatest overall level of satisfaction.

utility maximization rule A formula that illustrates the combination of two goods that maximize a consumer's utility. Can be extended to any number of goods and implies that customers do best when they try to ensure that the last dollar they spend on each type of good they purchase yields the same level of added satisfaction.

variable cost A cost that changes with the firm's level of production. Synonym for total variable cost.

wage The price of labor per unit of time. The vertical axis in labor markets is labeled as "wage." Wages are considered a variable cost for firms in microeconomics. In macroeconomics they are a component of the income method of calculating GDP and are considered fixed in the short run but variable in the long run.

wage taker Firms that hire labor in perfectly competitive labor markets are wage takers; they can hire any quantity of workers desired for a market wage rate. This stems from the fact that in these markets there are a large number of firms hiring similarly qualified workers. Thus, these firms face horizontal (perfectly elastic) labor supply curves equal to marginal factor cost.

wealth An important determinant of consumption. Wealth is the total value of a household's assets minus all its liabilities.

Index

A

Ability to pay principle, 159
Absolute advantage, 44–45
Accounting profit, 91
Aggregate demand, 265
  changes in, 214–215
  components and their behavior, 203–215
  as a concept, 200
  multiplier effect and, 211–213
  slope of, 201–202
Aggregate supply
  output and, 216–218
  shift of, 218–219
  in the short run and the long run, 219–222
Allocative efficiency, 77–78, 103
Allocatively efficient, 47, 147
AP Economics Exams
  free-response section, 9
  multiple-choice section, 8
  scoring process for, 9–10
  strategies for, 10–13
Asset demand, 237
Assets, 234–235
Automatic fiscal policy, 251
Automatic stabilizers, 251
Autonomous consumption (AC), 205

B

Balance of payments accounts, 287–294
Balance of trade, 293–294
Balance sheets, 234–235
Banks
  assets, liabilities, and balance sheets, 234–235
  demand for money, 236–238
  fractional reserve banking, 232–233
  interest as price of money, 236
  money multiplier, 233
  purpose of, 232
  required reserve ratio, 233
Base year price level, 191
Benefits received principle, 159
Best response, 123
Black markets, 79
Bonds, 230–231
Business cycle, 63–64

C

Capital, 35
Capital stock, 36, 180, 260
Cartels, 120
Central banks, 241
  money supply and, 246
Circular flow of economic activity, 48–50, 125–126, 183–184
Closed economy, 184, 213
Collective bargaining process, 141
Collusion, 120
Command system, 32
Commodity money, 229
Comparative advantage, 43–46
Complement, 53
Complements in production, 57
Consumer choice, 81
Consumer goods and services, 34
Consumer price index (CPI), 191–192
Consumer surplus, 76
Consumption, 49, 180
  consumer confidence and expectations, 207
  disposable income (DI) and, 203–204
  interest sensitive, 207–208
  marginal propensities to save and consume, 205–207
  savings function and, 204–205
  wealth and, 207
Contractionary fiscal policy, 250–251
Corporate profits, 182
Cost-push inflation, 189
Crash Course for AP Microeconomics, 3
Crash Course for Macroeconomics, 3
Cross-price elasticity of demand, 74–75
Crowding-out concept, 259–262
  cause of, 259–260
  consequences of, 260–261
  impact of deficits and the public debt, 261–262
Current account, 288–290
Cyclical unemployment, 196

D

Deadweight loss, 77–78, 149, 154, 163–166
Deflation, 189
Demand, 51–54, 60, 150
  cross-price elasticity of, 74–75
  effects of shifts, 60–63
  income elasticity of, 74
  price elasticity of, 71–74
Demand curve, 51, 53
  utility and, 83
Demand enhancement strategy, 141
Demand function, 52
Demand-pull inflation, 189
Demand schedule, 51

Depreciation, 36, 180
Depressions, 63
Derived demand, 126–127
Diminishing marginal utility, 51
Discount rate, 245
Discouraged workers, 195
Discretionary fiscal policy, 251
Diseconomies of scale, 89
Disposable income (DI), 203–204
Dissaving, 205
Dominant strategy, 123
Dual mandate, 242

E

Economic growth, 42–43
- in aggregate demand and aggregate supply model, 280
- business cycle graph and, 277–278
- capital and, 283–284
- determinants of, 281–284
- entrepreneurial ability and, 284
- labor and, 282–283
- land and, 281–282
- long-run, 275–276
- policy, 285–286
- production function and, 276–277
- production possibilities curve, 279

Economic profit, 91
Economic resources, 34–36
Economics, defined, 28
Economic surplus, 76
Economic systems, 31–33
Economies of scale, 89
Economists, 28
Effective controls, 80–81
E-flashcards, 3
Elasticity, 71–75
Employed individuals, 195
Entrepreneurial ability, 36
Equilibrium, 58
- changes in, 59–60
- short-run and long-run, 223–224

Excludable goods, 157
Exclusive union model, 141
Expansionary fiscal policy, 250
Expectations change, 52
Expenditure method, 178, 180–181
Explicit cost, 37
Exports, 181, 211

F

Factor market graphical analysis
- marginal productivity theory of income distribution, 144–145
- monosony model, 139–141
- perfectly competitive factor market, 137–139
- union negotiated wages and minimum wages, 142–144
- unions, 141

Fair-return pricing, 115
Federal funds rate (FFR), 244
Federal Open Market Committee (FOMC), 242
Federal Reserve, 240–247
Federal Reserve Act of 1913, 241
Federal Reserve system structure and functions, 241–243
Fiat money, 230
Field of economics, 33–34
Financial account, 291–292
Financial transactions, 185
Firms
- fixed cost and average fixed cost, 86–88
- long-run cost structure, 89–91
- marginal cost, 88
- marginal product, 84–86
- profit/loss in graphical representation, 92
- profit maximization at MC = MR, 92
- short-run and long-run production decisions, 84
- short-run cost structure, 86–88
- total cost and average total costs, 88
- variable cost and average variable cost, 88

Fiscal policy
- aggregate demand and, 252–254
- aggregate supply and, 254
- automatic and discretionary, 251
- countercyclical nature of, 252
- expansionary and contractionary, 250–251
- foreign exchange (FOREX) markets and, 305–306
- interest rates and, 255–264
- with monetary policy, 264–265

Fisher equation, 263
Foreign exchange (FOREX) markets
- basics, 294
- capital flight, 302–303
- causes of shifts in, 299–301
- currency appreciation/depreciation, 298
- currency value and, 295
- current account and, 301–302
- demand for a country's currency, 296
- financial account and, 302
- fiscal policy and, 305306
- graphical calculation, 297–298
- macroeconomic policy decisions and, 303–305
- monetary policy and, 305
- supply of a country's currency, 296–297

Foreign factor income, 179
Fractional reserve banking, 232–233
Free response section, approaches to, 21–27

Frictional unemployment, 196
Full-employment output, 197
  economy and, 224–227
Fundamental economic questions, 29
Fundamental identity of national income accounting, 178

G

Game theory, 120
  problems, solving, 122–124
GDP deflator, 191
Gini coefficient, 171–172
Goods
  excludable, 157
  free-rider problem, 157
  public, 158–159
  rival and shared consumption, 157
Government purchases, 210
Government purchases (G), 181
Gross domestic product (GDP), 178–179
  components, 179–183
  domestic/in-home production, 184
  formal definition of, 184
  goods and services in, 184–186
  illegal black markets, 185
  imperfections, 188
  per-capita, 187–188
  real and nominal, 186–187
Gross national product (GNP), 179
Gross private domestic investment (I), 180

H

Hiring of labor, 138–139
Households, 81–83
Human capital, 35, 283

I

Imperfections, 188
Implicit cost, 37
Imports, 181, 211
Incidence of tax, 167
Inclusive union, 141
Income, 182
Income changes, 52
Income distribution
  Lorenz curve, 170–171
  sources of inequality, 169
Income effect, 51
Income elasticity of demand, 74
Income method, 178, 181–182
Induced consumption, 205
Ineffective controls, 80–81
Inefficient price and quantity, 152
Inferior goods, 52, 74
Inflation, 263
  calculation of, 192
  causes for, 189–190
  conversion between real and nominal values, 193
  defined, 189
  faster than anticipated, 194
  losers and winners, 194
Inflationary gap, 226
Interdependent behavior of oligopoly markets, 120
Interest, 263
Interest sensitive consumption, 180, 207–208
Intermediate goods, 185
Investment, 36
  changes in consumption and, 208–209
Investment demand curve, 209–210

K

Kinked-demand model, 121

L

Labor, 35, 282–283
  determination, 140–141
Labor force, 195
  participation rate, 282
Labor productivity, 282
Labor supply market
  individual and, 132–134
Land, 34, 281–282
Law of demand, 51
Law of increasing opportunity cost, 39
Law of supply, 54
Least-cost rule, 134–135
Liabilities, 234–235
Loanable funds market, 255–256
  demand for, 256–257
  supply of, 257–258
Long run, 64
Long-run aggregate supply (LRAS), 221–222
Long Run Average Total Cost (LRATC), 90
Long-run economic growth, 275–276
Long-run equilibrium, 223–224
Long-run Phillips curve (LRPC), 267–269
Low-hanging fruit principle, 55
Lump-sum tax, 161–162

M

M1, 231
M2, 231
Macroeconomists, 33
Marginal benefit (MB), 48, 75–76
Marginal cost, 48, 75–76
Marginal external benefit (MEB), 153
Marginal external cost (MEC) per unit, 165
Marginal factor cost (MFC), 133
Marginal physical product, 128
Marginal private benefit (MPB), 150
Marginal private cost (MPC), 150
Marginal productivity theory of income distribution, 144–145
Marginal propensity to consume (MPC), 205–207

Marginal propensity to save (MPS), 205–207
Marginal resource cost (MRC), 133
Marginal revenue (MR), 69–70, 73–74
Marginal revenue product (MRP), 127–132
  changes in, 132
  for imperfect competitors, 131–132
  for a price-taking firm, 129–130
Marginal social benefit (MSB), 150
Marginal social cost (MSC), 150
Marginal utility (MU), 81–82
Market-based solutions for market failure, 156
Market-clearing price, 58
Market equilibrium, 58–59
Market failure, 147
  deadweight loss, 149
  externalities and, 149–154
  fixing of, 154–156
  market-based solutions for, 156
  reasons for, 148
Market for goods and services, 288
Market labor supply, 133
Markets for financial assets, 290
Market size changes, 52
Market systems, 31
Maximum efficient scale, 90
Medium of exchange, 229
Microeconomists, 33
Minimum efficient scale, 90
Mixed market systems, 32–33
Monetary policy tools
  in foreign exchange (FOREX) markets, 305
  lending to commercial banks, 245
  open market operations, 243–244
  perspectives, 246–247
  reserve requirement, 245–246
Money
  forms, 230–231
  measuring supply of, 231–232
  types and purposes of, 229–230
Money market graphical analysis, 238–240
Money multiplier, 233
Monopolistically competitive market, 115–118
  breaking even in long-run equilibrium, 118
  demand and marginal revenue in, 116
  efficiency assessment, 118
  in long-run, 117
  profit maximization, 116
Monopoly markets, 104–115
  demand and marginal revenue in, 106–107
  efficiency of, 110–111
  maximizing profit and minimizing loss, 107–110
  natural monopoly and regulation options, 113–115
  price-discriminating monopolies, 112–113
  profit in, 110–111
  reasons for formation, 105
  revenue-maximizing and breakeven quantities, 111–112
Monosony model, 139–141
Multiple-choice questions,
  approaches to, 13–20
  avoiding common errors, 19
  identifying key words, 18–19
  predicting the right answer, 15–17
  process of elimination, 13–15
  tips, 20
  using graphs, 17–18

N

Nash equilibrium, 123–124
National income (NI), 179
Natural monopoly, 90, 105, 113–115
Natural rate of unemployment (NRU), 197
Negative externalities, 151–152
Neoclassical self-correction, 225
Net export effect, 202
Net exports, 181
Nominal GDP, 186–187
Nominal interest rates (NIRs), 262–264
Nonprice competition, 115
Normal goods, 52, 74
Normal profit, 91
Normative economic conclusions, 34

O

Official reserves account, 292–294
Oligopoly markets, 119–124
  interdependence and strategic behavior, 120
  solving game theory problems, 122–124
  versions of, 120–121
Opportunity cost, 36, 39, 44
  calculation of, 40

P

Payoff matrix, 122
Per-capita GDP, 187–188
Per-capita real GDP growth rate (rGDP), 276
Perfectly competitive factor market, 137–139
  union negotiated wages and minimum wages, 142
Perfectly competitive markets, 94–104
  changes in market demand, 100

efficiency of, 103–104
entry, exit, and long-run equilibrium, 101–103
firm, 94–96
firm's marginal revenue curve, 95
maximizing profit in short run, 96–99
shut down rule, 99
Personal consumption expenditures (PCE) index, 191
Per-unit subsidy, 56
Per-unit tax, 56, 154, 162–164
Phillips curve
AD-AS model and, 270–274
changes in inflationary expectations, 273
changes in long-run curves, 273–274
definition, 265
demand-pull and cost-push inflation, 270–271
long-run, 267–269
monetary and fiscal policy in, 272–273
short-run, 266–267
Physical capital, 35, 283
Portfolio investment, 291
Positive economic conclusions, 33
Positive externalities, 152–154
Potential output, 196
Preferences change, 52
Price ceilings, 78–79, 155
Price control, 78
Price-discriminate perfectly, 113
Price-discriminating monopolies, 112–113
Price elasticity of demand, 71–74
Price floors, 79–80, 155
Price index, 190–192
Price leadership model, 121
Price level, 190
Price taker, 94
Principle of diminishing marginal returns, 84
Private economy, 184
Producer price index (PPI), 191
Producer surplus, 76
Product differentiation, 115
Production possibilities curve (PPC), 37–43, 279
Production possibilities frontier (PPF), 37–43, 46–47
food production in terms of, 39–40
slope of, 39
using graphs, 41
Productive efficiency, 104
Productively efficient goods, 40
Product market structures
essential characteristics of, 92–94
monopolistically competitive market, 115–118
monopoly markets, 104–115
oligopoly markets, 119–124
perfectly competitive markets, 94–104
Profit, 83, 91–92, 182
Profit maximization
of firms, 134–136
rule, 135–136
union negotiated wages and minimum wages, 142–144
Profit maximization at MC = MR, 92
Profit-maximizing firms, 91–92
Proportional tax, 160
Proprietors' income, 182
Public goods, 158–159
Purchasing power, 263
Purchasing power parity (PPP), 188

Q

Quantity control, 78
Quantity regulation, 80
Quota, 80

R

REA AP All Access system, 1–2
Real GDP, 186–187
Real interest rates (RIRs), 262–264
REA Study Center, 2–3
8-Week AP Study Plans, 3–6
Recessionary gap, 224–225
Recessions, 63
Regressive tax, 161
Rent, 182
Required reserve ratio, 233
Reservation prices, 43, 75–76
Reservation wage, 133
Resold goods, 186

S

Savings function, 204–205
Scarcity principle, 28–29, 36
Security, 230–231
Sellers' expectations, 57
Shortages, 59
Short run, 64
Short-run aggregate supply (SRAS), 221
Short-run equilibrium, 223–224
Short-run Phillips curve (SRPC), 266–267
Shut down rule, 99
Shutting down, 99
Socially optimal quantity, 147
Specialization, 46
Spillover benefit, 152–154
Spillover cost, 151–152
Stagflation, 189
Stocks, 230–231
Store of value, 229
Structural unemployment, 196
Substitute good, 52
Substitutes in production, 57
Substitution effect, 51
Sunk costs, 99
Suppliers, 57
Supply, 54–58, 150
change in quantity and, 55
effects of shifts, 60–63

elasticity of, 75
Surplus, 59

T

T-account, 234
Tastes change, 52
Taxes, 154, 213
and deadweight loss, 163–166
distribution of tax burden, 166
elasticity and tax burden, 166–169
as fixed or marginal costs, 161–162
income level and tax burden, 160–161
progressive nature of, 160
proportional, 160
regressive, 161
theories of collecting, 159–160
Total economic surplus, 77
Total factor cost, 133
Total product, 86
Total revenue, 69–70
Total utility, 81–82
Trade accounting, 287–294
Trade deficits, 181, 288
Trading ratio (or terms of trade), 46
Traditional economic system, 33
Transactions demand, 237
Transfer payments, 181, 186

U

Unemployed individuals, 195
Unemployment. *See also* Phillips curve
cyclical, 196
defining, 195
frictional, 196
structural, 196
Unemployment rate, 195
Union negotiated wages and minimum wages, 142–144
Unit of account, 229
Utility maximization, 82–83

W

Wage determination, 140–141
Wage-discriminate, 139
Wage seeker, 139
Wage takers, 137
Want-satisfying power, 34

NOTES

NOTES

NOTES

NOTES